FIRST-YEAR EXPERIENCE TEXT

The Ole Miss Experience

Editor: Natasha Jeter
Founding Editor: Leslie Showalter
Program Coordinator: Rachael Durham

Contributors: Lindsey Abernathy, Mariana Allushuski, Seph Anderson, Laura Antonow, Toni Avant, Bradley Baker, Jade Chalkley, Brownishia Clark, Casey Cockrell-Stuart, Donald Cole, Kevin Cozart, Erin Cromeans, Robert Cummings, Brittany Dawson, Melissa Dennis, Wesley Dickens, Laura Diven-Brown, Rachael Durham, Macey Edmonson, Bud Edwards, JoAnn Edwards, Kyle Ellis, Sierra Elliston, Norris "EJ" Edney, Martin Fisher, Karen Forgette, Jennifer Fos, Emma Gaddy, Susan Glisson, Wendy Goldberg, Travis Hitchcock, Kate Hooper, Natasha Jeter, Mariana Jurss, Leann Kendricks, Jazmine Kelley, Anne Klingen, Dewey Knight, Guy Krueger, Alex Langhart, Webb Lewis, Kyle Loggins, David Magee, Merrill Magruder, Rachel McClain, Kendall McDonald, Blair McElroy, Shawnboda Meade, Stephen Monroe, Ellie Moore, Tracey Murry, Alice Myatt, Natasa Novicevic, Cecilia Parks, Cadence Pentheny, Patrick Perry, Shelli Poole, Thomas Reardon, Ollie Rencher, Stacey Reycraft, Holly Reynolds, Rebekah Reysen, Shannon Richardson, JuWan Robinson, Jeremy Roberts, Nishanth Rodrigues, Valeria Ross, Leslie Showalter, Marc Showalter, Whitman Smith, Sovent Taylor, Katie Tompkins, Charles Tucker, Amanda Walker, Beth Whittington, Ryan Whittington, Nancy Wiggers, Noel Wilkin, and Robin Yekaitis.

A special thanks to University of Mississippi Communications — especially to the extraordinarily talented photographers.

ISBN #: 978-1-949455-26-7
Eleventh Edition

Printed in Canada
through a partnership with Friesens Printing

NOTE FROM **THE EDITOR**

Y ou are excited! We are excited! Welcome to the University of Mississippi! We are thrilled that you have made the decision to join our Ole Miss family. This is a very special year. Given that you are here with us, you have navigated through a senior year filled with "unexpected interruptions. For that, I say congratulations! You have already demonstrated a huge amount of resilience. You will need that strength as you navigate this new collegiate experience.

You come from various backgrounds, communities, and countries; you have different personalities, intellectual abilities, and talents. For some of you, doing well academically comes easily; for others, you may have to work a bit harder to be successful. The great thing about university life is that we are a community that is well equipped to support you as you matriculate through your new home, from Convocation to Graduation! Every part of the University of Mississippi experience has been thoughtfully planned to help ensure your success. Do not be afraid to learn new things, ask for help, meet new people, or make connections. Fully immerse yourself in the culture that is the University of Mississippi.

Natasha Jeter
Assistant Vice Chancellor
for Wellness and Student
Success

We have a number of spaces designed especially with you in mind. We have the Center for Student Success and First-Year Experience (CSSFYE) designed to facilitate your positive transition from high school to college. In addition to enhancing your academic skills, they will also help you acquire essential life skills. The Career Center will aid you by connecting your major to career opportunities. The Gertrude C. Ford Student Union is the heart of student life on campus, a space designed to support your co-curricular and extracurricular needs, improve nutritional health, facilitate student engagement within campus organizations, promote university involvement, as well as create safe, welcoming spaces for you to study, relax, or grab a snack or a meal with new friends.

Given that college life can be stressful, we know that learning to balance and create healthy habits is essential. The South Campus Recreation Center (SCRC) is a 98,000 sq. ft facility that houses a variety of activities and services to help you manage your physical health, promote university involvement, establish and maintain well-being, and engage you in the community. If you grow tired of our indoor spaces, take a break and enjoy a brisk walk or jog in the Grove or through the Circle. These are just a few of the many resources available to you on campus.

College is about growing, learning, and building relationships. I challenge you to start building organic relationships now. Invest in your networks (faculty, staff, friends, and mentors), watch them grow, and leverage them to achieve your goals.

Allow this text to be your guide. It will help you learn about the rich culture and resources that many have worked tirelessly to create to ensure your success. The campus resources contained at the back of this text will help you identify, navigate, and get assistance when you are confused, uncertain, or lacking direction. Remember, *I will is greater than IQ.* We are here to serve you. Enjoy your Ole Miss Experience.

Hotty Toddy,

Editor and
Assistant Vice Chancellor for Wellness and Student Success

Dear Students:

Welcome to Ole Miss and the First-Year Experience!

This course is designed to help our first-year students make a positive and successful transition to the University. We believe that through this course, you will improve your academic performance, acquire essential life skills, and explore careers and majors that may best suit your interests and abilities. During the semester, you also will learn about the history, mission, and values of the University of Mississippi; community service opportunities on campus and in Oxford, and how to be a productive and viable part of the Ole Miss community.

One of our former EDHE students described the First-Year Experience as "a wonderful way to become familiar with Ole Miss, acquire effective study skills, learn how to manage your time, and to discover who you are. It gave me a lot of connections, and I learned about so many helpful services I was actually able to use!"

This text focuses on the University of Mississippi with information about the history, traditions, and values, as well as academic and other support services available to you. The faculty and administrators of the University have assembled a virtual cookbook of the ingredients (resources) that are essential for your success. As a new member of the Ole Miss family, I encourage you to learn about the wonderful resources available to you and make good use of them now and for the next four years. We truly care about you and your success!

Hotty Toddy,

Rachael Durham
Assistant Director for First-Year Experience

3rd Floor, Suite P | Martindale Student Services Center | P.O. Box 1848 | University, MS 38677-1848
(662) 915-5970 | www.olemiss.edu | cssfye@olemiss.edu

7

CONTENTS

TRANSFER STUDENT SECTION

COVID-19 **Update and Reflection**

By Alex Langhart, Director of University Health Services

COVID-19 provided many challenges for institutions of higher learning across the nation. Throughout the pandemic, the University of Mississippi aligned its parameters and protocols for University operations with government orders as well as the IHL Safe Start Task Force, the U.S. Centers for Disease Control and Prevention (CDC), the Mississippi State Department of Health (MSDH), and the American College Health Association (ACHA). The University's response and planning were driven by the following guiding principles:

- Prevent the spread of the virus to safeguard our community by following guidance of public health officials and agencies,

- Resume an on-campus learning, residential and working environment that prioritizes the safety and well-being of the campus population,

- Fulfill our core mission of education, research, and service, and

- Enable our students to maintain progress toward earning their degrees.

The University's response was guided by the Incident Response Team representing many areas of campus operations. When it became clear that the response to COVID-19 requires more extensive and long-term planning, the Future Planning Task Force with working groups focused on academic planning and experiences, athletics, financial planning/implications, parameters and protocols, public education and awareness, student services and support. Later, the University created a Vaccine Distribution and Administration Task Force as well as a Work Strategies Task Force.

The campus parameters and protocols for Fall 2020 and Spring 2021 operations included properly wearing facemasks or appropriate cloth face coverings, maintaining physical distancing, and practicing proper hand hygiene. Additionally, in order to mitigate the potential spread of the virus, the University operated under a modified academic calendar.

Classroom capacities were reduced to comply with CDC and national public health recommendations, and courses were offered in one of four formats: face-to-face, hybrid, remote, or online. Given the space limitation necessitated by the protocols, some classroom changes and use of large spaces were needed.

Throughout the fall and spring semesters, the University offered free asymptomatic (i.e., without symptoms) COVID-19 testing for faculty, staff and students on campus. This testing and data collection added to the protections to keep our community safe.

In the spring semester the University stood up a vaccination site at the Tad Smith Coliseum, where more than 5,000 COVID-19 vaccines were administered to members of the campus community in an effort to get as many students, faculty and staff vaccinated as possible. UM health care professionals, including the University's nationally ranked pharmacy program, played a pivotal role in bringing clinical expertise from faculty and staff in administering the vaccine. Students from the School of Pharmacy, under the supervision of trained faculty and health care professionals, contributed to the successful operation of the site and received hands-on experience in a clinical setting.

To keep the University community plugged into the numerous and constant changes that occurred with COVID-19, a daily e-newsletter was created for faculty, staff and students. It eventually transitioned to a weekly newsletter as the pandemic continued. Additionally, the Public Education and Awareness Subcommittee developed and deployed strategies and materials to communicate changes in operations, expectations and health information in an effort to prevent the spread of COVID-19. These efforts included physical and digital signage, instructional videos, a C19 Ambassador program, student and employee informational modules, and a voluntary pledge.

On Feb. 26, 2021, Chancellor Glenn F. Boyce shared a message with the campus community that the growing adoption and distribution of multiple vaccines against the COVID-19 virus enabled the University to plan for a full resumption of in-person classes for Fall 2021 and a return of campus to pre-COVID-19 operations. The University continues to monitor the health and safety of the campus community and stands ready to adapt if necessary to evolving government orders and public health guidance.

Review daily updates here:
coronavirus.olemiss.edu

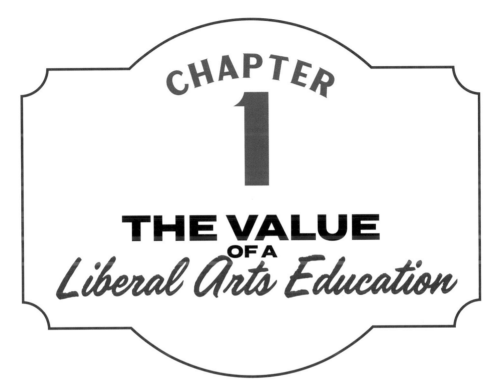

CHAPTER 1

THE VALUE OF A Liberal Arts Education

By Holly Reynolds

"Of all the
civil rights
for which the
world has
struggled and
fought for
5,000 years,
the right
to learn is
undoubtedly
the most
fundamental."
—W.E.B. DuBois,
1949

The University of Mississippi is the flagship liberal arts university in the state of Mississippi. What does this mean? And, what is the value of a liberal arts education?

From the origins of Western civilization comes the concept of a liberal arts education. The term comes from the Greek word *eleutheros* and the Latin word *liber*, both meaning "free." For free (male) citizens to fully participate in Athenian democracy, they needed certain skills in critical thinking and communication developed through a broad education in seven disciplines: grammar, logic, rhetoric, arithmetic, astronomy, music, and geometry. Such an education celebrated and nurtured human freedom and early democracy. The term liberal arts education does not mean an education that indoctrinates students in the political ideology of liberalism or the thoughts of those labeled as political liberals.

In modern times, we can look to the American Association of Colleges and Universities (AAC&U) for a contemporary understanding of this concept.

Liberal education is an approach to learning that empowers individuals and prepares them to deal with complexity, diversity, and change. It provides students with broad knowledge of the wider world (e.g. science, culture, and society) as well as in-depth study in a specific area of interest. A liberal education helps students develop a sense of social responsibility, as well as strong and transferable intellectual and practical skills such as communication, analytical and problem-solving skills, and a demonstrated ability to apply knowledge and skills in real-world settings. The broad goals of liberal education have been enduring even as the courses and requirements that comprise a liberal education have changed over the years. Today, a liberal education usually includes a general education curriculum that provides broad learning in multiple disciplines and ways of knowing, along with more in-depth study in a major." (aacu.org/leap).

You regularly will hear proponents of a liberal arts education cite some combination of the skills listed above as the mark of a well-educated citizen who is able to fully participate in our society, economy, and democracy. It is still about nurturing human freedom by helping people discover and develop their talents. Many of you have at least an implicit understanding that you enrolled at the University of Mississippi to acquire or deepen these areas of knowledge and skills mentioned above. Understandably, many students and parents are focused on preparing for the workforce in an ever-changing American economy. A liberal arts education is the best preparation for such uncertainty. Better yet, it prepares you for a meaningful life.

Faculty members developed a vision for the liberal arts education that is the basis for every undergraduate degree on campus. Look at the core curriculum and the learning outcomes listed in the Degree Requirements section of the Undergraduate Academic Regulations in the online catalog. There is a common core curriculum of 30 hours of course work that is the framework for your freshman year courses. This core curriculum sets the liberal arts foundation for your degree. And, when combined with the courses in your major and your co-curricular learning experiences, the core curriculum should enable you to:

1. study the principal domains of knowledge and their methods of inquiry;

2. integrate knowledge from diverse disciplines;

3. analyze, synthesize, and evaluate complex and challenging material that stimulates intellectual curiosity, reflection, and capacity for lifelong learning;

4. communicate qualitative, quantitative, and technological concepts by effective written, oral, numerical, and graphical means;

5. work individually and collaboratively on projects that require the application of knowledge and skill;

6. understand a variety of world cultures as well as the richness and complexity of American society;

7. realize that knowledge and ability carry with them a responsibility for their constructive and ethical use in society.

"At UM, all students must complete a general education curriculum that is strongly rooted in the liberal arts, which encourages creativity, critical thinking, empathy, and being a strong communicator. These skills are highly transferrable in industry and essential to our society, which becomes more and more complex each year." —Lee Cohen, Dean of the College of Liberal Arts

From this statement of values, we derive general education competencies.

- Critical thinking
- Ethical reasoning and ethical responsibility
- Mathematical reasoning
- Multicultural Competency
- Oral communication
- Written communication

Connect the courses you are taking this semester with the learning outcomes listed above. Sometimes it is very easy to make the connection due to the title of the course. In other cases you may need to look at the course objectives or description on the syllabus and think about your larger goals for your education. Now, imagine a web of 100-level through 400- or 500-level courses that connect together to form your undergraduate degree. The connections between these courses are real and come from the above list. You are not simply "checking off courses" on a degree sheet. You are building an interactive set of skills and content knowledge for a liberal arts education, whether it is for a degree in history, forensic chemistry, social work, or accountancy.

But you don't have to take my word for the value of a liberal arts education. Employers regularly espouse the positive qualities of a liberal arts education. Let's see how the skills and knowledge listed from the UM catalog show up on a few national employer surveys.

The National Association of Colleges and Employers (NACE) and the Association of American Colleges and Universities (AACU) conduct surveys of employers to determine the top skills or attributes and experiences sought among job candidates.

The NACE Job Outlook 2020 has the following attributes/skills supported by 70% or more of employers surveyed:

- Ability to work in a team
- Analytical/quantitative skills
- Communication skills
- Initiative
- Leadership
- Problem-solving skills
- Strong work ethic

Will you be prepared for what they value? How will your résumé and transcript reflect these attributes/skills? How will you highlight these experiences and demonstrate these skills in a cover letter, personal statement, or interview?

A recent Association of American Colleges & Universities (AACU) survey published in Fulfilling The American Dream asked executives and hiring managers what kinds of experiences they value the most in job candidates. The responses with over 50% support are shown below.

Gain What Employers Value

94%	Internship
83%	Community project with people from diverse backgrounds
81%	Collaborative research project with peers
78%	Service learning project in community
76%	Advanced senior project/thesis
72%	Multiple courses with significant writing
54%	Study abroad

Percent of employers likely to hire graduates with select experiences.

2019 survey by National Association of Colleges and Employers

The University of Mississippi campus is full of these opportunities. Faculty members across our campus intentionally foster these skills and opportunities. Student services staff members work diligently to help you connect with enrichment opportunities beyond the classroom. Seek out these opportunities while you are here, and reflect carefully about how you can demonstrate them to others.

Take these messages to heart. Be conscious of how each course and co-curricular activity will add these skills, values, knowledge, and experiences to your resume. Build a digital portfolio to showcase your preparation for future employment or graduate/professional school admissions committees. You are gaining a valuable education and preparing for a rich, meaningful life.

ABOUT THE AUTHOR

Holly Reynolds, Associate Dean in the College of Liberal Arts, Assistant Professor of Political Science.

Holly Reynolds earned her Bachelor of Arts in political science from Louisiana State University and Ph.D. in political science from Rice University. She joined the UM faculty in 1997 and became an administrator with the College of Liberal Arts in 2002. Dr. Reynolds' areas of specialization are comparative politics, Latin American politics, and transitions to democracy. She has received the Cora Lee Graham Award for Outstanding Teaching of Freshmen in the College of Liberal Arts.

LIVING THE CREED
AT THE UNIVERSITY OF MISSISSIPPI

By confirming your admission and enrolling in courses at the University of Mississippi, you have accepted the responsibility of being a member of our campus community. This campus community may be unlike any other community you have been a part of in your past. In fact, I hope it is different. I say that because placing yourself in a new environment is one of the most educational and transformational experiences you will ever have in life. It opens your eyes and your mind to those who are different from you, to alternative approaches to getting things accomplished, and it will force you to decide who you really are as a citizen of our world.

So, exactly what does being a member of this community mean? The Creed of the University of Mississippi can be your compass in answering that question.

The Creed of The University of Mississippi

The University of Mississippi is a community of learning dedicated to nurturing excellence in intellectual inquiry and personal character in an open and diverse environment. As a voluntary member of this community:

I believe in respect for the dignity of each person. I believe in fairness and civility.
I believe in personal and professional integrity. I believe in academic honesty.
I believe in academic freedom.
I believe in good stewardship of our resources.
I pledge to uphold these values and encourage others to follow my example.

You have moved into your residence hall or apartment and are living—at least initially—with complete strangers. You are going to class and are joining organizations with students from diverse backgrounds. You are likely to walk across campus and hardly recognize anyone. You are meeting students who look different from you and talk differently than you. You will find students who share your spiritual background and those who reject the existence of deities.

These experiences may scare you or force you to think twice about your decision to come to Ole Miss; I assure you, **this is the best decision you have ever made**. Keep an open mind; get to know others who, seemingly, are unlike you. Treat others as you would like to be treated, and you will find that you have more in common with them than you initially thought. You also will find that it is fun to learn about others' backgrounds, traditions, and heritage. These are the things that make each of us special and proud of our history. Everyone has a story. Listen and learn.

Social challenges are one thing, but a **large** number of first-year students indicate that they are overwhelmed academically. If you don't fall into this category, good for you! I hope you will extend your talents to your fellow students and help them with an algebra problem or another assignment – that would be living The Creed! If you do find your academics challenging, you are not alone. I recommend you talk to your professors, seek out support from the many academic resources we have on campus, or ask a friend to study with you and tackle assignments together. At the end of the day what matters most is that you allow yourself the freedom to explore new subjects so you can confidently select a future career.

Apply yourself, don't cheat yourself. If the topic is difficult (and we hope it is), your faculty expect you to ask more questions. Be curious and courageous with your academic career—you will never regret the choice to honestly expand your mind.

Being a member of this community requires you to possess an ethic of care. We expect you to:

> **care enough to respect yourself,**
> **care enough to respect others, and**
> **care enough to respect our campus.**

So, go to class and get what you are paying for – an education and an expanded world view that will make you a competitive applicant for your dream job. Take time to recognize the students, faculty and staff who walk by you on campus. Smile at others and say "hello;" as we say at the University of Mississippi— "Everyone Speaks!" Lastly, respect the buildings, the grounds, your residence hall, and your classrooms. There are thousands of staff members on campus who work hard to make our campus the most beautiful in the country—help them keep it that way. Whether it is a football Saturday in The Grove or a quiet Tuesday night early in the Spring, please be a positive role model and live our Creed. You can never go wrong if you use the Creed as a compass to guide your behavior, attitudes, and decisions.

We look forward to watching you live The Creed. We have high expectations for all of our students; we know you will meet, and likely exceed, them! We look forward to watching you grow and learn as a member of this amazing, diverse, exciting, and caring community.

Welcome to the Ole Miss family – We are thrilled you are here!

CHAPTER

2

UNIVERSITY
History

By Thomas Reardon and
Leslie Showalter

The University of Mississippi is the oldest and best known of Mississippi's public institutions of higher learning. The University has a rich history of producing scholars and leaders who have had influence on every segment of society. Today the University has buildings that house modern technology. Residence halls serve as homes to students, and intercollegiate sports can be enjoyed in some of the finest facilities in the country. The faculty is made up of men and women who come from all over the world and the total enrollment is more than 21,000.

The campus scene today is far different than it was in the founding, early years of the University of Mississippi. Ole Miss has survived the intrusion of power hungry politicians, wars, storms, riots, and the wear of the years. Today, she stands strong as a great university among her peers.

This is a brief look at the University of Mississippi since its founding in 1848. It is far from complete or thorough. For those interested in reading in-depth about the University and its history, David Sansing's *The University of Mississippi: A Sesquicentennial History* is a great account of the University's history. William Doyle's *An American Insurrection: The Battle of Oxford, Mississippi, 1962* is a riveting account of the integration of the University. For extensive coverage of the struggle of African-American students at the University, Nadine Cahodas' *Let the Band Play Dixie* is an excellent read.

The founding and early years

In February 1840, James Alexander Ventress brought a bill before the Mississippi State Legislature that would provide for the location of a university for the state of Mississippi. The bill was passed by both houses of the legislature and signed by Governor Alexander McNutt on February 20, 1840. In an address to the legislature in 1839, McNutt sent a message to the lawmakers in which he noted, "Patriotism, no less than economy, urges upon us the duty of educating our children at home. Those opposed to us in principle cannot safely be entrusted with the education of our sons and daughters." The birth of the University of Mississippi arose from the need to spend monies for "seminary lands" that had been sold by the state. There also was a sense of urgency to provide local higher education for students without the influence of those who did not embrace the "ways" of the state of Mississippi. Seeking to preserve a way of life, the founders believed that education is the process by which a culture ensures its existence and transmits itself across time. These founders' resistance to change, which they viewed as their right, if not their obligation, thus created the University of Mississippi as a bastion in defense of "the Southern way of life."

February 21, 1840, one day following the passage of the bill to establish a state university, the legislature appointed a special committee to locate a site for the new university. After almost a year, the committee came back to the legislature and presented a list of sites. After much deliberation, on January 27, 1841, Oxford was selected over Mississippi City (on the Gulf

PRESIDENT

GEORGE FREDERICK HOLMES (1848-49) Elected to serve as president when he was only 28, George Frederick Holmes is distinguished as the University's youngest president, its first president—and its most transitory president. He served only five months, due to illness in his family and difficulties in maintaining discipline on campus. Born in 1820 in Georgetown, British Guyana, Holmes was reared in England but journeyed to Canada and the United States in his late teens to teach and practice law.

President Holmes was a prolific writer; many of his essays were published in the Southern Quarterly Review before he was 25. He taught briefly at Richmond College and the College of William and Mary before coming to The University of Mississippi in 1848. Holmes helped inspire and organize the University's Hermaean Literary Society, which existed until 1946.

PRESIDENT

AUGUSTUS BALDWIN LONGSTREET (1849-56) Born in 1790, Augustus Baldwin Longstreet was the first of four Yale graduates to serve as president of the University, and he was the first of three presidents to be an ordained minister. A man of many trades, Longstreet worked as a lawyer, legislator, judge, and journalist in Georgia, where he started his own publication, The Sentinel, in Augusta. He also was a prominent author. His *Georgia Scenes*, a collection of humorous stories, was published by Harper in 1840. Longstreet served as president of Emory College in Oxford, Georgia, and of Centenary College in Shreveport, Louisiana, before being elected to the post at the University of Mississippi. During his tenure, several social fraternities were organized, the School of Law was started and a professorship of governmental science and law was added to the faculty.

Coast) by a vote of 58 to 57. The University was chartered by an act of the Mississippi State Legislature on February 24, 1844, and placed under the supervision of a board of 13 trustees, of which Ventress was the first appointed. James Alexander Ventress is known as the "father of the University" and Ventress Hall is named after him. The land for the new university was purchased from local land owners whose names were Stockard and Martin.

George Frederick Holmes was elected by the trustees as the first president of the University and on November 6, 1848, he welcomed the first students to the University of Mississippi. In an effort to avoid any appearance of indulging in aristocracy, the University had an open admissions policy, even to the extent of extending an offer of free admission to "any young man desirous of entering the University, but unable to pay for tuition." Eighty students, some no older than sixteen, became the first class of students. All were from Mississippi with the exception of one young man who was from Memphis, Tennessee. The open admissions policy proved a failure. Only 47 remained through the full term with five being expelled, eight suspended, 12 allowed to withdraw, and eight whose records show "absented themselves, whereabouts unknown."

Holmes's tenure as president of Mississippi's first state university was short lived. He left the University to return to Virginia in early March of 1849, and his absence was officially attributed to his ill health and that of his child. Perhaps more pertinent to Holmes's departure was the failure of an honor system that he had attempted to institute and the unruly nature of the students who first came to the University of Mississippi.

Augustus B. Longstreet replaced Holmes as president in 1849. Longstreet was a southerner by birth and had distinguished himself as a lawyer, judge, writer, and minister. Longstreet's tenure witnessed the first significant growth of the University from the original 80 students in 1848 to 232 students in 1856. Referred to by students as "Old Bullet" or "The Judge," Longstreet was a strict disciplinarian. After becoming involved in a dispute with political parties and criticized for being absent from the campus in his role as a businessman and clergyman, Longstreet resigned his position as president in 1856, and one year later became the president of the University of South Carolina.

F. A. P. Barnard and the Civil War

The next president of the University of Mississippi would leave an indelible mark on the institution. A young professor of mathematics and natural philosophy, Frederick Augustus Porter Barnard, a native of Massachusetts and a graduate of Yale, worked from 1831 to 1838 at the American Asylum for the Deaf and Dumb and at the New York

CHANCELLOR

FREDERICK AUGUSTUS PORTER BARNARD (1856-61)
Frederick A.P. Barnard was the University's first "chancellor" (the title was changed from "president" in 1858), and he was perhaps its most ardent and idealistic proponent. He aspired to make the University the greatest scientific institution in the world, establishing an ideal that has challenged and inspired his successors. Born in 1809, he graduated from Yale in 1828 and began teaching. In 1838, he accepted a position teaching mathematics and natural philosophy at the University of Alabama, and, in 1854, he accepted a similar position at the University of Mississippi. Shortly after assuming the presidency in 1856, Barnard convinced the Legislature to appropriate funds to order the largest telescope in the world for the University and to construct an observatory for it on campus. The observatory (now called Barnard Observatory), which today houses the Center for the Study of Southern Culture, was completed, but because of the Civil War the telescope was diverted to Chicago, where it remains today at Northwestern University. Barnard, a minister and musician, left Oxford during the Civil War and became president of Columbia University, where he remained for 25 years. He is the only University of Mississippi chancellor to be elected as an undergraduate to Phi Beta Kappa.

CHANCELLOR

JOHN NEWTON WADDEL (1865-74)
One of the University's original trustees and faculty members, Waddel was 36 when he came to the University of Mississippi in 1848, where he remained until the Civil War. An ordained Presbyterian minister, Waddel had served as commissioner of army missions for the Confederate Army in 1863 and had preached many sermons to troops. After the war, he was a highly influential and stabilizing force for the University and the community, encouraging the revival of the Alumni Association and student organizations. With the idea of revising the curriculum here, he visited leading universities in the North and East, ultimately achieving a new curriculum similar to that of the University of Michigan. Waddel was a graduate of the University of Georgia, where his father had served as president. He worked as a cotton farmer in Alabama, taught at the Willington Academy in South Carolina and established the Montrose Academy in Jasper County, Mississippi, before he was elected chair of the Ancient Languages Department at the University of Mississippi. He resigned the chancellorship to become secretary of education for the Presbyterian Church of the United States.

Institution for the Deaf and Dumb. In 1838, he accepted the chair of mathematics at the University of Alabama in Tuscaloosa and from 1848 to 1854 served as professor of chemistry and natural philosophy.

Barnard was elected to the faculty of the University of Mississippi in 1854 as professor of mathematics and natural philosophy. Barnard set about with all of his energy to make the University of Mississippi a great institution of higher learning. He disagreed with the existing system of student discipline as designed by Longstreet, especially the daily visitation to students' rooms by faculty members. With a free and flexible manner that won him the devotion of the students, Barnard saw the need for the students to have a life outside of the classroom and promoted the building of a student gymnasium and the establishment of literary societies. The gymnasium was one of the first in the nation for an antebellum college. For his focus on students, Barnard was praised by the student magazine "for endeavoring to infuse into the minds of students a love for...profound critical scholarship and high toned unblemished moral character."

Barnard wrote to the Board of Trustees of the University in 1858 and promoted an idea called "universitas scientiarum," which was a comprehensive plan to make the University of Mississippi "a true university that included all branches of science, medicine, agriculture, law, classical studies, civil and political history, and oriental learning." Although the faculty was dubious, the Board approved the "universitas scientiarum" plan with the exception of a training program for elementary and secondary education, a school of agriculture, and a school of engineering. With the adoption of this program, the title of "President of the University" was changed to "Chancellor of the University."

Throughout Barnard's tenure, the University was attacked by newspapers and lawmakers for being located in Oxford and for "pandering to the wealthy aristocracy." The attacks and constant criticism contributed to Barnard's weariness and frustration and led him to conclude that the University of Mississippi "was a thing too far above the ruling stupidity of the day to be a success." Barnard's status as chancellor was most severely damaged by the "Branham Affair."

Branham was a physician in Oxford and the son-in-law of former president Longstreet and the brother-in-law of faculty member L. Q. C. Lamar. Branham had held Barnard responsible for undermining the authority of Longstreet in his last days as president and had waited for the opportunity to seek revenge against Barnard.

May 12, 1859, while Barnard was out of town, two students entered Barnard's faculty house. One of the students, Samuel B. Humphreys, allegedly raped and brutally beat a slave of the

CHANCELLOR

ALEXANDER PETER STEWART
(1874-87) The only Civil War general to serve as chancellor of the University of Mississippi, Alexander Peter Stewart walked away from a $6,000-a-year job with the St. Louis Mutual Life Insurance Company to take the job here—which paid about $2,500 a year. Stewart's tenure was marked by firsts. Baseball was introduced to the University in 1876. The University's first Ph.D. was granted in 1877. The University became coeducational in 1882. And the first woman faculty member was appointed in 1885. Born in 1821, Stewart was a graduate of West Point Military Academy, and he taught mathematics at Cumberland University in Tennessee before the start of the Civil War. Stewart entered the Confederate Army as a major, was promoted rapidly and was appointed lieutenant general on June 23, 1864. Stewart was a commander in the Army of Tennessee and was distinguished in the battles of Shiloh, Perryville, Murfreesboro, Chickamauga, and Missionary Ridge.

CHANCELLOR

EDWARD MAYES

(1887-91) Edward Mayes was the first native Mississippian and the first University of Mississippi alumnus to become chancellor of the University. Born in Hinds County in 1846, Mayes served as a private in the Fourth Regiment of Mississippi Cavalry during the Civil War. When the University reopened after the war, Mayes was the first non-Oxford student to arrive—in October 1865. He was one of only 193 students enrolled at the University that year. After graduating in 1868, Mayes practiced law in Coffeeville and Oxford. He was selected to teach law at the University in 1877. During his tenure, Ventress Hall was constructed as the University's first library building. Mayes returned to his law practice at the end of his term, and he later served as dean of the Millsaps School of Law. Among his most notable writings is a history of education in Mississippi.

chancellor. Humphreys was called to a hearing before the faculty on May 23. He was found not guilty on counts of entering the chancellor's residence and assaulting the slave because at the time the word of a slave against a white man was not admissible in court. In a second vote of the court, Humphrey was "morally convicted." Barnard was not satisfied with the ruling of the faculty and took it upon himself to write Humphreys' parents and request that they withdraw their son from the University, which they did. The young man applied for re-admission in the fall, but Barnard denied his admission, which not only prompted a small rebellion by students but also provided Branham an opportunity to bring into question Barnard's stand on slavery and state's rights. Again, rumors were circulated that Barnard had denied Humphreys' testimony on the basis of "negro testimony."

Upset and frustrated, Barnard requested of Governor John R. Pettus that the charges against him, especially his stance on slavery, be subjected to the "fullest and most searching investigation." Pettus convened the Board of Trustees, who heard testimony in March 1860. Even though Barnard owned slaves himself, he had misgivings about the institution of slavery and would later denounce it. But on that day in 1860, the chancellor of the University of Mississippi stood before the Board of Trustees and declared, "I am as sound on the slavery question as any member of this board."

The Board of Trustees absolved

Barnard of the charges, yet he remained subject to criticism by the evangelical clergy and the press. When Mississippi seceded from the Union on January 9, 1861, Barnard found the beginnings of his way out of the University of Mississippi. Upon returning from Washington February 2, 1861, Barnard discovered a campus stirred by the fire of secession and the rumors of war. Flags of the Confederacy flew from windows, and students stole and burned books favoring the abolition of slavery on the campus grounds. May 1, 1861, the University Greys, later Company A of the 11th Mississippi Infantry, boarded trains for Corinth and left the University to defend "their way of life." Other students had enlisted elsewhere, and the campus was ghostly, prompting Barnard to write, "We are indeed inhabitants of solitude... Our University has ceased to have visible existence." During the Civil War, the University served as a hospital for both Confederate and Union troops.

In the fall of 1861, when only four students arrived to enroll, the Board held an emergency meeting in Jackson and voted to close the University of Mississippi. At that time, Barnard was relieved of his duties as the third president and the first chancellor of the University. In May 1864, Barnard was elected president of Columbia College and distinguished himself as a great educator. Barnard College was named in his honor.

F. A. P. Barnard fought numerous battles as chancellor of the University of

CHANCELLOR

ROBERT BURWELL FULTON
(1892-1906) Another University of Mississippi alumnus, Robert Burwell Fulton served as chancellor longer than any of his predecessors and deserves credit for establishing the School of Engineering (1900), the School of Education (1903), and the School of Medicine (1903). Born in 1849 in Sumter County, Ala., Fulton graduated with honors from the University of Mississippi in 1869. After teaching stints in Alabama and Louisiana, Fulton returned to Oxford in 1871 as assistant professor of physics and astronomy. He achieved full professor status in 1875 and was the first director of the Mississippi Weather Service. His leadership was largely responsible for the organization of the National Association of State Universities; he served as its president for five consecutive years. During Fulton's tenure, football was introduced to the University (1893), and the University's first printed annual was published (1897). Its name, The Ole Miss, soon became synonymous with the University of Mississippi.

CHANCELLOR

ANDREW ARMSTRONG KINCANNON

(1907-14) Born in Noxubee County in 1859, Andrew Armstrong Kincannon was the second Mississippi native to serve as the University's chief administrator. Striving to make the University a progressive school, he pointed to other top state schools around the country, such as the University of Michigan and the University of Wisconsin, to inspire an attitude of enthusiasm and growth. After graduating from the National Normal University of Ohio in 1884, Kincannon taught at Mississippi A&M College (now Mississippi State University), was superintendent of the new public school system in Meridian, and was president of the Industrial Institute and College (now Mississippi University for Women) before being elected chancellor of Ole Miss. During his tenure, the University grew in size and reputation: some of its younger graduates were among the first of a growing list of Rhodes Scholars; the School of Pharmacy opened in 1908; and, in 1911, The Mississippian, the University's student newspaper, was started under the auspices of the YMCA and two literary societies. But there was increasing animosity in the legislature toward the University: fraternities and sororities were banished by law in 1912.

Mississippi. His dream of "universitas scientiarum" was never realized, but it was the initial dream of the University becoming a great institution of higher education. In a way, his connections saved the University during the Civil War. While most of Oxford was burned by Union troops led by General A. J. "Whiskey" Smith in 1864, much of the campus was spared. General William Tecumseh Sherman, a friend of Barnard's with whom he had taught at Louisiana Seminary, had issued an order that the campus be spared. In a letter he had written to Barnard, Sherman noted — "When I rode through the grounds of the college, I thought of you... and... thought I saw traces of your life, of which I remember you spoke."

One of the buildings that was spared was the new observatory which was to house, at the time, the world's larg-est telescope. Today it is Barnard Observatory and houses the Center for the Study of Southern Culture.

Post-war years

The University of Mississippi reopened its doors to students in the fall of 1865 under the leadership of Chancellor John Waddel. The faculty members expected no more than 50 students, but were surprised when

86 showed up. The number of students grew over the academic year and swelled to 107 before the term ended. This new group of students was much like the entering class in 1848. Five were juniors, 41 were sophomores, 50 were freshmen. In addition, there were 40 "partial course" students and 57 preparatory students. The preparatory students were those who could not meet admission requirements to the University. Tuition and "fuel" expenses were $75 dollars a year, and students were charged $15 dollars a month for boarding fees.

National events brought about by the end of the Civil War and the emancipation of slaves began to change the landscape of higher education in Mississippi. The Morrill Land Grant Act of 1862 created Alcorn A&M College for the education of freed slaves. In addition, Mississippi Agricultural and Mechanical College, now Mississippi State University, opened its doors to students in 1880 and attracted the sons of Mississippi's blue collar workers, in contrast to the University in Oxford, which was seen as the school of the "aristocracy." Mississippi A&M came to be known as the "People's College."

In 1874, Alexander "Old Straight" Stewart succeeded Waddel as chancellor. His immediate challenge was to stop the alarming enrollment decline that was beginning to occur. The enrollment of 302 in 1873 fell to 208 in 1874, to 131 in 1875, to 125 in 1876. As a result of their concern for the University, the Board published a pamphlet entitled "Where Shall I Send My Son?" It

CHANCELLOR

JOSEPH NEELY POWERS
(1914-24; 1930-32) Joseph Neely Powers is perhaps best known as an educator for his role in establishing the agricultural high schools that would become the basis for the community college system in Mississippi. A native of Havana, Ala., Powers was born in 1869. He taught in several rural schools and later served as a principal and superintendent. Governor James K. Vardaman appointed Powers as state superintendent of education, a post to which he was subsequently elected. Powers enjoyed enormous popularity as chancellor of the University of Mississippi, although he was subjected to scandal and political favoritism during the political administrations of Governor Theodore Bilbo and Governor Lee Russell. He was voted out of office by the University's trustees in 1924 but was reappointed for a brief, turbulent period in the early 1930s. Powers is credited with the establishment of the School of Commerce. In another notable action, he permitted William Faulkner, the future Nobel Prize winner, to enroll at Ole Miss without a high school diploma—as a special student.

CHANCELLOR

ALFRED HUME

(1924-30; 1932-35) Alfred Hume was the first University of Mississippi chancellor to possess an earned doctorate, and he was perhaps one of the most dedicated to the University, devoting nearly 60 years of his life to the school. A Tennessee native born in 1866, Dr. Hume began teaching mathematics and astronomy at the University of Mississippi immediately after he received his doctorate from Vanderbilt University. Besides serving two terms as chancellor, he was called upon three additional times to serve as acting chancellor. Dr. Hume made many enduring contributions to the University. In 1927, he organized the graduate program into an administrative entity of its own. He started a significant building program, which included plans for the construction of Fulton Chapel, Bondurant Hall, the gymnasium, the high-school building, Lewis Hall, the School of Law, the cafeteria, six dormitories for men, one women's dormitory, Hemingway Stadium, and the Field House. Fraternities were allowed to reorganize. Most significantly, however, Hume is credited with preventing Governor Theodore G. Bilbo from moving the University to Jackson.

included a history and description of the University and made reference to the high morals and strong religious element "in the student body." Within the pamphlet, the public was assured by the faculty and citizens of Oxford that since the war "drinking, gambling, extravagance, and dissipation of every kind have been diminishing." The Board stated categorically, "There are no sons of rich men there." The pamphlet proved an effective recruiting tool. Enrollment jumped from 125 in 1876 to 471 in 1877.

The changing campus

The University would make a major change in 1882 when women were first admitted as students. They were not allowed to dine with men and were required to live off campus or in the homes of faculty members, and were provided separate study rooms. The first women students quickly established themselves as a presence at the University. In the first class to graduate with women students, Sally Vick Hill received the highest honors. In 1885, Sarah Isom McGehee was appointed the first woman faculty member at the University. She was a tutor of elocution. The Sarah Isom Center for Women and Gender Studies was established in her honor and memory in 1981 to address the changing roles and expectations of women students, faculty, and staff. The University has been a leader in providing educational opportunities for women. Eleven women entered the University when its doors were opened to women. Today, women make up more than half of the student body, and a woman has served as provost. Five women have served as vice chancellors.

Greek letter societies became a part of the University during Longstreet's term as president. He had been a member of the Mystic Seven at Emory University and helped establish the chapter at the University of Mississippi. Records show that Delta Kappa Epsilon was the first fraternity on campus and was established in 1850. By the time the Civil War started, there were nine fraternities on the Ole Miss campus. All closed with the onset of the conflict and the first to reopen after the war was Sigma Alpha Epsilon in 1866. In 1881, the Greek societies came under strong attack by the Board for appearing to exist only for the sons of wealthy men. These groups narrowly escaped banishment by the Board of Trustees.

The public began to lose faith in Chancellor Stewart because of his inability to control student discipline problems. Numerous complaints about student discipline were recorded. Throwing rocks at passing trains, annoying passengers at the depot, gambling, hazing of students, kangaroo courts, drinking, cheating, and disrespectful behavior toward faculty all became fodder for the state press, for sermons from pulpits and for general conversation. In 1876, it was reported that "tying balls of fire to the tails of

CHANCELLOR

ALFRED BENJAMIN BUTTS
(1935-46) A recognized scholar and law professor, Alfred Benjamin Butts was born in 1890. He received a B.S. degree from Mississippi A&M College in 1911 and a Ph.D. from Columbia University in 1920. While head of the Department of Education and Sociology at A&M, he spent summers teaching at numerous universities around the country, including at Yale, where he earned a law degree in 1930. Dr. Butts' most daunting task upon assuming the chancellorship in 1935 was to restore the University's accreditation, which had been lost during the Bilbo administration. This was achieved in 1941. Dr. Butts is credited with pulling the University through the Great Depression. To his credit, a substantial amount of construction was achieved despite economic difficulties: the Student Union (Weir Hall), the Physics and Astronomy Building (Lewis Hall), 21 new faculty houses, and 17 sorority and fraternity houses. Also during Dr. Butts' term, the name "Rebels" was selected for the football team.

CHANCELLOR

JOHN DAVIS WILLIAMS
(1946-68) John Davis Williams was chancellor for 22 years, and his influence on the University was profound. During the years of growth after World War II, he reorganized the administrative structure of the rapidly expanding University. He kept the University open and stabilized during the difficult period of integration in 1962. He saw the University experience a revival of athletics (the football teams were consistently successful during his term as chancellor). He helped the University celebrate its Centennial (an event highlighted by the publication of Dr. J. Allen Cabaniss' *A History of The University of Mississippi*). A Kentucky native born in 1902, Williams was the first and only chancellor to hold the Ed.D. (Doctor of Education) degree. In 1955, he oversaw the establishment of the Medical Center campus in Jackson and the transition from a two-year medical program to a four-year school that was fully accredited. Three years later (1958), the School of Nursing was added on the Jackson campus. Doctoral programs were authorized in biology, physics, political science, and psychology, and Carrier Scholarships were established to attract the best students. Also during his long tenure, the University built an alumni headquarters and celebrated its unique relationship with William Faulkner.

calves on dark nights to see them run across campus" had become a favorite pastime. This led to the prohibition of faculty keeping livestock on campus.

Stewart also found himself dealing with the problem of student housing. The dormitory system that constituted the mixing of boys from the "preparatory school," some as young as the age of 13, with older students, some of whom were now veterans of the Civil War, had long been a source of problems for the administration and faculty. Weekly room inspections were instituted, and the enforcement of this was uneven at best with some faculty members taking the duties seriously and others arguing that it was inconsistent with the atmosphere that should be promoted on a college campus. The inconsistent enforcement of this practice contributed to the student misconduct. Stewart decided to resign his position in July, 1886. In a bold move, the trustees abolished the chancellor title and allowed the faculty to elect a person from the faculty to serve as a chairman of the faculty. The faculty unanimously elected Edward Mayes, the first nativeborn Mississippian and alumnus of the University to so serve.

In 1889 another major reorganization of the academic

framework of the University took place. Degree requirements were changed, making nineteen departments (or schools) inside the Department of Science, Literature, and the Arts. There also was a Department of Professional Studies, but it consisted only of the School of Law. The title chancellor was reinstated, and Mayes continued serving in that position, with the full support of the board and faculty colleagues.

Mayes was unusually energetic and spoke to audiences throughout the state about the University. He earlier had written at length about the debt the state owed the University as a result seminary funds having been misused. Though he and Senator James Z. George, a supporter of Mississippi A & M, had earlier disagreed on this matter, Senator George later assisted the University "in securing... an additional grant of land from the United States Congress." Under the leadership of Mayes and with the assistance of funding from the state, buildings

CHANCELLOR

PORTER LEE FORTUNE JR.
(1968-84) Porter Lee Fortune Jr. was chancellor during a period of remarkable growth and development. Born in 1920, Fortune served as a naval officer during World War II and saw action in the South Pacific, where he was awarded the Bronze Star. After receiving his Ph.D. from the University of North Carolina at Chapel Hill, he joined the faculty at Mississippi Southern College (now the University of Southern Mississippi), where he later served as dean of the university and graduate school. During his first 10 years as chancellor of the University of Mississippi, Dr. Fortune saw enrollment increase by 40 percent and black enrollment increase from 17 students to 733 students. Dr. Fortune is remembered for helping to smooth the way for both black and white students during the civil rights movement. During his administration, funds were finalized for the construction of the Ole Miss Union; the Turner Health, Physical Education, and Recreation Center; the athletic dormitory; the chemistry building (Coulter Hall); Dorothy Crosby Hall; the Kate Skipwith Teaching Museum; Anderson Hall; the Lamar Law Center; and the J.D. Williams Library addition. The schools of Health Related Professions and Dentistry were added to the Medical Center during his chancellorship, as was the School of Accountancy on the Oxford campus. New programs under his administration included women's studies, African-American studies, communicative disorders, social work, and court reporting. Other legacies of the Fortune administration include the University of Mississippi Foundation, the Chancellor's Trust, and the Alumni Hall of Fame. But Chancellor Fortune may be best-remembered for promoting the development of the eastern part of the campus as a culture center—including the acquisition of Rowan Oak, the William Faulkner property, and the Skipwith property—which attracts visitors and scholars from around the world.

CHANCELLOR

ROBERT GERALD TURNER

(1984-95) The second youngest of the University's chancellors, Gerald Turner is credited with boosting the University's enrollment and with significantly increasing endowment funds. Spearheading the University's first capital campaign solely for academic enrichment and following that with a campaign to raise funds to bring athletics facilities to SEC standards, Dr. Turner oversaw a private fundraising effort that resulted in gifts to Ole Miss of more than $100 million. During his chancellorship, the University's endowment increased from $8 million to $64 million.

A Texan, Dr. Turner received his Ph.D. in psychology in 1975 from the University of Texas at Austin. He advanced rapidly through a succession of teaching and administrative positions at Pepperdine University and later served as vice president for executive affairs at the University of Oklahoma before being named chancellor of the University of Mississippi. During his administration, seven new academic programs were introduced and six federally funded national centers were established: the Jamie L. Whitten National Center for Physical Acoustics, the National Center for the Development of Natural Products, the Marine Mineral Research Institute, the Center for Computational Hydroscience and Engineering, the National Food Service Management Institute, and the Center for Water and Wetlands Resources. The Mississippi Supercomputing Center was established on campus, and externally funded research programs increased more than 300 percent. Twelve Barnard Distinguished Professorships were created from private funds, and the University's 23rd Rhodes Scholar, Mississippi's first African-American honoree, was named. Minority enrollment increased 85 percent, and the University received two Peterson Awards for Excellence in Graduate Admissions for Minority Students. More than $200 million in new construction was completed, initiated, or approved on the Oxford and Jackson campuses prior to his departure to become president of Southern Methodist University in Dallas, Texas, in May 1995.

were renovated, streets were laid, a new library was constructed, the first fraternity house (for Delta Psi) was built, the Mississippi Historical Society was founded (in 1890), and graduate student fellowships were created.

Mayes then made the tough decision to terminate Professors Hutson, Johnson, Quinche, Sears, and Latham because of continual complaints about their competence as teachers. It was a move that rankled some who thought the professors' years of service warranted a nobler end than firing. But Mayes followed through.

Although he had many enthusiastic followers, some of whom suggested him for various political offices, others never forgave Mayes for his decision. Perhaps because of this ill will (no doubt spurred by the fact that Quinche committed suicide shortly after his firing), Mayes elected to return to the law profession; he submitted his resignation in 1891 and joined a law firm in December of that year.

Chancellor Robert Fulton succeeded Mayes and took it upon himself to enhance the beauty of the campus. One of his most lasting and endearing contributions to the geography and spirit of the campus was a wooded area set aside in the center of the campus that would become known to generations of University of Mississippi students and alumni as "the Grove." With Fulton at the helm, the nature of life outside of the classroom changed dramatically. Ricks Hall, a women's dormitory was built, and the Parthenic Society, a women's literary society, was founded. Fulton also built a male dormitory for 200 students that included a large dining hall.

Student activities also became so popular in the 1890s that the YMCA began publishing a handbook for new students. Clubs and organizations included the Glee Club, the YMCA, the Mandolin and Guitar Club, the University Orchestra, and the Minstrels, a traveling music troupe. Academic clubs listed were the Science Club, the University Teachers Club, the Press Club, the Sketch Club, and the Dramatic Club. The Kodak Club, the F.O.X. Social Club, and the Cotillion Club were listed as social organizations. There were two "shooting clubs" included in the YMCA handbook. One was a gun club and the other was "unrestricted and open to all crap shooters." Women's clubs included were the Talkatani Club, the SSS Club, the YWCA, the Women's Athletic Association, the Tennis Club, and the Gymnasium Club.

The first student newspaper, The University Record, appeared in 1898 and was published once a week on Wednesdays. The Record folded in 1902 and was replaced by the Varsity Voice. In 1911, The Mississippian replaced the Varsity Voice, and it remains today as the student newspaper of the University of Mississippi and the oldest student newspaper in the state.

The University becomes Ole Miss

There would be no single event that would have a more lasting effect on the University of Mississippi than the naming of the initial yearbook published in 1897. In a contest to name the yearbook, which was dedicated to the University Greys, Elma Meek suggested the name OLE MISS. Within two years students and alumni

CHANCELLOR

ROBERT CONRAD KHAYAT
(1995-2009) A respected academician and administrator, Robert Khayat was a professor of law and served as associate dean of the School of Law, vice chancellor for university affairs, and director of the Sesquicentennial before being named chancellor of the University of Mississippi in 1995. He received his bachelor's degree in education from Ole Miss in 1961 and graduated with honors with his Ole Miss law school class in 1966. As a student-athlete, Chancellor Khayat demonstrated that athletes can succeed academically and be active in student life. During his undergraduate years he was tapped for membership in ODK, was active in the YMCA and served on ASB committees. Named an Academic All-American football player in 1959, he led the nation in kick-scoring in 1958 and 1959 and was selected to play in the 1960 College All-Star game. He played for the Washington Redskins from 1960-64 and was a member of the 1961 NFL Pro Bowl team.

Chancellor Khayat joined the Ole Miss faculty in 1969 as a law professor. While on leave from Ole Miss during 1980-81, he earned a master's degree in law from Yale University on a Sterling Fellowship. He returned as a law professor in 1981, advancing to the position of associate dean. He served as Ole Miss vice chancellor for university affairs from 1984-89. On leave from the University, he became the first president of the NCAA Foundation with a mission of promoting academic and personal development opportunities for college athletes.

He returned as law professor in 1992 and later began chairing the University's 150th anniversary celebration. The School of Law student body chose Professor Khayat as their 1993-94 Outstanding Law Professor of the Year, and the school's Mississippi Law Journal staff established a scholarship in his name in 1995.

He has served as Oxford-Lafayette County Chamber of Commerce president and was named Oxford's Citizen of the Year. The National Football Foundation presented him with the Distinguished American Award in 1987 and 1989. He also was featured in the 1987-88 and 1988-89 NFL yearbooks for achieving success after football, where he was cited as "one of the NFL's best examples of a successful scholar-athlete."

During his 14 years at the helm, Chancellor Khayat made an indelible impact on the University through enhancing the learning environment, increasing enrollment, and heading two capital campaigns generating almost $775 million in private support. The University created the Sally McDonnell Barksdale Honors College, Croft Institute for International Studies, Lott Leadership Institute, and Winter Institute for Racial Reconciliation while he was chancellor.

Chancellor Khayat spearheaded the effort that resulted in UM's becoming the first public institution of higher learning in Mississippi chosen for a Phi Beta Kappa chapter, thus establishing a climate of excellence for all endeavors at the University of Mississippi. Also during his tenure, Ole Miss hosted a presidential debate, announced its 25th Rhodes Scholar, and inaugurated the first black president of the alumni association.

were using the name of the yearbook as a name for the University.

Four years prior to the naming of the yearbook, the University played its first football game in 1893. Fulton is remembered for bringing many outstanding and memorable faculty members to the University of Mississippi, but none would rival Alexander

Bondurant for his role in the formation of the identity of the University. A Harvard-trained Latin professor, Bondurant introduced intercollegiate football to the University, coached the first team, and guided the program through its early years. The University of Mississippi played its first football game November 11, 1893, at University Park on campus against the Southwestern Baptist University of Jackson, Tennessee, before a large crowd. The "Oxford" team won 56-0.

Fulton had served honorably as chancellor but found himself embroiled in controversy over growing dissention between the Greeks and non-Greeks. The recommendation for abolishing the system went before the Board of Trustees, but Fulton intervened and became the target of public ridicule. Eventually, the Board voted to relieve Chancellor Fulton of his duties. Fulton was followed by Andrew Kincannon, who pledged in his early remarks to transform the University from an "aristocracy" to a "democracy." Kincannon established an Honor Council vested with authority over a wide range of discipline problems. This organization would be the predecessor to the Associated Student Body which still operates today. He also used the largest state appropriation to date to enlarge the infirmary, provide an updated water and sewage system for the campus, construct a laundry building, and build a new men's dormitory. Kincannon also dealt with accusations of misappropriation of University monies, a scandal involving paying football players. Perhaps the greatest controversy with which Kincannon had to deal was the decision of the state legislature to prohibit "secret societies" (fraternities). Charged before the state legislature for "encouraging dissipation, wasting money, discouraging study and scholarship, interfering with the literary societies, and destroying the college spirit by promoting cliques," the fraternities had little chance. The law would remain in effect until 1926 when the legislature passed a law allowing secret societies on campus. Kincannon dealt with the same issues that plagued many of his predecessors, and he resigned in 1914 stating that "he was unwilling for the school to become a political chattel."

CHANCELLOR

DANIEL W. JONES (2009-2015) Dr. Daniel W. Jones became the 16th chancellor of the University of Mississippi on July 1, 2009. Prior to his appointment, Dr. Jones was vice chancellor for Health Affairs, Dean of the School of Medicine, and Herbert G. Langford Professor of Medicine at the University of Mississippi Medical Center (UMMC) in Jackson. He served as the UMMC's chief executive officer for six years, overseeing its five schools and the medical center.

Dr. Jones is a native Mississippian who graduated from Mississippi College in 1971 and earned his M.D. in 1975 at the University of Mississippi Medical Center, where he also completed his residency in internal medicine in 1978. He entered into private practice in Laurel before going to Korea in 1985 to serve as a medical missionary.

Under Dr. Jones' leadership, the university undertook a major initiative to promote diversity across all of its campuses and launched an unprecedented construction boom, including new academic, residential and athletics facilities. Enrollment surged nearly 26 percent, and donations to the university hit record high levels.

During his six-year term, he focused on servant leadership and led UM faculty, staff and students to contribute thousands of hours to causes across the community, the state and around the world. At his 2010 inauguration, Chancellor Jones highlighted attracting faculty support as a priority. By 2015, the university assembled almost $40 million in endowed funds to provide ongoing support to strengthen teaching and research by UM faculty.

Dr. Jones is now the vice chancellor emeritus for Health Affairs and Dean Emeritus of the School of Medicine.

Joseph Neely Powers succeeded Kincannon in 1914, and by 1916 was enjoying an unusually high enrollment of 641 students. Unfortunately, the physical structure of the campus was inadequate to accommodate the large number of students, and the financial situation left by Kincannon made it difficult to provide new facilities. During World War I, many of the students left for service. Those who remained were busy preparing for military service, and the campus took on the appearance of a military base. After the war, campus enrollment swelled, and the legislature was forced to appropriate money to build and refurbish facilities. With this money, a new science hall was built, as well as three new men's dormitories and one women's dormitory. In 1923, enrollment on the Ole Miss campus reached more than 800 students.

Alfred Hume replaced Powers in 1924. His tenure as Chancellor would coincide with the 1927 election of Governor Theodore Bilbo, who wreaked havoc in higher education in

Mississippi. Shortly after his election, Bilbo initiated an effort to relocate the University to Jackson. Chancellor Hume fought him on this and in an address before the Board of Trustees, he eloquently pleaded, "Gentlemen, you may move the University of Mississippi. You may move it to Jackson or anywhere else. You may uproot it from the hallowed ground on which it has stood for 80 years. You may take it from the surroundings that have become dear to the thousands who have gone from its door. But, gentlemen, don't call it Ole Miss." The Board voted to keep the University in Oxford, which angered Bilbo, who removed Hume as chancellor and appointed former Chancellor Powers. In addition to Hume, 179 employees at the four major institutions of higher learning in Mississippi were

Ventress Hall

fired. This became known as "Bilbo's Purge." Because of Bilbo's interference in higher education, all institutions in the state lost their accreditation granted by the Southern Association of Colleges and Schools.

After Martin Conner was elected governor in 1931, a new Board of Trustees was appointed, Powers was dismissed, and former Chancellor Alfred Hume once again was appointed chancellor. He served only until 1935 when he retired to become chairman and professor of mathematics, positions which he held until he was 80 years of age. Hume Hall, home of the mathematics department, is named in his honor and memory.

Campus growth and the Rebels

Alfred Benjamin Butts became chancellor in 1935 and is recognized as the most visionary chancellor since Barnard. He was the first to assume the role of fundraiser for the University, which prospered under his leadership. In 1939, 55 building projects were underway on campus. Among the additions to the campus were Guyton Hall, the cafeteria (Johnson Commons), a gymnasium, an athletic field house, a women's dormitory, six men's dormitories, a new law school, University High School, and an 18,000 seat football stadium, Hemingway Stadium. In addition, Weir Hall was built as the first student union building and housed the bookstore, the post office, the Grill, a game room, a barber shop, a clothing store, and meeting rooms.

Chancellor Butts steered the University through World War II. The enrollment on campus dwindled from more than 1,400 in 1941-1942 to a mere 800 students in 1944. Many professors had been called away in the service of their country. During

CHANCELLOR

JEFFREY S. VITTER

(2016–2019) Following a national search, Dr. Jeffrey S. Vitter was named the 17th chancellor of the University of Mississippi and Distinguished Professor of Computer and Information Science in October 2015. A native of New Orleans and renowned computer scientist, Dr. Vitter graduated in mathematics with highest honors from the University of Notre Dame in 1977 and earned a Ph.D. under Don Knuth in computer science at Stanford University in 1980. He also holds an M.B.A. from Duke University.

He served previously for five and a half years as provost, executive vice chancellor, and Roy A. Roberts Distinguished Professor at the University of Kansas. Prior to joining KU, he served in leadership and academic roles at Texas A&M, Purdue, Duke, and Brown universities.

Under the leadership of Chancellor Vitter, the university earned and reaffirmed its Carnegie R1 "Very high research activity" designation, worked to tackle societal problems through multidisciplinary research networks, and hosted annual Technology Summits to position UM as a leader in STEM education.

Under Dr. Vitter's direction, UM pursued a $1 billion construction program with new spaces for academics, athletics, student activities, healthcare and essential services; collaborated with Mississippi communities to elevate community and economic development through the M Partner initiative; and advocated successfully for passage of the Healthcare Collaboration Act. A strong proponent of the UM Creed, he launched several initiatives to foster respect and diversity at the University. The Chancellor's Advisory Committee on History and Context was established to foster dialogue about the university's history with the goal of making the campus more welcoming for all.

Also under Chancellor Vitter's tenure, several notable changes occurred at the senior leadership level, including the hiring the university's first-ever vice chancellor for development and first-ever vice chancellor for diversity and community engagement. Additionally, he elevated the athletics director position to a vice chancellor designation to more accurately reflect the all-encompassing role of the position.

A recognized expert in big data and data science, Vitter returned to the faculty in January 2019 as a distinguished professor of computer and information science.

the war, University students served in medical units for both the Army and the Navy, the Specialized Training and Regiment Unit, and a unit of the Army Specialized Training Program. Campus life went on as normally as it could during the war years. With most of the male student body enlisted in military service, new roles fell to women on campus. For the first time in the history of the University, a woman, Maralyn Howell Bullion, was elected president of the Associated Student Body. Subsequently, women also were elected for the first time to the positions of editor of the yearbook and the student newspaper. One hundred and thirty-seven Ole Miss men lost their lives in World War II.

While Dean Malcolm Guess had promoted a campaign to create a friendly campus by having placards placed around campus stating, "Ole Miss, everybody speaks!", the

The stained glass window at Ventress Hall.

campus might have seemed anything but friendly in the aftermath of the war. During the 1945-46 academic year, enrollment surged to 2,005, the largest enrollment in the history of the University, and two and a half times that of the preceding year. Tensions were high with long lines, inadequate housing, and a shortage of teachers.

In addition to dealing with the challenges of the burgeoning student body numbers, Butts also faced growing criticism for his retention of Harry Mehre as football coach. After the 1945 season and Mehre's third consecutive losing football campaign, alumni became disgruntled and put pressure on Butts to fire Mehre. Also, Butts had received reports that Mehre had been inebriated at the Florida game earlier that year. The chancellor had made the decision to fire Mehre but under pressure the coach submitted his resignation on December 5, 1945. Students had become so frustrated with the chancellor and the football coach that they burned both in effigy after the firing. The Board of Trustees dismissed Butts in January, 1945.

Chancellor J. D. Williams, football and integration

John Davis Williams became the twelfth chancellor of the University of Mississippi in June, 1946. He faced the same challenges that had brought about Chancellor Butts' firing. Before he left the office of chancellor, Butts appointed Harold "Red" Drew head football coach. When Drew left to take the same position at the University of Alabama in 1947, Chancellor Williams promoted Ole Miss Assistant Coach John

CHANCELLOR

GLENN F. BOYCE

(2019–Present) In October 2019, Glenn F. Boyce was appointed by the IHL board as the 18th chancellor of the University of Mississippi. Dr. Boyce, who holds undergraduate and doctoral degrees from Ole Miss, brought more than 37 years of experience across secondary and post-secondary education in Mississippi to the position. He served previously as IHL commissioner for three years, and as associate commissioner for academic affairs. He had also served as president of Holmes Community College for nine years.

Early in his tenure, Dr. Boyce enjoyed several key successes, including securing a $26 million naming gift from Jim and Thomas Duff of Hattiesburg for the construction of a state-of-the-art science, technology, engineering and mathematics (STEM) facility on the Oxford campus. The gift significantly contributed to private support in Dr. Boyce's first year, growing to more than $127.2 million, up 26 percent from the previous fiscal year. The naming of Keith Carter as vice chancellor for intercollegiate athletics and the hiring of Lane Kiffin as head football coach were also broadly applauded.

With a student-centric focus, Chancellor Boyce prioritized instituting regular meetings with student leadership, including the Associated Student Body and Graduate Student Council. He hired the university's first-ever vice chancellor for enrollment management for the newly created Office of Enrollment Management, which brought together Financial Aid and Undergraduate Admissions to reflect current best practices in higher education and prioritize university-wide enrollment work and financial aid strategies.

On June 18, 2020, the State Institutions of Higher Learning Board of Trustees voted to approve the university's proposal to relocate the Confederate Monument from the Circle in the heart of campus to the cemetery on campus near Tad Smith Coliseum. Chancellor Boyce was committed to the relocation as a meaningful change in order to strengthen the campus' positive, productive and welcoming educational environment for all. The relocation was completed in July 2020.

During Chancellor Boyce's tenure, two prominent buildings on campus underwent name changes, including the naming of the Gertrude C. Ford Ole Miss Student Union in honor of the Gertrude C. Ford Foundation's deep and long commitment to the university. Additionally, the Martindale Student Services Center was renamed the Martindale-Cole Student Services Center in honor of Donald R.

Cole, a former student activist who returned to Ole Miss as a caring mentor and administrator for decades.

Another major highlight was the opening of the University of Mississippi Medical Center's (UMMC) seven-story Kathy and Joe Sanderson Tower at Children's of Mississippi. The new tower more than doubles the square footage of the state's only children's hospital and will play a key role in training the next generation of pediatricians and physicians.

Dr. Boyce led during a very challenging and ever-changing period as the university navigated the impact of the global COVID-19 pandemic. The university's response efforts focused on taking steps needed to reduce the impact of the virus in the campus community while, at the same time, keep students on track toward earning their degrees.

Howard Vaught to the position of head coach. Williams' decision to promote Vaught would have long-lasting, positive effects on the University of Mississippi. As head coach from 1947 through 1970, Vaught compiled an amazing record. His teams were 190-61-12 with three national titles. In addition, he won six Southeastern Conference titles, 18 bowl games, and coached 27 All Americans. The 1959 Ole Miss team was voted by the Southeastern Conference as the Team of the Decade.

Football in the 1950s and 1960s was a facet of Ole Miss that shaped the image of the University. Another was that in 1959 and 1960, Ole Miss had back-to-back Miss America winners in Mary Ann Mobley and Lynda Lee Mead. The combination of winning football teams and beauty queens led Sports Illustrated to feature the University in a 1960 article entitled, "Babes, Brutes, and Ole Miss: Successful football and dazzling Miss Americas are the products of Mississippi's hell-for-leather tradition."

Ole Miss beauty queens and gridiron victories were only a part of the administration of Chancellor Williams. Williams faced burgeoning student numbers as war veterans returned to college. From the late 1940s through the 1960s, the campus expanded at an amazing rate. Dormitories for women and men were built. An engineering building, a school of education, an alumni center, and a continuing education center were built. The building of the University library, which now bears Williams' name, was the most significant construction project of his administration.

Throughout its history, the University had dealt with major challenges, but no two were more difficult or had a more lasting effect than the issues of political interference and race. Civil rights became a major issue on the national landscape in the late 1940s and throughout the sixties. It was during the University's centennial in 1948 that the Confederate flag became a part of Ole Miss athletics. In the 1950s, students celebrated Dixie Week with a reenactment of secession, Robert E. Lee beard-growing contests, mule races, and ceremonial consumption of mint juleps.

In 1950, the student editor of The Mississippian, Alvin Krebs, wrote an article supporting the integration of the University. Krebs became a target of scorn and derision and a cross was burned on the lawn of his dormitory. Throughout the decade of the 1950s, the issue of race would resurface again and again. One of the most glaring examples of paranoia involving race at Ole Miss occurred in 1958 when both a current and a former state legislator charged members of the Ole Miss community with subverting the "Mississippi way of life." The two filed a 36-page document to the Board of Trustees, charging Director of Religious Life, Will Campbell, for playing ping pong with a black man; the dean of the Law School for publicly stating that Mississippi must obey the Supreme Court; a School of Education professor for bragging about being born in the North and for making fun of a female student with a southern drawl; and the chair of the history department for challenging the military strategy of Robert E. Lee. They also suggested that Ole Miss might be a "Communist cell." Chancellor Williams met with the Board of Trustees in 1959. The board cleared the University of all charges.

1962

When a young African-American Air Force veteran from Kosciusko decided to enter the University of Mississippi, a significant chapter in Ole Miss' history would be written. James Meredith saw Ole Miss as a symbol of white prestige and power, a "finishing school for the sons of the elite." After 18 months of Meredith's persistence, the University's delay tactics, and innumerable legal battles, Judge John Minor Wisdom ordered James Meredith admitted to the University of Mississippi on June 26, 1962. The University did all within its power to block Meredith's admission.

The Meredith monument located on the Universitycampus.

After lengthy legal wrangling, Meredith prepared to enter the University in September 1962. September 29, 1962, Governor Ross Barnett, a staunch segregationist, addressed a crowd of 40,000 fans in Jackson Memorial Stadium at half time of the Ole Miss – Kentucky football game. Stirring the crowd into frenzy, Barnett avowed, "I love Mississippi. I love her people, our customs. I love and respect her customs." In secret,

Barnett had been communicating earlier in the day with President John F. Kennedy and his brother, Attorney General Robert Kennedy, about how to get Meredith safely on to campus.

Meredith arrived on campus Sunday, September 30, accompanied by a phalanx of U. S. marshals. He was placed in Baxter Dormitory where he would live during the school year. In the meantime, as students began arriving back on campus after the weekend and the football game in Jackson, a crowd started to grow in front of the Lyceum. Many of those who gathered in the Circle were not Ole Miss students. As the night wore on, violence ensued. Gunshots were fired sporadically at the U.S. marshals. Bricks were thrown. Both rioters and marshals were injured. Cars were overturned and burned. In the end, two people were killed, the inner campus was scarred, and on Monday, October 1, 1962, James Meredith enrolled in the University of Mississippi.

There have been numerous articles, books, and documentaries produced about the integration of Ole Miss. It was a dark time for the University. *An American Insurrection: The Battle of Oxford, Mississippi, 1962*, by William Doyle, is an excellent account of the events of that time.

Enrollment dropped on campus from 5,042 in 1962 to 4,707 in the fall of 1963. In the fall of 1964, the University enrollment rebounded, and 5,159, the largest number of students to that date, entered Ole Miss.

The sixties

Chancellor Williams continued to lead the University through its recovery. He faced problems that were familiar to most university presidents. Students misbehaved, participated in panty raids, and tested the limits of the administration's patience. In October 1967, 800 students marched on the town square in support of legalizing beer in Oxford. Another "beer riot" occurred in December when students became rowdier, smashing parking meters, turning over trash containers, and hurling bottles. In the end, 58 students were arrested.

The assassination of Dr. Martin Luther King, Jr. on April 4, 1968, had a profound effect on the African-American students at Ole Miss. From the time that James Meredith entered the University in 1962 until 1968, there was little public notice of the black students on campus. Black student life was non-existent compared to the numerous opportunities offered to white students. Tensions ran high on the weekend following the death of Dr. King, and black students protested when the American flag was not lowered to half mast. Soon after, the black students sent a memorandum to the new chancellor, Dr. Porter Fortune. In the memorandum, the students cited an atmosphere of bigotry, bias, and prejudice, and accused administrators, officials, teachers, and workers of the University of perpetuating that atmosphere. In the memorandum there were 16 demands, including hiring black faculty and staff, granting a charter for the Black Student Union, and recruiting black athletes.

After a tense two-year period, the situation came to a climax when on the night of February 25, 1970, 61 black students marched onto the stage at Fulton Chapel where a traveling group, Up With People, was performing. All were arrested, and later that night another 28 were arrested for continuing the protest at various locations. When the Lafayette County jail was filled with students, the remaining students were bused to the state penitentiary at Parchman. In the fall of 1970, Ole Miss hired its first black faculty member, signed its first black athlete, and established a Black Studies Program. Within the next few years, the University met almost all of the demands of the students' memorandum.

During the 1960s there was minimal Vietnam war protest. What was billed as the "biggest anti-war demonstration in Mississippi," attracted 200 students because it was competing against the pep rally prior to the Ole Miss – Alabama football game. Only 200 students showed up in Fulton Chapel to hear faculty members, alumni, and students speak out against the war.

In 1974, the University abolished curfew for women students. This had been preceded by the abolition of a dress code for women that disallowed wearing shorts. Women who were walking across campus to a physical education class were forced to wear a raincoat over their shorts. Also abolished was the practice of "signing out" dates. Women who left residence halls with dates had been required to list where they were going and with whom.

Chancellor R. Gerald Turner

After 16 years as chancellor, Porter Fortune retired in 1984. The Board of Trustees of Institutions of Higher Learning elected R. Gerald Turner to serve as the fourteenth chancellor of the University of Mississippi. When Chancellor Turner took office, he had three primary goals for the University: increase the University's endowment, reverse the enrollment decline, and repair the University's public image. Perhaps Turner's greatest gift to Ole Miss was his ability to make alumni believe in the responsibility of giving back to the institution. He launched the Campaign for Ole Miss and worked arduously to raise funds for the University. He spoke to alumni groups, visited civic clubs, called on corporation CEOs, spoke at schools and churches, and spent endless hours away from the University selling its merits. After two and a half years, the Campaign for Ole Miss was completed and exceeded original expectations. A total of $61.7 million was raised for the University. Two years later, Turner initiated the Drive for Athletics and appointed Archie Manning chair of the drive. This fundraising effort resulted in $11.6 million raised for athletics and the subsequent construction of Oxford-University Baseball Stadium, the Starnes Athletics Training Center, and the Palmer Salloum Tennis facility.

Turner went beyond private giving and sought federal funding for campus projects. He relied on the support of Mississippi's powerful congressional delegation. During the 1980s and 1990s, the Center for Computational Hydroscience and Engineering and the Center for Wetlands Research were expanded. In addition, the Jamie Whitten National Center for Physical Acoustics, the National Center for the Development of Natural Products, and the National Food Management Institute were established on campus. The National Center for the Development of Natural products is a part of the Pharmacy School and is now named for Senator Thad Cochran.

Chancellor Turner sought to meet the second of his goals by initiating a broad and expensive recruiting effort. This new program proved highly successful and enrollment rose from 8,715 in 1984 to 11,033 in 1992. During this time, there was a significant increase in the number of out-of-state students who chose to attend Ole Miss. Dr. Turner also made a commitment to recruit African-American students and doubled the number from 536 in 1984 to approximately 1,000 in 1992. From 1984 to 1990 the number of African-American graduate students rose from 22 to 305.

Turner's toughest challenge was improving the public image of the University. He led unsuccessful efforts to eliminate the Confederate flag from athletic events. He also had an ongoing battle with the fraternity system when, in the 1980s, there were reports of fights between football players and fraternities, hazing, an alcohol-related death, and other incidents. Even though the decision to cease the annual Shrimp and Beer Celebration had been made before Turner took over as chancellor, he was blamed by students and alumni for its demise.

Embroiled in controversy over the association of the administration to the University Foundation and for firing the football coach for NCAA rules infractions, Gerald Turner accepted the presidency of Southern Methodist University in the spring of 1995. Turner made courageous and bold decisions on behalf of Ole Miss, and though not popular with many alumni and students, his contributions to the University of Mississippi are significant.

Chancellor Robert C. Khayat

The benefits that Ole Miss students enjoy today are the results of more than 160 years of hard work, sacrifice, leadership, and vision. Chancellors, faculty and staff, students, and alumni over the years have dedicated themselves to making the University of Mississippi a great university.

No person has done more to enhance Ole Miss than Robert C. Khayat, the fifteenth chancellor of the University. As an undergraduate, Khayat was a popular student who excelled in football and baseball. He was a member of the 1959 team of the decade and made All-SEC in baseball. Prior to becoming chancellor in 1995, Khayat had been a professor in the law school, associate dean of the law school, and vice chancellor for University Affairs. Khayat wasted little time in achieving his goal of making the University of Mississippi one of the nation's premier universities. During

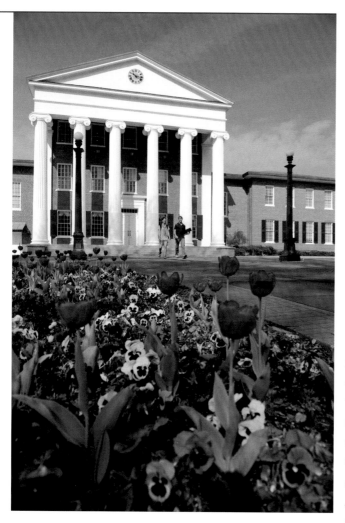

his term as chancellor, Khayat raised $778 million for academics and athletics. Due to his success in fundraising, the University prospered with the opening of the Sally McDonnell Barksdale Honors College, the expansion of Vaught-Hemingway stadium to 60,000 seats, the expansion of Oxford-University baseball stadium, the establishment of the Croft Institute for International Studies and the Trent Lott Leadership Institute, the renovation and expansion of the J. D. Williams Library, the creation of the School of Applied Sciences, and the establishment of the Overby Center for the Study of Southern Politics and Journalism. In addition, during Khayat's tenure the University was the first public university in Mississippi to be granted a chapter of Phi Beta Kappa. The Gertrude Ford Center was built and quickly recognized as one of the premier performing arts centers in the South.

One of Khayat's lasting legacies is his leadership to rid Ole Miss of its association with the Confederate flag. He brought alumni, students, faculty and staff members, and coaches together in this effort. It was not an easy task, and many in Mississippi blamed Khayat for doing away with a part of Southern heritage. Khayat's life was threatened for taking the courageous stand.

While Khayat worked tirelessly to enhance academics and athletics, he also put emphasis on enhancing the beauty of the Ole Miss campus. In 2008, the Ole Miss Landscape Services Department was awarded the Scenic Communities of Mississippi award by the Mississippi Urban Forest Council. The campus has been recognized by national publications as one of the most beautiful campuses in the United States, and was listed as The Most Beautiful Campus by Newsweek in 2011.

In May 2008, the University of Mississippi opened its doors on all campuses to a record enrollment of 17,601 students, and *Forbes* magazine ranked it as one of the Top 25 universities in the United States. September 26, 2008, the eyes of the world were on the University of Mississippi when the first Presidential Debate was held in the Gertrude Ford Center. Every major national network and media outlets from around the world came to Oxford. Tom Brokaw, Katie Couric, Shepard Smith, Bob Schieffer, and other news giants covered the event. Classes were canceled the afternoon of the debate, and more than 6,000 came to the Grove to participate in the Rock the Debate festival that featured music, speakers, southern food, and a live telecast of the debate on two giant screens.

Khayat embodied the characteristics of many of his predecessors. He shared Barnard's dream of making the University a great institution. Like Chancellor Fulton he valued and maintained the beauty of the campus. He capitalized on Butts's and Turner's commitments to fundraising. Many of Khayat's predecessors led the University through turmoil and tough times. As chancellor, Khayat did the same with resolve and vision.

Chancellor Daniel W. Jones

As with numerous other chancellors, Dr. Dan Jones's first year was eventful — if not tumultuous. Early in his first year, Chancellor Jones was approached by students who complained about the chanting of "The South Will Rise Again" at the end of the traditional pre- and post-game anthem "From Dixie with Love" which had been played at football games for 20 years. The song "From Dixie with Love" is a combination of "Dixie" and "The Battle Hymn of the Republic," the anthems of the Confederacy and the Union during the Civil War. Disgruntled because the foam-headed cartoon character, Colonel Rebel, had been dropped as the on-field mascot in 2003, a small group of students started the chant at the end of "From Dixie with Love." Students who entered the University after 2003 picked up the cheer, and it became more audible. For some, it was seen as a harmless expression of southern pride. For others, it evoked memories of segregationists in the 1950s and 1960s singing "Glory, glory segregation. Glory, glory segregation. The South shall rise again" to the tune of "The Battle Hymn of the Republic."

Prior to the Northern Arizona game in November 2009, Chancellor Jones issued a statement warning students that "From Dixie With Love" would no longer be played if the chant continued. Students ignored the warning and chanted it loudly after the song was played. On Monday after the game, Chancellor Jones asked the band to quit playing the song.

"Here at the University of Mississippi, there must be no doubt that this is a warm and welcoming place for all," Dr. Jones wrote in a letter to the University community. "We cannot ever appear to support those outside our community who advocate a revival of racial segregation. We cannot fail to respond."

Although supported by many, Jones's decision was met with outrage from some within and outside of the University community. The issue came to a head November 21, 2009, when 11 members of the Ku Klux Klan protested on the steps of Fulton Chapel on the day of the Ole Miss–LSU football game with tens of thousands of people on campus. The KKK was shouted down by a crowd of more than 300 onlookers and were taunted with shouts of "Go to hell, KKK!" A group of counter protesters led by the Associated Student Body and One Mississippi, stood 50 yards away. They wore T-shirts that read, "Turn your back on hate," and read out loud, over and over again, the Ole Miss Creed. The counter protest crowd numbered approximately 200 and included students, faculty, staff, alumni, and football fans, including some from LSU.

In the fall of 2009, ASB president Artair Rogers and Cardinal Club president Peyton Beard approached Chancellor Jones about a new on-field mascot for athletic teams. Dr. Jones agreed to consider it if the students voted to have one and they did.

On April 15, 2011, the University dedicated the Robert C. Khayat Law Center. The featured speaker was best-selling author John Grisham, an Ole Miss law graduate and a former student of Khayat's. The new law center was built at a cost of $50 million and covers 130,000 square feet. It is located at the southwest corner of the campus. The first law school classes were held in the Lyceum in 1854.

In keeping with Chancellor Jones' investiture theme of service, the Associated Student Body, under the leadership of President Virginia Burke, sponsored the University's initial Big Event. The Big Event is a day of service modeled after a program begun at Texas A&M University. More than 1,200 students spent Saturday morning, March 26, 2011, volunteering in Oxford and Lafayette County. The next year, more than 3,000 students completed 300 community projects as part of The Big Event. Today, the Ole Miss Big Event is the largest single day of community service in the state.

Despite success in the metrics typically used to evaluate leaders in higher education, Chancellor Jones had a strained relationship with the Board of Trustees of the Institutions of Higher Learning. He was notified in the spring of 2015 that his contract would not be renewed. There was a public outcry against the Board's decision, including a large on-campus rally organized by students and attended by students, faculty, staff, and alumni. A few months later, Dr. Jones accepted the position of professor of medicine, director of clinical and population science, and the inaugural Mr. and Mrs. Joe F. Sanderson, Jr. Endowed chair in obesity, metabolic diseases, and nutrition for the Mississippi Center for Obesity Research at the University of Mississippi Medical Center.

Recent Years

Provost and vice chancellor for academic affairs, Morris H. Stocks, was named interim chancellor, and a national search for the next chancellor was launched by the IHL Board. In October 2015, Dr. Jeffrey S. Vitter was named the seventeenth chancellor of the University of Mississippi and Distinguished Professor of Computer and Information Science. He assumed office January 1, 2016, and quickly appointed a transition team and launched a comprehensive listening and learning tour known as the Flagship Forum. Four pillar themes emerged from these meetings, forming the foundation of strategic planning efforts and forging a path to advance the University's flagship status as a great public international research university.

A native of New Orleans and renowned computer scientist, Vitter graduated in mathematics with highest honors from the University of Notre Dame in 1977 and earned a Ph.D. under Don Knuth in computer science at Stanford University in 1980. He also holds an M.B.A. from Duke University. He previously served for five and a half years as provost, executive vice chancellor, and Roy A. Roberts Distinguished Professor at the University of Kansas. Prior to joining KU, he served in leadership and academic roles at Texas A&M, Purdue, Duke, and Brown.

During February of Dr. Vitter's first year as chancellor, the University received Carnegie R1 "highest research activity" designation — a status afforded to only the top 2.5% of the nation's colleges and universities. Also during his first year, Chancellor Vitter hosted multiple powerful events, including the U.S. Department of Education's Back-to-School Bus Tour, the first ever University-wide Town Hall, the CEO Technology Summit, and the Innovation and Entrepreneurship Panel.

A frequent social media user, Chancellor Vitter communicated about what was happening on campus and engaged thousands of University stakeholders through his messages. A strong proponent of the UM Creed, he launched several initiatives to foster respect and diversity at the University, including the establishment of the Chancellor's Advisory Committee on History and Context.

After only three years in office, Chancellor Vitter resigned effective January 2019. Vice chancellor for administration and finance, Larry Sparks, was named interim chancellor and was asked to serve until IHL conducted a national search for the next chancellor. A native of Oxford and an Ole Miss alumnus, Sparks joined the UM administration in 1997 and has served as the university's vice chancellor for administration and finance since 2006. A notable issue during Sparks' tenure was a proposal originated by several student leaders within ASB and the Black Student Union to relocate the Confederate Monument from University Circle to the Civil War Cemetery near Tad Smith Coliseum. The proposal gained support from all student and faculty governing bodies on campus. The statue was moved on July 14, 2021.

In October 2019, Glenn Boyce was appointed by the IHL board as the 18th chancellor of the University of Mississippi. Dr. Boyce, who holds an undergraduate and doctoral degree from Ole Miss, brought more than 37 years across secondary and post-secondary education in Mississippi. He had served previously as IHL commissioner for three years, and as associate commissioner for academic affairs. He had also served as president of Holmes Community College for nine years. Early in his tenure, Dr. Boyce enjoyed several key successes, including naming of Keith Carter as vice chancellor for intercollegiate athletics, the hiring of Lane Kiffin as head football coach and securing a $26 million naming gift from Jim and Thomas Duff of Hattiesburg, for the construction of a state-of-the-art science, technology, engineering and mathematics (STEM) facility on the Oxford campus. Dr. Boyce also committed to continue efforts to pursue the proposed relocation of the Confederate Monument.

ABOUT THE AUTHORS

Thomas Reardon, *Dean of Students Emeritus*

Thomas Reardon worked in higher education for more than 30 years. Known to everyone at Ole Miss as 'Sparky,' Dean Reardon is retired.

Leslie Showalter, *Assistant Vice Chancellor for Student Affairs Emerita*

Leslie Showalter retired in 2019 after working more than 30 years in higher education. During her long career, she taught and mentored hundreds of first-year college students. Creating and editing The Ole Miss Experience was a labor of love.

CHAPTER 3

RACE AND THE UNIVERSITY of Mississippi

By Susan M. Glisson and
Charles H. Tucker

> "History, despite its wrenching pain, cannot be unlived, however, if faced with courage, need not be lived again." — Maya Angelou

F air warning: some things in this chapter are going to be uncomfortable. Not because it is a radical concept – science has been proving it in bits and pieces for years – but because it addresses something most of us learned from our friends, family, and the media while we were growing up and now accept as bedrock fact.

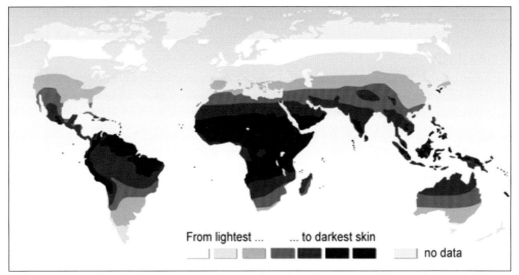

From lightest ... ... to darkest skin

no data

As it turns out, skin color is almost completely a function of how much UV sunlight an ethnic group receives in the fall. More sunlight means darker skin. (Anthropologist George Chaplin)

Race is complex.

Biologically, there is no difference, but culturally, race is still a huge issue. In 2003 an international team of scientists completed The Human Genome Project, a 13-year undertaking to map the human genetic blueprint. They discovered a lot of things, and are continually discovering more as they analyze their results. But one of the biggest things they discovered is this – there is no genetic difference between the so-called "races." None. Nor could they find any biological distinctions. According to scientists the differences in appearance, hair color and texture, skin tone, etc., are all superficial and are adaptations to climate and other environmental conditions. In short, humans come in one style – human. Many different scientific teams in many countries have verified these results and expanded upon them since then.

How it all started

If science proves there is no biological distinction between the "races," where did the idea come from, then? We invented it. Not us in this classroom, of course, but our ancestors. In other words, it is a social construction invented as a way to organize and eventually control people.

Although some of the first recorded accounts of the concept arose around 500 years ago during the Middle Ages, anthropologists and psychologists believe it goes back to the earliest days of mankind, back to when mankind lived in small nomadic groups, hunting and gathering, constantly on the move. Theirs was a cruel, scary world, filled with predators and harsh weather. Food was hard to come by and in short supply, as was water, in some cases.

It was during this time when various tribes first encountered people who were new to them.

Sometimes these encounters were pleasant. But most often they were not. The strange people would take their food by force, or not allow them access to the water.

Out of protection, and in constant competition for meager resources, these ancestors of ours developed a sense of "outlanderism," the automatic belief that anyone who was not a part of your tribe was an outlander and might be coming to harm your people and take your resources.

Here's an interesting bit of psychology: no species ever forgets a danger. Through one mechanism or another, it passes the memory down from generation to generation. Unfortunately, that memory remains in place in the subconscious, even when circumstances change and the once useful defense mechanism is no longer necessary. It is through this particular mechanism, outlanderism, that some scientists believe the once protective notion that people who do not look like you must mean you harm became a dangerous context for intergroup relations as time evolved. Mankind viewed the world as having two basic categories of people in it – "us" and "them," with "them," the outlanders, being anyone a particular group did not know, live in the same place as, recognize, or, in some cases, physically resemble. Because an outlander could sometimes look like one of them, it essentially focused on people from other groups, that is, people they did not know. This system worked for a while.

The transition between "outlanderism" to racism as a social order evolved through the development of anti-semitism, religious intolerance by Christians for Jews. The early church, which eventually grew into the Catholic Church, initially believed that Jews could convert to Christianity and thus become acceptable. Over time, a much more insidious conviction developed, that Jewish souls and bodies were unconvertible and that evil was in their blood. That being the case, then they must be a different type of creature, and a bad one at that, they reasoned.

It was in the late nineteenth century with the creation of the classification of "race" that things began to get nasty. While outlanderism was essentially a protective

"At UM, all students must complete a general education curriculum that is strongly rooted in the liberal arts, which encourages creativity, critical thinking, empathy, and being a strong communicator. These skills are highly transferrable in industry and essential to our society, which becomes more and more complex each year."

—Lee Cohen,
Dean of the College of Liberal Arts

reaction, race was used in a far more sinister way. Governments used the created classification of race to falsely define some populations as inferior and to justify discriminating against them and withholding resources for their support and development.

It is important to note that before this time race wasn't always attached to skin color. The British, for example, considered the Irish, Scots, and Welsh as separate and distinctly inferior races. They were outlanders or others, people not of their group, and therefore morally inferior and more like animals than humans. That belief still lingers on among some in the British Isles today.

The Big S (And, no, we don't mean Superman.)

Another development that influenced the concept of race was the enforced and unpaid labor system of race-based slavery. Slavery existed prior to racism. The Greeks and Romans and Egyptians had slaves.

Some African and Native American tribes enslaved conquered enemies. In the British Isles, the British conquered the Scots and the Irish and made slaves of them all. In fact, virtually every culture that has ever existed has used slavery to increase its labor pool. But it wasn't until the fifteenth century that race and slavery were linked.

Imagine if your community relied on slave labor to bring in additional crops that you needed to feed your people. And imagine that, over time, you had difficulty preventing these slaves from escaping. You see, you had stolen them from neighboring tribes or conquered people who, by and large, looked a lot like you. If they managed to escape and make their way back home, it was easy for them to blend in and hide among the other villagers. Or worse, hide for a while, scrub off in a stream someplace, find some clothes and pretend to be a free man in another village. Who would know? In Europe, that was a real issue. What to do…?

The solution, or so it seemed to the conquerors in Western Europe, was to force others who did not look like them into unpaid labor. But where to find them?

Somewhere… across the sea, somewhere….

During the late fifteenth century, Europe began exploring the globe. Columbus, Magellan, and other explorers sought out new lands and reported back, describing lands ripe for the taking. Sponsored by governments and private corporations (yes, they were around way back then), Europeans sailed into North and South America and the Caribbean and after encountering and, in some cases, completely annihilating native populations by virtue of their superior firepower and disease, discovered mineral and culinary treasures that they'd never seen before – silver, gold, jewels, spices, CHOCOLATE!

But, unlike the travel brochure-like descriptions of the explorers, that wealth was not simply lying on the ground waiting to be carried off. It had to be mined, harvested, packed, and loaded. That required hard, sometimes dangerous work.

It wasn't long before the Portugese and Spaniards, followed by the British, French, and Dutch hit upon an answer – let's use these conquered people as free labor! They don't look like us, so they can't blend in with us. And if they do run off, we can find them easily. And if we happen to be over there, we can conquer some more.

This launched an economic boom in Europe.

Europeans justified this unsettling proposition by evolving concepts of color-based race. In other words, the merchants who were making money off slave labor defended their actions by saying that what they were doing was a form of labor that targeted only inferior populations who, therefore, deserved such treatment. After all, if they were equal, they would look like us.

The Portuguese, followed by the Spanish and the British Empires, began to barter for and steal Africans for a growing slave trade.

This slave trade grew in force as these same merchants, explorers, and conquerors reached shores that were new to them. Largely enslaving or killing the native populations living in these new lands, these slave traders began a vicious triangle. They captured or bought Africans, largely from West Africa, and brought them across the "Middle Passage" of the Atlantic Ocean to what they called the "New World," the islands of the Caribbean, and the eastern shores of North America.

The enslaved persons who were not able to survive being constantly shackled, fed poorly, and beaten were simply cast overboard to their watery graves. Scholars estimate that slave traders forced as many as 25 million Africans from their homelands to make this terrible journey. Only 11 to 13 million made it to the New World. Of that great number, traders brought only about 400,000 enslaved people to the new British colonies in America; the rest worked on sugar plantations in the Caribbean in conditions so horrific that most died soon after arriving.

Ironically, it was in the so-called Age of Enlightenment during the late seventeenth and early eighteenth centuries that race and slavery became inextricably intertwined. While slavery as a labor system of unpaid, forced labor, had existed for centuries, it was Western Europeans who refined it by using presumed racial inferiority to justify the enslavement of African people.

In general, this combination meant that "blackness" was inferior and what was not black was superior.

Life in the New World

So, as Britain founded thirteen colonies in the New World during the seventeenth century, each colony used slavery as a labor system and protected that system legally.

In addition, the British also allowed indentured servanthood as a form of labor in the colonies.

Indenture meant that you could sign on to work for a set period of unpaid labor, but after serving your time, you could become free. Only Europeans could be indentured servants.

The difference between slavery and indenture was that black people were deemed slaves, because of their presumed inferiority, and only white people could

work their way into freedom. So, the United States grew based on a continuum of unpaid and paid labor: at one end were those deemed black and unfree and at the other end were those deemed white and free.

In the New World, the plantation economy developed slavery because of a lack of available laborers. Gradually understanding the dangers and abuses of the indenture system, individual business operations sought out a steady and plentiful supply of labor.

Despite claims that "all men" were created equal and deserving of liberty, our founding fathers did not believe blacks should be included in those claims. And so, they founded our country on a profound contradiction: they simultaneously declared that "all men are created equal" while legally protecting the rights of whites to own other human beings, who were black. To remove any doubt about the existence of this contradiction, they codified it in the new nation's Constitution, which declared that enslaved persons were not even fully human, while boasting that the document would "secure the blessings of liberty to ourselves and our posterity."

This journey to create the idea of race, having now moved from otherness to declaring that other human beings are inferior to justify mistreating them, continued to evolve. In the eighteenth and nineteenth centuries, Southern defenders of slavery, including Thomas Jefferson, described the institution as a "necessary evil." After the invention of the cotton gin in 1793, which made harvesting and processing cotton much easier, Southern slaveholders claimed a need for increased enslaved labor to meet the growing demands of Europe for its cotton. Remember this point: it's important.

Just as slavery grew, so too did its dissenters. Along with rebellions by enslaved persons, there was a growing and intensely successful global movement to abolish slavery. This prodded defenders of slavery to reject the "necessary evil" doctrine and to declare instead that slavery was a positive good, that it brought Christianity and civilization to a "savage" people.

Scholars have noted the paradox that racism exists more easily in a society, such as the United States, that aspires to equality. It was because of this principled claim that our society had to find a justification for why some could not be considered equal. Thus, these two competing ideas fought for supremacy in the American mind.

As the two philosophies grew— slavery versus freedom, inferiority versus supe-riority – the opinions, strategies, and tactics of both sides became entrenched. Pro-slavery theologians used Christianity, particularly verses from the Old Testament, to justify slavery. Control over slaves increased; slaveholders prevented slaves from learning to read, and slave patrols monitored open roads to help return escaped slaves to their plantations. In addition, pseudo-scientists published annals attempting to link phrenology, or the size of one's head, to intellectual capacity and declared enslaved blacks to be inferior due to presumed smaller brains. Pro-slavery economists suggested that enslaved persons must be happier than paid Northern laborers because their owners provided their food and shelter. (The numbers of slaves who attempted to resist or escape belied this assertion, however.)

Go West, young man!

As the nation expanded into new territory across the continent, the issue of slav-ery grew more divisive. Armed conflicts over whether a new state would be "free or slave" foreshadowed the Civil War. With the acquisition of the Louisiana Purchase, free states became concerned that slave states would have an unfair advantage. Thus emerged the Compromise of 1820.

The compromise had two parts: the northern part of Massachusetts became Maine and was admitted to the Union as a free state at the same time that Missouri was admitted as a slave state, maintaining a balance of 12 slave and 12 free states.

The second part of the compromise consisted of an imaginary line that was drawn at 36 degrees 30 minutes north latitude. This line came to be known as the Mason-Dixon Line. According to the compromise, all parts of the Louisiana Territory lying north of the Mason-Dixon Line would be free. There was a loophole, however. The act provided that fugitive slaves "escaping into any... state or territory of the United States...may be lawfully reclaimed and conveyed to the person claiming his or her labour or service" — and in the free territories, "slavery and involuntary servi-tude ... in the punishment of crimes" was not prohibited.

Meanwhile, in Mississippi

This is where that important bit about slave labor and cotton we told you about earlier comes into play. In Mississippi, cotton had become THE cash crop. Large plantations produced bales and bales of cotton, harvested by crews of slave labor, which were sold at a very tidy profit to the textile mills in New England and Europe.

The plantation owners who reaped the profits of those crops built palatial estates, complete with antebellum mansions and fruit orchards. They married and had children. These children grew up and were for the most part educated at local schools (except for some of the girls, who were sent back East to finishing schools). The young men were sent off to a university. Their parents could afford to send them to the best schools, so they went away to Harvard, Yale, and, in some cases, Oxford and Cambridge in England. There, they studied, partied, attended some classes, and eventually returned home.

But many were not the same when they returned. Some of the young men it seems, actually read their assignments on philosophy, religion, and political science. Upon their return, they looked at the social system of Mississippi and the "southern way of life" based on slavery, and found it wanting. They made these misgivings known to their parents, who were less than pleased. After all, their parents were at the top of the social order that their heirs wanted to topple. The parents then did what many parents do when their children question their decisions – they blamed the teachers. Their solution was simple: create their own schools that taught a philosophy more in keeping with theirs.

Professor Charles Eagles wrote in *The Price of Defiance*: "There was also a sense of urgency to provide local higher education for students without the influence of those who did not embrace the 'ways' of the state of Mississippi. Seeking to preserve a way of life, the founders believed that education is the process by which a culture ensures its existence and transmits itself across time. These founders' resistance to change, which they viewed as their right, if not their obligation, thus created the University of Mississippi as a bastion in defense of 'The Southern Way of Life.'"

On February 20, 1840, the Mississippi State legislature passed a bill to establish a state university to do just that. In short, The University of Mississippi was created explicitly to perpetuate the philosophy of race-based slavery and white supremacy.

Up on Capitol Hill...

The abolitionist versus pro-slavery debate continued to rage. First there was the Compromise of 1850 and the infamous Fugitive Slave Act. According to the compromise, Texas would relinquish the disputed land it had gained after the U. S. War with Mexico (remember the Alamo?) but, in compensation, be given 10 million dollars — money it would use to pay off its debt to Mexico. Also, the territories of New Mexico, Nevada, Arizona, and Utah would be organized without mention of slavery. (The territories would make that decision for themselves when they applied for statehood.) The slave trade would be abolished in the District of Columbia, although slavery would still be permitted. Finally, California would be admitted as a free state.

In exchange for the pro-slavery faction accepting this imbalance, the Fugitive Slave Act was passed.

This controversial piece of legislation required citizens to assist in the recovery of fugitive slaves, no matter how long they had been living in a free state. Furthermore, it denied a fugitive's right to a jury trial. If former slaves (or free persons of color accused of being escaped slaves) protested or sought to prove their freedom, special commissioners heard the cases. These commissioners were paid $5 if an alleged fugitive was released and $10 if he or she was sent away with the claimant. The Act called for changes in the process for filing a claim, making the process easier for slave-owners. Also, according to the Act, there would be more federal officials responsible for enforcing the law.

The federal government continued to go to great lengths to protect the property rights of white Southerners to own black people. In 1857, the U.S. Supreme Court heard the case of an enslaved man who sued for his freedom after having been brought to a free state by his owner. In the ruling, known today as The Dred Scott Decision, the majority of the Court ruled that since blacks were "beings of an inferior order, and altogether unfit to associate with the white race, either in social or political relations, and so far inferior that they had no rights which the white man was bound to respect."

Just two years later, Charles Darwin published On the Origin of Species, which advanced the concept of evolution. Defenders of slavery appropriated Darwin's work to argue that whites had evolved to be superior while blacks had not.

In response, many Abolitionists moved from attempts to persuade others to join their cause through public meetings and newspaper articles to legal challenges. Some, like abolitionist John Brown, even suggested and engaged in armed conflict.

By the time of Abraham Lincoln's inauguration as President in 1861, eleven Southern states, including Mississippi, had seceded from the Union; each one of them noted prominently in their articles of secession that slavery was the main cause of their leaving the Union.

The University of Mississippi, which had been founded in 1848 to teach young men to uphold the ideology of slavery, shut down during the war and its entire student body joined the Confederacy as the "University Greys."

Post-war

While the end of the Civil War may have settled the question of the supremacy of the Union, it only complicated the nature of race. Where before one could safely, though not completely, assume that a slave was a black person, now everyone was "free," to the extent that no one was supposed to be forced to work for another without pay. Since slavery also had produced multiracial children, often through the rape of enslaved women by their owners, there were many new citizens who could pass as white.

And so began a new development in the evolution of the social construct of race: the idea of whiteness.

"White" is another sociological construct. But unlike most group descriptors, which focus on who does belong, "whiteness" focuses on who doesn't. It wasn't based on a fixed definition. Place of origin, skin and eye color, and hair texture could or could not be factors. In fact, some groups considered "white" today – the Irish, Greeks, and Italians, for example – were not initially included, but were assimilated over time.

"When a tradition gathers enough strength to go on for centuries, you don't just turn it off one day."
—Chinua Achebe

Southern states and municipalities began to enact laws to define who was white and who was black. In places with populations of multi-racial persons who could pass for western European (Louisiana, for example) the notorious "one-drop" rule meant that any person who had even one ancestor who had been held a slave, or who had African ancestry (free or not) was considered black. And those who were deemed black could not vote or claim many other rights of citizenship, and so could not legally challenge the laws that oppressed them.

In 1890, the state of Mississippi became the first Southern state after the Civil War to pass a new state constitution. It was the first Southern document to codify segregation, which meant the legal disenfranchisement of all blacks as well as an enforced legal separation in all aspects of daily life—from hospitals and schools, to whom one could marry and where one might be buried. Every other Southern state followed Mississippi's example and passed similar constitutions. Not to be outdone, federal authorities weighed in as well.

In 1896, the Supreme Court ruled in Plessy v. Ferguson, that "separate but equal" was the law of the land. The case had arisen from a man in Louisiana, Homer Plessy, who could pass for white and who hoped, through his case, to stop the flow of new laws that infringed on new rights of black citizens. The Plessy decision was a turning point in the developing concept of whiteness. It was clear that going forward all the advantages of citizenship would remain only for whites and would be denied to those defined as black. There was a caveat to this awarding of advantages; only certain privileges would be awarded to all whites. In the end, those rewards included just enough benefits to keep poor whites from joining with blacks to challenge the political, social, and economic power of elite whites.

In the wake of the 1890 constitution, white Mississippians used economic and physical intimidation, as well as legal restrictions, to discriminate against blacks. The Mississippi Delta, for example, which had been largely settled, cleared, and prepared for cultivation by freed slaves, and which could boast of predominantly black land ownership in the 1880s and 90s, became a political center of power in the state by the 1920s, dominated by white plantation owners whose sharecropping and tenant system of labor ensured that blacks and many poor whites would never earn enough to get out of poverty. These plantation owners obtained their land largely through illegal thefts or violent intimidation of previous black owners. It was during this same period of time that the University of Mississippi also became known as "Ole Miss," a name suggested by Elma Meek in a contest to name the yearbook. It quickly became the school's nickname, and eventually a controversial one, as its origin was a term of affection used to describe the wife of a plantation owner.

Jim Crow era

The 1890s to the 1940s can be described as a racist regime in the American South. The earlier attempts to use science to justify such treatment lived now in a eugenics movement, which was a global effort to create a "master race" of whites and manifested itself in the United States in immigration restrictions, the prohibition of interracial marriage, and forced sterilizations of black women. Indeed, during this same period, Nazi Germany in the 1930s modeled many of its laws, including those against intermarriage, or "miscegenation," on those of the American South. The newly forming apartheid regime in South Africa also modeled its laws on those of the American South. Segregation laws went far beyond controlling who could vote or whom one could marry, to determining where one could eat or live or go to the hospital—even what Bible you could touch when pledging an oath in court. Those who violated these ordinances met with economic intimidation such as losing their homes or job or with lynching. In fact, the state of Mississippi had more lynchings per capita than any other state in this period.

Despite the dark period of "Jim Crow" segregation in Mississippi, there were always many blacks and some white allies who challenged the segregated system. National efforts to challenge the system supported state work and in the wake of World War II, significant changes began to occur. In Mississippi, led largely by black war veterans such as Medgar Evers and Amzie Moore, who had fought for democracy abroad but returned home to second-class status, local organizers challenged segregation. Many suffered economic intimidation and sometimes violence or death, but they refused to give up the struggle.

While the predominant ethnic groups in the state were blacks and whites, there always have been other ethnic groups present. Within the racially stratified system of both Mississippi and the country at large, immigrant populations moved into the state and worked hard to be defined culturally as whites to gain the privileges of white skin. Italian parents in the Mississippi Delta had to sue the state in the 1950s for their children to be considered white and therefore allowed to attend white schools. Jewish and Chinese settlers straddled between the two predominant cultures, working in arenas that served both populations but were never truly accepted by either. And much later, on the Gulf Coast, Vietnamese immigrants created homogeneous enclaves of fisherfolk in an attempt to protect themselves from the larger, divided culture. This pattern repeated itself around the country, framed by different waves of immigration at different historical periods. But each new population was judged and defined through the lens of the black and white division.

The aftermath of World War II initiated changes nationally and within the state. Because of the combined efforts of both state and local black leaders and their white allies, calls for civil rights reform increased. The National Association for the Advancement of Colored People (NAACP) launched a judicial initiative to dismantle segregation methodically in education, beginning with higher education in the 1940s. In the wake of the Holocaust, many who had previously engaged in or tolerated racism now saw its horrible ultimate conclusion and began to work to prevent similar developments. And increasingly, during the Cold War and the decolonization of Asia and Africa, the United States was under great pains to show that daily life under capitalism and democracy lived up to its stated ideals to resist the propaganda of the Soviet Union and its claims of the supremacy of communism.

In 1948, reformers within the Democratic Party successfully included, for the first time in a political party, civil rights in the Democratic Party platform. In response, half of the Alabama Democratic delegation and all of the Mississippi Democratic delegation walked out of the convention in protest.

These white supremacist protestors created a new political party that year called the "Dixiecrats." To show their support of the Dixiecrats, the Ole Miss student body began to fly Confederate flags, and the band played the song "Dixie" at athletics events.

Increasingly, the symbols of The University of Mississippi sent a message that the campus was a haven for those who opposed civil rights for all. Simultaneously, for some courageous black citizens like James Meredith, who called the University "the temple of white supremacy," their intent to desegregate the public facility grew as well. In 1954, as the Supreme Court issued the Brown v. Board of Education decision, which declared that the doctrine of "separate but equal" in schools was inherently unequal, Medgar Evers applied for admission to the University's law school. Its segregation policy prevented his admission, but his courageous application brought him to the attention of the NAACP, which hired Evers to become its first full-time field secretary for admissions. Less than ten years later, Evers assisted James Meredith in his attempts to enroll in the University.

In 1955, at least two white men in Tallahatchie County murdered fourteen-year-old Emmett Till, a black child from Chicago visiting his uncle for the summer. The men had been told that Till had whistled at one of their wives and this transgression of racial customs was enough for them to sentence him to death. His mother insisted that Till's casket remain open at his funeral so that the world could see what racism, the prejudice plus the power of whites in Mississippi, had done to her child. A photo appeared in the black magazine Jet, and Mississippi's reputation as a bastion of white supremacy only increased.

Civil rights groups began to determine ways to target the state for reform, while defenders of what they called the "southern way of life," sought to resist such efforts. It was perhaps inevitable that a climactic confrontation would occur. In 1962, that showdown happened at Ole Miss. Kosciusko, Mississippi, native James Meredith applied for admission to the University that year. While the University began a process of denying Meredith admission on the basis of his race, supported by then Mississippi governor Ross Barnett, national civil rights groups sought the intervention of President John F. Kennedy. Kennedy and his representatives negotiated with Barnett for Meredith's safe admission, but the clash intensified as many Oxonians and students as well as citizens across the state rallied for Barnett to defy the President. They were joined by protestors who came from other states to defend white supremacy at Ole Miss.

On September 30, Meredith came to campus under the protection of U.S. Marshals. Returning crowds of students, many of whom had been encouraged to resist Meredith's admission in a speech by Governor Barnett at the football game in Jackson on the previous weekend, learned of Meredith's presence on campus and began to gather in protest in front of the Lyceum. Bricks that had been delivered for new construction on The Circle became weapons in the hands of students. Students also fashioned Molotov cocktails to throw at the U.S. Marshals surrounding the Lyceum. Injured marshals retreated into the Lyceum and were soon joined by students who had been detained.

As the night wore on, other protestors from around the state and region joined the riot; many brought guns. Students began to retreat from The Circle and the armed insurrection of the remaining protestors began. Calm came only when federalized National Guard members, many of them native Mississippians, ignored their own biased training against blacks and slowly took control over the campus. The violence was not contained on campus alone that night; many black Oxonians reported later that rioters invaded their communities and inflicted injuries. On campus, many were injured and two people were killed: a French reporter and a local repairman. No one has ever been found responsible for their deaths.

On the morning of October 1, 1962, Meredith officially enrolled in the University, becoming the first black student to be allowed to attend the school. His safety that year required armed soldiers, who guarded him on campus; other Army personnel patrolled the streets of Oxford to keep order. Students enrolled at the time harassed Meredith throughout the year. Those who lived above his room in Baxter Hall would bounce basketballs on the floor throughout the night. When Meredith entered the cafeteria to eat meals, students turned their backs on him. And if he sat at a table of students, they would all leave. The few who attempted to reach out to him received death threats in return. Despite this intense pressure, Meredith persevered. Since he had transferred from Jackson State College, he graduated in the spring of 1963, wearing a button upside down that protestors had worn as a message to keep him out of Ole Miss. It said, "Never."

In the wake of the events of 1962, student enrollment dropped. Faculty who spoke out in support of Meredith, such as Professor James Silver, were forced to leave. Silver would write of the realities of segregation and the events on campus in his book *The Closed Society*. For many black leaders in the state, the book was an important first public acknowledgment by a white Southerner that segregation was wrong. There would be no single event that would have a more lasting effect on the University of Mississippi than the desegregation of the University in 1962.

The University has struggled to overcome that dark time. Many of the black students who attended the University after Meredith in the 1960s and 1970s also suffered harassment and intimidation. Some who protested such treatment were expelled. Black enrollment finally began to increase significantly in the 1990s, under the tenure of Chancellor Robert Khayat, who personally visited predominantly black high schools and churches to recruit students.

Sometimes the University has been too hesitant to move forward, forced to negotiate between alumni who have nostalgic views of the past and new students who bring differing perspectives on race. And sometimes, its efforts have gone unnoticed by a nation that would rather keep Mississippi as a scapegoat for negative race relations. Many of the battles over its racial past and present have come over the symbols of the University. Over the years, conflicts about the Confederate flag and the playing of the song "Dixie," have ignited the campus. So, too, did conflict raged over the official team name and mascot of the University, the "Rebels" and "Colonel Reb." Many view these symbols as connected to a robust and familial past, while others view them as relics of a time when blacks were not allowed on campus. This is no longer the official mascot. In 2010, the mascot became the Black Bear and seven years later the Ole Miss football mascot was changed to Landshark Tony.

In 1997, then-President Bill Clinton inaugurated an unprecedented national conversation on race. "One America: The President's Initiative on Race" marked the first time a sitting president had called for such a dialogue without the catalyst of a major crisis. It suggested, on a federal level, the importance of dealing positively with race relations on a daily basis. Accepting the challenge to prod grassroots efforts, The University of Mississippi hosted the only deep-South public forum for One America. Preceded by dialogue, groups representing ten constituency topics ranging from the arts to education to religion, the event highlighted elected delegates from each group. Sharing the insight and hopes of the more than 160 participants, the representatives crafted a frank yet civil discussion on one of our nation's most difficult subjects.

The President's staff hailed The University of Mississippi's experience as the single most successful of the entire Initiative year. That recognition encouraged the University to formalize its dialogue process with the creation of an institute to promote racial reconciliation and civic renewal. Founded in 1999, the William Winter Institute for Racial Reconciliation works in communities and classrooms, in Mississippi and beyond, to support a movement of racial equity and wholeness as a pathway to ending and transcending all division and discrimination based on difference. The William Winter Institute for Racial Reconciliation is now located in Jackson, Mississippi. An additional result of the One America success included the awarding of a Phi Beta Kappa chapter to the campus, whose original application had been turned down in 1962 because of the riot.

In 2002, the University undertook its own initiative on race. Called "Open Doors," the year-long series of events commemorated the desegregation of the University. An opening public event on October 1, 2002, focused on an apology by Chancellor Khayat for the exclusion of blacks from the University along with a moving ceremony led by Khayat and James Meredith to dedicate the space between the Lyceum and the J. D. Williams Library. More than 2,500 participants heard keynote speaker Myrlie

Evers-Williams, whose husband, Medgar, had been assassinated in their Jackson driveway in 1963; Evers-Williams extolled the attendees to be bold in seeking racial justice and healing. During the weekend-long event, the University undertook an oral history initiative about its past and welcomed back unsung heroes of its integration, such as the U.S. Marshals and soldiers who had protected Meredith, as well as the few students and white allies who had encouraged integration, including *Daily Mississippian* editor Sidna Brower Mitchell and Episcopal priest Duncan Gray. Workshops and lectures continued throughout the year and an International Conference on Race concluded the 40th anniversary commemoration.

The University hosted the first Presidential debate of the 2008 campaign. The historic event, which included the nation's first black presidential nominee of a major party, Barack Obama, reflected the strides made by the University in race relations. Because of the success of those efforts, the Presidential Commission determined that the unavoidable references to race that would occur during the event would be handled respectfully and honestly by the University. The event, coupled with the 40th anniversary commemoration success, began to turn public opinion in favor of the University, which had fully accepted its role and obligation to lead the nation in developing positive race relations.

On November 6, 2012, a growing crowd of students, largely white, gathered on campus to protest the re-election of President Barack Obama. Grainy cell phone footage quickly circulated evidence of their anger, through social media, and once again, in lightning quickness, the nation began to distance itself. Initial media reports on the morning of November 7 assumed that nothing had changed at the University. But this time, student leaders from One Mississippi, supported by faculty, staff, and administrators, made a call for peace and unity and were able to coalesce more than 700 participants that night at a candlelight vigil in front of the Lyceum. While it is clear that we have much work to do to continue to move forward in race relations, a new generation of students is learning from the past and refusing to repeat it.

Challenges will continue. While the vestiges of legal segregation are gone, the social and economic legacies of racism remain, both in Mississippi and the nation at large. Thirty-three percent of children in Mississippi, disproportionately black, live in poverty. In most quality of life indicators such as housing, education, health care, economics, and criminal justice, black Mississippians are much more likely to suffer the brunt of inequity. These structural inequities are undergirded now not necessarily by racist intentions, but through implicit bias or policies enacted in the past that discriminated based on difference.

Implicit biases are the unconscious attitudes formed as early as childhood, based on society's cues about racial prejudice. They are reinforced through social segregation, the tendency we have as human beings to stay in groups that are composed largely of people who look like us. Despite intentions to promote equality and inclusion, these attitudes can remain hidden catalysts for our behavior because our brains are wired for implicit bias. Filtering through the billions of pieces of information that bombard us by the minute, our brains learn to make short cuts, based on cultural messages. If the larger culture sends messages of inferiority, that difference is bad, that equality is only for some people, our brains pick up on those messages, whether we want them to or not.

Thus it is important to understand several ideas: none of us who are alive today invented "race" or racism. But since race as a social construct is a human creation, it can be replaced by something better, a more perfect human creation. And while we did not invent racism, we have inherited a responsibility to understand its effects and to undo them, especially the unearned privileges that those with white skin share.

Racism has been remarkably resilient in adapting to new contexts, so it requires us to be continually vigilant to undo it. If we know the difficulties, such as implicit bias, that make understanding and change challenging, we can begin to unlearn those behaviors and learn new ones that are inclusive and just. All it takes is intention, and a willingness by us to be a part of a safe space that allows for open and honest questioning to build relationships despite perceived differences. It also requires us as a society to work intentionally to undo generations of disadvantage and oppression so that there is an equal playing field for everyone. Supreme Court Justice Harry Blackmun argued in a 1978 decision that upheld affirmative action: "[I]n order to get beyond racism, we must first take into account race. There is no other way. And in order to treat some persons equally, we must treat them differently. We cannot—we dare not—let the Equal Protection clause perpetuate racial supremacy."

FIND OUT ABOUT YOUR IMPLICIT BIAS HERE — HARVARD IMPLICIT BIAS TEST TO SEE YOUR HIDDEN BIASES: IMPLICIT.HARVARD.EDU/IMPLICIT/

What if, in the end, we began to think of our identities as not based in our physical characteristics, as solely in the realm of our bodies, or even in some essentialized concept of culture, but based in our spirits, in the highest values to which we aspire? What might the world look like then?

DR. DONALD COLE
MY UNIVERSITY OF MISSISSIPPI EXPERIENCE

I entered the University of Mississippi in 1968 as a freshman with the blessings and concerns of my parents and many other community friends and leaders. I was a young, black man excited about attending the University of Mississippi, our state's flagship institution. The University had been integrated for about six years, but I did not realize that it was not yet fully integrated. At the time of my enrollment, there were still many staff members who had never served an individual like myself; faculty who had not taught a black person; and students who had not sat in a classroom with a black person. Naive to this, I entered with optimism and enthusiasm, but within weeks my optimism and enthusiasm were eroded by event after event of demonstrated racial displeasure for my presence on campus. I was not alone in experiencing this unchecked hostility, but complaints by my fellow black students and me didn't seem to matter. Our pleas for help to allow us to feel that we belonged and mattered fell on deaf ears.

These unmet requests by students of color led us to stand together. During a time when the entire country was experiencing protest (Vietnam War, women's issues, civil rights), black students enrolled at the University banded together to protest against the tacit acceptance of behaviors that demeaned black students on campus. We asked for increased recruitment of black students, integration of the faculty, and integration of athletics teams. The national culture at the time was "march and protest," and we did. One such march resulted in all the protestors being arrested and jailed. Some were taken to the state penitentiary at Parchman. Subsequent University judicial procedures suspended eight students, and (unfortunately) I was one of those suspended from the University. This forced me to enroll in another university to complete my undergraduate and master's degrees, but I applied for admission to a doctoral program at the University of Mississippi in 1977.

My eligibility to enroll after having been suspended was questioned, but I was granted admission. Upon my return to campus, I recognized that much about the University had changed. Black faculty had been hired, black athletes were part of the intercollegiate teams, and the University was working to disassociate itself from the confederate flag. I remained in the background during my graduate days; quite different from the outspoken student who entered in 1968. I graduated in 1985 with a doctorate in mathematics.

Although I failed to obtain a bachelor's degree from the University of Mississippi, I succeeded in earning my doctorate. In 1993, I was invited to apply for, and was then hired, as Assistant Dean of the Graduate School and associate professor of mathematics. Today, I am a proud alum and retired member of the University's academic community. I have a unique personal timeline of our institution's struggle and success with racial dialogue from the 60s to today. With still much work ahead, I am proud of the progress that we have accomplished and that we have positioned ourselves to be a national leader in racial reconciliation.

STRONGER TOGETHER:
HEALING, ALLYSHIP, ACTION
By Norris "EJ" Edney

In the months leading up to your enrollment at the University of Mississippi, our national, local, and university communities have wrestled with complex social and political debates about a number of issues. The long-standing history of inequity and injustice in America continues to affect every aspect of our lives. The killings of George Floyd, Breonna Taylor, Ahmaud Arbery, Tony McDade, and countless others have brought to bear the painful reality of racial injustice in America (1). The impassioned debates over the place of confederate iconography in our forward progress evidences the breadth of our collective opinion about how we honor our history (2). And COVID-19 has revealed deeply rooted disparities in our public health and safety systems (3). These are big problems with complicated solutions. It is important to remember that in times like these, when debate over societal injustices and inequities pervade our discourse, education can provide us with valuable tools for promoting healing, allyship, and action that creates a better world(4).

Your time as a student at UM can equip you with the knowledge, skills, and competencies to do just that. You will become even more aware of the systems and structures which either perpetuate or remedy inequities in our society as you embark on this educational journey. Your awareness of injustice and inequity will grow alongside your humility in recognition that there is much to yet learn. With careful consideration and guidance, you can structure your learning in ways that prepare you to create the change you want to see in the world.

When you see a problem in society that evokes your passions, learn as much as you can about it. There will be countless opportunities for you to play an active role in your learning as you consider your own place in shaping the social realities around you. Check out the *All in. All Year*. Calendar to see if there is an event or speaker you find interesting(5). Meet some of the staff and student leaders in the Center for Inclusion and Cross Cultural Engagement and tell us about your interests, we will work together to find opportunities to support your learning(6). Talk to your academic advisors(7), faculty, and career center professionals(8) about your interests; they may be able to lead you to coursework or other opportunities that will help you immerse yourself in the subject matter. Join or start a student organization that focuses on the issues that mean a lot to you(9). Or seek opportunities to engage your interests in the community through collaboration with organizations in the Lafayette Oxford University community(10). Whatever paths you choose, we hope that you use your time at the University of Mississippi to galvanize your commitment to actively shaping society for the better.

NOTES:

1. A brief history of racial violence in the United states: http://anthonysiracusa.org/an-encyclope-dia- entry-on-lynching-to-appear-in-press-in-critical-understandings-in-education-encyclope-dia-critical- whiteness-studies-brill-publishers-2021/

2. History of confederate iconography: https://www.theatlantic.com/ideas/archive/2020/06/ole-misss- monument-white-supremacy/613255/

3. COVID 19 health disparities: https://www.cdc.gov/coronavirus/2019-ncov/need-extra- precau-tions/racial-ethnic-minorities.html

4. Stronger Together: Healing, Allyship, Action framework: https://inclusion.olemiss.edu/stronger- together/

5. All in. All Year. Calendar: https://inclusion.olemiss.edu/all-in-all-year/

6. Center for Inclusion and Cross-Cultural Engagement Website: https://inclusion.olemiss.edu/

7. Ask an Advisor portal: https://cssfye.olemiss.edu/advising/askanadvisor/

8. Set an appointment with Career Center via Handshake:

9. Sign into FORUM to explore ways to get involved: https://olemiss.campuslabs.com/engage/

10. Engage with the Office of Community Engagement: https://diversity.olemiss.edu/engaged/ce-team/

EXCERPT FROM:

White Privilege—Unpacking the Invisible Knapsack

By Peggy McIntosh

I decided to try to work on myself at least by identifying some of the daily effects of white privilege in my life. I have chosen those conditions that I think in my case attach somewhat more to skin-color privilege than to class, religion, ethnic status, or geographic location, though of course all these other factors are intricately intertwined. As far as I can tell, my African American coworkers, friends, and acquaintances with whom I come into daily or frequent contact in this particular time, place, and time of work cannot count on most of these conditions.

1. I can, if I wish, arrange to be in the company of people of my race most of the time.
2. I can avoid spending time with people who I was trained to mistrust and who have learned to mistrust my kind or me.
3. If I should need to move, I can be pretty sure of renting or purchasing housing in an area that I can afford and in which I would want to live.
4. I can be pretty sure that my neighbors in such a location will be neutral or pleasant to me.
5. I can go shopping alone most of the time, pretty well assured that I will not be followed or harassed.
6. I can turn on the television or open to the front page of the paper and see people of my race widely represented.
7. When I am told about our national heritage or about "civilization," I am shown that people of my color made it what it is.
8. I can be sure that my children will be given curricular materials that testify to the existence of their race.
9. If I want to, I can be pretty sure of finding a publisher for this piece on white privilege.
10. I can be pretty sure of having my voice heard in a group in which I am the only member of my race.
11. I can be casual about whether or not to listen to another person's voice in a group in which s/he is the only member of his/her race.
12. I can go into a music shop and count on finding the music of my race represented, into a supermarket and find the staple foods which fit with my cultural traditions, into a hairdresser's shop and find someone who can cut my hair.
13. Whether I use checks, credit cards, or cash, I can count on my skin color not to work against the appearance of financial reliability.

14. I can arrange to protect my children most of the time from people who might not like them.
15. I do not have to educate my children to be aware of systemic racism for their own daily physical protection.
16. I can be pretty sure that my children's teachers and employers will tolerate them if they fit school and workplace norms; my chief worries about them do not concern others' attitudes toward their race.
17. I can talk with my mouth full and not have people put this down to my color.
18. I can swear, or dress in second hand clothes, or not answer letters, without having people attribute these choices to the bad morals, the poverty, or the illiteracy of my race.
19. I can speak in public to a powerful male group without putting my race on trial.
20. I can do well in a challenging situation without being called a credit to my race.
21. I am never asked to speak for all the people of my racial group.
22. I can remain oblivious of the language and customs of persons of color who constitute the world's majority without feeling in my culture any penalty for such oblivion.
23. I can criticize our government and talk about how much I fear its policies and behavior without being seen as a cultural outsider.
24. I can be pretty sure that if I ask to talk to the "person in charge," I will be facing a person of my race.

25. If a traffic cop pulls me over or if the IRS audits my tax return, I can be sure I haven't been singled out because of my race.
26. I can easily buy posters, post-cards, picture books, greeting cards, dolls, toys, and children's magazines featuring people of my race.
27. I can go home from most meetings of organizations I belong to feeling somewhat tied in, rather than isolated, out-of-place, outnumbered, unheard, held at a distance, or feared.
28. I can be pretty sure that an argument with a colleague of another race is more likely to jeopardize her/his chances for advancement than to jeopardize mine.
29. I can be pretty sure that if I argue for the promotion of a person of another race, or a program centering on race, this is not likely to cost me heavily within my present setting, even if my colleagues disagree with me.
30. If I declare there is a racial issue at hand, or there isn't a racial issue at hand, my race will lend me more credibility for either position than a person of color will have.
31. I can choose to ignore developments in minority writing and minority activist programs, or disparage them, or learn from them, but in any case, I can find

ways to be more or less protected from negative consequences of any of these choices.

32. My culture gives me little fear about ignoring the perspectives and powers of people of other races.

33. I am not made acutely aware that my shape, bearing, or body odor will be taken as a reflection on my race.

34. I can worry about racism without being seen as self-interested or self-seeking.

35. I can take a job with an affirmative action employer without having my co-workers on the job suspect that I got it because of my race.

36. If my day, week, or year is going badly, I need not ask of each negative episode or situation whether it had racial overtones.

37. I can be pretty sure of finding people who would be willing to talk with me and advise me about my next steps, professionally.

38. I can think over many options, social, political, imaginative, or professional, without asking whether a person of my race would be accepted or allowed to do what I want to do.

39. I can be late to a meeting without having the lateness reflect on my race.

40. I can choose public accommodation without fearing that people of my race cannot get in or will be mistreated in the places I have chosen.

41. I can be sure that if I need legal or medical help, my race will not work against me.

42. I can arrange my activities so that I will never have to experience feelings of rejection owing to my race.

43. If I have low credibility as a leader I can be sure that my race is not the problem.

44. I can easily find academic courses and institutions which give attention only to people of my race.

45. I can expect figurative language and imagery in all of the arts to testify to experiences of my race.

46. I can choose blemish cover or bandages in "flesh" color and have them more or less match my skin.

47. I can travel alone or with my spouse without expecting embarrassment or hostility in those who deal with us.

48. I have no difficulty finding neighborhoods where people approve of our household.

49. My children are given texts and classes which implicitly support our kind of family unit and do not turn them against my choice of domestic partnership.

50. I will feel welcomed and "normal" in the usual walks of public life, institutional and social.

CHAPTER 4

DIVERSITY AND INCLUSION AT UM:
EXPLORING SIMILARITIES AND
Embracing Differences

By Kevin Cozart, Shawnboda Mead, Cadence Pentheny,
Stacey Reycraft, JuWan D. Robinson, and Robin T. Yekaitis

Congratulations on your enrollment at the University of Mississippi. You are now an official member of the higher education community. Today's higher education communities (colleges and universities) include students from all over the world. These students and other members of the university community embody a range of different perspectives, beliefs, cultural practices, languages, socioeconomic experiences, and traditions. The university community also has people who differ from one another based on race, gender identity, sexual orientation, political beliefs, abilities, and religious practices.

Diversity in higher education is comparatively different to what colleges and universities included just a few generations ago. It is likely that our college community's diversity is dramatically different from that of your high school community. For starters, the University of Mississippi's student body includes people from more than 90 countries. This chapter provides you with an introduction to diversity, equity, and inclusion. Additionally, it highlights the expectations and requirements for membership in your new and diverse community by exploring three questions:

1. **Who Am I?**
2. **Who Are We?**
3. **What does it mean to be All In at UM?**

Identity: Who Am I?

For many of you, college is the first time you have the opportunity to explore your identity away from the influences of family, friends, and hometowns, but what does that mean? What is identity?

Psychology Today defines identity as "the many relationships people cultivate, such as their identity as a child, friend, partner, and parent. It involves external characteristics over which a person has little or no control, such as height, race, or socioeconomic class. Identity also encompasses political opinions, moral attitudes, and religious beliefs, all of which guide the choices one makes on a daily basis." Building on this definition, your identity when you begin college is mostly inherited from your family and your community where you grew up. While many individuals start to make decisions for themselves as teenagers, which can change their identity, those choices are often limited by their environment.

One popular theory on identity creation from the field of sociology is that of social constructionism, which states that societies construct certain concepts like identity and the associated terms such as gender, ethnicity, race, etc. For example, one who is born in Mississippi is known as a Mississippian and all that it entails, but what does it mean to be a Mississippian, and how is that related to social construction of identity? First of all, the State itself is a social construction; a little over two-hundred years ago elected officials decided what the geopolitical boundaries of the state would be. Unlike other parts of the world, the boundaries were not formed to link individuals with a shared religion, culture, etc. as the northern part was heavily Protestant Anglo-Saxon and Scots-Irish settlers, and the southern half was more Catholic Spanish and French migrants—a pattern that still holds for the most part today. Enslaved people and Native Americans were also found through-

> # Who am I?
>
> *Psychology Today* defines identity as "the many relationships people cultivate, such as their identity as a child, friend, partner, and parent.

out the state but were not considered then to be Mississippians. Since its founding, Mississippi has also seen influxes of Chinese to the Delta region, Vietnamese to the Coast, and Hispanic migrants. Regardless of ethnicity, religion, etc., everyone born here is a Mississippian by birth, an identity that has been constructed and reconstructed over the past two hundred years to mean something radically different from what it meant when the state was founded in 1817.

This same logic can be applied to any number of components of one's identity. For instance, what does it mean to be a Christian? Muslim? Jew? Buddhist? Or how about a Republican? Democrat? Conservative? Liberal? Ultimately it is important to understand that many parts of your identity have been defined for you by those around you and if you venture outside of your usual environment, those definitions might change.

Why is this important? Part of the collegiate experience is exploring your identity, which might be quite different than when you finish because of new relationships or changes in your political opinions or religious beliefs. Some of these changes are prompted by interactions with other students and/or faculty and staff who have

significantly different identities from your own for the first time in your life.

The challenge before you is to be open to hearing and listening to new ideas, to cultivate relationships of varying types with people who are different from yourself, and to understand that only you can ultimately decide for yourself who you are.

Identities: Who Are We?

The University is made up of numerous identities and yet we all share a common identity because of our shared experiences as students, faculty, staff, and alumni of the university. That identity intersects with and sometimes competes with our other identities. What do we mean by that? For example, because of the University's past history, Black students may have to justify why they want to attend the University. While not for the same reasons, a student from the northeast or west coast might get asked, "how did you end up here?" which still requires a justification. In both of these examples, a component of one's identity, or sub-identity, interacts with another part and changes their experience as part of that latter identity.

While there are numerous identities present at the University, they can be separated into three main categories of sub-identities: Individual, Group, and Relational.

- **Individual** sub-identities are those that are internal and not related to outside individuals or groups. Some examples include sex, gender/gender identity, sexual orientation, and disability, but also include eye and hair color, height, weight, etc.

- **Group** identities are those that reflect you are part of a larger group and can be broken down into two main groups: Involuntary and Voluntary:
  - *Involuntary* group identities are categories like ethnicity, nationality, citizenship, and socioeconomic status; external categories that we often think of being born into.
  - *Voluntary* group identities are categories like religious affiliation, political affiliation, social and professional organizations, etc.; these usually reflect choices we can or have made for ourselves.

- **Relational** identities are those that speak to your relationship with another such as sibling, child, grand-child, parent, grandparent, friend, spouse, classmate, etc.

> # Who are we?
> The University is made up of numerous identities and yet we all share a common identity because of our shared experiences as students, faculty, staff, and alumni of the university.

Regardless of the type of sub-identity, there are times when one might be more dominant than another, but it is never inseparable from and unaffected by the others. These intersections create vastly different lived experiences from others who might have only slightly different sub-identities. For instance, if two people share a gender, ethnicity, socioeconomic status, and religion, but one's denomination is more conservative than the other, their lives and the way they interact with the world can be remarkably different.

Important things to note about identities:

- Certain identity labels may appear in different groups, but mean something different. For instance, someone can be ethnically or culturally Jewish, but might not be a practicing member of the Jewish faith and the opposite may also be true.

- Some involuntary group identities such as citizenship and socioeconomic status can be changed through external or internal factors but we are all born into an identity.

- Hispanic and Latino/a are often used interchangeably, but do not have the same meaning. A person with Hispanic ethnicity can trace genetic ancestry to Spain. A Latino/a is someone who traces their ancestry to Latin America and includes those with European, African, Native American descent and more.

- Whiteness as a single group identity is a relatively new concept. For much of America's history, European immigrants mostly settled with others from their own country of origin and kept those identities (English, French, German, Irish, Italian, and Polish just to name a few) with White Anglo-Saxon Protestants (WASP) as the dominant cultural group. While they all considered themselves to be American, they didn't necessarily label themselves to be "white" and sometimes were actually even excluded by others. The rise of white as a perceived singular group in the United States is a reaction to two trends: 1) the increasing percentage of the population that does not trace its ethnic roots to Europe 2) the active push for full inclusion and equity for ethnic, religious, gender, and sexual minorities in American culture.

■ Not all identities are visible or easily discernible through casual interaction. This can include race/ethnicity, gender identity, sexuality, disability, religious affiliation or lack thereof, and others. Identity is personal and individual. Ultimately, you should not assume that you know someone's identities.

Your opportunity

You are now part of a wonderfully diverse environment at the University of Mississippi. Some of your fellow students, hall mates and roommates, your professors, and later on your co-workers and supervisors, neighbors, nurses, doctors, lawyers, or landscapers will be "those others." While you are a student at the University of Mississippi, you have the perfect opportunity to develop and practice those skills that will help you to be accepting and inclusive, to be an effective member of your workplace and community, and to learn to be a "good citizen." There is an old saying, "Knowledge, practice, attitude." It suggests that to effect positive change in your behavior, it is important to first understand yourself, to practice good habits, and to stand accordingly in the world.

At the University of Mississippi, we strive to be ALL IN when creating an inclusive community for everyone. Each and every one of you brings diversity that adds incredible value to our campus. And, each of you has a responsibility in ensuring that every member of our community feels welcomed and respected. In short, inclusion is everyone's business!

In the next section, you will learn more about what it means to be ALL IN at UM.

All In at UM: Navigating a Diverse Campus and World

All new students add their unique identities, experiences, and ideas to the diversity on our campus. We all share similarities and differences that make us who we are. Spending time learning about people who have different experiences increases our ability to be innovative and critical thinkers. Taking the time to discover the things that we have in common strengthens our understanding of our shared values. During your years here, some of the most powerful lessons will be learned when you embrace and appreciate ideas and viewpoints that are not our own. We know that when groups with individuals from different backgrounds come together to achieve a common goal they have the best chance at success.

All In at UM

As a student at the University of Mississippi, you will find we believe in our community being ALL IN. What this means is simple —

A – Adopt Inclusive Language

L – Listen Closely

L – Look to make a difference

I – Include others in activities

N – Nurture new experiences and perspectives.

A – Adopt Inclusive Language.

Words can sometimes be just as powerful as actions and can leave a big impact. Use words that create an environment that makes people of all backgrounds and identities feel respected and valued. Avoid making stereotypes and using language that is offensive or derogatory. Certain common expressions can unintentionally be hurtful to aspects of one's identity or to a specific group of people. If you hear someone using such language, speak up, don't be silent. Let the person know that what they're saying is not okay and takes away from the inclusive environment we strive to foster at UM.

L – Listen Closely.

There's a big difference between hearing and listening. Listening is actively wanting the person you're speaking with to feel that your attention is theirs for the moment and you find value in what they have to say. When you hear perspectives that are different from yours, seek to learn new points of view, instead of focusing on what you plan to say next. If someone shares about their lived experiences related to their identities, listen to understand and believe that their reality is true.

L – Look to make a difference.

At the University of Mississippi, we're big into the small, everyday things we can do to make a difference in someone's day and create a campus that is welcoming for everyone. Hold the door open for the next person, ask how someone is doing and listen for their answer. Get to know someone who has different identities and beliefs from you, and invite someone who is sitting or eating alone to join you. Also remember, this is your campus. Make your voice heard and take actions to make a positive impact at UM so that everyone feels comfortable here. The things you do can really brighten someone else's day and even leave a lasting legacy at our university.

I – Include others in activities.

If you're planning a get-together, working on a group project, or in a student organization, try to get other people who don't look like you, who are from different states and other countries, to get involved. When engaging with others, look around. Does everyone seem comfortable speaking out loud or contributing to the work? If not, ask that person for their opinions and ideas and try to incorporate them. These intentional acts can make everyone feel like they belong and are welcomed here.

N – Nurture new experiences and perspectives.

You've heard it time and time again that college is all about breaking out of your comfort zone. Learn about people from various backgrounds and identities by exploring the local community, doing community services, and attending cultural events. You can even take a class and attend a guest lecture about a particular topic or group to learn more about people across differences. Ask people who might be different from you how they think, or what they would do in a situation, or how their experiences have shaped them. Take advantage of our 370 student organizations to explore a new interest and build new relationships. Get to know the diverse community around you, and the University of Mississippi will feel more like home in no time!

We want to welcome each of you incoming students into our community. You have found a place to feel yourself, express your identity, and meet people from different cultures and backgrounds. Going forward in your college career, we support you in all you do and hope to be, and we want you to remember...ALL IN AT UM!

So...are you ready to be ALL IN? The following sections will help you further explore what you can do to contribute to a welcoming and inclusive campus environment.

Pathways to Equity

In January 2021, the University unveiled an institutional diversity, equity, and inclusion plan, *Pathways to Equity*, which lays the foundation addressing three Overarching Goals:

- Advance Institutional Capacity for Equity
- Cultivate a Diverse and Equitable Community
- Foster an Inclusive Campus Climate

Given the University's history, context, and importance to the state, it is imperative that we show immense leadership in ensuring all individuals can thrive on our campus. Further, it is beneficial to the University's immediate and long-term success to embrace its responsibility in cultivating a diverse environment that ensures all members of our community have what they need to be successful. To learn more about *Pathways to Equity*, visit chancellor.olemiss.edu/pathways-to-equity/.

Bigotry, Racism, and Microaggressions

Even though our population has become diverse, discussions focusing on race and race relations can still be sensitive ones. Conversations about race may elicit emotions ranging from rational to irrational, from love to hate to indifference.

> **Bigotry is the "irrational suspicion or hatred of a particular group, race, or religion" (Rogets II, 1995).**

A bigot is a person who exhibits intolerance and animosity towards those of differing beliefs or opinions and is adamant about the accuracy of his or her own views. Bigotry generally refers to someone who is hostile to those of a race, ethnicity, nationality, sexual orientation, or religion other than his or her own. Racism, per the definition of the Anti-Defamation League, is "the belief that a particular race is superior or inferior to another, that a person's social and moral traits are predetermined by his or her inborn biological characteristics." Stereotyping is defined by the Oxford English Dictionary as "something continued or constantly repeated without change." It is easy to make assumptions about groups of people, basing those assumptions on stereotypical characteristics that we ascribe to particular identities. These stereotypes may be based on our own experiences, impressions gained by characters in movies or TV programs, or perhaps even discussions with family and friends.

Bigotry, racism, and stereotyping can lead to microaggressions and more explicit acts of bias. Microaggressions are "the everyday verbal, nonverbal, and environmental slights, snubs, or insults, whether intentional or unintentional, which communicate hostile, derogatory, or negative messages to target persons based solely upon their marginalized group membership" (Sue, 2010). In "35 Dumb Things Well-Intentioned People Say: Surprising things we say that widen the diversity gap," Dr. Maura Cullen discusses intent vs. impact. Even well-intentioned microaggressions can cause harm and have a lasting impact. Well-intentioned statements such as "I don't see color" and "What are you?" may minimize the cultural heritage of others. While microaggressions are generally discussed from the perspective of race and racism, any marginalized group in our society may become targets including people of color, women, LGBTQ+ persons, those with disabilities, religious minorities, and more.

> **Microaggressions are "the everyday verbal, nonverbal, and environmental slights, snubs, or insults, whether intentional or unintentional, which communicate hostile, derogatory, or negative messages to target persons based solely upon their marginalized group membership" (Sue, 2010).**

Microaggressions can be based upon any group that is marginalized in this society. Below are a few examples (Sue, 2010):

- An Asian American, born and raised in the United States, is complimented for speaking "good English." (Hidden message: You are not a true American. You are a perpetual foreigner in your own country.)
- A blind man reports that people often raise their voices when speaking to him. He responds by saying, "Please don't raise your voice; I can hear you perfectly well." (Hidden message: A person with a disability is defined as lesser in all aspects of physical and mental functioning.)
- A female physician wearing a stethoscope is mistaken as a nurse. (Hidden message: Women should occupy nurturing and not decision-making roles. Women are less capable than men.)
- A white man or woman clutches her purse or checks his or her wallet as a Black or Latino man approaches or passes by. (Hidden message: You and your group are criminals.)
- A young person uses the term "gay" to describe a movie that she didn't like. (Hidden message: Being gay is associated with negative and undesirable characteristics.)
- When bargaining over the price of an item, a store owner says to a customer, "Don't try to Jew me down." (Hidden message: Jews are stingy and money-grubbing.)

Disability: A Social Justice Issue

Approximately 61 million Americans, or 26% of the population, have a disability. This makes people with disabilities the largest minority group in the country.

The definition of disability has evolved over time; however, people with disabilities are still subject to negative perceptions about the meaning of disability. Some view disability as a problem with the person and expect that people with disabilities should learn to live in the world as it is. Others see those with disabilities as tragic victims who should be pitied and taken care of. The disabled community rejects both of these definitions of disability.

Those with disabilities view disability as a social justice issue. Under the social justice model, disability is not caused by the limitations created by the illness, injury, or condition of the person and instead is a result of poorly constructed physical, social, attitudinal, educational, and economic environments that limit or prevent the full participation and inclusion of those with disabilities. The social justice model of disability was created by those with disabilities in reaction to preventable, artificially created barriers that limit access to employment, education, housing, and other activities that are easily available to those without disabilities.

Disability Statistics

Thirty years after the passage of the ADA, disability-related disparities continue to affect people with disabilities. According to the National Council on Disability (NCD), 32% of adults with disabilities are employed full-time, compared to 73% of adults without disabilities. The NCD also reports that those with disabilities "live in poverty at twice the rate of people without disabilities." The Cornell University Center on Disability Statistics reports that the high school graduation rate for students with disabilities is 67%. The high school graduation rate for non-disabled students is 85%. In addition, according the Center for Disability Statistics, only 15.2% of people with disabilities have a bachelor's degree or higher compared to 35.2% of people without disabilities.

As an example, imagine a person who uses a wheelchair has a job interview. That person gets to the building in which the interview is to take place, only to find that there is no accessible entrance to the building. Because there is no accessible entrance, this person is not able to get to his job interview and therefore is not hired. Some will look at this situation and think, "If that person weren't in a wheelchair, they could have gotten to the interview." This perception views the problem as belonging to the person. Others who view disability as a social justice issue will look at that situation and think, "If only there were an elevator, that person would have gotten to the elevator." The perception acknowledges that the problem is not the wheelchair but instead is the inaccessibility of the building.

Disability Etiquette

Many people hesitate to interact with those who have disabilities because they have no experience doing so. They may feel self-conscious, uncomfortable, or awkward, afraid of doing or saying something wrong. Below are some general tips that might help alleviate some of the discomfort that might occur when interacting with a person who has a disability:

- Don't make assumptions of what a person with a disability can do; experiences and abilities vary from person to person.
- Don't use antiquated and demeaning terms or phrases such as handicapped, crippled, special/special needs, wheelchair-bound, lame, dumb, hearing impaired, or suffering from a specific disability; also, don't use euphemistic language like differently abled or learning difference.

- Use "person-first" language such as a person who has low vision or uses a wheelchair. However, it is important to recognize that a person with a disability may choose to use "identity-first" language.
- Speak directly to the person with the disability, not an individual who may be accompanying the person (sign language interpreter, personal care assistant, etc).
- Respect personal space and equipment/adaptive technology; don't lean on a person's wheelchair or grab the person's arm.

Gender Pronouns

A pronoun is a word that refers to either the people talking (like "I" or "you") or someone or something that is being talked about (like "she," "it," "them," and "this"). The English language (as well as many others) has gender-specific personal pronouns, traditionally "he/him/his" for the masculine and "she/her/hers" for the feminine. Some folks, especially transgender, non-binary, and gender non-conforming individuals, choose to use gender neutral pronouns, such as "they/them/theirs," "ze/zir/zirs," or "per/per/pers."

Singular "They"?

Contrary to popular belief, the use of the pronoun "they" to refer to a single person has existed in English speech and writing for centuries. Because most of us are taught when we're learning to read and write not to use "they" as singular, it can definitely be hard to wrap your head around. When you first meet a person who uses "they" pronouns, it will probably have to be something you are very conscious about practicing. However, I can promise you that you already use singular "they" every single day—just unconsciously! Think about phrases like "Did someone leave their coffee cup at the table?" or "I'll call them back when I have a second." Normal!

Correctly using someone's pronouns is one of the most basic ways to show your respect for their gender identity, and really, them as a person. When someone is misgendered (referred to with the wrong pronouns), it can make them feel disrespected, invalidated, alienated, or even in danger—often all of the above. So yes, it is helpful to know that singular "they" is indeed grammatically correct—but even if it weren't, wouldn't you just want to do what is really the simplest thing possible to show another person that you respect them as a human being for who they are? Using someone's correct pronouns also matters just as much as calling them by the right name.

How do I know someone's pronouns?

A person's pronouns don't always "match up" with their gender identity and/ or expression. Just like gender identity, you can't know (and therefore shouldn't assume) what a person's pronouns are before they tell you.

It's also important to note that instead of straight-out asking, it's often better to give people the opportunity to tell you their pronouns themselves. Some people may not feel safe sharing this information right away, so a great way to show them that they can is by incorporating pronoun usage into your own introduction, i.e.: "I'm Meg, I'm from Utah, I studied English in college, and my pronouns are they/them!" If people are confused as to what gender pronouns are, this can also be a teaching opportunity, and an easy and powerful way to express allyship.

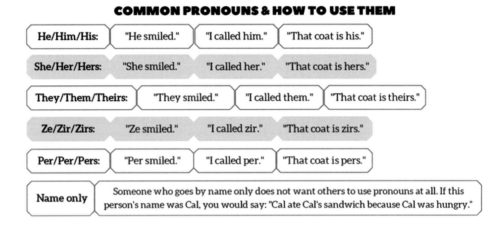

COMMON PRONOUNS & HOW TO USE THEM

He/Him/His:	"He smiled."	"I called him."	"That coat is his."
She/Her/Hers:	"She smiled."	"I called her."	"That coat is hers."
They/Them/Theirs:	"They smiled."	"I called them."	"That coat is theirs."
Ze/Zir/Zirs:	"Ze smiled."	"I called zir."	"That coat is zirs."
Per/Per/Pers:	"Per smiled."	"I called per."	"That coat is pers."
Name only	Someone who goes by name only does not want others to use pronouns at all. If this person's name was Cal, you would say: "Cal ate Cal's sandwich because Cal was hungry."		

Best Practices for LGBTQIA+ Allyship

- Don't assume that everyone around you is cisgender and/or straight.

- Always use the name and pronouns that someone has asked you to refer to them by.

- Be an open-minded and active listener, and speak up when you notice cruelty or discrimination.

- Confront your own prejudices and biases, even (especially!) when it is uncomfortable to do so.

- Apologize (briefly and sincerely) if you make a mistake. Mistakes are going to happen, for all of us, so apologizing, learning, and moving forward matter.

- Do some research and learning on your own. There are so many free resources and sources of information out there. This takes some of the responsibility off of marginalized people from feeling like they have to educate all the time, which can be very tiring.

- Believe that all people, regardless of gender, sexuality, or any other aspects of identity, are deserving of dignity and respect.

The Bias Education and Response Team (BERT)

While freedom of expression and the open exchange of ideas are important to the University of Mississippi, actions and behaviors that are bias-motivated, prejudiced, or otherwise disrespectful can negatively impact individuals or groups. The Bias Education and Report Team is a non-judicial team of faculty, staff, students, and administrators that supports members of the University of Mississippi community who bring forward allegations of bias. The primary role of BERT is to connect those impacted by bias incidents to the appropriate resources and support.

Bias-related incidents are defined as alleged threats or acts of harassment or intimidation, whether verbal, written or physical, which are motivated by a bias against a person or property in whole or in part because of that person's age, color, ability, marital status, national or ethnic origin, political affiliation, race, religion, sex (including pregnancy), socioeconomic status, gender identity, gender expression, sexual orientation, veteran status, family medical or genetic makeup or information, intellectual perspective, criminal background, and potentially other identities or identifiers.

Members of the university community who have experienced or witnessed perceived/alleged bias incidents are encouraged to complete a Campus Climate Concern form. The form will give you the opportunity to share the details of the incident including the impact it has had on you and/or others. BERT will review all submissions to determine appropriate next steps. BERT is not an investigative, adjudicatory, or disciplinary body and does not function in lieu of any disciplinary or complaint processes within or outside of the University. To learn more about BERT, visit bert.olemiss.edu.

Diversity at UM and Beyond

For many, college campuses are the most racially, politically, socially, and economically diverse environments. This is often an exciting time and opportunity for great learning. Simultaneously, many students are learning the skills needed to engage with peers, faculty, and staff that have different backgrounds, experiences, and values than their own. As you read the University of Mississippi's Diversity Statement, you will see a clear commitment by our campus to ensuring all faculty, staff, and students are able to engage in a diverse community and thrive as they navigate their experience.

University of Mississippi Diversity Statement

The University of Mississippi embraces its public flagship mission of inspiring and educating our diverse and vibrant community where all individuals are able to intellectually, socially, and culturally thrive through transformative experiences on our campus and beyond. In fulfillment of this mission, we demonstrate the following commitments to diversity, equity, and inclusion:

- Diversity is an affirmation of the intersecting individual, social, and organizational identities that make our community vibrant and transformational. We commit to openly increasing, embracing, and recognizing the full spectrum of diversity at all levels of our institution.

- Equity is directly addressing the social, institutional, organizational, and systemic barriers that prevent members of marginalized groups from thriving in our community. We commit to be both proactive and responsive in mitigating barriers so that all members of our institution are able to reach their full potential.

- Inclusion is actively and intentionally creating a welcoming campus where all individuals feel they have a supportive and affirming space to learn, grow, and engage. We commit to fostering a campus environment that fully supports, values, and engages the intersectional identities of every member of our community.

As you navigate your college experience, each student must embrace this process fully. Here are two considerations as you navigate your college experience:

Classroom Learning. No matter your major, minor, or overall interests, learning is central to the college experience. Your classrooms will offer you an opportunity to be introduced to complex ideas, concepts, and challenges that deepen your knowledge and prepare you for your future beyond campus. While you are engaging with the multitude of topics in your classes, commit to embracing the diverse perspectives and experiences within each of your classes, which allows you to have the most robust learning experience and allows you to critically think about the topics presented. Each student has their own background and experiences that inform how they process and perceive the world around them. Hearing and thoughtfully engaging diverse perspectives and experiences allows for the most powerful learning experience and deepens your own knowledge and understanding. In each course, consider a few questions to ask yourself:

- How have my own identities and experiences informed my connection to this information?

■ What assumptions did I make as I processed the presented topic? Did I make space for an experience of an underrepresented group to be included? How is that different or similar than my assumptions?

■ How can I find opportunities to thoughtfully engage with the perspectives of underrepresented authors, scholars, and/or peers on my given topic? How might these perspectives deepen my learning?

Leadership and Involvement. Learning also happens beyond the confines of your classroom. Your learning can be furthered by getting involved in experiences on campus such as joining a Registered Student Organizations (RSOs), going to cultural/ heritage events, and participating in leadership development experiences. All of these, and many more, experiences offer you a chance to explore and expand your interests and knowledge. Further, these are opportunities to engage with diverse peers, faculty, and staff. As you join organizations, you will be able to work with other leaders on engaging and transformative programs. This is an incredible opportunity to learn how to work with others from different backgrounds and to learn about your role in supporting an inclusive environment for all. As you participate in student involvement and engage in leadership experiences, consider a few questions:

■ What programs can I attend or participate in that will help me learn about experiences of underrepresented communities?

■ How are student leaders perceived based on their different backgrounds? How might I support leaders from all backgrounds?

■ What does thoughtful collaboration look like with cultural organizations? How do we enter equitable and mutual partnerships?

■ What role does my organization have in ensuring our campus is supportive of students from all backgrounds?

There are many resources available at the University to support you in this process. On the next page of this section, you can find a list of campus resources prepared to provide opportunities for you to explore diversity, equity, and inclusion. Ample opportunities also exist for you take courses on race, gender, sexuality, socioeconomic status, global affairs, and other topics that allow you to engage with a diverse range of identities, experiences, and groups. These courses can be found in academic departments such as, but not limited to, the following:

African American Studies

The Croft Institute for International Studies

Department of Higher Education

Department of Psychology

Gender Studies

The Intensive English Program

International Studies

Modern Languages and Culture Studies

Sally McDonnell Barksdale Honors College

Sociology and Anthropology

Southern Studies

Study Abroad

The Diversity Bonus

The University of Mississippi's investment your learning about and engagement with diversity, equity, and inclusion is in complete fulfillment of our institutional mission to transform lives, communities, and the world. In order to achieve this, we must be sure all members of our campus are able to thrive and contribute their knowledge, talent, and experiences in pursuit of the most robust and impactful learning environment. The University must also help prepare graduates that are equipped for transformative leadership in their given field and industry. Our graduates will be expected to meaningfully engage with diverse and interdisciplinary teams in order to unlock the "Diversity Bonus." *The Diversity Bonus* is a book by Professor Scott Page, Ph.D. that illustrates that diverse teams produce the best responses to complex tasks and challenges, even outweighing the impact of individual intellect. All across industries, leaders are exploring ways to unlock the not-so-hidden power of diversity and seeking employees who can work well with others from a multitude of backgrounds, experiences, and identities to achieve the goals. During your time at UM, you will have ample opportunity to be learn the skills needed to be prepared for these opportunities.

In the following section, you'll find valuable resources to support you during your time as a student at the University of Mississippi.

Campus Resources

The Division of Diversity and Community Engagement

Established in 2017, the Division of Diversity and Community Engagement (DCE) coordinates the University of Mississippi's efforts to create and support a diverse, inclusive, and welcoming environment for all members of the community, including students, staff, faculty, and alumni. Under the leadership of Interim Vice Chancellor Shawnboda Mead, DCE envisions a more equitable, engaged, and self-transforming university, community, and world. The division moves toward this vision while supporting the mission of UM by transforming people, institutions, and communities. It does so through partnership, access, and engagement that fosters belonging, enriches learning and development, enhances research, and creates equitable opportunities for all.

The Center for Inclusion and Cross-Cultural Engagement

The Center for Inclusion and Cross-Cultural Engagement (CICCE) opened in 2014. Located in the Ole Miss Student Union, the Center offers students a welcoming environment to interact, exchange ideas, and engage in programming and meaningful conversations that celebrate the cultures and heritages of our diverse community. The CICCE provides opportunities that prepare you for success in a multicultural society. From academic resources to peer mentoring and cultural programming, there is something for everyone. The desire is that, as a community, we interact with one another from a place of appreciation and acceptance, where all members are valued. The University of Mississippi is likely to be the most diverse community you will ever be part of in your life. The Center encourages you to embrace the difference and diversity around you.

The Office of Student Disability Services

In collaboration with the larger campus community, SDS assists the University in its commitment to protect the civil rights of students with disabilities and to assist with the design of more welcoming and inclusive environments. SDS is responsible for determining support for a student's disability-related need for accommodations and for facilitating, through an interactive process with students and faculty, the removal of unintentional curricular and programmatic barriers.

The Sarah Isom Center for Women and Gender Studies

The Sarah Isom Center for Women and Gender Studies was established at The University of Mississippi in 1981 to address the changing roles and expectations of women students, faculty, and staff. The University has provided educational opportunities for women longer than any other state university in the South. When UM opened its doors to women in 1882, eleven women registered for classes; one of these became the valedictorian of her class. In 1885, Professor Sarah McGehee Isom became the University's first female faculty member. Named in her honor, the Isom Center continues the tradition of promoting education and opportunities for women, who today constitute more than half of the UM student population.

Today, the Sarah Isom Center for Women and Gender Studies educates about issues of gender and sexuality, promotes interdisciplinary research, and advocates for diversity, equity, and inclusion.

Veteran & Military Services

Veteran & Military Services works to solve the complex issues surrounding military-connected students in higher education. This office works with all military-connected students to help navigate the college experience, focusing on helping identify pathways to success both in and out of the classroom. The staff within VMS help to advocate for students in a variety of situations, from working with the Department of Veterans Affairs to get education benefits, to serving veterans with every facet of the veteran experience. The office and staff are able to provide services for education benefits, obtaining VA appointments, disability and compensation solutions, medical assistance with VA healthcare, survivor and end of life benefits, VA home loans, a food pantry, lounge, free printing, and a place to connect with students from all walks of life. By serving the whole person, VMS aims to be a one-stop-shop for all military-connected students, including Active Duty, Guard, Reserve, Veteran, and dependent students.

The Office of International Programs

The Office of International Programs (OIP) is housed within the Division of Global Engagement. In addition to international recruitment and admission, OIP provides information and documents to support nonimmigrant student visa applications and assists international students and scholars with their cultural as well as educational adjustments, so they can complete their educational goals.

Multi-cultural or ethnicity organizations: The University of Mississippi has many organizations composed of multi-ethnic memberships. These organizations host events and provide opportunities to dialogue about multicultural topics. Each of these organizations is registered through the Ole Miss Student Union. To view the website for these organizations and/or locate contact information, visit olemiss.campuslabs.com/engage/.

African Caribbean Organization

Black Graduate Professional Student Association

Black Student Union (BSU)

Cultural Connections Club

Cultural Connections Mentorship Program

Friendship Association of Chinese Students and Scholars

Indian Students Association

International Ladies Club

International Student Organization

Latin American Student Organization

Men of Excellence

Model United Nations

Muslim Students Association

PRIDE Network

Society of Black Sociologists

Student Accessibility Coalition

Taiwan Student Association

University of Mississippi German Club

University of Mississippi Gospel Choir

University of Mississippi Russian Club

Cultural events are held annually on the campus of the University of Mississippi. The Center for Inclusion & Cross Cultural Engagement's *All In. All Year.* calendar highlights on-campus and community diversity and inclusion programs. The following is a listing of some of the events that are held throughout the year:

Disability History Month

Hispanic Heritage Month

LGBTQ History Month

Native American Month

Black History Month

SarahFest

Celebration of Achievement

Fiesta Latina

Pride Camp

Lavender Graduation Ceremony

Get Involved Now

Homecoming Step Show

India Night

International Fest

Sister2Sister and Brother2Brother Leadership Retreats

CICCE Cross Cultural Excursions

Globalization in Higher Education[i]

- "1,075,496 international students studied at U.S. colleges and universities in 2019–20"

- "In 2019, the continued growth in international students coming to the U.S. for higher education had a significant positive economic impact on the United States. International students contributed more than $44 billion to the U.S. economy, according to the U.S. Department of Commerce"

- "347,099" U.S. students studied abroad for academic credit in 2018–2019"

On language diversity: Linguists estimate that there are 7,117 living languages[ii] and that 43% of the population is bilingual. While English is the most common spoken language, 66% of the people who speak English learned it as a second language. The most common "native" language is Mandarin Chinese. As compared to English as a native language, almost 2.5 times as many people in the world speak Mandarin Chinese. The most common native languages spoken in the world are: 1) Mandarin Chinese 2) Spanish 3) English 4) Hindi 5) Bengali (India and Bangladesh) and 6) Portuguese. Meanwhile, many languages of smaller ethnic groups are no longer spoken by the children of these groups. Almost 40% of the languages in the world are considered in danger of dying out.[iii] This is partly due to the increasing globalization of our economies and the global importance of the English language and Western (especially U.S.) culture. However, cultural diffusion has not been a one-way affair. For example, the English language contains words from more than 240 other languages. In less than one generation, the cultural influences of Asia and Latin America especially, have dramatically changed life in North America. (e.g. boogie, safari [African]; ketchup, wok [Asian]; coleslaw, frolic, furlough [Dutch]).

---

[i] https://www.iie.org/en/Why-IIE/Announcements/2020/11/2020-Open-Doors-Report

[ii] https://www.ethnologue.com/guides/how-many-languages

[iii] https://www.visualcapitalist.com/100-most-spoken-languages/

ABOUT THE AUTHORS

Kevin Cozart *(he/him/his), Operations Coordinator for the Sarah Isom Center for Women and Gender Studies*

A native Mississippian, Kevin Cozart has been a member of the University's staff since 2004 and has served on the the the University's Staff Council, advisor for the UM Pride Network and OUTGrads, president of the Graduate Student Council, and co-director of the ALLIES program. A UM graduate, Kevin holds master's degrees in journalism with an integrated marketing communications emphasis and higher education and student personnel with a minor in gender studies. He is the winner of the 2019 UM Lift Every Voice Award. He routinely uses film and other forms of visual media as bases for exploration of issues related to gender and/or sexuality. He currently serves on the board of directors for the Oxford Film Festival.

Shawnboda Mead *(she/her/hers), Interim Vice Chancellor for Diversity and Community Engagement*

A native of Prentiss, Mississippi, Shawnboda Mead joined the University of Mississippi in July 2014, and is responsible for advancing institutional diversity, equity, and inclusion goals. Dr. Mead provides leadership and coordination of UM's strategic efforts to create an inclusive and welcoming environment for all members of the community. Dr. Mead earned a bachelor's degree in educational psychology from Mississippi State University and a master's degree in student affairs/higher education administration from Western Kentucky University. She holds a doctorate in higher education administration from UM and has over 17 years of experience in higher education.

Cadence Pentheny *(they/them/theirs), Coordinator for LGBTQIA+ Programming & Initiatives for the Center for Inclusion & Cross Cultural Engagement*

Cadence is primarily responsible for LGBTQ+ programming and initiatives within the CICCE, as well as supporting various

ABOUT THE AUTHORS

diversity education initiatives across campus. They hold a bachelor's degree in sociology and women's, gender, and sexuality studies from Franklin & Marshall College in Lancaster, Pennsylvania, and a graduate certificate in human sexuality through the University of Minnesota. They are passionate about art in all its many forms, especially its roles in social justice movements. In their free time, they also enjoy finding odd home decor at thrift shops, walking, reading, writing, making art, collecting and caring for plants, and listening to podcasts.

Stacey Reycraft *(she/her/hers) Director, Student Disability Services*

Originally from Crested Butte, Colorado, Stacey Reycraft moved to Oxford in 1987 to complete her undergraduate degree at the University of Mississippi. Stacey has over 24 years of experience in the area of disability in higher education, with a focus on disability as a social justice and civil rights issue. She has also worked on broader issues of disability. She served as the chair of the City of Oxford Mayor's Commission on Disability for 10 years and was the founder of the Mississippi Association of Higher Education and Disability. She has also worked extensively for the international Association on Higher Education and Disability, serving as the program reviewer, presenter, and volunteer. Stacey holds a bachelor's degree in English and a master's degree in higher education, both from the University of Mississippi.

JuWan D. Robinson *(he/him/his), Project Manager for Diversity Education and Strategic Initiatives, Division of Diversity and Community Engagement*

JuWan grew up in Bessemer, Alabama, and joined the University of Mississippi in 2017. In his current role, he is primarily responsible for leading diversity education in the Division of Diversity and Community Engagement and works collaboratively across campus on the advancement of diversity, equity, and inclusion efforts. JuWan holds a bachelor's degree in

ABOUT THE AUTHORS

secondary education from the University of South Alabama and a master's degree in higher education/student personnel from the University of Mississippi. He is currently a doctoral student in higher education at the University of Mississippi.

Robin T. Yekaitis *(she/her/hers), Access Services Advisor, Student Disability Services*

Robin Yekaitis joined Student Disability Services at the University of Mississippi in 2006. She collaborates with students in pursuing their academic goals by identifying barriers in their academic environments and determining accommodations necessary to provide access to their courses. She also provides training to faculty and staff on disability access, inclusion, and equity. She earned a bachelor's degree in history from Mississippi University for Women and has taken courses towards a master's degree in higher education and student personnel at the University of Mississippi. In addition to being active on campus, Robin serves on the Mayor's Commission on Disability Issues (Oxford, MS).

Special Acknowledgements:

- Previous contributions to chapter: Toni Avant, Valeria Beasley-Ross, Ge-Yao-Liu, and Greet Provoost

- Creators of *All In at UM* Campaign: Dr. Tanya Nichols and Jacqueline Schlick, Division of Diversity and Community Engagement

CHAPTER 5

HOTTY TODDY

AND Other Traditions

By Seph Anderson and Thomas Reardon
Updated by Bradley Baker
and Martin Fisher

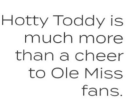

Hotty Toddy is much more than a cheer to Ole Miss fans.

The Alma Mater of the University of Mississippi is a beautiful song that has been sung and played at athletic events, commencement ceremonies, the inauguration of chancellors, funerals and memorial ceremonies, class reunions, and other special events. The song has great meaning and is held sentimental by alumni of the University. It was written in 1925 by Mrs. A. W. Kahle and her husband.

When the Alma Mater is played, there should be an attitude of respect. Those in attendance should stand, remove hats or caps, and sing the words.

In recent years, singing of the Alma Mater has become a game day tradition at sporting events like football and men's basketball. At the end of the contest, the team sways and sings in unison with the student section as the Pride of the South plays the Alma Mater.

THE ALMA MATER

Way down south in Mississippi, There's a spot that ever calls Where among the hills enfolded, Stand old Alma Mater's halls.

Where the trees lift high their branches, To the whisp'ring southern breeze. There Ole Miss is calling, calling, To our hearts' fond memories.

With united hearts we praise thee, All our loyalty is thine, And we hail thee, Alma Mater, May thy light forever shine;

May it brighter grow and brighter, And with deep affection true, Our thoughts shall ever cluster 'round thee, Dear Old Red and Blue.

May thy fame throughout the nation, Through thy sons and daughters grow, May thy name forever waken, In our hearts a tender glow,

May thy counsel and thy spirit, Ever keep us one in this,

That our own shall be thine honor, Now and ever dear Ole Miss.

Heighty! Tighty! Gosh A Mighty!
Who in the hell are we?
Rim! Ram! Flim! Flam!
Ole Miss, by Damn!

The Legend of Hotty Toddy

Nothing may be more shrouded in uncertainty than the origins of Ole Miss's Hotty Toddy cheer. The first print appearance of the cheer surfaced in a 1926 Mississippian, but the true origin of the famous school cheer has no such definite beginnings.

In 1931, an Ole Miss music professor named Arleen Tye wrote a spirited song appropriately titled "Ole Miss." Important to note is that the song's chorus was, "Hi-ty Ti-ty Gosh a'mighty, Who the heck are we?"

While parts of the chorus are similar to today's version of Hotty Toddy, the remainder of Tye's "Ole Miss" doesn't make as much of a connection.

Ole Miss historian Gerald W. Walton poses a potential connection to World War II by suggesting, "Many associate the cheer with one used during World War II. Battle Cry and Band of Brothers contained versions of: Highty, Tighty, Christ almighty, Who the hell are we? Zim Zam, god damn, We're airborne infantry."

However, quite possibly the strongest and most logical connection actually stems from another university, Virginia Tech. Specifically, the Virginia Tech Regimental Band which began to be called the Highty-Tighties in 1919:

How did the cadet band come to be known as the "Highty-Tighties?" The cadet band website suggests:

The origin of the name has been hotly debated for years — some claimed it was part of a cheer, others claimed it sprang from a trip to Richmond where the Corps and Band marched in honor of Field Marshal Foch, the supreme allied commander of WW-I. Supposedly the drum major had dropped and then recovered his baton while rendering a salute in front of the reviewing stand and someone in the crowd yelled hoity-toity. Southwest Virginia slang had supposedly turned this into Highty-Tighty. Like many legends there are bits and pieces of factual information from several events woven into a story — but the accepted story is, that just like "Hokie" began as part of a cadet cheer, so too, the name "Highty-Tighty" began as part of a cadet cheer.

As for that cadet band cheer, suggested to have come from a cheer when the band was housed in Division E of Lane Hall, cadet sources claim it originally went something like this:

Highty-Tighty! Christ Almighty!
Who the hell are we?
Rip, Ram, God Damn!
We're from Division E!

In all likelihood, the well-known Ole Miss cheer we know today developed over the years from several of these potential origins. In the end, it's the mythical nature of the cheer that adds to its legend.

Let's Call Them the Rebels

In a 1929 student-only contest by the *Mississippian* to name the team, Ole Miss student Dick McCool suggested the team be called the "Flood," in reference to the 1927 Mississippi River flood. After reviewing an estimated 800 student entries, the contest committee decided to go with the "Flood."

However, the new team name simply didn't catch on in the years that followed. Having been referred to as the "Mighty Mississippians," "Flood," "Red and Blue" and "The Southerners" for periods of time prior to the program's first bowl appearance in the 1936 Orange Bowl, head coach Ed Walker was looking for a strong team name to further establish the program's presence on a national stage.

A major reason behind Walker's insistence was likely the name by which one sportswriter had casually referred to the Ole Miss team. David Sansing notes in *The University of Mississippi: A Sesquicentennial History*:

> *After an unimaginative sportswriter referred to the Ole Miss football team as the "Mudcats," the student newspaper decided it was time for another contest and a new name. In the 1936 contest, a committee of sportswriters selected the name Rebels, which was submitted by Ben Guider of Vicksburg. The name was a natural and quickly captured the imagination of Ole Miss students, fans, friends, alumni, and sportswriters.*

The five finalist options put before the sportswriters through *Mississippian* sports editor Billy Gates' poll, were the Confederates, Ole Miss, Raiders, Rebels, and Stonewalls. In the end, Rebels received 18 votes, Raiders received two votes and Ole Miss received one vote. Ever since that momentous final vote, University of Mississippi squads have been called the Rebels.

James "Blind Jim" Ivy – "Perpetual Dean of Freshman Class"

The legend of James "Blind Jim" Ivy at Ole Miss began back in 1896, a mere three years after Bondurant coached the school's first football team. However, the peanut vendor's legend was actually born at an Ole Miss Baseball game. With Ole Miss losing to the University of Texas, Ivy began to loudly cheer for the Rebels. Come the end of the game, Ole Miss had prevailed, and Ivy was credited for helping to rally the red and blue.

From that day forward, Ivy would be an integral part of the campus fabric. Called the "Perpetual Dean of the Freshman Class" for his close affiliation and care for the freshman class each year, he was known to give an opening address to the freshmen each fall and to lead the pajama parade, among other contributions.

Alongside a picture of Blind Jim with the freshman class, the 1924 Ole Miss states, "For over thirty years he has been one of the truest and most optimistic Ole Miss supporters. His courage is inspiring, and the spirit with which he has cheered the team has many times given heart to the weak and encouraged us to fight to the finish even though it were a losing one."

Blind Jim would remain a mainstay on the Ole Miss campus for nearly sixty years. Primarily a peanut vendor on campus for decades until a single food service company assumed all such duties in 1931, Ivy was considered one of the most loyal and truest Rebel supporters.

As much as Ivy cared for the University, its students and athletic teams, the feeling was mutual. Dr. Gerald Walton writes in *The University of Mississippi: A Pictorial History:*

In 1936, when he (Ivy) was about to lose his home to foreclosure, students and alumni raised about $425 to help him. In 1955, Ivy became too ill to attend Homecoming. A committee was formed to see to his needs; they raised more than $1,100, later used to pay for his medical and burial expenses.

When Ivy died October 20 of that year, the Daily Mississippian ran a huge front-page banner headline and news story. Because he had gained celebrity status by then, several regional newspapers also reported the news of his passing, along with history. His memorial service at Second Baptist Church in Oxford, an all-black church, was a precedent-shattering integrated affair attended by more than five hundred people. The crowd was so large that many people could not even get in the door.

The headline in the Oxford Eagle the next day read, "Blind Jim Mourned by Both Races."

Moreover, an entire page in the 1955 The Ole Miss is dedicated to the fervent Rebel. Ivy is quoted as famously saying, "I've been following the Rebels for 50 years and I have never seen them lose a ball game yet." The dedication goes on to read, "Everyone who comes to Ole Miss knows Jim, and more than likely, if you have ever talked to him he will remember you also. He is known all over the United States for his undying loyalty for the Rebels. When things are not going so good for us out on the field, it is Jim who is the first to give a rousing Rebel yell and raise the Ole Miss spirit again."

Lock the Vaught

Prior to kick off on Saturdays in Vaught-Hemingway Stadium, Rebel fans lock arms and sway in rhythm with the football team. Like many traditions, this one began as an idea from a handful of students. The first couple of games in the 2009 season, only small portions of the student section swayed with the football team, but it grew in popularity each week. Today, thousands of fans lock arms and participate in "Locking the Vaught," a relatively new tradition that appears to be here to stay for years to come.

Frank Everett quote

During your time at the University, you probably are going to walk into an office and see on the wall Frank Everett's quote about Ole Miss. You might notice it on the wall of the main staircase in the Union. And, most likely, you will hear it quoted in a speech before you graduate.

Everett, a lawyer from Vicksburg, gave these remarks as part of his introduction of Chancellor Porter Fortune at an alumni event in 1971. It was so well received that it was published in the Sunday paper two days later.

The opening paragraph is most frequently quoted:

There is a valid distinction between "The University" and "Ole Miss" even though the separate threads are closely interwoven. The University is buildings, trees, and people. Ole Miss is mood, emotion and personality. One is physical and the other is spiritual.

One is tangible, and the other intangible. The University is respected, but Ole Miss is loved. The University gives a diploma and regretfully terminates tenure, but one never graduates from Ole Miss.

Gamedays in The Grove

While Ole Miss students, faculty, and staff enjoy a tranquil, serene Grove most of the year, on six or seven Saturdays each fall the Grove becomes the scene of the finest tailgating experience to be found on the planet.

Having been applauded by The Sporting News as "The Holy Grail of Tailgating" and by Business Insider as one of the "Top 50 Trips to take in the United States," the Grove has truly become a national tailgating treasure.

It is yet another part of what makes being an Ole Miss student so special. Where some people come to experience the Grove once in their lives and others come for a few games each fall, you're afforded the opportunity to enjoy the majestic natural landscape throughout the school year.

The Grove's not only the place you'll experience your first home football weekend as part of the Ole Miss Family, but it is also where you will sit during commencement when you graduate.

The Grove is known as the premier site in the country for football tailgating. In fact, Sports Illustrated ranked it as #8 on the list of all-time best sports experiences.

The Founding Father of the Grove: Chancellor Robert Burwell Fulton

Former Chancellor Robert Burwell Fulton, an alumnus himself, is the person responsible for first preserving and growing the 10-acre campus landscape. It all began in 1889, when work began on a campus library. While the library was being built, now known as Ventress Hall, a nearby wooden fence enclosed the "inner circle" of campus.

Not too long after the library was finished, as new chancellor, Fulton had the temporary fencing removed and made the decision to advance the campus east in the direction of what was at the time the railroad and train depot. Not only did he extend the campus beyond the "inner circle," but he also decided to enhance the newly-included campus grounds by adding a variety of trees and shrubs to the area.

In the 1902 *Ole Miss*, University of Mississippi student S. Lamar Field wrote a fitting poem, "Our Campus," about the natural beauty of the campus Fulton helped grow:

> The chilling blasts have passed us by:
> The gentle Spring greets us with cheer;
> A panorama fills the eye
> That looks upon the views now here.
>
> The artist's hand, so deft and skilled,
> And with imagination's aid,
> Were weak to please the soul that's thrilled
> By beauty such as here is laid.
>
> Though fancy's ideal high may be,
> If bound by earth's or nature's views,
> No grander sight her eye can see.
> Nor grander scenes her wishes choose.
>
> The pink horizon in the East
> Is brightened by the rising sun;
> The shadow of the night has passed.
> A cheerful song of birds begun.
>
> The grass an emerald carpet rare,
> And rich with diamond dew-drops bright,
> Aglow with brilliance everywhere,
> Creates a most imposing sight.
>
> The weeping willow's graceful bow
> To huge, gigantic, stately oak,
> Salutes the squirrel seated low
> As he, in glee, chats with his folk.
>
> The sky, a canopy of blue.
> With grace, is bent above the scene;
> The sun beholds the brilliant view
> And smiles upon this plot of green.
>
> At last, but greatest of it all.
> The Co-Ed comes, so rare and bland;
> Upon this scene dark shadows fall
> And leave it for the artist's hand.

It's telling that more than 100 years after Field wrote "Our Campus," his words and description remain ever so true.

The 1899 *Ole Miss* contains an entry entitled "The Devil Knows," in which a student writes about being visited by spirits in the original University chapel (now the Croft Institute for International Studies). Having been used as a hospital during the Civil War, many students believed parts of the campus were haunted by those lost during war.

Particularly interesting, though, are the references made about the land between the chapel and old train station. The writer suggested: "Everyone who visits the University of Mississippi is struck with the beauty of the place. Perhaps June and October never find a more splendid situation for their gorgeous displays in all our picturesque Southland than within that sacred Grove of the goddess of wisdom. But those mighty forest trees and vine-clad buildings often wear a gruesome aspect under the shade of night that banishes all memory of their beauty by day.

The University chapel was used as a Confederate hospital during the Civil War, and within that building and the surrounding groves, the deadly misfortunes of that fatal strife were in ample and ghastly evidence. Perhaps some cool-headed student residing upon that campus today has never noticed the weird and uncanny influence which those historic groves exert by night. If such is the case, I would ask that student, bearing in mind the mournful war record of the place, to choose some dark, starless night, best of all midnight in October, when a low east wind is mourning among the treetops and the sere autumn leaves float slowly to the earth, whispering vaguely the while, choose such a night as this, and take a walk all alone around the chapel building and on down through those dark woods past the Dead House in the direction of the railroad depot."

The reference to "mighty forest trees and vine-clad buildings," along with the suggestion that students "walk all alone around the chapel building and on down through those dark woods past the Dead House in the direction of the railroad depot," almost assuredly refers to the area now known as the Grove.

The Glade Becomes The Grove

While the earliest of Ole Miss yearbooks reveal information that suggest the Grove has long been known as the "Grove," a photo in the 1928 Ole Miss shot behind the then-Law building and towards the train depot is entitled "The Ancient Law Building, From The Glade."

Whether referred to as the Grove or the Glade through the early 1930s, a photo in the 1935 Ole Miss shows a backdrop of the grassy plot labeled "The Grove." Moreover, the 1996 annual states, "In 1935, the Grove gets its name." Regardless of what faculty, staff, students, and locals called the 10-acre green spot, by 1935 the Grove or Glade would officially become the "Grove." It's remained the same ever since.

Tribute to Chancellor Fulton's Vision

The 1907 Ole Miss yearbook was dedicated in Fulton's honor and proclaimed:

And may these words sincerely show
The love, the pride that men have failed
At times to feel when power paled
And greatness moved at ebb and flow

You loved these trees, these walks, this life;
You gave for them unswerving work
And untold thought which in them lurk;

That dares to scar this pulsing heart
Of Mississippi. Broad and brave.
You made it; drove in calm the wave
That washed it safe in every part.

It speaks in us, tho' some may chide;
It speaks in us, tho' some may complain;
It speaks in us one word not vain –
It speaks the love no heart can hide.

It is remarkable that an alumnus, chancellor, and most importantly an individual who showed great affinity and love for the University of Mississippi is responsible for the Grove as it's known today. Well before tailgating in the Grove would even first take shape in the 1950s, Fulton's students knew their leader was doing something great.

The Beginnings of a Tailgating Tradition

Prior to the 1950s, tailgating and gameday camaraderie among students largely took place at fraternity and sorority houses on campus. However, legendary head coach John H. Vaught helped ignite a football frenzy at Ole Miss after his inaugural season at the helm in 1947.

In that season with the red and blue in 1947, Vaught's team won the school's first SEC Championship and claimed the school's first bowl game victory in the Delta Bowl, among other accomplishments. While there is not a specific year or game in which tailgating first took root in the Grove, there's no question the early successes of Vaught and Ole Miss First-Team All-Americans tailback Charlie Conerly, end Barney Poole, fullback Kayo Dottley, and quarterback Jimmy Lear, amped up football excitement.

Come the 1950s, gameday crowds grew, and cars, trucks, and RVs began to park in the Grove for a true "tailgate" picnic alongside throngs of other fans on campus to watch the upstart Rebels. Patrons popped open their trunks, unfolded their card tables, opened their picnic baskets and coolers, and simply enjoyed the atmosphere of gameday in the Grove.

Tailgating in the Grove would continue over the next couple of decades until vehicles descended upon a rain-soaked Grove to tailgate before the October, 26 1991 homecoming game against Vanderbilt. With cars, trucks, and RVs having driven all over the grounds that afternoon, the Grove had been turned into nothing more than a muddy mess.

While vehicles first parked in the Grove to tailgate out of necessity to accommodate growing gameday crowds, it was clear to University officials that the Grove was beginning to suffer as a result of hosting so many vehicles.

Ahead of the very next home game in what had been another rainy week in Oxford, a decision was made by University administrators to no longer allow vehicles to be parked in the Grove.

More than twenty years later, that decision has turned out to be a wise one, as tens of thousands of college football fans now descend upon the Grove each time the Rebels play at home. From the rush of people setting up their tents and tailgating equipment beginning at 9:00 p.m. on Friday nights, to Ole Miss students donning their Sunday best for an afternoon in the Grove, gameday in the Grove has become a major affair.

Examining the Grove Grounds

In terms of specific types of grass in the Grove, the two predominant grasses are tall fescue and Bermuda 419. In noting the diverse climate and shade of various areas in the Grove, Landscape Services' website states:

"Generally, Landscape Services uses a tall fescue blend that can handle the deep shade of the Grove as well as the hot summer heat. Although tall fescue is a cool season grass and does great in the spring and fall, it does a fair job in deep shade if kept moist during the summer. Also, Bermuda 419 is used in full sun areas in the Grove."

As of early 2014, there were in excess of 150 trees in the Grove and some 75 in the neighboring Circle.

A variety of oak species is far and away the most prevalent in both areas. Specific to the Grove, the two most prevalent species of oak are the willow oak, followed by the water oak. It takes only a quick look above to notice the immense size of so many Grove trees. While willow oaks can near 130 feet at maturity, water oaks grow to only around 90 feet.

Many of the larger oaks likely were planted in the early part of the twentieth century, meaning there is only so much longer the stately trees have to live. The next time you walk through the Grove on your way to class, look to the sky to appreciate the towering beauty.

New trees continue to be planted that will grow larger in time, but unfortunately there's no way to replace aging trees that have helped give the Grove indistinguishable character. One day, they'll be gone.

Protecting and Preserving the Grove

In 1983, a student group called "Save the Grove" made efforts to preserve the Grove from damage being caused by revelers pulling their vehicles into the Grove to tailgate. Just one year earlier in 1982, tailgating in the Grove had been ruled off limits entirely while a lengthy landscaping project took place.

Ahead of tailgaters arriving for the Memphis State game in 1983, their first time tailgating since the Grove was ruled off limits during the previous season, members of "Save the Grove" went out and strategically laid blankets around trees in the Grove to try and keep vehicles away.

A few years later, the senior class of 1986 made its class project "Preserve the Grove." Among several different fundraising efforts, members of the class charged five dollars to everyone who wanted to park and tailgate in the Grove.

Finally, as previously mentioned, vehicles were forbidden in the Grove following the muddy mess that was created when tailgaters parked in an extremely wet Grove during the 1991 Vanderbilt game.

Today, the Green Grove Initiative, founded in 2009, through the University of Mississippi Office of Campus Sustainability is doing its part to keep the Grove green. During each home game student volunteers walk from tent to tent with Green Grove recycling trash bags and encourage tailgaters to do their part to keep the Grove green.

UM Landscape Services shares the following gameday facts and figures:

Landscape Services places 500 thirty-five gallon plastic waste cans and approximately 200 cardboard boxes in the 10-acre Grove and Circle areas on the day before each home game.

More than 200 additional fifty-five gallon barrels are placed around the campus perimeter to assist with refuse demand.

An additional 12 to 30 dumpsters (20 or 30 yards each) are placed on campus to remove all waste that is generated in the Grove and around campus.

In 2012, Landscape Services removed a total of 489 tons of waste from the Grove. This is the equivalent of 16 M4 Sherman tanks (30 tons). The Central Arkansas game produced 42 tons of waste while the Texas game produced 87 tons. The 87 tons removed from the Texas game is greater than the weight of an empty space shuttle (82.5 tons).

The collective efforts of these groups are clearly helping keep the Grove clean and green, so that the treasured campus space may continue to be enjoyed for decades to come.

The Walk of Champions

In the heart of the Grove lies the affectionately-named "Walk of Champions," a brick-paved path beginning near the Ole Miss Student Union and crossing through the Grove.

Upon being hired as head coach in 1983, Billy Brewer began walking with his players from the old athletics dorm (Kinard Hall) across campus to the stadium before every home game. While the Rebels' Saturday strolls to the stadium were first comprised of different game day routes, the path Brewer took with his team beginning in 1985 would become a Saturday staple.

Looking for a way to try and include his coaches and players in the pre-game revelry of the Grove on game day, Brewer felt leading his coaches and players through the fan-frenzied Grove would add to the players' game day experience. The players, coaches, and fans alike enjoyed the atmosphere, and a new gameday tradition was born.

Approximately two hours before kickoff at every home game, Ole Miss team buses pull up alongside the Walk of Champions entrance to the cheers of thousands of fans. Those lucky enough to stand alongside the actual brick-path get to do more than just watch coaches and players make their way through the crowd. The path-side patrons get the opportunity to reach out and high-five their coaches and players.

Named in honor of the 1962 undefeated, national champion Ole Miss Rebels, Walk of Champions has become a time-honored tradition in the Grove.

The Pride of The South

Just over an hour after fans have cheered Ole Miss coaches and players traveling down the Walk of Champions, there is another game day experience in the Grove.

Nestled just steps behind Ventress Hall inside the Grove, in an area surely to have been part of that which Fulton had fenced off when the library was being built in 1899, the University of Mississippi Band, The Pride of the South, performs its pregame medley in an area to the right of the Grove stage.

Initially formed as merely a small, student-led campus organization, the University of Mississippi Band became an official institutional organization in 1928. That year, Chancellor Alfred Hume selected Roy Coates to be the first Director of Bands to serve with faculty status.

Interestingly, the UM Band website suggests, "Coates's initial marching band used instruments, uniforms, and equipment donated by the National Guard. Not until 1934 did the Rebel Band own full dress uniforms, purchased by funds solicited by the general student body."

Crimson of Harvard and Navy Blue from Yale

So how did Ole Miss's colors become red and blue? When Ole Miss began playing football in 1893 and was training to play five games that year, the players discussed what colors to wear. According to Dr. A. L. Bondurant, the first coach of Ole Miss football, one of the managers spoke up and noted "that the union of the Crimson of Harvard and the Navy Blue of Yale would be very harmonious and that it was well to have the spirit of both of these good colleges." From that day forward, Ole Miss's colors have been red and blue.

Eternally Undefeated, No. 38 Chucky Mullins

The legacy of Ole Miss Rebel Roy Lee "Chucky" Mullins is as rich and storied as any that preceded or may follow him at the University.

The legend of "Chucky" began in Russellville, Alabama.

Having lost his mother at a young age and without a father in his life, Mullins was raised by family friend and local recreational center worker Carver Phillips and his wife. Under the excellent care of the Phillipses, Chucky would make a name for himself growing up as an athlete in Russellville.

When Ole Miss Head Coach Billy Brewer offered Mullins a football scholarship, little did he or anyone else on the Ole Miss campus know what type of impact the exuberant young man and athlete would have on the place he loved so much.

Redshirted his freshman year, No. 38 Chucky made it his mission to show coaches just what he was capable of doing on the football field. The next season as a sophomore, Mullins began to make a name for himself and found playing time on both special teams and defense.

On October 28, 1989, the Rebels hosted Vanderbilt for Homecoming on a beautiful fall day in Oxford. However, spirits on the Ole Miss campus would quickly turn grim when Chucky failed to get up after what initially appeared to be a routine defensive collision.

A stunned crowd at Vaught-Hemingway Stadium sat in silence as Mullins didn't pop back up after the play. Something was wrong, very wrong. Mullins was taken off the field on a stretcher to the local hospital before being airlifted to a hospital in Memphis. It was there that it was revealed the Rebel had shattered four vertebrae in his cervical spine. It was a daunting discovery for a young man just hours earlier so full of life.

After undergoing operations and spending 114 days in the hospital, Mullins was transferred to the Spain Rehabilitation Center in Birmingham where he underwent extensive rehabilitation work. Never down or discouraged, the upbeat young man was determined to return to the Ole Miss campus to earn his degree and to be back around his teammates.

As is chronicled in Micah Ginn's film, *Undefeated: The Chucky Mullins Story,* one of the highlights of both Mullins's and his team's time following the devastating injury came at the 1989 Liberty Bowl in Memphis.

It was in the tunnel of the Liberty Bowl that Mullins was brought in and wheeled off the ambulance to wish his teammates well against Air Force, and memorably stated, "It's Time" before every Rebel in shouting distance erupted in cheer.

Mullins returned to Oxford in 1990 and began taking classes again in the spring of 1991. His undefeated spirit served as daily inspiration to both Ole Miss students he would visit with on campus and certainly his teammates. Things were as back to normal as he could have hoped, and Chucky was happy.

Sadly, on the morning of May 1, 1991, he stopped breathing and was immediately rushed to the hospital where he would pass away only days later from a blood clot.

While his time on earth and with his Ole Miss teammates and family had ended, the "never quit" attitude that defined the spirited competitor and human being would live on.

Today, Chucky's spirit remains alive and well at Ole Miss. Since 1990, a leader on the Rebel defense has been selected each year by coaches to receive the Chucky Mullins Courage Award. Additionally, the award winner receives the honor of wearing Mullins's No. 38 during the upcoming season.

While No. 38 was retired in 2006, and no player wore the jersey through the 2010 season, the retired number made its way back onto the jersey of the award winner beginning in 2011 and every year since.

Today, Ole Miss coaches and players are reminded of Mullins's legacy and can-do attitude during each home game as they touch the Chucky Mullins statue above the inscription "Never Quit" when entering and leaving the locker room.

The Ole Miss Creed

As the University approached the year 2000, there was discussion among Chancellor Robert Khayat and others about the development of a creed for the University. A committee of students, faculty, staff, alumni, and community members was appointed, and it undertook the task of writing a statement that succinctly explained what the University believed. After consulting the University of South Carolina about The Carolinian Creed, the task force held focus groups with campus, University, and local constituencies. More than 1,500 persons participated in lengthy, sometimes intense, discussions about what Ole Miss valued and believed.

After the committee reviewed the information provided by the first focus groups, another round of discussions was conducted. The initial draft was presented to the chancellor and the executive management council in late 2002, and in 2003, the University of Mississippi officially adopted The Ole Miss Creed.

The Ole Miss Creed is the standard by which members of the University community attempt to live.

Since its adoption, it has been used as a basis for discussion in trying times and often is used by instructors in classroom situations. The senior class of 2005 left as its class memorial The Ole Miss Creed monument in front of the Lyceum.

THE OLE MISS CREED

The University of Mississippi is a community of learning dedicated to nurturing excellence in intellectual inquiry and personal character in an open and diverse environment.
As a voluntary member of this community:
I believe in respect for the dignity of each person.
I believe in fairness and civility.
I believe in personal and professional integrity.
I believe in academic honesty. I believe in academic freedom.
I believe in good stewardship of our resources.
I pledge to uphold these values and encourage others to follow my example.

The University Memorial Ceremony

In 2008, Chancellor Khayat issued a proclamation that designated "University Memorial Day" would be observed on the last Thursday of classes of the spring semester. As with any community, the University is saddened by the loss of one of its members. At the end of the work day on University Memorial Day, the University community gathers in Paris-Yates Chapel for a ceremony to remember those who have died in the past calendar year. Those remembered include students, faculty, staff, faculty/staff emeriti, and special friends of Ole Miss.

During the ceremony, names of the deceased are read and friends or family members place a gardenia in water in their memory. The Peddle Carillon tolls once for each of those being remembered.

Rebel Run

Rebel Run is a game day tradition at Ole Miss where fans welcome freshmen to the campus by inviting them to a free game and the opportunity to run across the football field before kickoff. Each year, thousands of students participate in this exciting event.

Red, Blue, and Green

Chancellor Dan Jones signed the American College and University Presidents' Climate Commitment in 2014. Chancellor Khayat had first signed the agreement in 2008. The University of Mississippi also has become a LEED (Leadership in Energy and Environmental Design) campus and vigorously promotes sustainability efforts through programs of energy conservation and recycling, as well as sponsoring Green Week each Spring.

The Landshark Becomes Our Official Mascot

In September 2017, the Associated Student Body (ASB) sponsored a campus-wide student vote to determine whether or not there was student support for changing the school's mascot from the Black Bear to the Landshark.

More than 4,100 Ole Miss students took part in the ASB poll, with 81% of student voters indicating they were in support of changing the University's official mascot to the Landshark. As a result, on October 6, 2017, Chancellor Jeffrey S. Vitter officially announced that the University would move forward with the Landshark as the school's official mascot.

The Landshark Legacy

At Ole Miss, Landshark is a term that was first adopted by the Rebel football team's defensive unit. As part of that identity, defensive players celebrate big plays by putting a hand to their forehead in the shape of a shark fin. A battle cry of "Fins Up" also contributes to the players' persona. With the popularity of both the players and the hand gesture, Ole Miss fans and student-athletes from other sports embraced the spirit of the Landshark, and in October 2017, the University announced the Landshark as the official mascot of the Ole Miss Rebels. The Landshark mascot was unveiled at the start of the 2018 football season.

Roots of the Landshark at Ole Miss date back to 2008. After four straight losing seasons, the Rebel football team returned to national prominence with a 9-4 record and a victory over 7th-ranked Texas Tech in the Cotton Bowl. Leading the charge was a defensive squad that ranked fourth in the nation in rushing defense and included All-American Peria Jerry and eventual All-SEC standout Jerrell Powe.

The term Landshark originated that season from senior linebacker Tony Fein, an Army veteran who served a one-year tour in the Iraq War before arriving in Oxford. A two-year letterman after transferring from Scottsdale (Ariz.) Community College, Fein was the 2008 recipient of the Pat Tillman Award by the Military Order of the Purple Heart. Fein passed away in October 2009, but his legacy at Ole Miss continues through the Landshark. olemisssports.com/trads/landshark.html

The Ole Miss Big Event

Service has been a part of the Ole Miss Community since the school's beginning in 1848.

UMSFusion, an annual service event developed in 2003, gave students of the University of Mississippi an excellent opportunity to volunteer in the Oxford/ Lafayette community. As this event continued to grow year after year, it became evident that the students of Ole Miss were committed to providing assistance and service to the members of the surrounding communities.

After visiting Texas A&M University in College Station, Texas, in 2010, student leaders and staff from Ole Miss were excited by the idea of a large-scale, one-day community service project similar to Texas A&M's "Big Event." Soon thereafter, the decision to take service to the next level in Oxford and Lafayette County was made by the leaders of the ASB and the Division of Student Affairs. In Spring 2011, more than 1,200 students participated in the first Ole Miss Big Event. Braving wind, rain, and hail, students gathered in the Union to kick off the BIGGEST community service project in Ole Miss history. On March 31, 2012, in only the second year of the event, more than 3,000 students volunteered to work in 300 community projects to say, "Thank you Oxford and Lafayette County." In just a few years, The Ole Miss Big Event has become an important and valued tradition of the University and the surrounding community.

The Columns Society

Begun in 2008, The Columns Society is a group of 15 men and 15 women selected from the sophomore and junior classes to serve as the official student hosts for the University. The Society is based upon the principles of humble service, leadership, and integrity. The Columns Society serves the University of Mississippi at all

functions where it is desired to have students welcome guests and visitors to our campus.

The Columns Society, coordinated by the Division of Student Affairs, provides services to the offices of the Chancellor, the Provost, the Vice Chancellor for Student Affairs, Athletics, Alumni, and Development.

Named after one of the prominent symbols at the University of Mississippi, the columns that support the Lyceum, The Columns Society seeks to advance the University of Mississippi through humble service. No opportunity to serve the University is considered too small. Membership in the Columns Society is highly selective and requires a significant commitment to serve Ole Miss, always with humility and integrity.

RebelTHON

Over 150,000 kids will be admitted to Blair E. Batson Children's Hospital (Jackson, MS) or its affiliated clinics each year, with an average of 410 admitted every day. That's 410 kids thrown into chaos, 410 caregivers having to pause daily life for illness, 410 childhoods interrupted every day. Understanding the importance of the work being done at Batson's, Ole Miss students stepped up to do their part to help.

Each spring, Ole Miss RebelTHON, a student-led, volunteer organization and part of the Children's Miracle Network, puts on a 12-hour dance marathon to support the children at Blair E. Batson Children's Hospital. However, the dance marathon is only a small part of the students' involvement. RebelTHON hosts a number of fundraisers and awareness campaigns each and every year to raise funds and let students know how they can become active participants with RebelTHON.

In 2020, RebelTHON raised $252,571.89 - more than a quarter of a million dollars! Since its start in 2013, RebelTHON has raised over $1,000,000 - all for Blair E. Batson Children's Hospital. In the eight-plus years of RebelTHON's existence, donations have supported the hospital's AirCare Flight Team, upgrading patient and family areas and the $180 million hospital renovations that will alter the state's medical care for Mississippi children.

The organization celebrates the strength of the kids who have seen the worst but given their best, celebrates the parents who love and support their kids through the most difficult times and celebrates the doctors and nurses who work every day to make a world without childhood illness a reality. As stated on RebelTHON's website, "We are this generation fighting for the next, and we will keep dancing until every child at Batson has the opportunity to be a kid again."

"When you join us in supporting the campaign for Children's of Mississippi, you'll be giving Mississippi's sickest children new hope. There's no better feeling than knowing you played a part in giving a child a chance to grow up."

— Abby and Eli Manning,
Batson's Growing Campaign Honorary Chairs

ABOUT THE AUTHORS

Seph Anderson, *former Financial Aid Advisor*

Seph Anderson received his B.B.A. (marketing) and M.A. (higher education and student personnel) from the University of Mississippi. He serves students and families in the Office of Financial Aid at Ole Miss.

Thomas Reardon, *Dean of Students Emeritus*

Thomas Reardon worked in higher education for more than 30 years. Known to everyone at Ole Miss as 'Sparky,' Dean Reardon is retired.

CHAPTER 6

TIPS FOR SUCCESS AT Ole Miss

Original Contributors: Dewey Knight, Leslie Showalter,
Whitman Smith, & Katie Tompkins
Updated (2020) by: Rachael Durham, Leanne Kendricks,
Rebekah Reysen, and Jeremy Roberts

elcome to the University of Mississippi and EDHE 105 or 305. We are so excited that you chose to take this course as we know it will be truly beneficial to you during your first semester at Ole Miss. We hope that the atmosphere of this course will aid in making you feel more comfortable in asking questions, expressing your concerns, and learning to navigate through this new "season" of your life. This course is designed to help you in your transition to college and the University, and we will start by discussing some good habits you can begin to develop to aid you during your time in college and beyond.

SIX HABITS THAT LEAD TO SUCCESS

1. Go to class: Every day, go to class, even when it's hot, cold, raining, or snowing. Sure, you know this is important, but we remind you because every year there are students who don't go to class, and the results aren't good. Did you know, for instance, that you can fail a course based solely on poor attendance? Many professors require attendance and will lower final grades if students miss more than two or three classes. Will going to class certainly guarantee you an A? No, but skipping class almost certainly guarantees that you will NOT earn an A. While going to class is a great first step, also make sure to come to class prepared. Bring something to write with, even if you plan on using a laptop to take all your notes; you never know when you might need a writing utensil to take a pop quiz or sign in for attendance.

2. Read your syllabus: Read each syllabus carefully and write down the important dates and deadlines in your planner. It's a good idea to read each syllabus several times. There may be assignments in the syllabus that the instructor never mentions, which you are responsible for just the same. The syllabus is your road map to completing the course successfully. After you have read it over a few times, highlight important assignments, deadlines, room changes, days you don't have class, etc. Next, get out your planner. Write

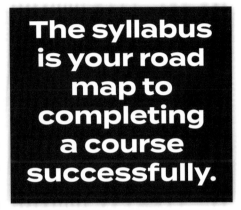

The syllabus is your road map to completing a course successfully.

the assignments from *every syllabus* in your planner. You might use different colors for different courses (red for math, blue for EDHE 105 or 305, green for history). When you are finished, you will be surprised how many assignments and tests hit at the same time. This is your clue to begin projects and papers well in advance of deadlines.

3. Use a planner: Time management begins with the use of a pocket calendar, smart phone calendar, or paper planner as a reminder of classes, appointments, meetings, and errands. Now, not everyone is the same in how they plan and organize, so find something that works best for you and stick with it. If you sleep seven hours a night, you have 119 hours a week to do everything that you need to do. That, of course, includes everything from going to class, eating, sleeping, athletic events, getting ready to go out, going out, time-in-transit, studying, club meetings, social media, texting, video games, shopping, laundry, telephone and television time, and everything in between. You must use all 119 hours a week to schedule everything you must do. Then you must stick to your schedule, which should give you an idea of your true priorities. Study time should be scheduled at a ratio of two to three hours of study per hour of class. Moreover, a daily "to do" list should be made each day, either when you wake up in the morning or each night before you go to bed. The list should be kept short, no more than five or six items, both academic and personal. It's a good idea to prioritize the items and be specific, such as read five pages in psychology.

4. Make connections: Begin making contacts with three important groups of people: faculty, staff, and students.

- **Faculty:** These are the professors, instructors, and graduate assistants teaching your classes. They make out tests and decide if there is going to be a pop quiz on Friday morning. They calculate and assign your grades. Introduce yourself, and show an interest in the class. Engage in conversations outside of the classroom about intellectual issues. Successful relationships with faculty are key to your college success.

- **Staff:** These are the people who perform administrative tasks, take care of the buildings and grounds, manage the University's resources, plan for the future of the institution, and even teach a course or two along the way. Get to know them as they typically know the ins and outs of the University and can help you in a variety of ways.

- **Students:** These are the people sitting next to you in class, living in your residence hall or apartment complex, walking along the campus sidewalks, and eating lunch at the next table. Introduce yourself, smile, and make an effort to get know people who are different from you. College is the perfect time to begin lifelong friendships; the process begins with you.

5. Take care of business: You might remember this advice from orientation, but it is worth repeating. As a college student, you have the absolute freedom to make your own choices, but with freedom comes personal responsibility. You can't enjoy the freedom of independent living without the responsibility that comes with making your own decisions. Procrastination is one of those barriers that stops you from taking care of business. The term procrastination (derived from a Latin word meaning "to put off for tomorrow") entered the English language in the sixteenth century, and by the eighteenth century, Samuel Johnson was describing it as "one of the general weaknesses" that "prevail to a greater or lesser degree in every mind." The problem seems to be getting worse. According to Peirs Steel, a business professor at the University of Calgary, the percentage of people who admitted to difficulties with procrastination quadrupled between 1978 and 2002.

Philosophers are interested in procrastination for another reason. It's a powerful example of what the Greeks called *akrasia*—doing something against one's own better judgment. Professor Steel defined procrastination as willingly deferring something even though you expect the delay to make you worse off. The essence of procrastination lies in not doing what you think you should be doing, a mental contortion that surely accounts for the great psychic toll the habit takes on people. This is the perplexing thing about procrastination: although it seems to involve avoiding unpleasant tasks, indulging in it generally doesn't make people happy. In one study,

65 percent of students surveyed before they started working on a term paper said they would like to avoid procrastinating: they knew both that they wouldn't do the work on time and that the delay would make them unhappy.

OVERCOMING PROCRASTINATION

- **Break large tasks into smaller ones.**

- **Work for realistic periods of time.** If you work best at one-hour intervals, don't try to cram in two hours of study.

- **Don't rely on energy drinks or drugs to power through a study marathon (like all-nighters).**

- **Mix activities.** Switch subjects after a while, or try to alternate between doing things you enjoy with things that you find challenging or boring.

- **Create an effective place to do your school work.** Make your work place comfortable but not too comfortable. Try to keep distractions to a minimum (such as phones, TV, and friends).

- **Reward yourself when you finish a task on time. Start NOW!**

"By failing to prepare you are preparing to fail." —Benjamin Franklin

6. Embrace Adversity: We know that the transition to college can be difficult, and you may hit some bumps along the way. **Homesickness**, **roommate issues**, and **the common cold** are particularly some of the first things students struggle with when they attend college. Here are some tips on how to better handle these things.

Homesickness

Being away from home and in college can be exhilarating and exciting, but at the same time it can be quite scary and intimidating. With all of the newness and excitement of college, you may also long for some of the familiarity of home. Missing your friends and family (even pets!) is completely normal. All new students experience some form of homesickness during their first semester or first year away. Homesickness looks different on each person and may hit at different times throughout the first year. Homesickness can hit if you are 10 or 1,000 miles away from home. All students deal with homesickness in different ways, too. But just know that it is completely okay to feel this way as you are transitioning into a completely new way of life.

Here are some tips that may aid in helping you overcome your homesickness:

- **DO NOT** stay in your room. Being alone feeds homesickness.
- **DO NOT** avoid contact with people.
- **DO NOT** continually call home, call friends at home, or worse, go home. This feeds the feeling that you cannot make it in college. Fight through it, and stay on campus!
- **DO NOT** think you are in this alone—see above! There are many faculty, staff, and fellow students here to help.
- **DO NOT** think something is wrong with you. Homesickness is a normal part of being a new student.
- **DO** talk to people when you are on the bus. It's a great way to meet people.
- **DO** seek out new friends on your floor or at your apartment complex. Invite them in, or walk around and meet them.
- **DO** go to class! You need to keep a normal routine as much as possible.
- **DO** seek help—your community assistant, a professor you know, someone in Student Affairs (hint: your EDHE instructor), or the free and confidential University Counseling Center. We are here to help.
- **DO** continue to eat, exercise, and sleep (at night, not during the day).
- **DO** spend time outside.
- **DO** stay in Oxford for weekends. This is when you really have time to work on new relationships.
- **DO** volunteer to help others. This is a surefire way to quit thinking about yourself.

Roommate Issues

Whether you are living with your best friend or someone totally new, your chances for roommate conflicts are the same. This may be enhanced if you have never shared a room with another person. The key is to communicate your feelings and agree upon some basic rules. Talk with your roommate early about study habits, sleep habits, housecleaning, and personal space. Working out the details of sharing a small living space, sooner rather than later, will make life much more pleasant. Practicing this now will help you gain some good communication skills for future roommates, too. And, don't be surprised that when you voice a complaint, your roommate has a complaint or two about you.

Fatigue & the Common Cold

If there was ever an expression that summed up new college students, it is "burning the candle at both ends." Of course, that means the candle burns out twice as quickly. It's understandable that you want to go to every event, meet tons of new people, go to football games, and in general not miss out on anything fun. And, there is no one to stop you from trying to do everything. After all, you are living with hundreds of fellow students and not your parents. Eventually, the college lifestyle will catch up with you, and you will be more tired than you have ever been and probably sick, too. Being sick and tired away from home is hard, and something you likely have not experienced.

Try to create a balance of social activities, exercise, personal hygiene, and healthy eating. Eat a variety of foods, because a steady diet of pizza, cheeseburgers, fries, and soft drinks can lead to a sluggish, sick feeling. Wash your hands often, keep your room or apartment reasonably clean, and try for at least seven hours of sleep most nights. Residence hall and apartment living at a minimum put you in close proximity with a lot of people, so the inevitable virus is bound to hit at some time or another. When you feel sick, go to the Student Health Center to see a physician or nurse practitioner. (*Check the resource guide at the end of the text for location and office hours.*)

It takes work to be a successful college student. EDHE 105 and 305 and this textbook will help you work smart and make the most of your Ole Miss experience. Dr. Ken Sufka, professor of psychology and pharmacology, advises, "Learning is not a spectator sport." Don't stay on the sidelines; get involved in your classes and campus life *today*!

We hope you will keep these six simple habits in mind not only during your first semester here at Ole Miss, but also each and every semester moving forward. We feel that these are the key components to making your transition here much easier and hope to aid you in success during college.

TIME MANAGEMENT

Time management is key. The first tip to be successful with time management is to start by memorizing ten little two-letter words; **"If it is to be, it is up to me."**

Here are 10 steps to utilizing that mantra to its fullest:

- **Get—and use—a planner.** No matter what kind it is, make sure you have one and you use it—EVERY DAY.

- **Set goals.** Determine what you want to accomplish and set goals to accomplish it. Setting goals makes you more inclined to follow through with your plans and accomplish your tasks. Your life is a series of choices and decisions. You are actually managing these choices, not the flow of time.

- **Prioritize.** Once you determine what you want to accomplish, you must prioritize your tasks. Figure out what must be done and what can be put on hold. Focus on the most important tasks before proceeding to the less important ones. Prioritizing makes you less inclined to procrastinate.

- **Learn to say no.** You can determine how to spend your time or you can let others plan it for you by default. Knowing your priorities helps you stay focused. You are not being selfish if you choose to schedule your time according to your goals. Be careful with over-commitment, and don't attempt to do too much. Remember that every time you say yes to something, you are automatically saying no to everything else you could have done with that time.

- **Let yourself relax.** Schedule certain days that are just for you. Don't study on those days, and don't make obligations to anyone else. Instead, use this time to do something that you really enjoy. It is important to have personal time—it can be renewing.

- **Plan ahead.** Do you have a large research paper due the last week of the semester? Work backward in your calendar and figure out how much time you need to write it, how much time you'll need to research it, and how much time you'll need to pick your topic. If you think you'll need six weeks for the entire project, work backward from the due date and schedule the time into your calendar before it's too late.

- **Utilize spare time.** If you have to wait in line or for class to start, use that extra time to review your notes or study for an exam. Have an hour between classes? Study in the coffee shop, the library, or the Grove. Don't waste any time! You can accomplish a lot during this extra "found" time. This will allow extra time to complete larger tasks.

■ **Know when you are most productive.** Everyone has a time during the day when they are most productive. Whether this time is in the morning or at night, use it to tackle your most demanding tasks. Do less challenging activities when you have less energy.

■ **Plan for the unexpected.** Sure, you just might be able to pull off two papers and a presentation during midterms week. But what happens if you catch the flu the night you're supposed to be pulling the all-nighter? Expect the unexpected so you don't have to spend more unplanned time trying to fix your mistakes.

■ **Don't give up!** Like any other skill, it takes time to learn how to manage your time. Even time management experts have days when their whole schedule falls apart. If yours does, don't give up on time management. Instead, pick up the pieces and start again the next day. Review your schedule at the end of each week to see what did and what didn't work for you. Build on your successes as you develop plans and time management strategies for the following weeks.

ALTERNATIVE COURSE OPTIONS

For most of you, your first year of college is the first time in your life that you have been in control of your schedule, managed your own time, and exclusively made your own decisions about what you do throughout the day. The idea of *not* having to be in specific places at specific times can be intoxicating, and for some students, long mid-afternoon naps begin to feel like a necessity rather than a luxury. For other students, more personal time is an opportunity to work, have an internship, or engage in more student organizations.

In this brave new world, options such as online courses and independent study may seem like a perfect fit. When handled responsibly, they certainly can be. However, too often students jump into these type of courses without understanding the requirements and expectations, and what they envision as a surefire way to make a good grade without a regularly scheduled time commitment can end in disaster. Online and independent study courses are not recommended for freshmen, but if you consider this option later in your academic career, the following information will be helpful.

Online Courses

For most online classes, the majority of course content is available through the web, but there might be a required live element. Many online courses require proctored tests. A few even have a required online meeting in a virtual classroom or in a live classroom setting. Online learning is flexible and convenient, but it also is more challenging.

Persistence: Students who are successful in online courses are those willing to work through technical problems. They seek help and assistance when needed, keep a daily course work schedule, and continue through challenges. To help with persistence and avoid technical problems, confirm technical requirements and test your computer to make sure it works with all the online tools, and know whom to contact for assistance with any issue you may have.

Time-management and preparation: Avoid procrastination by developing a plan of action for assignment completion and having a daily "to do" list. Read your course syllabus to create these lists. Schedule time for yourself to log in to your course two to three times a week and schedule study times and time for assignments/discussions. To be successful in an online course, a student must be independent, self-motivated, disciplined, and responsible.

Communicate and connect: Use communication tools built into Blackboard to communicate with your instructor. In the course syllabus, the instructor also will provide other ways to contact him or her. In traditional classes, instructors have visual cues and body language to know when a student is struggling. The online environment does not allow for these cues, so reach out. If you do not reach out, your instructor will not know. The same goes for your fellow classmates. Get to know your classmates, and create connections with them. The social tools and applications available today make building a learning community relatively easy.

Appropriate study environment: No matter the format of the course, whether it is online, hybrid, flipped, or traditional, every student needs a suitable study environment. Create your perfect study environment by locating a quiet space, avoiding games (consider uninstalling games on your computer), turning off your phone, and avoiding surfing the net or social media.

Be active, be present: Time management plans of action and "to do" lists will help you be active and present in an online course. Professors teaching online courses expect students to log in to their online course two to three times a week. Check regularly for discussion posts, course announcements, course materials, and other important information. While checking for updates in your online course, get involved in a discussion and respond to your classmates' postings. This will enhance your learning experience and make you a more active member of that online community.

Independent Study

Most independent study (iStudy) courses are available online through Blackboard (Bb), but there are classes that are paper-based, with many courses available in both formats. Students enroll in iStudy courses by submitting a registration form, and lessons are submitted, graded, and returned to the student. The student must take a proctored midcourse test (some courses have two course exams) and then submit the remaining lessons. A final exam is given, and the student receives a grade for the course. Students typically have one year from the date of enrollment to complete the course but semester options are also available.

When considering iStudy, remember:

- There are two options for iStudy courses: Semester and Flex. Semester courses take place during the time frame of the academic semester in which the course is offered. Flex courses begin at the time of enrollment and are to be completed within a calendar year.
- There are many restrictions and requirements placed on financial aid, and it is imperative that students using financial aid consult with the Financial Aid Office to determine eligibility, possible delayed aid disbursement, and completion deadline requirements. Do this before registering for an iStudy course.
- Tuition for a semester-based iStudy course is included in full-time tuition. The tuition fee for a three-hour semester credit under the full-year Flex option is a separate fee. More information can be found through the iStudy website outreach.olemiss.edu/istudy.
- iStudy courses require students to be self-motivated and good with time management. It is critical to keep moving ahead with readings and assignments. The course should be started as soon as you have your materials.
- Students must have approval from their academic dean's office to enroll in iStudy.
- Students are generally limited to two iStudy courses at one time. However, some academic areas further limit course enrollment, so you should always check with your academic advisor before planning to enroll in iStudy courses.
- If a student does not complete his or her course in the Semester based iStudy, no extensions are available. However, Flex based iStudy courses offer extensions with additional costs.

ABOUT THE AUTHORS

Dewey Knight, *Associate Director for the Center for Student Success and First-Year Experience Emeritus*

Dewey recently retired from the University.

Leslie Showalter, *Assistant Vice Chancellor for Student Affairs Emerita*

Leslie Showalter retired in 2019 after working more than 30 years in higher education. During her long career, she taught and mentored hundreds of first-year college students. Creating and editing *The Ole Miss Experience* was a labor of love.

Whitman Smith, *Director of Admissions Emeritus*

Whitman trained, taught, and mentored hundreds of students and leaders through Orientation and Admissions, taught the first-year experience class for 20 years and enthusiastically promoted the University of Mississippi everywhere he went. He lives in Oxford with his family and is happily retired.

Katie Tompkins, *Prospect Research Analyst for University Development*

Katie is originally from Florence, Alabama, but now calls Oxford her home. She earned her B.A. in English from Ole Miss in 2002 and a J.D. from the University of Mississippi School of Law in 2006.

Rachael Durham, *Assistant Director for First Year Experience*

Rachael is originally from Memphis, Tennessee, but now calls Oxford home. She earned her B.A. in journalism with an emphasis on public relations in 2008 and her M.A. in higher education/student personnel in 2012, both from the University of Mississippi.

ABOUT THE AUTHORS

Leanne Kendricks, Academic Mentor for First Year Experience

Leanne is originally from Georgia, but now calls Oxford home. She earned her B.A. in anthropology, with a minor in mathematics, in 2016, and her M.A. in higher education/student personnel in 2019, both from the University of Mississippi. Leanne also serves as a point of contact for Ole Miss Opportunity Scholars.

Rebekah Reysen, Assistant Director for Academic Support Programs

Rebekah received her undergraduate degrees in psychology and theatre from Purdue University, and her master's degree and Ph.D. in counselor education from the University of Mississippi. She is a National Certified Counselor (NCC), Licensed Professional Counselor (LPC), Distance Certified Counselor (DCC), and has published articles in a variety of counseling journals. Dr. Reysen coordinates programs for academically at-risk students and is passionate about helping students navigate their way through college.

Jeremy Roberts, Learning Specialist for Academic Support Programs

Jeremy has a degree in English and hospitality management for the University of Mississippi. He has a master's in health and sports science from the University of Memphis, and an MBA from Delta State University.

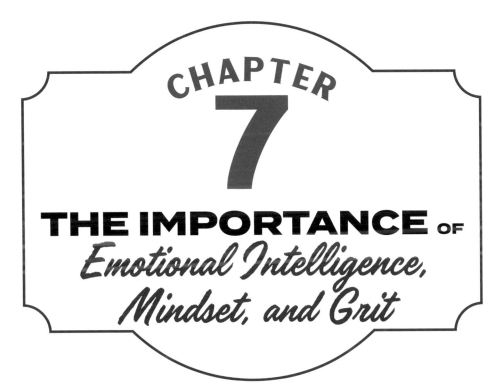

CHAPTER 7

THE IMPORTANCE OF
Emotional Intelligence, Mindset, and Grit

By Patrick Perry, Rebekah Reysen,
and Rachael Durham

Think about a recent event that made you happy. Now think about an event that made you sad. Finally, think about an event that made you angry. If you are able, remember specific details of each of these events. Let's go a little deeper and do you remember making any decisions after each of these events? If so, were you aware of your emotions during the decision-making process? Were the decisions you made small or perhaps more significant? Would the decisions you made at that time be the same if your emotions were different or if you had been in more control? The first part of this chapter explores the role emotions play in decision-making and your ability to be successful or not based on your ability to manage emotions.

Emotional intelligence is defined as "a set of emotional and social skills that influence the way we perceive and express ourselves, develop and maintain social relationships, cope with challenges, and use emotional information in an effective and meaningful way" (Multi-Health Systems, 2011). Many times, we associate successful people with their intellectual ability. Intellectual ability does contribute to success but having a high IQ does not necessarily guarantee success. What about the ability to identify and control emotions, especially when making decisions? In the 1980s, the psychologist Dr. Reuven Bar-On struggled with the fact that there were individuals who possessed strong intellectual skills but were unsuccessful while others with average skills were successful (Stein & Book, 2011). Bar-On's research led to him to create a measure called the Emotional Quotient or "EQ" (Stein & Book,

2011). The research of Bar-On resulted in the creation of the Emotional Quotient Inventory (EQ-i), an assessment that provides individuals information about emotional strengths and areas for potential improvement.

Why does developing my Emotional Intelligence matter?

Research indicates that a person's intellectual ability (IQ) develops until around seventeen years of age but Emotional Intelligence, often referred to as "EI" may develop throughout the lifetime (Stein & Book, 2011). This is important because through practice and experience you may develop your emotional intelligence skills. Research indicates that having certain EI skills can positively impact your ability to be successful and graduate from college as well as other healthy living habits. In a study conducted by Sparkman, Maulding and Roberts, the EI skills of social responsibility, impulse control and empathy were predictors of enrollment and graduation (2012). National Career Services noted that although technical skills and knowledge can be taught, "soft skills" are what employers would like to have in employees' skill set (2015). The soft skills identified by National Career Services as most commonly sought by employers include: communicating, making decisions, showing commitment, flexibility, time management, leadership, creativity and problem-solving, being a team player, accepting responsibility and the ability to work under pressure (2015). Some research studies indicate that EI may also have a positive effect on your mental and physical health (Stein & Book, 2011). To summarize, research supports the fact that developing your EI skills may increase your level of success in college and your success and well-being in life.

How do you develop your emotional intelligence?

You will have many opportunities in college to develop your EI. Your choice to get up for an 8:00 a.m. class instead of sleeping late is exercising your impulse control. Making the decision to talk to your roommate about an issue in a meaningful and productive way instead of being angry or silent demonstrates your skill in assertiveness. Understanding that a poor grade may be due to your lack of effort versus the thought that the instructor is at fault for giving too difficult of a test is an indication that you are strong in your reality testing. When faced with multiple decisions under stress and being able to thrive and find solutions, demonstrates your problem-solving skills. The key is that you must exercise emotional intelligence skills. To become better at managing your emotions you have to practice and see what works and what does not work. This can be difficult because it means identifying your strengths as well as areas in which you may improve. Just keep in mind that although managing your emotions effectively is not easy, it will lead to higher levels of success in college and life.

"We all go through
something in life.
Sometimes you have
to push past the pain."
— Antoinette Tuff,
Lives saved using her
Emotional Intelligence

I encourage you to listen to the entire 911 recording of the incident to more fully understand the extent of Ms. Tuff's heroic actions on that day.

Thinking About Growth Mindset

Like Antoinette Tuff, how you approach a situation can have an impact on the outcome of that situation. How you think about yourself, talk to yourself and your willing to learn new things all play a crucial role in your success in school. You have to be willing to work, to grow, and to learn new things. No one else can do it for you. But, do you have a growth mindset in your growth and development?

What is a growth mindset anyway?

According to Dr. Carol Dweck, a psychology professor at Stanford and pioneer researcher on Mindset (2006), "In a growth mindset, people believe that their most basic abilities can be developed through dedication and hard work—brains and talent are just the starting point. This view creates a love of learning and a resilience that is essential for great accomplishment." So, you can learn and develop if you put your "mind" to it!

But what does that really mean?

Take a look at your language. How you speak to yourself and about yourself plays an important role in your success.

ANTOINETTE TUFF:
EMOTIONALLY INTELLIGENT TOUGH

The story of Antoinette Tuff and her actions to save students' lives at the Ronald McNair Learning Center near Atlanta, Georgia, in 2013 demonstrates how important effective management of emotions can be in a life and death situation. On the morning of August 20, 2013, Michael Hill entered the Ronald McNair Learning Center Elementary School with a weapon and hundreds of rounds of ammunition with the intent to harm those inside. Ms. Tuff, a bookkeeper at the school substituting for the receptionist on that particular day, was told by the gunman to call 911 and to state that he was going to start shooting (CNN, 2014). Ms. Tuff, instead of panicking, began a "calm" and "matter of fact" dialogue with the gunman that eventually led to his surrender (CNN, 2013).

During the time after Mr. Hill entered the elementary school until his surrender Ms. Tuff went through many emotions along with Mr. Hill. Her ability to listen and talk in an empathetic way with Mr. Hill saved many lives. Ms. Tuff calmly explained to Mr. Hill at several different times that he was not in this alone and that she cared for him and about his specific life circumstances. Ms. Tuff told Mr. Hill, "we all go through something in life" (CNN, 2014). Ms. Tuff's calmness and caring dialogue with Mr. Hill allowed her to be successful in convincing him to surrender without a single person being injured that day.

Scenario:

This morning you checked Blackboard and saw that you made a C- on your most recent WRIT 101 assignment. Then, during a student organization meeting, you received some negative feedback from your members on a new initiative you suggested the organization implement. Not to mention on the way back to your residence hall, you realized you forgot to move your car from the incorrect lot and you received a parking ticket. Once you get to your room, you try to talk to your roommate about your day and he/she sort of brushes you off.

What do you think? How do you feel?

Well, most people would automatically feel unlucky, maybe even unworthy. You may feel that you don't belong, or you're ready for the day to be over and a "redo" tomorrow. You may call yourself an "idiot" or say something along the lines of, "No one cares about me." But, let's reframe that. In a growth mindset, you could try, "Tomorrow, I will speak with my instructor to see what I missed in this paper so that I can be better prepared for the next assignment," or, "Maybe my roommate had a bad day, too." You can also say, "I was in a rush this morning to get to class on time and forgot to move my car. I will give myself a pass this time, pay my ticket, and remember to be sure to park in the correct lot moving forward." It's all about your language, realizing that making mistakes is human nature, and you can always learn something if you put your mind to it.

Are you going to quit? No, because you have Grit!

Former Ole Miss Football Coach Billy Brewer told Roy Lee "Chucky" Mullins "You're not big enough, you're not strong enough and you're not fast enough to play football at Ole Miss" (ESPN Storied, 2014). Chucky Mullins replied, "If you give me a chance, I'll never let you down" (ESPN Storied, 2014). Earlier in this textbook you learned about Chucky Mullins and the challenges he faced in his life. Chucky was a role model for his determination, positive attitude and grit. Recent research suggests that grit can play a significant role in your achievement of goals. Merriam Webster defines grit as firmness of mind or spirit; unyielding courage in the face in hardship or danger (2015). Angela Duckworth defines grit as passion and perseverance for long-term goals; sticking with your future, day in and day out not just for the week, not just for the month but for years and living life like it is a marathon, not a sprint (AP Conference 2013).

Grit, like emotional intelligence, may be developed through practice and can have a positive influence on your current and future level of success not only in college but also in life. Chucky Mullins had countless opportunities in his life to give up when he faced adversity but he chose to persevere and push forward instead, and with a smile. How do you face adversity and failure? Think about something that has posed a barrier to you being successful in something. As you progress in college and in your life you will face numerous obstacles and your capacity to stick it out when faced with challenges and failure is a measure of your grit.

"If you're not failing every now and again, it's a sign you're not doing anything very innovative." – Woody Allen

How Do I Develop Grit?

Educators and researchers are trying to better understand the extent to which grit plays a role in success. Most agree that if you have characteristics of grit, generally you are more likely to be successful in achieving goals. Of course, this makes sense, right? If you have a goal and you are persistent working towards the goal you are more likely to achieve the goal. Do you think you are gritty? If so, great! Could you be grittier? Consider the following example of grit.

In an article by Tyler Tervooren, he describes how, as a child, he would take things apart that were broken to see how they worked and then try to repair them himself (2015). He started with the computer his parents purchased but over time he developed the confidence to attempt to fix pretty much anything. This process involved a lot of failure but by breaking and repairing things he was developing grit (2015). I am not encouraging you to break your computer so you can take it apart and try to fix it! However, it is important to develop your grit by attempting to do things that you may be uncomfortable doing if that is what is necessary to reach your goals. Think about the goals you have set for yourself. Some of things you will need to do to accomplish your goals will undoubtedly test your grit. Through practice and repetition, you will be more successful and will become grittier and grittier.

Start Building Grit Today!

Successful individuals acquire grit in small ways every day. Angela Duckworth said, developing grit is "a marathon, not a sprint" (Xhelo, 2013). Taking this interpretation literally, for those of you who played sports in high school,

you know that being a strong runner, soccer player, football player, etc. takes practice, repetition, and persistence. As the Greek Philosopher Aristotle once said, "We are what we repeatedly do. Excellence, then, is not an act, but a habit." Running an actual marathon begins Day 1 with something small, like walking for 20 minutes a day a few days out of the week. Similarly, in the case of your academics, writing a 10-page research paper may seem like a lot to tackle, but like the marathon, you can break it up into steps which can help you complete the process without too much of a headache.

Write a 10-Page Research Paper

Day 1: Gather information that you can use to discuss the topic of your paper. Find at least a few resources that you can cite. Take notes on those resources.

Day 2: Create an outline for your paper and include the information you found Day 1. Don't forget that asolid paper includes an introduction and conclusion in addition to the body of your paper.

Day 3: Expand on your outline. Begin adding details to each of these sections. By now your outline should be at least a couple of pages long. Turn these notes into complete sentences and you will have another couple of pages.

Day 4: Edit your previous work and then write 3 more pages.

Day 5: Finish your paper.

Day 6: Give your manuscript a good editing session. I also recommend taking your paper to the Writing Center for review.

Day 7: Edit your manuscript a second time. After that, you should be done!

As you can see, you can get a lot of work done in small increments. Most of the steps above can be accomplished in less than an hour each. Some people prefer to wait until the last minute to get an assignment accomplished, but this will likely result in poor quality work. Additionally, this is a prime opportunity for something bad to happen when it is least expected, such as coming down with the flu, or your car getting a flat tire. If this happens, then you will totally miss your opportunity to get an A on your assignment, and not getting a good grade on this paper will then impact your overall course grade.

If you want to set goals effectively, you can think about the SMART Goals acronym: Specific, Measurable, Attainable, Realistic, and Time Bound (Drucker, 1954; Doran, 1981).

Here is how writing a paper can follow this method:

Specific - Write a 10-page paper for English class.

Measurable - Work on the paper for an hour a day until the paper is complete (about one week).

Attainable - You can attain your goal by working on your paper for an hour a day.

Realistic - Writing a high quality 10-page paper is definitely possible!

Time Bound - The paper must be complete within a week.

Don't Forget about Passion

As you recall, grit is defined as perseverance AND passion for long-term goals. Do not forget the passion part. The great thing about being the unique person that you are (there is only one of you!) is that you can be enthusiastic about whatever you

want. And, you can make a difference in society by translating what you are passionate about into a future career.

What are you passionate about? Start thinking about how all of the activities that you do on a daily basis translate into being a successful college student. The book *The A Game* by Dr. Ken Sufka (2011), which you should have in addition to this textbook, can point you in the right direction. Go to class. Take your own notes. Don't sit in the cheap seats. Make mind maps. Know what you don't know, etc. Practice these tips on a daily basis.

And beyond that, I want you to think about how passionate you are about being a college student. Are you willing to study for at least a couple of hours each day? Enjoying what you are studying in your major can make a huge difference in persisting to graduation.

Many students struggle with trying to find the right major (Scott, 2016). If you already know what you want to do, that's great. More power to you! But if you don't know what to major in, or feel like your major is not a good fit, I want you to consider going to the Career Center, where you can sit down with an advisor and brainstorm potential majors and careers. (For more information, please consult the Career Center chapter in this text.)

The Center for Student Success and First-Year Experience's (CSSFYE) Academic Support Programs are another campus resource available to help you improve your study habits. You can attend one of their free Student Success Workshops on time management, test preparation and analysis, and note taking strategies. To schedule a meeting or attend a workshop, go to their website: cssfye.olemiss.edu/student-support-programs/.

You can build success one day at a time in simple, SMART steps. Success is based not only on perseverance and habits, but on passion - who you are as a person and what you like to do. As Mahatma Ghandi once said, "Be the change that you wish to see in the world." We have great confidence in you!

ABOUT THE AUTHORS

Patrick Perry, *Director of Luckyday Scholarship Progam*

Patrick received his undergraduate degree in geography, his master's degree, and Ed.D. in leadership from the University of Memphis. Since 2008, he has been the director of Luckyday Scholarship Programs at the University of Mississippi. He enjoys working with students to identify the best resources needed to reach their goals.

Rebekah Reysen, *Assistant Director for Academic Support Programs*

Rebekah received her undergraduate degrees in psychology and theatre from Purdue University, and her master's degree and Ph.D. in counselor education from the University of Mississippi. She is a National Certified Counselor (NCC), Licensed Professional Counselor (LPC), Distance Certified Counselor (DCC), and has published articles in a variety of counseling journals. Dr. Reysen coordinates programs for academically at-risk students and is passionate about helping students navigate their way through college.

Rachael Durham, *Assistant Director for First-Year Experience*

Rachael is originally from Memphis, TN, but now calls Oxford home. She earned her B.A. in journalism with an emphasis on public relations in 2008 and her M.A. in higher education/student personnel in 2012, both from the University of Mississippi.

CHAPTER

8

COMMUNITY STANDARDS AND

Community Expectations

By Tracy Murry, Brittany L. Dawson,
and Brownishia Clark

The University of Mississippi seeks to promote a stimulating and demanding educational and social environment in which a diverse student body with a wide range of individual interests, values, and abilities can live, interact, learn and develop based on the mutual understanding, trust, respect, and concern for the well-being and dignity of self, others, and the community. To belong to a positive community, each person must demonstrate responsible exercise of personal and academic freedom and adhere to individual accountability for words and actions.

Students are responsible for compliance with all federal and state laws, applicable county and municipal ordinances, and all rules, regulations, and written policies of the University of Mississippi. College jurisdiction, including jurisdiction to impose disciplinary sanctions, extends to any conduct which occurs on the campus and to any conduct that occurs off campus that adversely impacts the University of Mississippi, the University Community, or the pursuit of the mission of the University.

COMMUNITY STANDARDS

Office of Conflict Resolution and Student Conduct

The Office of Conflict Resolution and Student Conduct (CRSC) provides a comprehensive array of approaches to support The University of Mississippi's values of civility, respect for human dignity, and the honoring of community standards.

Conduct Rules and Regulations

All policies can be found on the University of Mississippi's Policy Directory located at https://policies.olemiss.edu. While the following is not a list of all policies related to student non-academic behavior, it is a list of the most common and important policies of which students should be aware:

Smoke-Free Campus Environment

Alcohol

Drugs and Drugs Paraphernalia

Presentation of Identification

Fraud or False Identification

Disregard for University Authority

Disorderly Conduct

Assault and Battery

Harassment

Stalking, including Cyber-Stalking

Hazing

Respect for Property

Theft

Arson, Explosive Devices, and Emergency Equipment Possession of Weapons

Unauthorized Entry

Responsibility for Guests

Title IX

Student Organizational Conduct

Game Day and Game Day Activities

Events Observance of Local, State, and Federal Criminal Law Violation of Other Applicable University Policies

Alcohol, Drugs, Tobacco, and Related Policies

The University of Mississippi is a very social environment which is celebrated and promoted by most of the community members. However, as positive and inclusive as the environment may attempt to be, our community must be prepared to address concerns that often occur when alcohol and/or drugs are present within a community.

It is important to remember that the decision to possess, consume, and, possibly abuse substances may be a personal choice. Such a choice does have an important impact on the individual student, the people directly interacting with the student, and the campus community at large. While policies exist to address alcohol and/or drugs on our campus, it is important to understand the impact that these substances have on the health and safety of students and the campus community.

Many students choose to be substance-free. These students have the right to have their choice supported, promoted, and tolerated by other community members. These students have the right to feel comfortable, safe, and welcomed to all events, activities, and to the campus as a whole.

Policies related to alcohol, drugs, and/or tobacco use exist to support student and community wellness. Each violation is seen as a potential threat to a healthy community and to the success of an individual student.

Important policies:

Alcohol:
- Illegal Possession
- Underage Possession
- Illegal Consumption
- Underage Consumption
- Visibly Overcome by the Consumption of Alcohol
- Driving while Under the Influence
- Illegal Distribution

Drugs (Illegal and Prescription substances):
- Illegal Possession
- Illegal Use
- Illegal Distribution, Sale, Manufacture, and Delivery of Illicit Drugs
- Drug Paraphernalia
- Visibly Overcome by the Consumption of a Substance
- Driving Under the Influence of a Substance

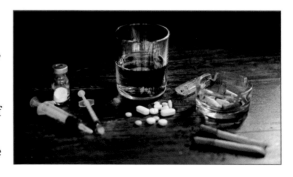

Other Important Policies:
- Game Day and Game Day Activities and Events
- Fraud or False Identification
- Smoke-Free Rules and Regulations
- Unregistered Events

Safety and Well-Being Amnesty:

A safety and well-being amnesty policy benefits the campus by encouraging community members to make safe and responsible decisions in seeking medical attention or treatment to any situation that may involve alcohol or drug use. The policy seeks to encourage individuals and student organizations to seek the necessary medical attention for community members who have over consumed alcohol or drugs. The  purpose of the safety and well-being amnesty is to diminish fear of disciplinary and conduct sanctions in such situations. This policy allows for University officials to practice discretion on a case-by-case basis to determine whether to grant amnesty from charges and sanctions by the Office of Conflict Resolution and Student Conduct (CRSC).

Under the safety and well-being amnesty, a student or student organization who seeks emergency assistance on behalf of self, another community member, or a friend experiencing an alcohol or drug-related emergency will not be subject to disciplinary action under the University's policies. If a party with authorization over a particular dwelling proactively requests a "sweep" of their premises by the canine unit then that organization will not face conduct charges.

Although students who qualify for the safety and well-being amnesty are exempt from the charges and sanctions from the CRSC, they may still be responsible for completing educational measures in relation to their alcohol or drug consumption. Educational measures may include, but are not limited to: parental notification if under the age of 21, alcohol and drug education, or a written project. Students who qualify for safety and well-being amnesty will still be required to meet with a University official.

However, when the call for medical assistance is made by a University employee acting within the scope of their responsibilities, medical amnesty will not be applied. In addition, law enforcement agencies may act within their own jurisdictions in enforcing local, state, and federal laws.

No Contact Letters:

A No Contact letter is a directive from a University official that prohibits people from contacting each other, either in person, through a third party, or through written or electronic communication. A No Contact letter can be amended or removed at any time. Anyone can request a No Contact letter or the University can issue a letter based upon a report, investigation, adjudication, or resolution of an incident.

Both parties receive the same request and instructions. In other words, Student A is asked to have no contact with Student B. Student B receives a letter instructing Student B to have no contact with Student A.

The No Contact letter is often a first step of involving University officials when a conflict between two students is not being resolved by the students themselves. The No Contact letter may be the only action taken by the University but it also does not limit or prevent any other investigations and conduct action from taking place.

Incident Reports:

Any person may submit an incident report to the Office of Conflict Resolution and Student Conduct (CRSC) when the individual would like help and support in resolving a conflict and/or when an individual believes that another student has violated a policy or policies that fall within the University of Mississippi's authority and jurisdiction. CRSC will make attempts to resolve the conflict or to refer the incident report to a person or office that may be better equipped to respond to a particular incident. CRSC will also review the incident to determine if the behavior described in the incident report is a matter that falls under the University of Mississippi's Student Conduct Process.

> **The Office of Conflict Resolution and Student Conduct provides a comprehensive array of approaches to support The University of Mississippi's values of civility, respect for human dignity, and the honoring of community standards.**

Informal Resolutions:

In most cases, when a student is charged or accused through the conduct process, the complainant (the reporting party) and respondent (the student/organization against whom a complaint has been initiated) are informed of options for resolution: formal and informal. Formal resolution involves a hearing with the University Judicial Council. Informal Resolutions are opportunities outside of the formal hearing process. The two most common forms of informal resolution are mediation and administrative agreement.

Mediation:

All parties actively work with a conduct officer and/or other officials to resolve the matter. In this process, there is a focus on all parties having a voice in the process and in the resolution of the conflict or violation. Mediation can be very positive and satisfying but can be time consuming and may end in unresolved conflict that will then need to be resolved in other ways.

Administrative Agreement:

In this option, a conduct officer meets with a respondent or accused students. After discussing the incident, the information, and process, the conduct officer can offer an administrative agreement. The respondent can accept responsibility for the policy violation and accept the sanction or remedy offered by the conduct officer. This option is quick and allows the respondent the opportunity to accept responsibility for the violation and to immediately address a remedy for the violation through the sanction.

Formal Resolution:

Complainants and respondents are allowed to make statements, present information, and ask/answer questions in the formal resolution process. The hearing panel will review all relevant testimony and information to determine responsibility and, if necessary, will issue a sanction for a violation. The decision is based on a preponderance of the evidence (more likely than, not standard) and the majority vote.

University Judicial Council Hearing:

The University Judicial Council (UJC) is the primary fact-finding and decision-making body in the University conduct system. The UJC, acting through a panel of at least six members (five members plus the chair), hears and decides cases involving alleged individual or organizational violations of University policy. Decision of the UJC are final yet subject to appeal.

Appeal Process:

Outcomes involving violations of University policy heard by the University Judicial Council (UJC) may be appealed to the Appellate Consideration Board (ACB). Cases submitted for appeal will be considered by a panel of at least three members of the UJC, vice chancellor of student affairs or assistant vice chancellors of student affairs.

There are four grounds for an appeal:

1. procedural irregularity that affected the outcome of the matter
2. new evidence that was not reasonably available at the time the determination regarding responsibility or dismissal was made, that could affect the outcome of the matter
3. The University Judicial Council had a conflict of interest or bias for or against complainants or respondents generally or the individual complainant or respondent that affected the outcome of the matter.
4. The sanctions imposed by the University Judicial Council were not appropriate for the violation that the respondent was found to have committed.

The decision of the ACB is final.

Advisors:

Students are permitted and encouraged to consult with an advisor at any time during the conduct process. An advisor can be anyone identified and selected by the student such as a relative, faculty, staff member, student, friend, or attorney. An advisor should be an individual that will help the student feel comfortable and will support the student throughout the process. While the advisor should aid the student, the student maintains the responsibility to participate and make decisions. The advisor cannot access information without consent of the student and cannot speak for or represent the student. Advisors are beneficial in helping a student prepare for meetings and hearings, talking through decisions the student must make, and advising the student on options presented during the process.

Sanctions:

When a student accepts responsibility, or is found responsible for a violation, the student must receive a sanction. Sanctions are designed to promote the University's educational mission. A sanction should be impacted by all circumstances surrounding an incident, including aggravating or mitigating factors such as a student's or organization's prior conduct history, harm caused or danger posed to the University community, and/or whether the misconduct was committed because of the actual or perceived race, color, ancestry, ethnicity, religion, national origin, gender, sexual orientation, sexual identity, gender expression, or genetic identity of a person. The Office of Conflict Resolution and Student Conduct promotes Restorative Justice philosophy when sanctioning. This approach focuses on four principles:

- **Inclusive decision-making:** All participates should have a voice or role in determining a sanction.

- **Active accountability:** Respondents are encouraged to take responsibility and attempt to make amends.

- **Repair Harm:** Restorative Justice aims for reparation and healing to hear harmed parties, not to punish or bring down offenders.

- **Rebuild Trust:** Restorative Justice rebuilds relationships so that respondents can be trusted again and harmed parties can feel safe again.

COMMUNITY EXPECTATIONS

To ensure that disagreements do not devolve into endless and unproductive arguments and potential violence, members define and subscribe to sets of rules and behaviors. It works similarly at the University of Mississippi. To protect and sustain our spaces of learning, experience, and exploration and to avoid chaos and harm, participants must accept and adhere to certain guidelines. The college campus, in addition to existing as its own society, prepares students for the many public, professional, and private societies outside of the University. Learning and integrating civil behaviors now will absolutely assist students in advancing in their future careers, communities, and relationships. Here are some easy guidelines for civility. Johns Hopkins University professor, P.M. Forni, has created a solid list of ways to ensure civility. Many of the ideas expressed and elaborated on in this section are drawn from or inspired by his thoughts:

- **Pay Attention**: Focus on the individual speaking. Avoid cell phone usage while engaged in face-to-face conversations. Appearing distracted can encourage misunderstanding and convey disrespect.

- **Listen:** Be an active listener and attempt to understand/appreciate what is being said. Do not focus only on your thoughts or listen only to respond. Be a positive partner in the conversation.

- **Be Inclusive (language and action):** Be mindful of conversations and respectful of what is being said and heard in a public space. Attempt to avoid gestures or speech that signal secrecy or exclusion.

- **Be Patient:** Remain calm, think before responding, and convene thoughts and ideas that reflect positively on the individual and the community. Negative emotional responses inhibit rational thinking and lead to frustration and conflict.

- **Be Respectful:** Each person's words have the power to comfort, inspire, and move people. Avoid cutting off or interrupting someone who is speaking and wait for an appropriate opportunity to engage.

- **Do Not Harass People:** Do not verbally or physically threaten people in speech or by writing threatening letters, text messages, emails, or leaving disturbing voicemail messages. Gather emotions before approaching people regarding difficult situations. Do not encourage sexism, racism, homophobia, ethnocentrism, or classism.

- **Respect Others' Opinions:** Avoid belittling differing opinions. Also, avoid assuming that everyone must think the same. Criticism of opinions should be listened to intently and rationally. A person can acknowledge, even appreciate, different viewpoints before express their own opinion. This is known as "qualified disagreement."

- **Expanding Horizons:** College campuses are designed to expose community members to various ideas, beliefs, and customs. Each member should make time to learn more about backgrounds or cultures to expand their own perspective, belief systems, and interpersonal skills.

- **Work Collaboratively:** To maximize learning and skills development and effectiveness for course assignments, campus activities, and curricular events, make sure to work in a collaborative manner.

- **Respect Other People's Time:** Avoid being late for classes, meetings, work, and campus events. Being tardy to class signals disrespect and is disruptive and distracting to professors and classmates.

- **Accept and Give Constructive Criticism:** Speak and write with words that are intentional, thoughtful, and purposeful for advancing someone's progress. Identify the problematic action or idea and do not criticize or attack the individual. Avoid resorting to obscenities and name-calling. Try to be empathic and deliver criticism in a way that is helpful to the person. Remember to respect the work of others through positive comments.

- **Respect the Environment**: Strive to keep the campus environment clean; recycle; do not use materials that harm the environment; and adopt a conservationist attitude. Avoid wasting water and energy sources.

- **Protect Your Communities**: Uphold these standards of civility. Avoid doing and saying things that damage the reputation, productivity, integrity, and safety of the community.

SOCIAL MEDIA AND CIVILITY

- **Avoid the Mistake of Assuming Anonymity:** Every communication that is made and every site that is visited is recorded and can be accessed. While a person is entitled to free speech under our country's constitution, the person is not immune to the consequences of their actions while online or on social media.

- **Consider How Internet Images and Statements Might Affect Your Professional and Personal Futures:** With increasing ease of access to the Internet and social media, employers, colleagues, and friends can access information and images about any person. Be mindful of any online "footprint" or personality.

- **Avoid Impulsive Behavior:** Re-read messages before sending them. To maintain civility and credibility, consider the impact of each and every word before hitting send, especially in a highly emotional state.

- **Assess the Credibility of Online Information:** Check information and rely on facts rather than assumptions. Make sure that before acting or reacting to online information or social media, gain as much credible information as possible to create the most reasonable and effective response.

- **Make Ethical Choices:** While active on the Internet and in social media, maintain an ethical compass. Strive to be self-reflective about activities on the Internet and on social media.

- **Avoid Using Electronic Devices When Inappropriate:** Difficult personal and educational conversations and productive labor are best accomplished in person. Using text messages, Twitter, Facebook, and email to communicate can often lead to misunderstandings and miscommunications. Textual communication rarely communicates the intended tone.

- **Avoid Addictive Use:** Always consider the amount of time spent on the Internet and social media. Think about whether the time spent on the Internet and social media is productive or if it is inhibiting communication skills, sociability, and mental state. If this is difficult to do, consider consulting with a counselor.

THE BENEFITS OF CIVILITY

Acting civil is not a mere demonstration of being polite; it provides many benefits to all members of a society or community. Civility guarantees:

- **Respect for all regardless of who they are and what they believe.**
- **A safe environment that promotes learning and self-discovery.**
- **An ability to more effectively navigate through campus issues.**

ABOUT THE AUTHORS

Tracy Murry, *Director for the Office of Conflict Resolution and Student Conduct*

Tracy Murry is a graduate of Louisiana State University (LSU) and Northwestern State University. Mr. Murry has been director since summer of 2016.

Brittany L. Dawson, *Assistant Director for the Office of Conflict Resolution and Student Conduct*

Brittany L. Dawson is a two-time graduate of The University of Memphis. Ms. Dawson is currently enrolled as a Ph.D. student at The University of Mississippi, in the Higher Education program.

Brownishia Clark, *Graduate Assistant for the Office of Conflict Resolution and Student Conduct*

Brownishia Clark is a graduate of The University of Mississippi and currently enrolled in the Masters of Higher Education program.

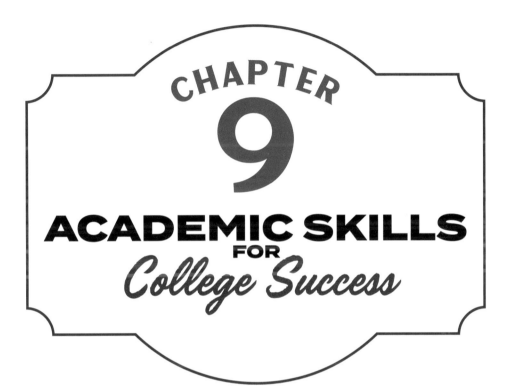

CHAPTER 9

ACADEMIC SKILLS FOR College Success

By Jeremy Roberts, Rebekah Reysen,
& Dewey Knight

S tudents who are new to college life often report being shocked by the amount of time they are required to invest in their coursework. Many students believe that the effort they put into studying in high school will translate into performing well in college, but often times students need to adjust their work ethic in order to maintain a high level of academic performance. For example, college lectures are often much different than those in high school, which means that students will need to acquire new academic skills in order to perform well in their coursework.

Many college professors, including those at the University of Mississippi, rely on lectures for relaying information to students about course topics. Professors may rely on in-person presentations or even pre-recorded lectures. Some lecturers may include various types of visual aids (PowerPoints, videos, handouts, etc.) in their presentations, whereas others may speak freely from behind a podium. No matter what the delivery method, professors are considered the experts in their respective fields, so students will need to remember that much of what is said by professors in the classroom is going to be very important information to recall later on. To be able to remember information for upcoming tests, students take in the information from the professor's lecture, write their notes, study the material, and prepare for exams and projects. This process of taking in information on the students' end is what we refer to as a form of listening – a process that requires us to be active participants.

In order to become a more ***effective*** learner, you will need to become an active learner. As we begin this section of the text, focus on the following key concepts. Incorporating these concepts into your daily studying practice will definitely help you meet your academic goals.

Active listening vs. Passive hearing

The term "active" is defined as being engaged in a specific process, one that is characterized by energetic participation within that process. The term "passive," on the other hand, is defined as when a person does not participate in the process at hand. Listening is an active process. Passively, one can hear simply by being conscious (awake) and perceiving sounds. Listening goes beyond just hearing as it involves thinking about the information. Listening requires energy, being alert, and being engaged. Hearing and listening are not the same thing. Hearing is a physiological response, while listening involves proactively seeking to understand, think, and analyze. In short, when you listen you are actively involved!

The most successful students learn to listen selectively. They focus on ideas, not just words. Throughout a lecture, they ask themselves, "What are the most important points the instructor is trying to get across?" Selective listening involves an awareness of what is and is not important enough to write down.

You will never be able to take down every word the professor utters and you should not even if you could.

Instead, in discerning what is important (selectively listening), respond to the cues given by the instructor. These so-called listening cues are both verbal (what the instructor says) and non-verbal (what the instructor does).

LECTURER'S SIGNALS...

- **Writes on the board**
- **Repeats information**
- **Speaks more slowly**
- **Gives a definition**
- **Lists a number of points/steps**
- **Explains why or how things happen**
- **Describes a sequence**
- **Refers to information as a test item**
- **Changes tone of voice**
- **Uses body language**
- **Uses visual aids**
- **Refers to specific text pages**

Note making vs. note taking

The most effective class notes are actively made, not just taken passively. Learning to make notes effectively will help you to improve your study and work habits as well as remember important information. Often, students are deceived into thinking that because they understand everything that is said in class, they will remember it. This is so wrong! Write it down!

As you make notes, you will develop skills in selecting important material and in discarding unimportant material. The secret to developing this skill is through repetition. Check your results constantly. Strive to improve. Notes enable you to retain important facts and concepts and to develop an accurate means of arranging information.

Once done with notes in class, another way to remain active is to transform your notes for studying such as through using various study aids like flash cards/index cards, concept maps, SQ4R, and Cornell Notes; never just rewriting them for the sake of doing so, though. Also, handwritten notes are proven to be more successful in the note making process than using your computer because you are more actively engaged with the process.

Ask questions in class

- Avoid irrelevant questions.

- Maintain focus. Don't ask a question about what was just said if you weren't paying attention.

- Give your instructor a place to start. Preface what you don't understand by saying what you do understand.

- Think of a question and ask it!

A good note maker learns the instructor's style. Some lecturers start with a written outline, follow it, report key ideas, do not get off topic, and end on time. Other lecturers start with no outline, meander through various topics, write on the board, and sum up the lecture at the end of class. Pay close attention to the signals (verbal and non-verbal) that the lecturer sends.

ABBREVIATIONS AND SYMBOLS

&	and
<	less than
>	greater than
b/c	because
w/	with
w/o	without
@	at
#	number

Avoid distractions

Active listening is dependent on your being focused during the lecture. You must avoid distractions both external, and internal. External distractions include windows and doorways, classmates, cell phones (yours should never be active during class), seating choice, room temperature, and outside noises. Internal distractions are all within your control – make sure that you exercise the control that is yours. Avoid negative self-talk!

Negative self-talk

- So, who cares?!?

- I'm never going to remember all of this.

- I should never have taken this class.

- I wonder what I will do after this class...

- What a stupid question!

- I wish I weren't here...

Make the Most of Difficult Lecturers

Lecturer Characteristics	Suggestions for Students
Jumps from topic to topic; unorganized.	• Reorganize notes *after* each class. • Have three-ring binder with the aim of using a separate sheet of paper for each topic; reorganize the pages after class. • Record (with permission), and use the recording to help you reorganize the notes, by topic, after class.
Talks over students' heads; uses complex words and ideas.	• Review chapter to be covered. • Ask lots of questions. • Talk with the instructor outside of class to seek explanations.
Talks too fast.	• Review notes after every class — use text to fill in what you missed. • See the instructor during office hours to review what you missed or don't fully understand. • Ask the instructor to slow down and/or to repeat information.
Talks with a foreign accent.	• Sit in front of the room near the instructor. • Talk to the instructor one-on-one. This will help you get used to the instructor's manner of speech. • Ask the instructor to repeat the information.
Boring **— presents information in a lifeless, boring manner.**	• Sit near the instructor. • Bring colorful supplies — at least create lively notes for yourself. • Ask questions and urge classmates to ask questions to enliven the presentation.
Condescending or impersonal towards students.	• See if you can talk to and form a relationship with the instructor. • Ignore it. • Seek help and personal affirmation out of class.
Is unprepared.	• Go to tutoring to fill in gaps. • Read and study the textbook before and after class. • Ask lots of questions and show interest. This might spur the instructor to prepare better for class.
Doesn't want to be bothered explaining material.	• Be persistent; keep asking questions. • Personally talk to the instructor after class — try to establish a working relationship. • Seek help from a tutor or another student.

Once you have your notes from class, it is time to start the studying process. Here is where you can use the information listed above with flash cards/index cards, concept maps, SQ4R, and Cornell Notes to make your studying more active. Give yourself time to study. Set up a schedule that works with your current weekly schedule that allows you to have multiple times devoted to studying. Consider the Pomodoro Method by Francesco Cirillo: Study for 25 minutes, then take a 5-minute break, then get back to studying for 25 minutes, then take another break. Complete this process 4 times to see how much information you retain. Quiz yourself on the material or use the help of a friend to quiz yourself.

Preparing for an Exam

It is important to review your notes at least once a week; don't wait until two or three days (or nights) before an exam for your review. Taking tests, quizzes, and final exams are an inescapable part of college. Strong, effective test-taking skills are crucial for college and career success. You may have noticed that test-taking is different at the University level from it was in high school or at some community colleges. Typically, university courses have fewer tests than high school or community college courses. This may seem like good news, but the reality is that college tests cover more material, sometimes half of the course content, so preparing for tests requires more study hours over an extended period of time.

Test preparation cannot be accomplished in one night.

Some professors award students' grades based solely on test score(s). Homework assignments and class participation will help you understand and apply what you are learning, but there are courses where your test score will be the primary or only factor in assessment. Look at the syllabus for each of your classes at the beginning of the semester and record all important dates (quiz, test, and exam dates are the most important) in your planner, cell phone calendar, or computer. By doing this, you can be prepared, and tests will not sneak up on you.

To effectively prepare for tests:

- Begin preparing on the first day of class.
- Identify the days and times of all your exams for the whole term in your planner. Find out exactly what material the test will cover.
- Understand that specific types of preparation are required for specific types of tests. Make a study schedule.
- Begin serious reviewing several days before the test. Maximize your memory.
- Get everything ready the night before the test.
- Manage your energy so that you're ready to focus and work quickly. Have a productive, positive attitude.
- Study with other students.
- Remind yourself of your long-term goals.

- Arrive at the classroom early, but not too early. Don't use drugs or energy drinks to stay awake.

- Don't let open-book or take home tests lull you into thinking the test will be easy!

Types of Test Questions

Test questions can be categorized as objective or subjective questions. Objective questions require a lower level of thinking because they tend to ask for facts and concepts that usually appear in the form of multiple choice, true/false, fill-in-the-blank, and/or short answer. Subjective questions are those which ask for your opinion about the material or challenge you to think of the material in a new way – essay and critical thinking questions are examples of subjective questions.

It is crucial to read all test questions carefully but especially when reading a multiple-choice question. Mark special words that are found within the question such as "not," "always," and "only." Cross out answers that you know are definitely wrong, and if you are guessing, make sure to eliminate answers that are misspelled.

Pay attention to "all of the above" and "none of the above" answer choices. If you can determine that two answers are correct, then "all of the above" is probably the correct answer. If two of the answers are not correct, the answer is probably "none of the above."

Here are some of the best ways to approach different types of test questions:

OBJECTIVE

Matching: When answering matching questions, make sure to read through both columns and determine whether there are multiple matches to a word in the list. Review the list after you've answered to make sure that all letters are in their correct space.

True/False: These questions can be difficult even though there are only two possible answers. Read through the questions carefully and note words such as "frequently," "sometimes," and "a few" because these words usually indicate a true statement. Words such as "never," "only," and "always" usually indicate a false statement. If a true/false question is causing a lot of difficulty, go with your gut instinct.

Fill-in-the-blank and Short Answer: These require you to recall definitions, key terms, or items in a series. Read the question carefully, and spell terms correctly.

SUBJECTIVE

Problem Solving: These questions can be detailed, and it is important to mark the specific steps and directions in the question. Determine what information is needed to answer the question and then break the question into parts. Also, write down each process or operation to be performed so you can more easily work through each stepof the question. Once you believe you have come to an answer, review your work.

Essay: These questions are popular in college because their answers call for a deeper understanding of the material. Make sure to answer all parts of the question, and your answer should be the length the teacher suggests. Before writing, make an outline of what will be covered in the essay to make sure you do not leave anything out. Too often, students make the mistake of not providing enough details in their answers. Essay questions demand more, not less. Because essay questions are long and take extra time to grade, a well-organized essay will stand out and make it easy for the professor to identify the key points of your argument. Make every effort to write legibly too, so the professor doesn't have to struggle to read yourwork.

If you do not succeed on a test despite having spent adequate time preparing, schedule an appointment with the instructor, go over the test, and learn what and how you can improve for the next test. Always take the initiative to learn from past mistakes to improve in the future.

Preparing for Final Exams

First confirm your final exam schedule by going to the Registrar's website (registrar.olemiss.edu).

Remember, your finals may be scheduled for days and times other than your regularly scheduled class times.

To avoid becoming overwhelmed by final exams, use time management skills discussed in previous chapters and throughout the semester to help you maximize your preparation for finals. Two or three weeks before exams, sit down and make a new calendar for the end of the semester. By using a calendar for all the specific assignments that need to be completed and lessons that need to be studied, you can better estimate how much time is needed to complete each task. Aim to have at least five days before exams begin to completely concentrate on finals. Do not try to finish projects, write papers, and study for finals at the same time. It cannot be done!

It is easy to lose momentum at the end of the semester and to think that the best thing to do is rest before a final exam. This is not true. The best thing to do is push through the last two weeks of school and prepare and study as much as possible. Set priorities by looking at where you stand in each class and calculating what score you need on each exam to succeed. You should focus on any courses where you have a borderline grade because the final exam can make a major difference in the grade you earn for the course.

Test-Taking Anxiety

A serious issue that can arise when taking a test is test-taking anxiety. Recognizing if you have this anxiety is the most important part of being able to control and conquer it. Some of the symptoms include perspiration, sweaty palms, headache, upset stomach, rapid heartbeat, and tense muscles. Anxiety can cause difficulty in organizing your thoughts, reading and understanding questions, and remembering key words. Anxiety also causes mental blocking. The best way to combat these anxiety symptoms is to avoid laziness, procrastination, and daydreaming. Build self-confidence by studying well in advance of the test. Procrastination only increases test anxiety. The Student Health Center, COPE, Psychological Services, and the University Counseling Center can help you if you believe you are suffering from test anxiety.

Last Minute Advice on Exams

It is always important to speak with your instructor in the weeks leading up to the exam by attending office hours, any study sessions, or before or after class. They hold the key to what will be on the exams, quizzes, and even homework for that matter. When in doubt, always ask questions.

Attending tutoring sessions done by many departments on campus can also help students with preparing for finals in speaking with their peers who have successfully completed the courses (the same with Supplemental Instruction sessions).

Study when you are sharpest and build in breaks. Rome was not built in a day and studying for an exam with a large quantity of material to review cannot be done in just one day.

Actively going through your notes, studying, and then putting together a final list of questions you have about the material to then speak to your instructor is important for all exams (regular exams in classes, midterms, and finals). Using any of the study aids mentioned in this chapter will help you throughout the progression of the semester - starting strong and ending on a positive note!

ABOUT THE AUTHORS

Rebekah Reysen, *Assistant Director for Academic Support Programs*

Rebekah received her undergraduate degrees in psychology and theatre from Purdue University, and her master's degree and Ph.D. in counselor education from the University of Mississippi. She is a National Certified Counselor (NCC), Licensed Professional Counselor (LPC), Distance Certified Counselor (DCC), and has published articles in a variety of counseling journals. Dr. Reysen coordinates programs for academically at-risk students and is passionate about helping students navigate their way through college.

Jeremy Roberts, *Learning Specialist for Academic Support Programs*

Jeremy has a degree in english and hospitality management for the University of Mississippi. He has a master's in health and sports science from the University of Memphis, and an MBA from Delta State University.

Dewey Knight, *Associate Director for the Center for Student Success and First-Year Experience Emeritus*

Recently retired from the University.

CHAPTER 10

OUR *Libraries*

By Melissa Dennis

"A university is just a group of buildings gathered around a library."
—Shelby Foote, *Civil War historian and American novelist*

The University of Mississippi Libraries include the J.D. Williams Library and the Science Library. You can find the J.D. Williams Library in the center of campus where it serves as the main library for everyone. You can visit the Science Library in the Thad Cochran Natural Products Research building where it contains the pharmacy, chemistry, and biochemistry collections. Both libraries are open to the public. Our libraries support research, teaching, and learning at the University. This means **we are here to help you find, evaluate, and cite sources for your papers as well as help you through the research process at any point.**

In addition to visiting us in person, you can take advantage of our extensive online library. Discover what library services and resources we offer through our website: libraries.olemiss.edu. For many of our services, you may choose the convenience of accessing our online library anytime. However, some students find that visiting our libraries on a regular basis helps them succeed. We provide a lot of study space options, research help, and unique collections that you cannot experience without visiting in person. We hope you choose to use the libraries on campus and online throughout your time at Ole Miss. This chapter will help you navigate your library experience online and in person.

We're Not Your High School Library

If you walk into the J.D. Williams Library and feel a little overwhelmed, you are not alone. You may think you already know how to use a library because you frequented the one in your high school or even your local public library. But we are not a school library or a public library, we are a large academic library. Like most large academic libraries, we use the Library of Congress Classification System (LCC) to organize over two million books and other materials in our buildings. High schools and public libraries use the Dewey Decimal System because they are organizing a much smaller collection. So, it's likely you have never had to find books using the LCC and it may be intimidating at first. Let's talk about how to use the LCC to find a book in the library.

The LCC system arranges books by their call number. **A call number is a book's address: it's a unique set of letters and numbers that you can use to find a book on the shelf.** Call numbers are assigned based on the subject first—not the title or the author. This is a main reason that academic libraries use the LCC. We understand that you will more often need to find resources by subject than by title or author. The LCC system arranges books by subject so that when you find a section in the library with the call number for one book that appealed to you, you have now found many books on that same subject. This makes browsing a large print collection easier and faster.

> ### QUESTION?
>
> **How does our library organize books?**
>
> Our library uses the Library of Congress Classification System (LCC)—an alphanumeric classification system that was first developed in the late nineteenth and early twentieth centuries to organize and arrange book collections of the Library of Congress. The LCC uses call numbers to organize materials.

A Closer Look at a Call Number

The LCC categorizes books by subject, and all subject headings are assigned a letter (from A–Z). Therefore, all call numbers begin with a letter. You need to know which section of the library to find this letter to begin finding your book. A = General Works, B = Philosophy, C = Auxiliary Sciences of History, D = World History and History of Individual Countries (except the Americas), E and F = History of the Americas, etc.

Of course you don't have to memorize the LCC to find books in the library, just always write down the entire call number or take a picture of it with your phone before you walk into the stacks. No two books have the same call number, but just writing down "PS 3500" or "E 185" will lead you to several hundred books in that section. You need the whole address (call number) to find the exact location of each book in the library.

We're More Than Just Books

Finding a book is just one reason to visit our libraries. We have lots of other resources and services available to help you succeed in college. The J.D. Williams Library has three main floors and three mezzanine floors (only accessible through the East side of the building). Here are noise levels, call numbers, services, and spaces for each floor:

First Floor

- **Noise Level:** Talking is okay.

- **Call Numbers:** R – Z, and also M (Music) and the Juvenile Collection (written for ages 0 – 18)

- **Services & Spaces:**

  - **Access Services Desk**, located at the West entrance of the building (fountain side), is where you can check out books, pick up books you have requested from other libraries (Interlibrary Loan), find course materials your teacher put on reserve, and clear holds on your library account (we charge a fee for unreturned items, but don't worry, we will email you to let you know when items are approaching their due date and when they are overdue).

  - **Classrooms 106D and 106E** are located at the South side of the building at the end of a long hallway. Many classes book these rooms for library instruction and research days, but student groups and other units on campus frequently use these rooms for private meetings and public workshops. Open "Classroom Calendar" on the library's homepage to see when your EDHE 105/305 class is visiting the library.

  - **The Commons** is the large open space in the center of the first floor where most campus tutoring services take place. The Commons also have a printing station, scanning station, lots of computers, and group study rooms. These open spaces are not reservable online.

  - **Government Documents** are located near the IDEALab on the East side of the building. This is a large collection of millions of federal and state books, maps, pamphlets, microforms, and other materials we receive on a continuing basis from U.S. government agencies and agencies from the State of Mississippi. In 2018 we were awarded Best Federal Depository in the Nation.

- **The IDEALab** is located directly beneath Starbucks on the East end of the building. Workshops are listed on the library's homepage and many of them require you to register because they fill up so quickly. This is a creative space with virtual reality, poster printing, 3-D printing, sewing, robotic kits, soldering station, design and editing software, and more. IDEALab hours are listed on the library's homepage.

- **Research & Instruction Offices** located on the far South side of the building in rooms 103, 105, and 106A next to the Classrooms 106D and 106E. R&I librarians visit classes to talk about the research process and how to use library resources. We also create online research guides and tutorials and love to work with students by appointment, so please "book us" on the library's Subject Librarian page to reserve time with us. We are here to help you find the resources you need, so don't be afraid to make appointments with us. You can also chat with us anonymously using the Ask a Librarian chat on the library's homepage.

- **STUDIOone** and the editing room are in the Commons. Reserve this video studio and video editing room on the library's homepage. We can help you use the equipment, too, so don't worry if it's your first time using rooms like these.

> ## QUESTION?
>
> **What can you find in the Department of Archives and Special Collections?**
>
> 1. Original documents or primary sources
> 2. Blues archive
> 3. Mississippi collection
> 4. Material related to the University of Mississippi
> 5. Diaries, letters, scrapbooks, and financial records
> 6. Publications, photographs, recordings, and manuscript collections

Scan the QR code to find out how to currently access our print collections and to play the online escape room game: Escape UM Libraries.

Second Floor

- **Noise Level:** Talking is okay in the Baxter Room and Starbucks, but overall this is a quiet-talking only floor.
- **Call Numbers:** J–Q, not L or M
- **Services & Spaces:**
  - **Baxter Room** is next to Starbucks and a popular space for group study. This room also has computers, printing station, and magazines, journals, and newspapers to browse.
  - **Rooms 201 and 212A** are reservable group study rooms through the library's home page "Reserve a Space." Rooms can be reserved by individuals, but you need at least two people in a group room to avoid being removed when space is limited.
  - **Pilkington Room** is a large study area next to the main staircase with a blue accent wall and rotating student art collection. It's a great place to meet friends for quiet study.
  - **Starbucks** is located at the East end of the building. Watch the live webcam on the library's homepage to see how many people are waiting to place orders in line.

Mezzanine A

- **Noise Level:** Quiet talking only.
- **Call Numbers:** L (Education)
- **Services & Spaces:**
  - **All Gender Bathroom**
  - **Private Faculty Carrels**

Third Floor

- **Noise Level:** No talking/whisper only is preferred on this floor.
- **Call Numbers:** A–H
- **Services & Spaces:**
  - **Administration Suite** is located at the East end of the building above Starbucks. This is where you can fill out an application to work in the library, visit with the Dean of the Libraries, or drop by the Harrison Room that is attached to this suite and often available as an open study space. An All Gender Bathroom is in the Harrison Room.

- **Archives and Special Collections** department located at the East end of the building. Hours: Monday–Friday, 9:00 a.m.–4:00 p.m. The Faulkner Room, a popular venue for workshops and special events, is in this department. You are welcome to visit the Archives, especially to see this year's annual exhibit on Space Exploration, but appointments are preferred for research help. Browse special collections, including all Ole Miss yearbooks, on the library's homepage "Archives." Because items housed here are unique, they cannot be checked out, but you can view them in the department or online.

QUESTION?

How can you contact a librarian?

1. Email
2. Instant message (chat)
3. Phone
4. Reference Desk
5. Personal consultation
6. "Ask a Librarian" link on website
7. Find subject librarian for your major on the library's website

- **Bike Room** is located next to the Jesse White Room and has treadmills and stationary bikes that can be used while reading or studying. This is a great space for anyone who wants to study and exercise lightly at the same time.

- **Jesse White Room** located next to the Bike Room is another open study room available for individual study. Rooms 301 and 302 are reservable group study rooms on the South side of the building. Rooms can be reserved by individuals on the library's homepage, but you need at least two people in a group room to avoid being removed when space is limited.

Librarians teach you how to find and evaluate credible sources, cite them correctly to avoid plagiarism, and critically assess information.

Mezzanine B

- Noisc Level: Silence is preferred.
- Call Numbers: None
- Services & Spaces:
  - Faculty private carrels
  - Library storage
  - Nursing Mother Room B16. You can check out a key to this room at the Access Services Desk on the 1st floor.

Mezzanine C

- Noise Level: Silence is preferred.
- Call Numbers: None
- Services & Spaces:
  - All Gender Bathroom
  - Graduate student private carrels
  - **This is the Graduate Student Floor and should not be used by undergraduate students.**

Ask A Librarian

Librarians are experts in finding and evaluating information and we are available to help you in several ways. First of all, we know the LCC system and all of the ways to find materials in our buildings and on our website. This is the main reason you can find an "Ask a Librarian" link on many of our web pages. **We want you to always remember that you can ask us to help you find what you need.**

- **CHAT** with us through an anonymous instant messaging service Monday–Thursday, 9:00 a.m.–6:00 p.m., Fridays, 9:00 a.m.–1:00 p.m. and Sundays, 5:00 p.m.–8:00 p.m.

- **EMAIL** us your questions at asklib@olemiss.edu and we will get back to you ASAP.

- **CALL** us at 662-915-5855 if you want to talk over the phone.

- **VISIT** us after you book a time for a research consultation by selecting your personal librarian (assigned by UM department/major) at "Subject Librarians" on the library's homepage. We can also meet in Zoom.

Librarians teach you how to find and evaluate credible sources, cite them correctly to avoid plagiarism, and critically assess information. Librarians are faculty; we engage in research and produce scholarly works like other professors at the University. In other words, we understand the expectations your instructors have and know how to help you succeed in your classes. Whether you need to book us for a research consultation or ask us a quick question through Chat, you can get help by asking a librarian.

During your time at the University you may discover the libraries are great places for thinking, creating, collaborating, writing, reading, napping, or gaming. No matter how you spend time here, please remember the libraries are public spaces for you to share with the Ole Miss community. You are always welcome at UM Libraries; enrich your academic experience by using them.

QUESTION?

Why do I need to cite something I found online or read in a book?

Whether you use someone else's words or ideas directly or indirectly in your academic work, you always need to properly cite them to distinguish where your thoughts end and theirs begin. Citing your sources demonstrates to your professors 1) that your argument is valid because you are using credible sources and 2) that you respect and understand the research process enough to give other people credit for creating the sources that you selected.

ABOUT THE AUTHOR

Melissa Dennis, Head of Research and Instruction Services and Associate Professor

Melissa Dennis received her B.A. in English from the University of Mississippi and her M.L.I.S. from the University of Southern Mississippi. She coordinates library research and instruction services at UM-Oxford, UM-DeSoto, UM-Boonville, UM-Tupelo, and UM-Grenada.

CHAPTER 11

READING
College Texts

By Stephen Monroe

"Reading is the route to intelligence."

– Robert Scholes, The Crafty Reader

I f you want to be smarter than other people, you simply need to read more than other people. There is no secret to knowledge. And knowledge has nothing to do with an ACT score. Right now, you should forget—leave behind—your ACT score, whether it was high or low or in between. It means nothing now. You are here, in college, and you can become anything you wish. Do you want to be a doctor? A journalist? A political scientist? An accountant? Read widely. Read books about your chosen profession and about everything else. If you read actively and selfishly, you will learn how to think. Your mind will grow full and strong like the Catalpa tree outside the Union. If you don't read, or if you read minimally or lazily, you will gain nothing and your mind will become runny and soft like undercooked eggs.

Benefits of Reading

The benefits of reading are obvious. If you need proof, however, you should look to a landmark report from 2007. *To Read or Not to Read: A Question of National Consequence* draws upon decades of scientific and statistical evidence to make a compelling, research-based argument for the benefits of reading.

The report finds that voluntary, regular reading correlates strongly with the following:

- Gainful employment, promotions, and career satisfaction;

- Active participation in social, cultural, and civic life;

- Contributions through volunteer service and charity work;

- Job security, even during economic downturns;

- Freedom. (I'm not kidding: only three percent of adult prisoners read proficiently).

In America, reading will not only make you smarter, it will make it easier for you to build a successful, happy life.

You will, at times, need to read when you'd rather be doing something else.

Reading When You Don't Want to Read

My mom always said, "Sometimes in life you have to do things you don't want to do." As a kid, I hated this idea, and I was sure that she was wrong. Well, she was right.

In college, you will need to read books about subjects that don't immediately interest you. You also will need to read at times when you'd rather be doing something else. Maybe it's the first warm day of spring and Frisbees are flying in the Grove. The only problem: you have a test tomorrow in your least favorite subject. You have put off reading the textbook, which you know was a mistake, but you are now trying to rally. You want to do well on the test, but you dread the thought of reading all of those piled up pages. How do you motivate yourself to read in this scenario?

You have to find your own answer to that question. Each of you will be motivated by different thoughts and emotions. Some may be negative: the fear of a shameful return to your hometown and family at the end of this first semester. Some may be positive: the hope of a triumphant return to your hometown and family at the end of this first semester.

Reading is difficult work. If you feel relaxed while reading, you are doing it wrong.

No matter where you find your motivation, you do need to find it. It takes energy and determination to read actively and effectively, especially when you are short on time or when there are seemingly better things to do.

The Practice of Reading

Dozens of researchers have "invented" various methods of reading school textbooks. The most famous of these methods may be SQ3R, which is shorthand for survey, question, read, recite, and review. You may have learned this method in high school. By breaking down the complicated process of reading into seemingly easy-to-follow steps, methods like SQ3R can be useful. Furthermore, they are designed to be straightforward and easy to learn. For details, you can look to the web, where many universities offer information on SQ3R and other reading methods. This module from Oregon State University is a good example:

https://success.oregonstate.edu/learning/reading

You also can take advantage of free workshops offered on our own campus by the Center for Student Success and First-Year Experience. Their DIY Learning Tools Workshops often cover reading strategies. https://cssfye.olemiss.edu/academic-success-workshops/

Truth be known, you can memorize the best reading system in the world and still be a horrible reader. Reading, especially in college, is difficult work. It requires an active mind. If you feel relaxed while doing it, you are doing it wrong.

Reading Actively

Have you ever been reading along, only to suddenly realize that you've not been paying attention?

You look back and see an entire page or two that you've "read" but that you can't remember? We've all done this, and we should all learn from our mistakes. Such listless reading is bad. It is the opposite of active, beneficial reading.

WALT WHITMAN was right. Real reading is not "a half sleep." It is, instead, "an exercise." If you want to get into shape, will you go to the Turner Center or the South Campus Recreation Center to gently roll a very light weight across the floor? Will you stand still on an unplugged treadmill? Will you take a nap by the swimming pool? No. Instead, you will push yourself. You will crush out serious reps in the weight room. You will go hard on the treadmill for forty minutes. You will swim laps until your arms hurt and your lungs burn. If you want to get into shape, you will exercise. The same is true with your reading. If you want benefits — if you want to get smarter — you will lift the heaviest ideas, struggling to understand them. You will keep your eyes wide open and your body tense as your mind races. You will pull yourself through the tough passages. You will go for at least forty minutes. You will yank and tug at the words on the page. You will agree. You will disagree. You will care. If you lose focus for a moment and miss a page, you will double back and read that page again until you've got it. You will not be relaxing, you will be exercising your mind. You will be reading.

Walt Whitman was right. Reading is an exercise. If you want to get your mind into shape, you must lift the heaviest ideas, struggling to understand them.

CREATING THE CONDITIONS FOR ACTIVE READING

How to create the conditions for active, effective reading:

Read when well-rested and alert. Too tired to read? Take a twenty-minute nap followed by one shot of espresso.

Read in a quiet place. If you think you read best while streaming shows, you are lying to yourself. You cannot read actively or effectively while watching The Office. Close every television app. If you need background noise, try listening to Mozart or Brahms. Even better, download an hour's worth of nature sounds. Try searching "rain" on your favorite music app."

Read in a comfortable, but not too comfortable, spot. Under the covers of your bed in your pajamas in a completely reclined position is too comfortable. In a hard chair in a hot room in your fanciest Sunday clothes is not comfortable enough. Find something in between.

Read alone. Get away from everyone. Schedule around your roommate or get out of your room. Campus is huge. We have lots of nooks and crannies, and we even have a really cool place designed just for readers: the J.D. Williams Library.

Read while disconnected from the world. This is not the time to post on Instagram or kid around on Snapchat. Turn everything off. Don't look at your cell phone. You just looked. Don't look at your cell phone.

ACTIVITY

Try this: go to the J.D. Williams Library and browse the shelves. Do not stop first at the online catalog. Go right to the stacks (the shelves) and browse the old fashioned way. Don't hurry, just look around. If a book looks interesting, for whatever reason, pull it down. Flip through it. What kind of book is this? When was it last checked out? Read the first few paragraphs. Now, put it back on the shelf. Wander around the library, browsing at your own pace. Don't hurry. Don't think about going someplace after the library. Just chill for a while in the library.

It's one of the few places where you can really be alone and quiet and not bothered by anyone. Keep browsing. Pull down random books until you find one that makes you curious, until you find a book that you might like to read. Now, check out that book. Take it back to your room. Don't show it to anyone. Don't talk about it. Keep it to yourself. Within the week, find time to read your book. No, it doesn't have anything to do with your classes. No, it will not help your grades. Yes, you will have to skip doing something else in order to read it.

How about not watching television tonight? Not playing Madden? How about skipping a party on Saturday by pretending that you are sick? Do whatever you need to do to read this book. Why? Because you found it. Because no one else is making you read it. Because no one else expects you to read it. Read it because you went into a library with a million books and you found this one book in particular. Read it selfishly; read it only for yourself.

> "I find television very educational. Every time someone switches it on I go into another room and read a good book." —Groucho Marx

Marginalia

My mom always said, *Don't write in your books*. As a kid, I hated this idea. I wanted to write in my books, and I was sure that my mom was wrong. Well, on this point, she was wrong.

You should write in your books (as long as you own them). Highlighters can be helpful, but there is no better tool than a sharp pencil. Use the margins to write notes to yourself, to record your reactions to particular ideas or passages, and to underline unfamiliar words.

Perhaps because some people consider writing in books to be nearly criminal (my mother), it is somewhat difficult to find fully developed systems of marginalia. This really isn't a problem, however, because you can simply develop your own. I use an exclamation mark to note a passage that bothers or alarms me, a question mark to mark a passage that I don't understand, D to signal a word or term that I need to define — you get the idea.

Indeed, such marks can be extremely useful when you are reviewing a particular reading assignment. If you have read carefully and left yourself reminders of your thoughts, you can take a few minutes before class to refresh your memory and walk in ready to contribute to the discussion or to listen more intelligently to the lecture.

Conclusion

There are many good reasons to read actively and energetically. Perhaps the most important at the moment: succeeding in college and earning your degree. Between now and graduation, you will spend hundreds of hours reading. If you do it well, you will make good grades and accomplish your goals. You also will learn more about the world and about yourself than you can now imagine. Enjoy the exercise. Happy reading.

ACTIVITY

Discuss active reading and personal systems of marginalia and note taking.
Read and discuss the following poem by Billy Collins.

Marginalia
By Billy Collins

Sometimes the notes are ferocious,
skirmishes against the author
raging along the borders of every page
in tiny black script.
If I could just get my hands on you,
Kierkegaard, or Conor Cruise O'Brien,
they seem to say,
I would bolt the door and beat some logic into your head.
Other comments are more offhand, dismissive -
"Nonsense." "Please!" "HA!!" —
that kind of thing.
I remember once looking up from my reading,
my thumb as a bookmark,
trying to imagine what the person must look like
who wrote "Don't be a ninny"
alongside a paragraph in The Life of Emily Dickinson.
Students are more modest
needing to leave only their splayed footprints
along the shore of the page.
One scrawls "Metaphor" next to a stanza of Eliot's.
Another notes the presence of "Irony"
fifty times outside the paragraphs of A Modest Proposal.
Or they are fans who cheer from the empty bleachers,
Hands cupped around their mouths.
"Absolutely," they shout
to Duns Scotus and James Baldwin.
"Yes." "Bull's-eye." "My man!"
Check marks, asterisks, and exclamation points
rain down along the sidelines.
And if you have managed to graduate from college
without ever having written "Man vs. Nature"

By Dr. Natasha Jeter

The practice of assigning incoming students "common reading"—asking them to read the same book before they arrive on campus—is a widely adopted practice that is support by has gained popularity in recent years as colleges and universities have sought new ways to improve the first-year experience (American Library Association, 2003; Ferguson, 2006; Laufgraben, 2006).

Reading and discussion are integral parts of every student's college education, and the common reading experience provides students with the chance to read a compelling book, express opinions and questions about the book, and listen and react to others' differing opinions. Classes engage in small group discussions about the content and often have the opportunity to participate in service learning, and other community engagement opportunities related to the content of the selections. The ability to listen, respectfully engage in discussions, and to articulate an opposing viewpoint are important skills necessary for success in higher education. Our EDHE 105 and 305 classes have been the center of this learning practice; and in recent years other departments and divisions have joined in and also provide us in engaging curricular and co-curricular experiences around the common reading. Our common reading is used to foster students' exploration of values and ethics, increase awareness of cultural diversity, deepen feelings of being part of a community, and integrate social and academic campus experiences.

Join us in reading - The common reading assignment is developed to encourage students to relate personal experiences with what they read, to develop the ability to express viewpoints, draw parallels between content in the book, people they know in their families, communities, and the University. It is a great way to synthesize concepts and connect with the broader community.

The Selection

The University of Mississippi Common Reading Experience began with the 2011-2012 school year, and continues in 2021-2022 with the selection of World of Wonders: In Praise of Fireflies, Whale Sharks, and Other Astonishments by Dr. World of Wonders by Dr. Aimee Nezhukumatathil. Every first-year student receives a copy of the selected text at orientation to finish before the school year begins in August. Instructors from the Department of Writing and Rhetoric, First-year Experience, and others utilize the text in their classes. This year, students will receive an electronic copy followed by a hardcopy when they return for the Fall 2021 semester. More than just a text, this year's selection will be foundational to conversations about kindness, respect, love and civility.

"World of Wonders: In Praise of Fireflies, Whale Sharks, and Other Astonishments," a celebrated new collection of essays

by Aimee Nezhukumatathil, UM professor of English and creative writing.

"This is especially meaningful because this book starts and ends with love--recollections of the outdoors and the various animals and trees that have captivated me," Nezhukumatathil said. "But it ends right here in Oxford, Mississippi, a place where my family and I now call home. The university's own incredible Tree Trail and champion catalpa tree get a mention here too."

"It makes me smile to no end that readers all over the world have connected with these short, illustrated essays of the outdoors." She said the book answers the central questions of "What and where is home for you? How can you find love and safety again in a place when you are transplanted or facing a new situation?"

"These are universal concerns," Nezhukumatathil said. "I try to remind people to practice having wonder in their lives as adults because so many of us had that curiosity and excitement about learning as children. It's not only vital towards opening our hearts when there is so much division in the news, but it's also free to do so."

Dr. Aimee Nezhukumatathil
Photo credit: Caroline Beffa Photography

She said she's a poet at heart, not a scientist, but has always loved being outdoors.

"I have loved the dazzling outdoors all my life," Nezhukumatathil said. "There is so much that I don't know about the natural world, but I view that curiosity as a good thing, a place where I feel alive and my pulse quickens because I genuinely want to know the hows and the whys of creatures and plants with whom I share this planet."

She said she would never have been able to write this kind of book without "the time and headspace" that the John and Renée Grisham Writer-in-Residency at UM gave her.

"As I mention in the book: I could feel a shift in my body the first day we opened the door and stepped foot in Oxford, like tiny magnets in me lined up and snapped to attention because I was finally where I needed to be," Nezhukumatathil said. "I could feel it in my bones...a landscape full of blue sky and whirls of thick kudzu and cricket song."

Since its debut in September 2020, the book has been a smash hit, including being chosen by Barnes & Noble as its Book of the Year. Following the Barnes & Noble recognition, "World of Wonders" jumped to No. 5 on the prestigious New York Times Best Seller List for Nonfiction. The book was named to year-end best book lists published by BookPage, Esquire, NPR and The Wall Street Journal, among others.

UM Chancellor Glenn Boyce said it's particularly exciting the UM community will dive into such a beautiful and widely acclaimed book from an accomplished member of its campus. The university owes its profound thanks to selection committee, and especially to Nezhukumatathil for "gracing us with this extraordinary work," the chancellor said.

"This year's Common Read will give rise to curiosity and conversation, and you will experience joy while reading and discussing this book," Boyce said. "I'm excited for the new insights and understanding that we all will gain from this shared community experience."

"It calls on us to take delight and pleasure in nature while touching on issues of family, travel and identity."

Stephen Monroe, chair of the Department of Writing and Rhetoric and of the Common Reading Steering Committee, said the book is sure to inspire and challenge the community.

"Reading a book together is always an act of wonder and discovery," Monroe said. "Aimee has given us an especially profound place to gather. I thank the selection committee—and the provost and chancellor—for choosing this resplendent text for the 2021 Common Reading Experience."

Natasha Jeter, assistant vice chancellor for wellness and student success and co-chair of the CRE selection subcommittee, said the collection of essays is an especially fitting one.

"It speaks to our sense of wonder; is inspirational and will lift our spirits as we emerge from the woes of the pandemic," Jeter said. "Dr. Nezhukumatathil masterfully uses nature and the beauty of the environment to teach us more about life and love.

It is my hope that our community will be motivated and inspired by her literary work; and allow us a place to gather, connect and be transformed."

REFERENCES

American Library Association (2003). One book one community: Planning your community-wide read. Chicago: American Library Association. Retrieved from http://publicprograms.ala.org/orc/pdfs/onebookguide.pdf

Ferguson, M. (2006). Creating common ground: Common reading and the first year of college. Peer Review, 8(3), 8–10.

Laufgraben, J.L. (2006). Common reading programs: Going beyond the book. [Monograph No. 44]. Columbia, SC: University of South Carolina, National Resource Center for the First-Year Experience and Students in Transition.

"If art is to nourish the roots of our culture, society must set the artist free to follow his vision wherever it takes him. We must never forget that art is not a form of propaganda; it is a form of truth. ... In serving his vision of the truth, the artist best serves his nation."
– President John F. Kennedy, 1963

The Gertrude Castellow Ford Center for the Performing Arts

Chancellor Robert C. Khayat (1995-2010) envisioned an arts facility that would serve the University of Mississippi community by offering opportunities to attend performances by world-class artists and to express themselves through their own creative efforts. With an initial gift of $20 million from the Gertrude C. Ford Foundation in 1998, and an additional investment of $20 million from the State of Mississippi and the University of Mississippi, the Ford Center for the Performing Arts was completed in 2003. The 88,000 square foot, six story facility, houses two theatres, dressing rooms, a green room, large storage areas in the basement, and administrative offices. It officially opened on Friday, March 24, 2003 with an inaugural gala hosted by Chancellor Khayat and starring Morgan Freeman as master of ceremonies. A cast of University alumni appeared together with a dozen university ensembles from the departments of Music and Theatre.

The Ford Center is guided by its mission to "enrich the intellectual and cultural environment of the University of Mississippi and the region by providing a venue for programming in performing arts, public affairs and the humanities. The Ford Center will complement the University's commitment to excellence in education, research and service while celebrating imagination, innovation and creativity."

The University of Mississippi considers the social and communal nature of live performances to be an important part of a student's education. Interaction or communication between audience members and the performers provide a visual expressivity that extends beyond the end of the performance. As a touring house, the Ford Center presents national touring productions of Broadway musicals, plays, ballet, modern dance, opera, jazz ensembles, symphonies, choral groups, and international artists. As a producer, the Ford Center incubates and serves as a catalyst for collaborative projects between the University and the community. The facility also serves as a venue for campus and local productions, University functions, lectures, and meetings.

On September 26, 2008, the University of Mississippi hosted journalists from around the world as the site for a presidential debate. The first debate between Barack Obama, a Democratic senator from Illinois, and John McCain, a Republican senator from Arizona, was broadcast live from the Gertrude C. Ford Center for the Performing Arts. With more than 150 events annually, performances include Morgan Freeman, Hal Holbrook, Art Garfunkel, Mary Stuart, The Blind Boys of Alabama, B.B. King, and Lewis Black. Noted lecturers such as

Prince Edward, the King of Jordan, Janet Reno, Cornell West, James Earl Jones, Thomas Friedman, John McCain, and Tom Brokaw are among a growing list of authors and noted intellectuals who have appeared in the Ford Center.

Located in the Ford Center, the UM Box Office handles ticket sales for all performances on campus, including those presented at the Ford Center. The Box Office is open from 10:00 a.m. – 4:00 p.m., Monday through Friday, and an hour before performance/event times. **Students receive discounted prices for all shows.** Check online (fordcenter.org or olemissboxoffice.com) for performance times and ticket order information, or call (662) 915-7411.

The Ford Center welcomes all individuals to enjoy its beautiful atmosphere and the accouterments of an exceptional performing arts facility. As a student at the University of Mississippi, you have the opportunity to explore a variety of art forms and expand your understanding of the world around you.

You might be surprised at how a live performance can reach you on an intellectual or emotional level that is new and exciting. Sharing those experiences with friends can create a special connection that you may discuss and remember for many years. Be a Rebel and take a chance. Attend something you have never seen before.

Theatre Etiquette

It is best to arrive 15-30 minutes before curtain. This will allow time to purchase concessions, find your seat, and read the program before the show begins. If you are late, you may not be seated until intermission. Late arrivals disturb the performers and other audience members.

Take care of any personal needs before the curtain. It is discourteous to leave while the show is in progress or before the actors have taken their final bows.

Please sit in your assigned seat. This will avoid confusion for other audience members locating their seat.

Silence or turn off your cell phone before the show begins. It is distracting for everyone to hear a phone ring or see the glow from texting or sharing on social media during a performance.

Do not video or take photos. It is contractually forbidden for audience members to video or take photos during a performance. Professional theatrical companies take this infraction seriously.

Please cease talking when the music begins. The overture is part of the performance.

Please refrain from talking, humming, or singing along during the show.

If you need assistance, contact the nearest volunteer usher. If additional assistance is needed, the usher will notify the appropriate Ford Center staff member.

Only bottles of water and wine cups purchased at the Ford Center may be taken into the theatre; no food is allowed.

Following these ten Theatre Etiquette rules will help you, and others, enjoy the theatrical experience.

CHAPTER 12

WRITING AND SPEECH

Programs

By Division of Writing and Rhetoric faculty members,
including Robert Cummings, JoAnn Edwards, Karen Forgette,
Wendy Goldberg, Kate Hooper, Guy Krueger, Stephen Monroe,
Ellie Moore, and Alice Myatt

The **Department of Writing and Rhetoric (DWR)** is the home of the University's composition and speech programs. Its primary mission is to improve student writing and speaking. The DWR is part of the College of Liberal Arts, and DWR faculty and staff have offices in Lamar Hall. In addition to teaching writing and speech courses to most University of Mississippi students (listed in the undergraduate catalog as WRIT or SPCH courses), the DWR also is the home of the rhetoric major, the professional writing minor, and the University's Writing Centers, spaces that provide writing and composition peer consulting services for all disciplines on all campuses. The Oxford campus Writing Center is located in Suite C on the third floor of Lamar Hall. The Southaven and Tupelo campuses also have Writing Centers.

When it comes to successful academic and professional writing and oral presentations, experience proves that there is no one solution or magic key that automatically guarantees student writing/speaking projects will receive the highest possible grades. However, we do have some proven tips and strategies from our writing and speech instructors, and we share them with you in this chapter. Further, since much of the writing you do in your EDHE 105 or 305 classes will be reflective response essays, a brief guide on how to write effective reflective essays is included in this chapter (see Appendix A). Appendix B is an explanation of how to read and understand a writing assignment, and in Appendix C two University of Mississippi students share letters of advice about writing assignments. Appendix D gives some tips for making presentations.

The University of Mississippi (UM) Speaking Center was planned and developed by the Department of Writing and Rhetoric (DWR) as part of an UM General Education Committee initiative to demonstrate support for student's oral communication competency. In August of 2020, the virtual opening of the speaking center was celebrated. The Speaking Center now works in tandem with the Writing Center to promote strong oral communication on our campus.

The Speaking Center's highly trained peer consultants work alongside students on presentations in all disciplines. We provide access to one-on-one consultations, group workshops, and other speech communication-focused resources. Our services are delivered face to face and online. We cultivate individualized strategies with students to help them become independent, effective, and confident speakers.

Tip 1: Develop your critical reading skills.

Here's what Keith Hjortshoj, author of *The Transition to College Writing*, says about the importance of reading: Performance on examinations, problem sets, labs, research projects, and writing assignments depends heavily on knowledge acquired from texts of many kinds. As a consequence, effective reading probably represents the most crucial set of skills you can acquire in college, where reading everything thoroughly from beginning to end might not always be possible. Given a particular assignment, however, the question is not only "Should I read this?" Because if the answer is "yes," then you need to ask yourself other questions:

> *What am I reading?*
> *Why am I reading it?*
> *How can I read it most efficiently?*
> *How can I remember what I will need to know about it?*

These questions acknowledge that reading is not a single kind of activity. Reading can be done in many different styles, with different approaches and strategies, used for specific purposes and for particular kinds of tests (31).

Stated simply: your writing is only as good as your reading. In college, expect to read, read, and then read more. Understanding the what, why, and how of your reading will do much to ensure that your writing projects meet the goals of your assignments. You may find it helpful to read more of Hjortshoj's work, *The Transition to College Writing*; we include it in our list of resources. (Be sure to read "Reading College Texts.")

Tip 2: Understand your audience.

Writing is communication, and knowing your audience is vital to your success. As you write, consider, "Who will be reading this? What is the best way to reach my audience? How can I get my point across in an interesting, thought-provoking way?"

Tip 3: Talk with your professor.

Instructors are a valuable resource that students often overlook. Get in the habit of visiting them during their office hours, asking questions about anything that you don't understand. If you can't make it to their office hours, don't be shy about asking to set up an appointment.

Conferencing with your instructor when working on writing or speech assignments is one of the best strategies to understand what you need to do to improve. When you conference with your instructor, be sure to bring a full draft of your project. Also, it is a good idea to take notes when you conference with your instructor so you have a record of the meeting for later reference.

Tip 4: Use the Writing Center!

Many students find value in making regular visits to one of the University's Writing Centers located on the third floor of Lamar Hall. The peer consultants in the Writing Center are undergraduates who have experience in writing and in helping their peers. The writing consultants enjoy working with students during all stages of the writing process, from brainstorming ideas to the final revision. Many successful students begin going to the Writing Center with their first writing or speech assignment and continue making appointments with various consultants over the course of the semester and beyond. The goal of the Writing Center is to help students become better independent writers, so the consultants don't "proofread" papers or merely "correct" errors; they help you brainstorm, talk about research, explore resources, and answer your grammar and citation questions.

Here are some tips for using the Writing Center:

- **Make an appointment.** The Writing Center can often accommodate walk-ins, but don't count on it. It's better (and easy) to make an appointment.

- **Be on time.** Sometimes the Center is really busy. If you can't make it to your scheduled appointment, please call 662-915-7689 or visit the website to reschedule.

- **Bring a copy of your assignment and your work at any stage.** You can bring class assignments, paper assignments (both formal and informal), speeches, resumes, personal statements, letters of application, and just about anything you want to work on. Bring a typed paper, if possible. Handwriting can be challenging to read, and a typed paper is much easier to read and review.

- **Bring a list of writing concerns you've had in the past or that your teachers have noticed.** We can help you improve your understanding of those problems.

Tip 5: Use a good writer's handbook.

While there is no official handbook for DWR first-year composition classes, a writing handbook helps you regardless of your academic major. Becoming familiar with any good writing handbook will be an asset as you work with various types of writing assignments.

The Writing Center
is located on the third floor of Lamar Hall.

We offer free writing consultations to all UM students. No matter your home campus, you may make face-to-face or online appointments at any of our writing centers through our WCOnline system. We have physical locations at the Oxford, Tupelo, and Desoto campuses and offer online sessions to students at all UM campuses, including Booneville and Grenada. Consultations are available both online and face-to-face, and appointments may be made online at rhetoric.olemiss.edu/writing-centers/.

Follow us on **Twitter@OleMissWCenter** to keep up with special events or important messages concerning Writing Center services. (Note that we are unable to schedule appointments via Twitter.)

 Become a **Facebook fan of the Ole Miss Writing Center** and take a look at what's happening in the Writing Center.

Some recommended resources for writers:

- The "For Students" web pages at the DWR website:
- https://rhetoric.olemiss.edu/student/
- The University of Mississippi Writing Center website: https://rhetoric.olemiss.edu/writing-centers/ The Norton Online Guide for Writers:
- https://wwnorton.com/college/english/write/writesite/research/documentation.aspx The Online Writing Lab at Excelsior College:
- https://owl.excelsior.edu/ The The Purdue Online Writing Lab:
- https://owl.purdue.edu/

Books you may find helpful:

- Birkenstein, C. & Graff, G. (2014). *They Say, I Say: The Moves that Matter in Academic Writing*, 3rd ed. New York: W.W. Norton.
- Hacker, D. et al. (2015). *A Writer's Reference*, 8th ed. Boston: Bedford/St. Martin's.
- Hjortshoj, K. (2009). *The Transition to College Writing*, 2nd ed. Boston: Bedford/St. Martin's.
- Weinstein, L. (2012). *Writing Doesn't Have to Be Lonely: 14 Ways to Get the Help of Other People When You Write*. Cambridge, MA: One of a Kind Books

APPENDIX A
Writing an Effective Reflective Essay Response
by Karen Forgette and Guy Krueger

Why Reflection?

Much of the writing you do in EDHE 105 or 305 is reflective response writing. Reflective response writing asks you to consider how campus events or experiences influence your beliefs, attitudes, values, and ideas. In reflective response assignments, you critically examine an event or experience, analyze the interaction between that event or experience and your own prior knowledge and assumptions, and make explicit connections between what you already know and what you are learning in college.

Reflection is important because it empowers you to take charge of your own learning. As you make connections between your ideas and the world around you, you begin to analyze how your thinking is shaped by your environment. You also begin to evaluate your intellectual growth. Although reflective writing is more personal than other kinds of academic writing, it is no less challenging. Reflective writing requires sophisticated critical thinking and self-analysis.

In some college courses, such as the first-year composition sequence, you are required to write reflective response assignments. Though reflective response writing may not be explicitly required in all of your college courses, the reflective skills you learn in EDHE serve as powerful tools to help you identify and examine your own learning throughout your college career.

The Nuts and Bolts of Reflection

Reflective writing may be new to many college students; however, the steps that lead to other successful writing projects work equally well with reflective response writing. The first step is to understand exactly what it is you are being asked to write about. Reflective writing does not ask you to restate what you have done; rather, the goal is to try to better understand what your classroom work and your college experiences mean to you as a student and a learner. This type of writing, too, can benefit from a process, the same process students use when composing an argument essay or a research paper.

The first step to any successful writing process is to understand and think about the assignment before you write. ***Being asked to reflect on an event includes preparing for the assignment that follows the event.*** One tip to help your chances of writing a successful reflection paper is to ask yourself a few questions before the event:

1. **What do I expect the event to be like?**

2. **Have I ever attended an event like this before? If so, what, and what was it like?**

3. **What do I hope to learn by attending this event?**

4. **Can I prepare for this event in any way (e.g., bring a pen and paper or a way to take notes, bring my phone to take a picture, etc.)?**

By asking yourself some questions and preparing before the event, you put yourself in a better position to later reflect on what you experienced and how it was significant to you as a learner. If there is time, making a few notes in response to these questions or others is a great idea.

The next step to consider is attending the event. The types of events you attend vary, so you should be aware of what, and how, you can record information. For example, if you are attending a speaking event, you can probably take notes or even record the event if allowed. This way, you could have access to direct quotes, or, at the least, be able to recall some of the more important points. If the event is more active, say, Rebel Run, you may reflect solely from your memory, or perhaps from a couple of pictures. Whatever the case, it is important to think about your assignment as you attend an event, to remember that your task is to make meaning out of the event. In other words, remember that your goal in reflective writing is to explore the significance to you of an event, not simply to restate or summarize what you did.

Then, you need to compose your reflection. Without thinking about the significance of the event, your temptation may be to sit down and describe what happened. To avoid this, try to again ask yourself some questions. Here are some ideas:

1. **Did the event change your thinking or outlook, even in a minor way(s)? How? Be specific.**

2. **Did you experience something that interested, inspired, and/or upset you or caught your attention? Explain.**

3. **Did you experience something that reminded you of or made you think about your own life in any way(s)? Explain.**

4. **Did you learn anything about yourself? Explain.**

For example, you would not be writing a successful reflection paper if you attended Rebel Run and wrote about exactly what happened and ended by saying you had a good time. You could, however, write a successful paper by acknowledging that you were not looking forward to participating in an event with so many people you did not know but then realizing you had fun meeting new people and finding out about them. This type of reflection could allow you to explore how and why you interact with others and why you are nervous around new people. Of course, this is just one possibility of countless ways to construct a reflection.

In terms of structure, you should need no more than a few sentences, or, at most, a paragraph, to describe the event. The majority of your essay should be spent on more substantive ideas, such as what you learned and why that might be significant to you. Also, remember that reflection is often personal. Though you will turn in your work to your instructor, you should write to help yourself think about your own learning, no matter how small the impact on your knowledge or literacy might seem.

Finally, do not forget that your reflective responses are essays, though short ones. Thus, use the writing process to help you submit more polished and thoughtful work. Write at least one draft of your response and allow yourself time to read over your work to make sure you are addressing the idea(s) that has the most meaning to you and that the idea is clearly articulated. Also, leave time to edit and correct mistakes that may interfere with reading. Your final product should demonstrate not that you simply attended an event, but that you were able to make meaning of that event and reflect on the significance of that meaning.

Following is a sample reflective response that demonstrates the use of at least some of the steps listed in this section:

I attended the concert by Rain on October 27, 2011. Rain is a touring act of performers that dress up like, impersonate, and play music by the Beatles. The show took place at the Ford Center and looked to be sold out.

I was interested in going to see Rain because my parents listened to the Beatles a lot when I was younger, so I grew up learning to like a lot of their music. I felt like I would have more fun at a concert when I knew the music. I have been to other concerts where I was not familiar with the music and still had fun, but that is because I was with my friends. Since I went to this show alone, I was more comfortable knowing the songs.

What surprised me most about this concert, though, was that I did not know some of the songs played by Rain. Having heard a lot of Beatles music growing up, I thought I would know everything that was played, but I didn't. I heard of lot of music I know, like "Twist and Shout" and "Hey Jude," but I was lost during some of the songs. Most of the crowd seemed to know everything that Rain played though. I was the youngest person I could see in all of the people around me.

I think the thing that was most interesting to me was watching some of the people in the crowd. I liked the music, but I also enjoy people-watching. Some of the people were dressed up very professionally, but seemed to be reliving their youth. People were dancing, singing, and smiling like they were back watching the Beatles years ago. People were also very moved by the video screens, which showed important events from the time the Beatles' music came out.

Watching the people got me thinking about growing older myself. The people at the Rain show seemed to be so happy when they listened to the music and watched the show. I wonder if I will look back on my years and college and think I didn't enjoy them as much as I could. I also wonder if I don't pay enough attention to important events like the first black president or Occupy Wall Street. Will I listen to Lady Gaga or Ke$ha and remember their songs as fondly as the people in the crowd remembered the Beatles?

Overall, I had a good time and the concert made me think about myself a little more. I also realized I don't know nearly as many Beatles songs as I thought I did.

APPENDIX B
Decoding a Writing Assignment

Sometimes an assignment can look like it is written in a foreign language. With patience and practice, you will become more confident with what an assignment is asking and, as a result, your papers will improve. Look over the assignment below and review the margin notes.

Assignment - Medical Ethics: Now and Then by Matt Saye

(A) Read the article from *Wired Magazine* entitled "Seven Creepy Experiments That Could Teach Us So Much (If They Weren't So Wrong)" available at: **wired.com/magazine/2011/07/ff_swr/all/1**

1. (B) Describe the position on medical ethics taken by both the *Wired* article and *The Immortal Life of Henrietta Lacks* and (C) analyze both authors' positions on medical ethics. (D) Do the authors seem to have the same view of medical ethics? Are there any places where they disagree?

2. The article from *Wired* comes some 60 years after Henrietta Lacks' cells were taken from her without her knowledge. (E) Using evidence from both the article and Skloot's book, describe how medical ethics have changed in the intervening 60 years and analyze the consequences of these changes.

3. One of the main points made by Skloot in *The Immortal Life of Henrietta Lacks* is that Lacks' cells were taken without her knowledge or consent. (F) Do you think that any of the medical experiments described in the Wired article would be unethical if participants were willing subjects who had been properly informed of the dangers and consequences of the experiments, or is science bound by a "moral compass" regardless of consent?

F) Again, you are being asked for your opinion, and it is quite acceptable, in reflective response assignments, to begin a paragraph by writing, "I think," or "I believe." Just be sure to provide reasons and support for what you think or believe.

A) If an assignment asks you to read, then you should read actively.

B) Describe is one of the verbs professors often use in writing an assignment. Your response should be specific and include details.

C) This is another key verb. Analyze here means to break down the authors' positions to understand how and why their arguments are constructed.

D) Here, you are being asked for your opinion. When you give it, be sure to support your opinion with evidence from the text under question.

E) Using evidence means to give examples and citations from the texts to support what you say about the medical ethics and how they have changed. Be sure to provide titles and page numbers when you refer to those examples and use quotations from the texts.

APPENDIX C
What First Year Students Say . . .

Dear College Writer,

Having a hectic, demanding, and stressful schedule is something nearly every college student must learn to balance. In order to be successful in your writing, I would make a few suggestions. First of all, I would plan. Plan out your day—know exactly when you will have time to work, study, eat, and write. Secondly, do not wait until the last minute. You will overly stress yourself and end up with a poor grade if you procrastinate for too long. Another important suggestion for writing is to make it gradual. Do your research, prepare, and write drafts so that when it is time to write the final, you will be ready. Remember to stay motivated and always keep a good attitude and you will go far. Good luck!

Sincerely,

Hannah Harpole

Dear College Writer,

There are lots of things that you'll have to prepare for when doing a research paper, or a paper of any kind for that matter. One of the first things that you should prepare for is procrastination. When you receive an assignment you should start working on it the night you get it or at least two days afterward. The reason for this is because if you don't start on the assignment as soon as possible you'll procrastinate and find yourself doing it the night before the due date. Normally papers are better formatted and understandable when they are gradually thought out. If you wait till the night before, things seem cluttered and your grade will suffer.

Allen Ball

APPENDIX D
A Few Presentation Basics

You are in the middle of a tough semester, and on top of all your other responsibilities you have been assigned a stand-and-deliver presentation in one of your classes. Whether you find the challenge exciting or you find yourself anxious and uncertain, the same physical reactions are at play. Adrenaline is pumping and priming you for the extreme sport of public speaking. If you are less than happy about the requirement to speak in public, you are not alone. Since the 1973 Bruskin Study in the London Sunday Times, public speaking has consistently been reported as a top personal fear (Dweyer and Davidson 2012; Chapman University 2014-2016). No wonder employers continue to inform universities they need students who can verbally communicate well (NACE, 2011-2016). How can you learn to manage the physical and mental effects brought on by speaking in public? Take the time to make your presentations POP by planning, organizing, and practicing before you present.

PLAN your presentations around your strengths or the necessity of the situation. If you get to choose your topic, draw on your knowledge, interests, and passion. A solid command of your subject matter helps you speak with confidence and credibility. Even if your instructor or professor assigns your topic, find a way to relate to the subject and bring your unique talents to the experience.

Entrepreneur and marketing expert, Seth Godin, notes, "A presentation that doesn't seek to make change is a waste of time and energy. Before you start working on your presentation, the two-part question to answer is, 'who will be changed by this work, and what is the change I seek?'"(2013). The more you know your audience's attitudes and needs, the more likely you are to meet your speaking goal.

ORGANIZE everything in your presentation around a single focus, and send the audience home with one clear message. Organized presentations have an introduction, body, and conclusion—all supporting a thesis. Your thesis presents the main idea of your presentation in one clear sentence. Use the introduction to reveal your thesis, as well as orient your audience to the occasion. Develop the body around a series of points supporting your thesis. Finally, highlight why your thesis is relevant in the conclusion.

Increase the clarity of your message by arranging body points logically. Common ways to organize points are by topics, spaces, time spans, causes/effects, and problems/solutions. Bring points to life by offering examples, stories, explanations, and evidence. Making the point "we are running out of water" becomes far more interesting and engaging when you (1) explain the critical drought situation, (2) provide evidence showing water could run out within five years, and (3) demonstrate the effect of water shortage on food supplies.

Finally, use language with accuracy, expression, and style. Experiment with varied word choices, expand your vocabulary, and employ language your audience will understand. As you practice for your presentation, strive for fluency by banishing meaningless—like, you know—words. Every word should be a contributor.

PRACTICE your presentation to increase confidence and polish. Practice over time, not just over night. Cramming increases stress. Practice makes you more capable of delivering a confident, fluent, flexible presentation. Up to 90 percent of communication is nonverbal (Mehrabian, 1972). So practice actions and tone, as well as words.

Stand confidently by planting both feet on the ground, centering your weight, and making consistent eye contact. Make friends of mirrors and recording devices. Watch yourself objectively and analyze how you stand, the gestures you use, and what your face is saying. Full engagement of body language should make you feel less stiff and more naturally expressive. If you plan to move around the room, walk with purpose and avoid the temptation to pace.

> **"Ultimately, the presentation is about the message—not you. Once you have a topic, consider your speaking goal."**
>
> **Mary Kate Domino, Winner of 2014 Undergraduate Speaker's Edge**

Speak clearly by speaking in concise sentences and enunciating words.

Practice aloud, not silently to yourself. Time your presentation for a reasonable speaking rate. Project your voice, and breathe. Breathing helps you stay relaxed and supplies your brain with needed oxygen to recall the presentation you designed.

Connect to your audience with a sincere, expressive, conversational style. Avoid reading your speech. Limit speaking notes to key words and phrases. If you practice enough, you will know what you want to say. Standing in front of an audience with limited notes may be a bit unnerving at first, but the more you connect with your audience, the more empowered you will feel.

In general, audiences want you to succeed! When you deliver with confidence, audiences will react favorably. In fact, a study published by the Royal Statistical Society showed some people responded to confident delivery more than accuracy (Smith and Wooten, 2013). Of course, to maintain top credibility you need both. So build your confidence through preparation and rehearsal and give yourself permission to strive for connection instead of perfection during delivery.

Many people do not realize Dr. Martin Luther King, Jr. never planned to say "I have a dream" when he delivered his famous speech from the steps of the Lincoln Memorial in 1963 (Jones and Connelly, 2011). He added the refrain in response to a shout from the crowd, "Tell them about the dream, Martin. Tell them about the dream" (Jones, 2011). Dr. King moved his notes aside and reacted to the moment. "I have a dream," he shared. "I have a dream," he kept repeating. One of the most recognized speeches of the twentieth century followed.

Dr. King did not limit himself to the page; he transcended it.

You, too, can be inspired by the passion to connect your message to the audience. You simply need to be prepared for the moment. So, plan, organize, practice, and present your presentations with all the knowledge and passion you have to share. You can not only empower yourself and enliven your audience, but potentially gain an edge with employers one day when they see your ability and willingness to communicate well.

ABOUT THE AUTHORS

Robert Cummings, *Executive Director of Academic Innovation and Associate Professor of Writing and Rhetoric*

Robert Cummings received his Ph.D. in English from the University of Georgia, and he is the award winning author of *Lazy Virtues: Teaching Writing in the Age of Wikipedia*.

Joann Edwards, *Speech Instructor and Director of Forensics, Department of Writing and Rhetoric*

JoAnn Miller Edwards received her M.A. in theatre arts from the University of Mississippi in 1983. Edwards revived The University of Mississippi Forensics Program within the Trent Lott Leadership Institute in 2000. Since then, the team has garnered regional and national recognition, hosting the American Forensics Association National Tournament in 2003.

Karen Forgette, *Lecturer and Assistant Chair, Department of Writing and Rhetoric*

Karen Forgette's research interests include self-regulated learning, electronic portfolios, service learning, and learning communities. She serves as the coordinator of writing instruction for the FASTrack first-year cohort program at the University. She obtained her M.A. degree from the University of North Carolina – Chapel Hill.

Alice Myatt, *Assistant Professor, Department of Writing and Rhetoric*

Alice Myatt received her Ph.D. in English from Georgia State University with a concentration in visual rhetoric and composition pedagogy, to which she adds her research interests of learning in digital environments, writing pedagogy, and writing center studies.

ABOUT THE AUTHORS

Wendy Goldberg, *Core Lecturer, Writing 102 Curriculum Chair, Department of Writing and Rhetoric*

Wendy Goldberg is the coordinator and chair of the Writing 102 committee and works closely with all Writing 102 instructors. Her research interests include integrating pop culture, including comics and manga, in the classroom. Ms. Goldberg taught for six years at the United States Coast Guard Academy before coming to the University of Mississippi. She received her M.A. from the University of Connecticut.

Kate Hooper, *Core Lecturer of Speech, Department of Writing and Rhetoric*

Kate Hooper utilizes her background in performance and communication education to empower people through confident expression and meaningful connection. She holds an MFA from UCLA's School of Theatre, Film and Television and a graduate certificate in communication education from Minnesota State University, Mankato. Additionally, Kate draws from three decades of experience as a professional performer, coach, sales person, and independent contractor.

Guy Krueger, *Core Lecturer, Writing 101 Curriculum Chair, Department of Writing and Rhetoric*

Guy Krueger's research focuses on basic writing theory and praxis at institutions across America. Additionally, he is interested in assessment and placement in first-year composition (FYC) courses. Krueger has been at the University of Mississippi since 2010. Currently, he is ABD—English with a concentration in rhetoric and composition—Southern Illinois University – Carbondale.

ABOUT THE AUTHORS

Stephen Monroe, *Chair and Assistant Professor, Department of Writing and Rhetoric*

Stephen Monroe is chair and assistant professor in the Department of Writing and Rhetoric at the University of Mississippi, where he is an affiliated faculty member in the Center for the Study of Southern Culture, a steering committee member for the Sarah Isom Center for Women and Gender Studies, and director of the Willie Morris Awards for Southern Writing. His book, *Heritage and Hate: Old South Words and Symbols at Southern Universities*, will be published in June of 2021 as part of the Rhetoric, Culture, and Social Critique series from the University of Alabama Press.

Ellie Moore, *Instructor of Speech and Interim Director of the Specking Center*

Ellie Moore worked as a public speaking instructor for Laredo College in Texas and as a public debate instructor at the Universidad de Concepción in Angol, Araucanía, Chilé. She received her master's degree in communication studies from New Mexico State University in Las Cruces, New Mexico. In 2019, she received her Ed.D. in higher education from the University of Mississippi.

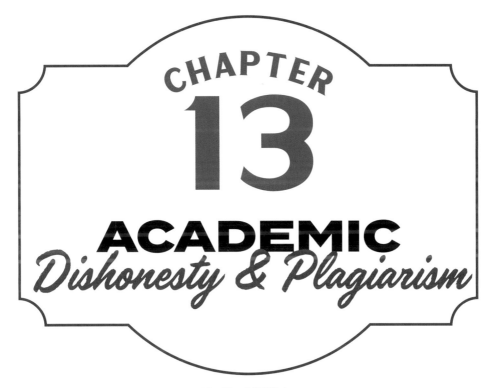

CHAPTER
13
ACADEMIC
Dishonesty & Plagiarism

By Noel Wilkin

We are living in a time when information is more accessible and prolific than in any other time in history. With a smartphone, computer, or tablet, people can find information on just about any topic or subject. This access generally is regarded as a good thing. It is important to realize, however, that while the information around us is wonderfully accessible, it is not ours. Credit for creating it belongs to someone else. My wife and I have a beautiful lithograph of a painting that hangs in our dining room. It is a painting of a farm; I see it every day. We bought it, and it belongs to us. Yet, that does not mean that I can lead people to believe that I painted it. In fact, I do not have the skills, knowledge, tools, or capability to create anything quite that beautiful on a canvas. This painting resulted from the artist's vision, experiences, creativity, and perspectives. What he chose to represent in the painting of the farm was based on his knowledge of farms, a view of an actual farm, and knowledge of what belongs on a farm. He chose to leave some details in, and leave some out. He chose the colors and the perspective. There was a lot of time, effort, and personal perspective that went into this painting. With this example, it seems simple and would seem strange to claim credit for creating the original painting. It should seem just as strange and unusual to claim credit for thoughts, perspectives, and ideas that belong to someone else whether they appear in an image, a painting, an illustration, a poem, a book, or a paragraph.

An individual's ideas, perspectives, skill, and knowledge are reflected in every picture or illustration we see and every phrase that we read. The words used, the structure of the sentences, and the order of information are all the creations of the original author. As a result, by reading and processing the work of others, the information shapes our perspectives and shapes the way we work and live. It also shapes how we think and how we write. This influence on our thoughts, ideas, and perspectives by others is an essential part of education. We learn from the work and creativity of others. Yet, when it is time for us to create, for us to extol our perspectives, the ideas, words, sentences, and creations must be our own.

Why does it matter?

In the example of the painting, if I were to tell people that I painted it, who would care? While it would probably not have much direct impact, it would certainly change people's opinions of me. In addition to perhaps leading people to believe that I was delusional, it would be an outright lie. It would clearly indicate to others that I was dishonest, lacking of character, and not worthy of trust. The same outcomes result when people inappropriately use the work of others and claim credit by presenting it as their own. Let's assume that a class was given an assignment to paint a farm scene and the assignment was to be graded. Simply turning in someone else's work is clearly a shortcut and dishonest. At an obvious level, if this were not discouraged it would be unfair to the other students who put in the effort to complete the assignment on their own. Fairness is not only valued at a societal level, it is an important element of assigning grades within classes. Yet, at an academic institution, dishonesty is a more egregious violation.

Your ideas, words, and creations must be your own.

While studying at the University, you are a member of a community that places tremendous value on getting things right, striving for truth, and being sincere (Horacek, 2009). Horacek (2009) argued that academic integrity is not simply a nice attribute of academic institutions, it is "absolutely necessary for getting difficult

The University of Mississippi creed emphasizes:

- dignity
- fairness
- integrity
- honesty
- stewardship

things done" (p. 12). Researchers at academic institutions struggle to discover the truth about our world and about our past, and make truthful predictions about our future. This new knowledge is not simply a blogger's opinion on reality. It is the foundational knowledge upon which people in our society base decisions, live our lives, and choose our actions. Asking and answering questions in principled and methodical ways (like the scientific method), are the hallmarks of this search for truth.

Getting it right is critical. As a student at the University, you are not only receiving an education, you also are a participant or initiate into this community of researchers (Horacek, 2009). These perspectives of fairness, integrity, and academic honesty are represented in the University's creed:

The University of Mississippi is a community of learning dedicated to nurturing excellence in intellectual inquiry and personal character in an open and diverse environment. As a voluntary member of this community:

I believe in respect for the dignity of each person.

I believe in fairness and civility.

I believe in personal and professional integrity.

I believe in academic honesty.

I believe in academic freedom.

I believe in good stewardship of our resources.

I pledge to uphold these values and encourage others to follow my example.

Standards and procedures

In addition to the Creed, which succinctly describes the University community's values and communicates to our community the ideals that we believe are fundamental to our success, we also have policies that outline what happens when academic honesty, fairness, and professional integrity are violated.

Standards of honesty

The University is conducted on a basis of common honesty. Dishonesty, cheating, or plagiarism, or knowingly furnishing false information to the University are regarded as particularly serious offenses. Disruptive behavior in an academic situation or purposely harming academic facilities also is grounds for academic discipline (Student Academic Conduct and Discipline, 2010).

This standard reflects the values of the community and is based on the premise that honesty is at the heart of our mission. Protecting it and ensuring it is a responsibility that is taken very seriously.

When violations occur, these policies guide appropriate discipline. The purpose of these policies and the associated discipline are to ensure preservation of a community that is conducive to the goals of the institution. As stated in the University's Academic Conduct and Discipline Policy, "The broad purpose underlying student discipline is to order University living in such a way that the interests of the student body as a whole and of the individual members are best served" (Student Academic Conduct and Discipline, 2010). This statement reinforces the fundamental philosophy regarding the discipline of students. Discipline is used to ensure that the interests of the institution are protected, and the interests of the student body and community as a whole hinge upon honesty.

Different universities will have similar expectations for academic honesty, although they might have different standards of discipline or processes by which cases of academic dishonesty are evaluated and sanctioned. Probably one of the most notable standards is that of the University of Virginia. Their honor code system dates back to 1842, and guilt results in expulsion from the university. "Any student found guilty of an Honor offense, or deemed to have admitted guilt after having left without requesting a trial, will be permanently dismissed from the University" (Honor Code at UVa, 2010).

Standards of Honesty

The University is conducted on a basis of common honesty.

. . .

Dishonesty, cheating, or plagiarism, or knowingly furnishing false information to the University are regarded as particularly serious offenses.

. . .

Disruptive behavior in an academic situation or purposely harming academic facilities also is grounds for academic discipline.

. . .

("Student Academic Conduct and Discipline," 2010)

Discipline of academic dishonesty at the University of Mississippi begins between the faculty member and the student. Upon discovery of academic dishonesty, faculty members will recommend a sanction after a discussion with the student. There are many possible sanctions that can be imposed or recommended. A few examples include failure on the work, failure in the course, grade reduction in the course, probation, suspension, and expulsion. If the faculty member is recommending a sanction of probation, suspension, or expulsion, then the chair, the appropriate dean, the registrar, the provost, and the vice chancellor for student affairs are notified. The provost will notify the registrar, who then will contact the student if the sanction is probation or suspension. The chancellor is notified by the provost if the recommended sanction is expulsion. The chancellor then contacts the registrar, who then will contact the student (Student Academic Conduct and Discipline, 2010). The student has the right to challenge the sanction through a process of appeal. Some schools within the University of Mississippi maintain honor code systems with their own processes. These include the schools of law, pharmacy, and engineering.

For the other schools and the college, this process is handled by the Academic Discipline Committee. Students should refer to the policy for specifics on this process and the timeline requirements for filing an appeal.

Academic dishonesty

The University houses a wide variety of diverse subjects and disciplines. Each subject fosters the discovery of truth and advancement of knowledge in many different ways. The disciplines, or subject areas, rely upon different methods of helping students grasp new concepts, and each offers students the opportunity to learn different information, content, and strategies of knowing. As a result, it is difficult to provide one definition that will encompass all examples of academic dishonesty. Definitions of academic dishonesty most often include two parameters: (1) "unauthorized assistance" and (2) "the work is graded" (Garavalia, Olson, Russell, & Christensen, 2007, p. 34). Examples of unauthorized assistance can include anything that is helpful in completing the assignment and forbidden by the instructor. It is easy to think of common examples like access to information during exams, looking on another's test during an exam, and obtaining the answers from others. Of course, this is differentiated from assistance that is commonly authorized such as the use of books in the library for the purpose of writing papers, appropriate assistance from team members in team-based assignments or work, a calculator in certain situations, etc. Therefore, the first step to understanding what is appropriate is to understand what assistance is authorized in given assignments. The second criterion involves the grading of the work. Assignments and exams help instructors to understand how a student is performing in a given course. They allow for the assignment of grades that are based on the student's performance and provide feedback to the students as to how well they are performing in the course. Use of unauthorized assistance affords the student an advantage that is not available to all students and violates the University's value of fairness. It also results in an inappropriate grading of the student's work and an inappropriate (i.e., unfair) assignment of a grade. As a result, instructors have a responsibility to the students they teach and to those who hire graduates to ensure that students are acquiring the knowledge and skills necessary to be successful; grade assignment is an indicator of successful acquisition of the knowledge and skills taught in the class. Assignments, papers, examinations, quizzes, and other assessment tools are essential to determine whether students are learning the material being taught and developing the skills commensurate with the grade assigned. This responsibility increases the importance of remaining vigilant in detecting, preventing, and disciplining cases of academic dishonesty by students.

Some schools within The University of Mississippi maintain honor code systems with their own processes. These include the schools of law, pharmacy, and engineering.

The University's standards of honesty specifically mention types of dishonest behaviors – cheating, plagiarism, or knowingly furnishing false information to the University. In each instance, these behaviors provide some form of unauthorized assistance, and the information is used to grade or assess the student. In instances of cheating, such as doing someone else's homework, purchasing a paper written by someone else, and copying answers during a test, it is easy to see how these behaviors gain an individual an unfair advantage and many can see why this is unauthorized assistance – thus making these examples of academic dishonesty. Similarly, providing false information to the University (e.g., giving inappropriate ACT scores, forging transcripts to provide false GPAs) seems reasonably straightforward as being dishonest and gaining unearned or inappropriate advantages. Other examples of academic dishonesty mentioned in the policy and other places (Types of Plagiarism, 2010; Garavalia, et. al, 2007) are included on the next page. Plagiarism, while in some instances may seem straightforward, can be more difficult to understand. Please note that academic dishonesty is not limited to these examples. However, this list is meant to describe the breadth of behaviors and activities that fall into the category of academic dishonesty. (See examples.)

Plagiarism

Those in academia have a high standard of scrutiny towards plagiarism, and yet, different academic disciplines will have different standards and different expectations when it comes to citations (Anderson, 1998) and to defining and assessing plagiarism (Blum, 2009). Blum attributed this high standard to the need to link information and build upon the foundation of others. "Proper academic citation provides a way for authors to trace their influences, to situate themselves intellectually, to prove that they have done their background theoretical reading, to demonstrate engagement in an ongoing community of inquiry, and to provide sources for readers who want to consult earlier thinkers or data" (Blum, 2009, p. 14).

While studying at the University, students should keep this in mind and realize their professors have this perspective when reviewing assignments and grading papers. As a professor, I expect students to provide that window into their reasoning when writing papers and completing projects. I also expect them to provide accurate citations of their sources. This allows me to fully assess the content of their work, the thought process that they had in completing the work, and the strategies used to assemble resources used to complete the work – hence it allows me to assess their ability.

A simple definition of plagiarism is, "the act of using the words of another without giving the originator credit" (Anderson, 1998, p. 1). Plagiarism "refers to appropriating any material – ideas, writings, images, or portions of those – and claiming to be the original creator" (Gilmore, 2008, p. 2).

SOME SPECIFIC EXAMPLES OF ACADEMIC DISHONESTY*

- Plagiarism
- Copying another's homework
- Allowing someone to copy or use your homework
- Copying answers to test questions
- Allowing others to do your work or homework
- Allowing someone to take your exam for you
- Handing in a paper that was purchased
- Handing in a paper written by someone else
- Taking a test for someone else
- Attempting to gain possession of a test prior to its administration
- Accessing unauthorized computer files, reference materials, files, previously completed work, notes during exams
- Stealing books or other University resources (from the library, museum, computer center, or other University facility)
- Harming or causing damage to facilities that support the academic environment
- Damage to books, laboratory equipment, computers, laboratories, or other facilities
- Fabricating references or citations
- Paraphrasing without acknowledgement
- Accessing an office without authorization in an attempt to gain an advantage
- Employing bribery, intimidation, or harassment in an attempt to gain an unfair advantage
- Falsely attesting that work has been completed when it has not been completed
- Falsely claiming attendance at functions or classes
- Falsely claiming attendance of others at functions or classes
- Altering grade reports
- Changing grade forms or class rolls
- Altering, falsifying, or misusing University documents
- Falsifying research data
- Disruptive behavior in class or at University functions
- Physically or verbally harassing an instructor or fellow student
- Interfering with an instructor's ability to teach or students' to learn
- Copying from the Internet

*Sources: (Student Academic Conduct and Discipline, 2010; Types of Plagiarism, 2010; and Garavalia, et. al, 2007) * Academic dishonesty is not limited to the examples in this list.*

Like many offenses, there is a range of plagiarism that can take place. Blum (2009) proposed a range that stretches from "deceptive" to "uninformed" (p. 27). Deceptive plagiarism examples would include "buying a paper" or "using someone's freely given paper" (Blum, 2009, p. 27). On the other end of the spectrum is uninformed plagiarism that would include "imperfect mastery of citation conventions" (Blum, 2009, p. 27). It could be argued that at the college level, students should have a good idea as to what should be cited and the manner in which it should be cited, or have the ability and motivation to look it up or ask the instructor. Learning about how to appropriately cite is still taking place in college. Students should become familiar with the reference style appropriate for their disciplines to ensure proper citation strategies and notations when using other people's work (e.g., Lipson, 2006; Hacker, 2009).

If an instructor suspects that some of a student's work has been plagiarized, the policy dictates a meeting with the student. Without a full analysis of the situation, it is difficult for an instructor to know where on the continuum a particular offense might fall. It may be easy to assume that the student has had unauthorized assistance on graded work. The policy requires a discussion with the student for the purpose of assessing where the offense falls on the scale and whether it matches the criteria for being considered academic dishonesty.

Strategies to prevent or avoid plagiarism

Students are encouraged to take active steps to prevent inadvertent or unintentional plagiarism. The prolific amount of information and ease of access, in addition to the need to support one's arguments and assertions with foundational knowledge, raises the importance of knowing how to appropriately use the thoughts and words of others to do one's own work. In writing, there are three options when using the ideas of others to support your work – quote and cite the original authors, paraphrase and cite the original authors, and summarize and cite the original authors. The pivotal role that citation plays increases the importance of learning an appropriate citation style for the discipline of study. Some of the more commonly used citation styles are the American Psychological Association (APA) Style, the Modern Language Association (MLA) system of citations, the *Chicago Manual of Style*, and others. Two concise references on citation style include *A Writer's Reference* by Hacker and *Cite Right* by Lipson.

Discerning when it is most appropriate to quote, paraphrase, or summarize words and ideas is an important skill eclipsed only by the importance of knowing how to appropriately do each. Some inappropriately assume that only full sentences borrowed from another source need to be quoted (Howard, 1999). Even the act of copying phrases (three- to five-word sections of sentences) from other sources patched together with synonyms or abbreviated thoughts based on the original author's work is considered plagiarism. While there is some debate over this type of writing, which has been called "patchwriting," and its role in learning to write, it meets the criteria for plagiarism (Howard, 1999, p. 11). Writers' references and handbooks are good sources of learning strategies for appropriate paraphrasing and summarizing. "A summary condenses information; a paraphrase reports information in about the same number of words as the source" (Hacker, 2009, p. 420). (Please note that Hacker [2009] is the reference used by the University's Center for Writing and Rhetoric.) These strategies espoused in writers' handbooks also assist in learning how to avoid this type of patchwriting when paraphrasing or summarizing. Because both should be in your own words, perhaps the most valuable recommendation is to "set the source aside, write from memory, and consult the source later for accuracy" (Hacker, 2009, p. 421). Additionally, the University's librarians have created a tutorial on plagiarism (Research Help Tutorial: Plagiarism and Academic Honesty, 2010).

Students are likely to improve their ability to appropriately cite supporting source information if they take the time to learn about plagiarism. There are no shortcuts to doing your own work; if it feels like a shortcut, then it probably is not appropriate. Allowing ample time to do the work correctly, cognitively reflecting on the body of information assembled, gathering all of the appropriate and authorized resources, and taking careful notes also are important strategies. Sloppiness and failure to take the time to appropriately reference materials as you take notes based on other sources can easily lead to inadvertent plagiarism. Once the information is extracted it is difficult to remember from where it came. As you take notes from sources and incorporate information, quotations and citations should be carefully noted.

Finally, don't hesitate to ask the instructor to clarify the materials that are approved, what citation style is appropriate, for assistance. Help is available from the instructor, from reference librarians, from the Writing Center, and from the Center for Writing and Rhetoric.

ABOUT THE AUTHORS

Noel Wilkin, *Provost and Executive Vice Chancellor for Academic Affairs, Professor in Pharmacy Administration, and Research Professor in the Research Institute of Pharmaceutical Sciences.*

Noel Wilkin received his B.S. and Ph.D. from the University of Maryland. Dr. Wilkin's areas of research include practical reasoning and its role in decision making, mechanisms to enhance optimal drug therapy, pharmacy entrepreneurship and management, and issues facing professional education.

CHAPTER 14

COMMUNICATION
and Technology

By Nishanth Rodrigues and Ryan Whittington
Additional contributions by Emma Gaddy and Webb Lewis

S tudents today live in a world of instant communication and immediate access to information. In fact, it is not unusual for students to be more comfortable with the use of technology than their instructors. After all, you were born into a world saturated with video games, personal computers, mobile devices, smart phones, and the World Wide Web, whereas previous generations began using these technologies as adults.

The EDUCAUSE Center for Applied Research (ECAR) Study of Undergraduate Students and Information Technology is a comprehensive study of technology use among undergraduate students. The 2019 report noted that students believe technology is critical to academic success and that they bring to campus a variety of small, portable, network-enabled devices. According to the study, 93 percent of students own laptops, 96 percent own smartphones, and 57 percent own tablets. Add to this e-readers, gaming devices, smartwatches, Internet of things, and students typically bring two, three, or four networked devices to campus—or more! Among the technology-based tools that students use are the library website, learning management systems such as Blackboard, e-textbooks, productivity tools, and software to manage citations and e-portfolios. In fact, the study found that most students (58 percent) said that learning works best for them when courses incorporate at least some online components. The majority of students agreed that their instructors typically use tech to engage them in the learning process (66%), use technology to enhance learning with additional materials (67%), and encourage the use of online tools to communicate/collaborate with the instructor or students in or outside class (62%); these responses were consistent across institution type and size. Technology is embedded in students' lives in all sorts of ways, such as to communicate with instructors and peers, access learning management systems, take notes in class, and much more. Patterns of technology use among UM students are similar to the national trends reported in the ECAR study.

What does this mean for you as a UM student?

For one, it means that there are incredibly exciting new ways for you to learn, communicate with instructors and friends, and engage in campus life. However, it also means that you need to be cautious with technologies or services that are new and unfamiliar to you. This chapter offers information and advice on navigating the Internet in ways that are most beneficial to you.

TECHNOLOGY AT OLE MISS

The "online" UM campus is rich with technology services for taking care of business and staying connected. The campus portal, **myOleMiss** (my.olemiss.edu), is a place where you can register for classes, accept financial aid awards, check midterm and final grades, order transcripts, and much more. Many UM instructors use **Blackboard** (blackboard.olemiss.edu) to post assignments and other class information. Some instructors use personal response systems or "clickers" in class to increase student engagement. You can check your email using **UM Gmail** (mail.go.olemiss.edu), and you can find out about campus news and events through **UM Today**, an online announcement board that includes messages relevant to you. **UM Box** (olemiss.box.com) is a cloud-based file storage and collaboration service where you can store documents, work with other students on group projects, and more. Features include the ability to automatically synchronize documents with your computing device (Box Drive) for a worry-free back up of your data. **RebAlert** is a notification system in which UM students receive text messages in cases of campus-wide class cancellations or emergencies. The **Ole Miss News** site (news.olemiss.edu) has the latest news and human interest stories from the University. Almost all of these services have mobile-friendly versions. An online map of campus (map.olemiss.edu) offers easy and quick access to information for building locations services, construction zones, parking, etc.

Any technology assistance is offered through our **Help Desk** (olemiss.edu/help-desk) located in Weir Hall. Self-help is available on the website.

OLE MISS SUPPORT TOOLS

WebID and password: Your Web ID is the same as your University email name (the part of your email address before the "@" symbol).

For example:

Email Address: johndoe@go.olemiss.edu

Web ID: johndoe

Your WebID and password give you access to myOleMiss, email, Blackboard, the campus wireless network, and many other services. Never share your password with anyone else, and don't access the account of another person. A comprehensive list of restrictions and cautions is available in the IT Appropriate Use Policy (olemiss.edu/ause.html).

Getting Started: You need an Internet browser to begin using Blackboard. Blackboard can be accessed via your University of Mississippi Web ID and password by visiting: blackboard.olemiss.edu/ You also can find a link to Blackboard at the bottom of the Ole Miss Homepage. Once you have signed on to Blackboard, the my UM home page displays the following six default modules: My Announcements; My Courses; My Tasks; On Demand Help and Learning Catalog; Report Card; Tools. You can personalize which modules display by selecting Personalize Page on the upper right side of the home page.

> ## Blackboard (Bb)
>
> What exactly is Blackboard? It is a social media software tool used in many courses at the University of Mississippi. Blackboard allows instructors to post content for a course, including assignments, article links, attendance, grades, syllabus, videos, and announcements. Blackboard also accommodates blogs, discussion boards, and journals for teaching purposes.

My Courses: Click on an individual course in the My Courses module to display the course home page with six menu items on the left side of the webpage: Homepage; Content; Discussion; Groups; Tools; Help. Instructors for individual courses might choose to add additional menu options such as Assignments or Information, or give different names to the existing menu options.

Some features of the menu on the left include the ability to access and submit assignments, view the syllabus, view grades, and email the instructor or other members of the class. If you do not see your course listed, it may be because your instructor has not yet made the site available. If you have registered for the course, check back later. Contact your instructor if the course is not available when the semester begins.

On Demand Help and Learning Catalog: This section of the Blackboard home page provides resources for using and understanding the many capabilities of Blackboard technology. Here you can find tutorials, short video clips, and other guides to help you navigate Blackboard. Additional technical assistance is available through the University of Mississippi Information Technology Helpdesk. Contact the Helpdesk via email (helpdesk@olemiss.edu) or telephone (662-915-5222).

Blackboard App (Highly Recommended): You can sync Blackboard to your smart phone by downloading the Blackboard app. One of the main advantages of having this application on your phone is that you will receive notifications regarding grades, course announcements, and content posting. For instance, if one of your instructors uploads a PowerPoint presentation that will be covered in class, you will receive an immediate notification, which will allow you enough time to read through and print the document to bring to class. Getting immediate notifications of course updates is a valuable tool, as it helps track your progress in your classes.

Ole Miss Email: Your Ole Miss Gmail account is a critical component of your life as an Ole Miss student. Through this account, you receive official communication from the University, as well as important notices from your instructors. As a student, you are expected to check your email at least twice a day, and faculty assume that you have received and read any communication sent via email. "I didn't get the email" is never an acceptable excuse, so make sure to check it frequently!

The IT Helpdesk website provides you with more information about your Gmail account at olemiss.edu/helpdesk/. Under the Frequently Asked Questions section, you can learn how to sync your Ole Miss email to your smart phone, so that you get immediate notifications upon receiving an email. It is strongly encouraged that you sync your email to your smart phone. You also may choose to forward your Ole Miss emails to your personal email account.

Lastly, it is wise to keep a separate email account for your personal emails so as to reduce the amount of spam and other non-academic information you receive.

myOleMiss: One of the most important features of your myOleMiss portal is access to course registration (you can read more about this in the Academic Advising chapter of this text). In addition to allowing you to register for classes, myOleMiss allows you to pay Bursar bills, apply for certain scholarships, accept financial aid awards, check your midterm and final grades, read and submit teacher evaluations, and check your registration holds. You are encouraged to take time at the beginning of the semester to become familiar with all of the tools offered through the myOleMiss portal.

LiveSafe App: The University has a partnership with LiveSafe, a mobile safety communications application. LiveSafe is a free mobile safety app that allows faculty, staff, students, parents, alumni, and even visitors at Ole Miss to report nonemergency or anonymous tips to the University Police Department (UPD). The app is available for free download for both iOS and Android devices. More information about the app is available at olemiss.edu/livesafe.

TECHNOLOGY BEYOND THE OLE MISS CAMPUS

Countless communication services and tools are available outside of the campus intranet. Popular social media networking sites such as Facebook, Twitter, Instagram, and LinkedIn, allow members of the Ole Miss family to connect with individuals and communities around the world. Messaging applications such as SnapChat, WhatsApp, and Facebook Messenger allow for even more intrapersonal commentary. Wikipedia (wikipedia.org) is one of the most well-known "wikis," or networks of interrelated online documents and information. Instant messaging is a popular way to communicate in real time using text-based tools, whereas software applications such as Google Hangouts (hangouts.google.com) and Zoom (olemiss.zoom.us) allow for voice and video conversations over the Internet.

PRIVACY AND PERSONAL SAFETY

With the abundance of online interaction comes new and challenging concerns related to privacy and personal safety. Listed next are some practical suggestions for protecting yourself online. See also the IT Security website (itsecurity.olemiss.edu), which contains recent alerts, security basics, tools, and resources.

- **Use discretion when posting information.** Don't announce that you are alone or out of town even among Facebook friends. Don't post or email anything that you wouldn't want to share with the public, including your parents, instructors, or potential employers. A common mistake is to inadvertently send a message to the wrong recipient, for example through automatic word-completion capabilities in email programs. Information posted online can be immediately duplicated and forwarded, creating a lasting record that cannot be erased.

- **Never give out private information.** Numerous "phishing" scams exist to try to extract personal information from you for the purpose of stealing your identity or your money. Often they are designed to direct you to a bogus website that looks very similar to the website for a legitimate institution. Never give out your social security number or password, and only give out your credit card information when you are absolutely sure that the site is trustworthy. The University will never ask you for personal information via email.

- **Manage your privacy settings.** Most social networking sites such as Facebook allow you to control who has access to your information. Take the time to learn what these settings mean and then proactively manage them to help protect your identity. Even so, remember that technology is not flawless. Properly-controlled privacy settings can occasionally fail and are therefore no substitute for practicing good judgment about what should and should not be posted on the Internet. Occasionally "Google" yourself to see what information is posted for public viewing.

- **Think about the impact to your reputation.** It is not unusual for employers to "Google" applicants to gain insight into their personalities and values. Be especially careful with any photographs that you post, and think about the impression they create with viewers who may or may not know the circumstances or setting. Keep in mind that once information has been posted on the Internet, it is virtually impossible to delete. Read the accompanying section in this Chapter ("The Good, the Bad, and the Awful of Social Media") to see some real-world examples of poor reputation management.

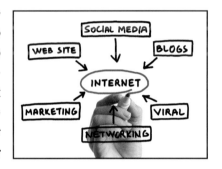

BE A GOOD CITIZEN ONLINE

Netiquette, or Network Etiquette, is a set of accepted practices that have evolved over the last 20 years defining good behavior on the Internet. There are many good books and articles that provide detailed netiquette guidelines. A few of the most important conventions for communicating in cyberspace are noted here.

Internet shorthand

When you send text messages or communicate online you will find a multitude of abbreviations and codes that serve as shorthand. There are several good sources for finding out what these mean, including NetLingo (netlingo.com). Common examples are bff for best friends forever, lol for laughing out loud, and idk for I don't know. Likewise, there is a convention in which writing in ALL CAPS means that you are SHOUTING.

Flame wars and spam

Be careful what you sign up for online. If you are faced with an enticing service that requests personal information and is not one that you went looking for, there may be a possibility that this service could "sell" your information to other third parties and result in additional SPAM coming your way.

Stay informed!

Be sure to check your Ole Miss email, including UM Today, daily. UM Today is used to communicate pertinent information about events on campus. Also, if you want to receive RebAlert emergency notifications, verify that your cell phone number is listed correctly in myOleMiss by going to Student -> My Profile and selecting Contact Information.

Respect others online

The UM Creed (https://olemiss.edu/info/creed.html) sets expectations for treating others with fairness, respect, and dignity. These expectations are just as relevant and important in the digital world as they are on the physical UM campus. Just as it is never acceptable in "real life" to threaten, harass, embarrass, or otherwise target another person, it is absolutely unacceptable to do these things using the Internet, digital technologies, or mobile phones. The UM Creed also sets expectations for good stewardship of resources. These expectations apply to digital environments, especially as related to network bandwidth usage and data storage.

Keep in mind that once information has been posted on the Internet, it is virtually impossible to delete. Party pictures you post today may well turn up in Google searches ten years from now.

Illegal downloads, copyright infringement, and cryptocurrency mining

Copyright law limits the right of a user to copy, download, distribute, edit, or transmit electronically another person's intellectual property, including written materials, images, videos, software, games, sounds, music, and performances, without permission. Violations of copyright law may include giving others unauthorized access to copyrighted materials by posting that material on social networking sites, or downloading from Internet websites or through Peer-to-Peer (P2P) file sharing any material owned by another without the owner's permission. Even if you do not intend to engage in infringing activity, installing P2P software on a computer easily can result in you unintentionally sharing files (copyrighted music, movies, or even sensitive documents) with other P2P users, and you may then be personally responsible for the legal and financial consequences.

University resources must not be used for personal financial gain. As such, community members are prohibited from using university resources (including computing equipment, network services, and electricity) for cryptocurrency mining activities outside of faculty-sanctioned research and course work.

Computer use and wellness

Social networking sites, video games, and other kinds of technology can be a fun way to stay connected with friends and entertain yourself, but when used excessively they can distract you from what is really important. Internet tools can enhance learning but when used in class independently from the instructor, e.g., to check BuzzFeed, read the *Daily Mississippian* online, or send and receive text messages, they can cause you to miss important concepts. It is easy to become overwhelmed with the amount of information that is being streamed to you. Finding a good balance between online communication and face-to-face relationships is essential, both personally and professionally. Learning to filter out the "noise" and even going "offline" periodically are critical to your personal productivity and overall sense of well-being.

The University's commitment is also reflected in the work of the UM Energy Committee and Active Transportation Committee, as well as in the newly updated UM Master Plan, which provides guidelines for sustainable growth at the university.

Last Words of Advice

Just like many other new experiences during your first year at Ole Miss, navigating these different online systems may be overwhelming. Remember that your instructors and advisors are here to help you, so do not hesitate to ask them questions about these systems. Your EDHE instructor is an excellent resource to help you become familiar with Blackboard, myOleMiss, and your Ole Miss email account.

EMAIL ETIQUETTE

It seems that the more popular and expansive social media and smartphone technology become, the less capable we are in producing appropriate and effective email communication. Many students equate email with the forms of communication they use more frequently (such as texting, tweeting, and Facebook messages), and they assume that email in college is just as casual. Big mistake, but easy to fix!

Consider your audience. When you send a text or tweet, it is most likely to a friend or family member. In college, emails are typically how you communicate with professors and instructors, potential employers, or administrators.

The email you send influences people's opinions of you and can influence the type of treatment you receive as a student. If you send inappropriate, offensive, or poorly written messages, professors and administrators usually remember them and you, but not in a good way.

Email Etiquette Basics Dos and Don'ts:

The Basics:
- Be concise and to the point.
- Answer all questions.
- Use proper spelling, grammar, and punctuation.
- Use complete sentences.
- Use proper structure.
- Use gender neutral language.
- Use correct name with appropriate title.
- Use his or her name with the appropriate title: Dr., Professor, Ms./Mrs./Miss, or Mr.
- Be sure to spell the name correctly.
- Address the person receiving the message properly
- Identify who you are.
- Use a signature.

The Don'ts
- Overuse the high priority option.
- Write in ALL CAPITALS.
- Leave out the message thread.
- Send an email without reading it first.
- Overuse Reply to All.

- Use abbreviations and emoticons.
- Forward chain letters or virus hoaxes.
- Request delivery and read receipts.
- Ask to recall a message.
- Discuss confidential information.
- Send or forward messages containing libelous, defamatory, offensive, racist, or obscene remarks.

Subject Lines
- The subject line should help the person receiving the message understand the reason for the message.
- Include a specific question or concern.
- Include a class assignment or title.
- Do not the leave the subject line empty.

Beginning Body
- The next sentence should explain who you are.
- Teachers or faculty members may be teaching hundreds students or several sections of the same course.
- Always sign your name at the bottom of the message; include your ID number.
- It is your job to explain who you are!

Incorrect Example:

Hey!!!

I didn't hear my alarm this morning and slept in. Oops! Did I miss anything important in class?

Correct Example:

Dear Ms. Morgenstern:

I overslept this morning and missed our EDHE class, section 106. I am really sorry and promise it will not happen again. I have gotten the class notes from Taylor and will be in class Wednesday morning, ready for the test. Again, I apologize for missing class.

Sincerely, John Brown #001-29-456

Professional Email Addresses and Signatures

Use your Ole Miss email address when communicating with University faculty and staff. If you must use a different personal address, remember that readers can see it, and they won't be impressed with your maturity if your personal address is kutiegurl@yahoo.com.

Never assume that your reader will know who you are without a proper email signature. Too often students treat email like texting and forget that their email address is NOT automatically connected to a name. I've heard many professors say that when they get a message from an email address that doesn't immediately reference a student name, they simply ignore it and move on. Their time is valuable, and they won't waste it trying to track down your identity. Provide your full name (not a nickname) and your student ID number at the end of your email message, and you will likely get a response.

Avoid personal statements about politics, religion, and other controversial topics in your email signature when communicating with faculty, staff, or current or potential employers. It is easy to delete these before you press send, and you avoid the risk of offending your recipient.

Subject Lines

Always provide a brief explanation of the nature of your email, such as "question about group project" in the subject line. An additional tip: Avoid subject lines that use phrases such as "urgent request." At best it annoys a professor when you've waited until the last minute, and at worst it makes them less likely to respond at all.

Greetings and Complimentary Close

"Hey!" is not an appropriate way to begin an email to a professor or staff member. Use "Dear Professor (insert his or her last name). If the recipient is a staff member or instructor, use the name provided on the course syllabus, or use the University directory to get the correct name. If you cannot find a name or are not sure of correct spelling, open with Dear "Sir" or "Madam." To close, use a common complimentary close such as "Sincerely," or "Yours truly."

Content

Be concise. If your question or request is buried in the third paragraph, it is possible that your recipient will never read that far. If you must include a lot of information, break it into short paragraphs or bullet points.

DO NOT use slang, text message abbreviations, emoticons, all caps, profanity, or any offensive language in an email. This is not a text message or your friend's Twitter account. Think of your emails as college papers. Write in complete sentences with correct grammar and punctuation, use spellcheck, and *always* proofread for errors. Your recipient will be impressed, and you will increase your chances of getting the response you need.

Remember

Always check to make sure you have typed the correct email address so your message gets to the intended recipient. Check your syllabus to see if your professor has rules about email, such as where to send it, what type of attachments are acceptable, etc. Do not assume your professor can open any attachment. If you are unsure, always ask well in advance of the assignment deadline and make other arrangements if necessary.

Email is forever. Always read your message before you send it. If you are upset, calm down before composing an email you might later regret. Once the message is sent, you cannot take it back.

Always acknowledge an email or reply from professors, staff members assisting you, potential employers, etc. When a professor goes out of his or her way to assist you and never receives an acknowledgment or thank you...it is remembered. A simple thank you now can equal a glowing recommendation letter in the future.

The Good, the Bad, and the Awful of Social Media

As an institution of higher education in the 21st century, we would be remiss if we did not talk about social media and the role it plays in dictating your personal and professional reputation. As members of Generation Z, you have all grown up using social media. In fact, a January 2018 Pew Research Center study found that 88 percent of online adults between the ages of 18–29 use Facebook, and 64% of all Internet users within that same age range use Instagram.

Thanks to smartphones and a world that has come to expect instant communication, your tweets, status updates, snaps, and Instagram stories can be shared across the Internet in a matter of seconds. While technology and social media have the ability to make our lives much easier in so many different ways, they also come with more than their fair share of pitfalls.

Social Media Crises on Campus

The University of Mississippi and its student body experienced the pitfalls of social media following election night in November 2012. Shortly after 10 p.m. on the evening of November 6, 2012, Ole Miss students took to social media to share their thoughts on the election and to describe a verbal exchange between supporters of Gov. Mitt Romney and President Barack Obama. What began as political speech turned into ugly incidents of racially charged speech fed in part by students' use of social media. In fact, the political exchange was soon being described on social media as a "riot."

Student tweets exaggerating, even fictionalizing, what happened and the resulting media coverage reached millions of people around the world, creating a sense with many observers that a riot actually had occurred at Ole Miss. The situation could have been avoided if those involved had reminded themselves that you cannot believe everything you read on Twitter, and you should not re-tweet information you don't know to be accurate.

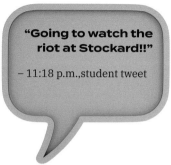

"Going to watch the riot at Stockard!!"

– 11:18 p.m.,student tweet

The rise of anonymous social platforms such as Yik Yak also have proven problematic on many educational campuses. In 2014, more than a dozen high schools and colleges charged students with threats of violence after "yaks" were made on the app. Almost all of these incidents were pranks, but to administrators and the authorities, all were quite serious. Students who made these threats felt that they were unable to be traced. However, Yik Yak personnel were cooperative with school officials and turned over IP addresses and GPS locations of those individuals, which led to felony charges and arrests.

These events proved detrimental for students, faculty, staff, alumni, and fans at all institutions, and while these are only a handful of examples, the bottom line is that students should never make false comments online—no matter the platform.

PRIVACY AND PERSONAL SAFETY

Reputation management

Have you ever typed your name into a Google search? If not, now is a good time to do it. It is not uncommon for potential employers, graduate school admissions offices, scholarship committees, and yes, even your parents, to seek out information about you on the Internet.

A Google search of a person's name can return photographs, status updates, and biographical information posted to any number of different social networking profiles. An embarrassing photograph or distasteful video taken at a party and posted on social media could restrict you from future job interviews, promotions, and certain career fields. Remember that screen grabs and other technologies have made it virtually impossible to remove anything from the Internet.

On the evening of March 7, 2015, members of the Sigma Alpha Epsilon fraternity at the University of Oklahoma learned firsthand just how disastrous their words could be for their organization, their university, and their fellow students. That night, members of the group were filmed singing a racist song on a bus. The nine-second video made its way to a number of different social media channels and quickly went viral. It sparked outrage nationwide and ultimately led to the closure of the University of Oklahoma SAE chapter and the expulsion of two fraternity members.

While both the university and the organization were swift to react to the heinous video, the long-term repercussions for the members of the fraternity and those targeted in the community remain. According to the parents of one of the students expelled, their son "made a horrible mistake and will live with the consequences forever."

Plenty of stories exist about individuals who later regret what they post to their personal social media profiles. But keep in mind, just because you land that first job or internship doesn't mean you should get lazy on social media.

In February 2016, a daycare employee in Arizona was fired when a controversial Snapchat she sent made its way back to the business's owner. The 19-year-old employee took a photo of her middle finger extended in front of a small child's face with the caption, "swear I love kids." The owner later relieved the employee of her duties.

Best Practices on Social Media

The proper and effective use of social media presents unequaled opportunities for the university community to share our story in an authentic, transparent and timely manner while building richer, more substantive relationships with people we may not have reached through traditional communication  channels. However, knowing a few tips will help you get the most out of your accounts as well as help you avoid any sticky situations on social media.

Give your timeline a "Scrub." A social media scrub is the act of looking through your personal social media history, your timeline, and identifying posts that may not represent who you are today. Some of you have had a social media account for nearly ten years and chances are you are not the same person you were when you began those accounts. As unfair as it may seem, you may be held accountable for something your 11-year-old self posted. Take some time and identify potential problem posts from your past and hide, delete or just make your account private.

Identify your views as your own. As members of the Ole Miss community, the things we say and do reflect directly upon the University. On your personal accounts, be clear to identify your views as your own if you have identified yourself as a member of the University community. A simple disclaimer in your profile is sufficient, such as, "Opinions are mine," or, "All views, posts, and opinions are my own."

Think before you post. Comments made on social media are not only a reflection on you, but also on any group or organization you represent. Remember, everything you post online is public, easily searchable, and will be online forever. Use good grammar when posting online. Mistakes are a reflection of you and your education. That doesn't mean you have to sound robotic, we are in Mississippi so there is nothing wrong with using conversational language. Just remember that your social media post will be the first impression you make with many of your peers, professors and potential employers.

Be respectful. Be constructive and respectful when discussing differing opinions online. Remember that even if your social profile is private, disparaging comments about others can often be traced to the original source. Do not engage in online arguments or debates. In other words, don't "feed the trolls." Your engagement on social media when dealing with differing opinions should be used to raise the level of debate on that space, not to simply take your opponent down by any means necessary.

Be accurate. Keep in mind that not everything you read on social media (or on the Internet) is true. Film director Spike Lee found out the hard way that misinformation can be commonplace on the Internet. In 2012, a man named Marcus D. Higgins used Twitter to inform celebrities of the address of George Zimmerman, a neighborhood watchman accused of shooting and killing teenager Trayvon Martin.

Lee re-tweeted Higgins' tweet to his 240,000-plus followers believing it was accurate. Instead, an elderly Florida couple with the same last name was forced into hiding when Lee shared their address with all of his followers (many of whom shared the address with their followers, and so on.)

Social Media Best Practice

Before your next post to your followers, just remember to think before you post, be respectful and honest, be accurate, and be kind.

LESSONS LEARNED
by Emma Gaddy

The year is 2013, and I am sitting in my 10th grade chemistry class. The principal of my high school walks in, whispers something to the teacher, approaches my desk, and slaps down two pieces of paper in front of me. She says nothing except, "I need to speak with you outside."

Long story short, earlier that week my principal, Mrs. Howard, made a decision that really, really upset me. What did I choose as my outlet to express my anger? Twitter. The two pieces of paper that she so aggressively slapped down on my desk were full-page printouts of my tweets, one of which read, "MRS. HOWARD IS AN IDIOT!" Needless to say, the conversation that happened outside of the classroom door was not a pleasant one, nor was the one I had with my mother that afternoon. This lapse of judgement cost me the respect of many of my peers, teachers, and leaders in the community, whose opinions I valued considerably. Fortunately, I outgrew the fifteen-year-old version of myself who was ignorant to the repercussions of her words. Now, I carefully consider the consequences of my actions before posting or sharing anything on my personal social media pages. Erin Bury, a marketer, entrepreneur, and one of Marketing Magazine's Top 30 Under 30 recipients, said, "Don't say anything online that you wouldn't want plastered on a billboard with your face on it." I know for a fact that if my face ever ends up on a billboard, "I HATE MRS. HOWARD!" are not the words I want shared to the masses.

Currently, I am working as a graduate assistant at University Marketing & Communications, and a part of my job includes interviewing candidates for our Social Media Ambassador program. The very first thing that I and my coworkers do after a student submits a resume is look them up on social media. We ask ourselves, "Does this candidate represent our brand? Are there any red flags? Would they represent our department and university with integrity?" This is common across all areas of the job market. According to a study performed by CareerBuilder in 2017, 70% of employers use social media to screen candidates, and 54% of employers have chosen to not hire a candidate based on their social media profiles. Needless to say, what you post on social media speaks volumes to who you are, both on and offline. Choose to post things that represent the best version of yourself, whatever that may be. Share opinions with discretion and try to understand the impact of your words. Remember, how you represent yourself is how you represent every facet of your life.

Be more discerning than I was at age fifteen. Whether that's archiving those few photos off Instagram that do not show you in the best light, choosing to not comment on every single Facebook post that expresses opinions different from your own, or not calling your principal an idiot on Twitter, it might be the difference between a life of opportunity and a life spent apologizing for your own poor judgement.

USING LINKEDIN

It is incumbent upon students and young professionals in today's ultra-competitive job market to evaluate how best to advertise their skills to potential employers. Whether it is an internship or full-time position you are seeking, social media can help to distinguish you as a top candidate. LinkedIn is one of the most powerful social networking tools available. The business-oriented social networking site launched in May 2003, and serves as a means for professional connections.

Creating a LinkedIn profile is simple and only requires a valid email address. Your LinkedIn profile is a resume that you can customize and is searchable by others. Before creating a LinkedIn profile, make a list of all previous work experience, including the name of the organization, your role within the organization, dates during which you were employed, and skills you acquired during the work. Also list all awards and honors you have previously received, as well as your involvement in any clubs, organizations, or academic societies.

When you are ready to create your LinkedIn profile, keep in mind that potential employers often identify candidates for positions based on work experience, education, and endorsements and connections with other LinkedIn users. Make sure your profile is complete with all of the relevant information. Once you publish your LinkedIn profile, it is time to begin building professional connections. You should request to connect with those who will be beneficial to your job-search goals, such as past supervisors who can endorse your skills, instructors who can speak to your academic credentials, mentors, and other professionals in your intended career field. As you begin to make connections on LinkedIn, consider requesting endorsements from your connections for specific skills that you have mastered. This will help your profile stand out to potential employers.

CONCLUSION

It is hard to believe that social media has been around for less than two decades. Studies now show that more than 95% of college students use at least one social media platform. Facebook has been around now for more than 15 years and continues to command nearly three billion monthly users. Twitter has seen a decline over the past few years but still is used by college students in a news gathering capacity. Instagram continues to grow rapidly among not only college students but also their parents and grandparents who are making the move over to the platform from Facebook. There will always be up and coming platforms like TikTok that make a huge wave out of the gates. Learning all we can about new platforms is important to understanding the impact they can make on us personally and within our campus communities.

Bottom line, social media is here to stay and as it continues to evolve and change the way we communicate, we must be vigilant and create a heightened sense of privacy in how we go about conducting ourselves on these platforms.

ABOUT THE AUTHORS

Emma Gaddy, *Graduate Assistant, University Marketing & Communications*

Emma Gaddy is currently a graduate student working towards her master's in integrated marketing and communications. She works as a graduate assistant at University Marketing & Communications, where she was also a Social Media Ambassador for two years. While earning her bachelor's degree, Emma was a member of the Ole Miss Rebelette dance team, Kappa Delta, and an avid fan of Chaney's Waffle Cone Wednesday. Follow me, let's be friends! @emmacarolg_

Webb Lewis, *Digital Content Specialist, University Marketing & Communications*

Webb Lewis (@WebbLewis21) has been referred to as the "Social Media Guy" around the Ole Miss campus. He is responsible for creating the content seen on the university's official social media channels. Webb received his bachelor's and master's degrees from the University of Mississippi and has been working with University Marketing & Communications since 2010. When not living on a social media timeline, Webb is spending time with his wife, Tiffany, and their son Jack.

Nishanth Rodrigues, *Chief Information Officer*

With more than 26 years of IT experience in academia, manufacturing, and professional health care, Rodrigues is an award-winning leader in information technology. Previously assistant vice president and chief technology officer at Michigan State University, he joined the University of Mississippi as chief information officer in 2017. Rodrigues earned his Master of Business Administration degree from Michigan State University and his bachelor's degree in network engineering from Davenport University. Rodrigues is a martial artist and a video gamer, both hobbies help keep his mind and body active.

ABOUT THE AUTHORS

Ryan M. Whittington, _Director of Marketing and Brand Strategy_

Ryan Whittington, an early adopter of just about every social media platform (yes, even MySpace @rmwhitti), received both bachelor's and master's degrees in journalism from the University of Mississippi. He has worked in University Communications since 2012. In his spare time, you can catch him looking for his next half marathon to run with his wife, Beth.

CHAPTER 15

ACADEMIC
Advising & Registration

By Mariana Allushuski, Kyle Ellis, Jennifer Fos,
Travis Hitchcock, and Beth Whittington

College students have high expectations of academic advising and quickly learn that the personal relationship between academic advisors and students is important for their success. Academic advisors and advising programs especially have a major impact on first-year students as they face the transition from high school to college or transfer from one institution to another. Academic advisors can serve as a primary support for new students, providing guidance in course selection, hold removal, and choosing a major, but academic advisors can offer much more than this to their advisees. Advisors have a wealth of knowledge regarding majors and campus resources; they are eager to help students achieve academic success.

Academic advising at Ole Miss

Although class selection is a major portion of academic advising, there is much more to the advising experience at Ole Miss. Advising is a partnership between the advisor and student regarding the student's classes, future plans, academic challenges and any issues outside of the classroom. Every University of Mississippi student is assigned an academic advisor based on major and must meet with his or her advisor at least once each semester. Some majors have faculty members within their department who serve as faculty mentors. The role of the faculty mentor is to assist students with more in-depth questions regarding internships, research, careers, or graduate school.

Freshman Advising

The majority of freshmen will have a professional advisor in the Center for Student Success and First-Year Experience (CSSFYE), while others will be advised by either a faculty member or professional advisor within their department. Students with a declared major who are advised in the CSSFYE during their freshman year will be assigned an advisor within their major at the beginning of sophomore year. Please refer to the chart below to locate your advisor.

Now that you have learned a little bit about academic advising, you may be asking yourself, "Who is my academic advisor?" Your academic advisor is determined by your major and your classification (freshman, sophomore, etc.). The easiest way to find information about your advisor is through your myOleMiss account. Start by searching for "Advisor" in the drop-down box on the right side of your screen. When you click on "My Advisors," you will see your advisor's name and contact information. As an undergraduate student at the University of Mississippi, you are required to meet with your advisor once every semester. Until you meet with your advisor, you will have an ADVISOR HOLD on your account, which will prevent you from registering for classes. Even though you are required to meet with your advisor only once a semester, you are encouraged to contact your advisor any time you have academic-related questions. Just as you expect your advisor to be knowledgeable about your degree plan, career options, University policies and campus resources, your advisor expects you to do your part as a student.

Here are some things you should do BEFORE you meet with your advisor:

Stay connected: Get in the habit of checking your Ole Miss e-mail at least once a day. Advisors usually send e-mails concerning important University dates, upcoming events related to your major, and when and how to make your advising appointment. You also can ask your advisor questions via e mail.

Do career-related research: As a new student, you may feel overwhelmed about the many major choices the University offers. Even though your advisor can give you information regarding different majors on campus, your advisor cannot make the decision for you. Remember, you are in charge and are the only one who truly knows what is best for you. Deciding on a major is an active process, which requires you to learn about yourself and about the field you are planning to study. Chapter 20 has some great tips on how to begin the process of career exploration.

Become familiar with the requirements for your major: The best resource for degree requirements is the official University catalog, which can be found at catalog. olemiss.edu. It may seem daunting at first, but the catalog is clearer than you might expect. Successful students take charge of their academic career and set goals for themselves. Even though your advisor is the expert, you should strive to become familiar with the academic requirements for your major.

CSSFYE ADVISING

General Studies
Freshman Studies

College of Liberal Arts
Biology
Chemistry and Biochemistry
Economics
English
Forensic Chemistry
Mathematics
Modern Languages
Political Science
Public Policy Leadership
Psychology
Sociology and Anthropology
Southern Studies

School of Business Administration
Banking and Finance
Entreprenuership
Economics
General Business
Finance
Management
Management Information Systems
Marketing
Marketing and Communications Strategy
Real Estate
Risk Management and Insurance

School of Applied Sciences
Applied Gerontology
Communication Sciences and Disorders
Criminal Justice
Dietetics and Nutrition
Exercise Science
Hospitality Management
Law Studies
Public Health & Health Sciences
Social Work
Sport and Recreation Administration

Patterson School of Accountancy
Accountancy

School of Engineering
Biomedical Engineering
Chemical Engineering
Civil Engineering
Computer Science

School of Engineering
Electrical Engineering
General Engineering
Geology
Geological Engineering
Mechanical Engineering

DEPARTMENTAL ADVISING
College of Liberal Arts
African American Studies
Art and Art History
Classics
Film Production
History
International Studies
Liberal Studies
Music
Philosophy and Religion
Physics
Religious Studies
Theatre Arts

School of Journalism and New Media
Integrated Marketing Communications
Journalism

School of Education
Early Childhood Education
Elementary Education
English Education
Health & Physical Education
Mathematics Education
Science Education
Social Studies Education
Special Education

School of Pharmacy
Pharmaceutical Sciences
Pharmacy

Health Related Professions
Allied Health Studies
Dental Hygiene
Health Informatics and Information Management
Histotechnology
Medical Technology
Medical Laboratory Sciences
Nursing
Radiological Sciences

Develop a list of questions: After looking at degree requirements for your major, you may have questions for your advisor. Make sure to write them down so you don't forget them!

ACTIVITY:

Which of these are good questions to ask your academic advisor?

"I am struggling in my Math class. What campus resources do you recommend?"
"Which class is easier?"
"I am thinking about taking a class at the community college close to my home this summer.
Will those hours transfer?"
"I heard Professor _____ is terrible! What do you think?"
"I am having trouble getting involved on campus. Do you have any suggestions for me?"
"These are the classes I am considering taking next semester. What are your thoughts?"
"Which classes would fulfill my social science requirement?"
"Can you get me into a class that is closed?"

During your advising appointment: After following the steps listed in the previous section, you should feel confident and prepared for your advising appointment. Consider the scenarios below: Can you pick out the strengths and weaknesses in these advising sessions?

Scenario 1: Jane walks into her advisor's office three weeks before her registration window opens. She sits down in the chair and pulls a notebook from her backpack. She opens to a page on which she has many questions written down and a list of classes that she wishes to take. The advisor helps her work through her questions, and then they go over the classes together. Jane and her advisor leave the meeting feeling as though progress was made.

Scenario 2: Bob walks into his advisor's office three days after his registration window has opened. He flops down in the chair and slumps down. He looks down at his feet as his advisor addresses him and tries to talk to him about his current grades and career aspirations. He tells his advisor to just give him some classes. The advisor tells Bob that this should be a collaboration between the two of them and he needs to help pick his classes. When asked about a major, he tells his advisor to pick a major that she thinks he should have. He continues to be nonverbal, noncommittal, and non-participatory. The advising session ends with Bob being advised toward a few classes but meaningful progress has not been made.

Confidentiality in advising: College students over the age of 18 are protected by the Family Education Rights and Privacy Act (FERPA), a federal law that protects students' educational records. Without your consent the University cannot release information such as your grades, bursar bill, schedule, or financial aid. However, many students choose to give the University permission to release information to their parents or legal guardians. You can change your FERPA permissions on myOleMiss by selecting the link "Access for Relatives/Guardians" under "My Profile."

After your advising appointment: Once you have met with your academic advisor, you have taken the first step towards registration. The next steps are checking your holds and your registration window on your myOleMiss account. Each semester you will be assigned a specific date and time when you will be allowed to register for classes, known as your "registration window." Holds prevent students from registering for classes. Some common holds you may encounter are below:

Once you have met with your advisor, cleared your holds, and your registration window has opened, you are ready for registration! Here is a refresher on registering for classes through myOleMiss. As you review this process, keep in mind that adding a class to "My Favorites" does not register you for the class. If you are ever in doubt, feel free to contact the Center for Student Success and First-Year Experience at 662-915-5970.

TYPE OF HOLD	WHOM TO CONTACT
Advisor Hold	Your academic advisor
Accounts Receivable Hold	Office of the Bursar (2nd Floor Martindale)
Bursar Hold	Office of the Bursar (2nd Floor Martindale)
Financial Aid Hold	Office of Financial Aid (2nd Floor Martindale)
Wellness Education Hold	William Magee Center for AOD & Wellness Ed (South Campus Recreation Center)
RebelADE Hold	William Magee Center for AOD & Wellness Ed
Student Conduct Hold	Conflict Resolution and Student Conduct (Somerville Hall)
Library Hold	J.D. Williams Library

Select student tab from toolbar.

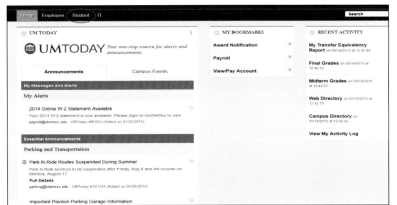

Under course registration section, select My Course Favorites. Students can click the green bookmark icon next to app to save to book marks for easy access later.

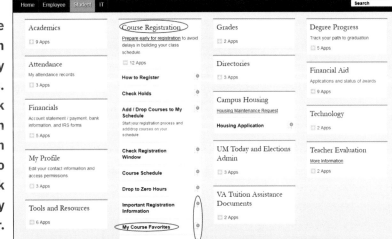

Alternately, students can use the search function to search for My Course Favorites.

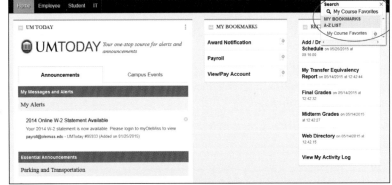

Click Add to My Favorites.

On the course schedule screen, insert course name/title or browse by department.

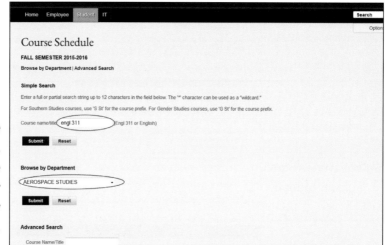

On the search results screen, select view all sections to see offered sections for the course.

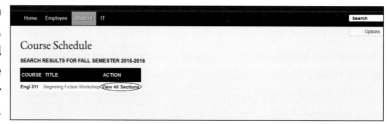

Check box(es) next to desired course sections and click on button to Add to Favorites.

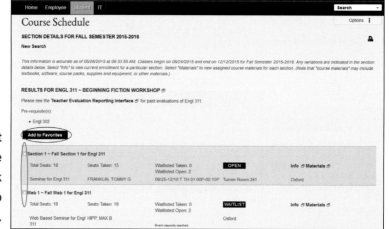

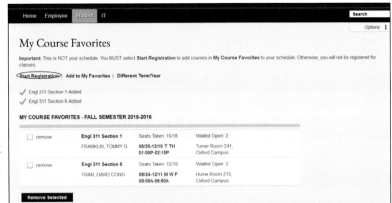

When ready, Click Start Registration.

Add / Drop Courses to My Schedule

Select the term and program for which you are registering.

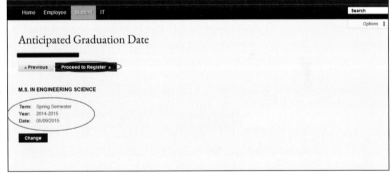

Review information for anticipated graduation date for accuracy and make changes if necessary. Then, click Proceed to Register.

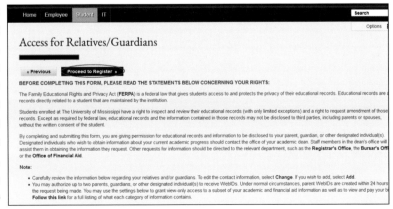

Restrict/Grant access to account for relatives. Relatives can be added at the bottom of the page and can have their information edited at any time. Click Proceed to Register

Make edits to your contact information (phone number, email address). Click Proceed to Register when ready.

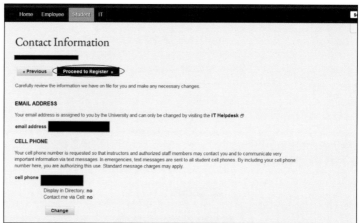

Be sure to carefully read the information about registration. Click Proceed to Register when finished.

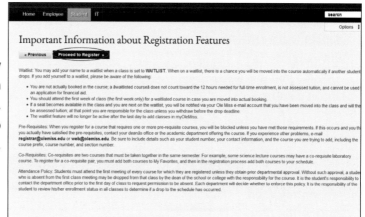

After viewing the registration agreement, scroll to the bottom and click Accept to Register.

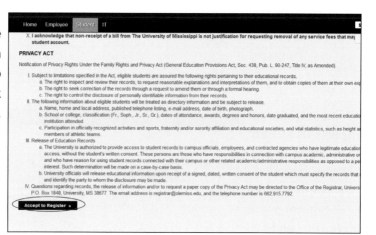

Click Add to add classes to schedule, and/or Drop to remove classes from schedule.

Check box(es) next to courses you wish to add and click Add to Schedule.

Calculating College Grade Point Average (GPA)

Trying to calculate and understand your college GPA can be difficult and confusing, especially since the calculations are done differently than in high school. The first thing you need to learn is that there are three different types of GPA calculated for college students: resident GPA, transfer GPA, and overall GPA. If you have transferred credits from another institution, the grades you have earned are reflected in your transfer GPA. Your resident GPA is your Ole Miss GPA and takes into account only classes you have taken at the University of Mississippi. Your overall GPA is a combination of your transfer and resident GPAs.

How is GPA calculated?

Your GPA is based on quality points. Quality points are grade points multiplied by the number of credit hours a course offers. You may remember grade points from high school, i.e., A = 4, A- = 3.7, B+= 3.3, B = 3, B- = 2.7, C+ = 2.3, C = 2, C- = 1.7, D=1, and F=0.

Let's say you take a biology lecture and biology lab and make an "A" in both courses. The lecture is worth three credit hours and the lab is worth one credit hour. First, convert both "As" to "4s." Now multiply each "4" by the number of hours earned from the class. The biology lecture is worth 12 quality points and the biology lab is worth four quality points.

TABLE 1

Class	Grade	Grade Point	Hours	QualityPoints
Bio. Lecture	A	4	3	12
Bio. Lab	A	4	1	4

I figured out my quality points. What now?

Once you calculate how many total quality points you have earned, you need to divide that number by the total number of graded hours (the number of credit hours you are taking, excluding pass/fail coures). For example, during the summer after high school graduation, you completed six hours of English credit at a community college (two classes) and earned a "B" in both. Then, for your first college semester, you take a three-credit hour algebra course and earn a "C+," a three-credit hour music appreciation course and earn an "A-," and a four-credit hour chemistry course and earn a "B." What is your overall GPA after the first semester? Remember, divide the total number of quality points by the total number of graded hours.

TABLE 2

Class	Grade	Grade Point	Hours	QualityPoints
English I	B	3	3	9
English II	B	3	3	9
Algebra	C+	2.3	3	6.9
Biology	B	3	4	12
Music App.	A-	3.7	3	11.1
French	B	3	6	18
Total			**22**	**66**

You should calculate an overall GPA of a 3.0.

What GPA do I need to maintain to be in good standing?

The general answer is 2.0 resident GPA. If your resident GPA falls below a 2.0 during your time as a student at Ole Miss, you will be placed on academic probation. During any semester that you are on academic probation, you must obtain a 2.0 semester GPA. Failure to do so could result in suspension from the University.

CONCLUSION

The relationship between an academic advisor and an advisee can be mutually beneficial. Students at the University of Mississippi should understand the basic components of the advising process, such as advising structure for their major, their assigned advisor, office location, and availability. Most importantly, you should be an active participant in the advising process. Have goals, plans, thoughts, and ideas about your ideal educational experience. Ask questions about your education plans.

Take advantage of having an advisor available to provide information and guidance on a wide range of academic matters. Working with your advisor, registering for classes, and understanding your grade point average are just three of the many new responsibilities associated with being a college student. Take a moment now to schedule an appointment with your advisor.

ABOUT THE AUTHORS

Mariana Allushuski, *former Academic Advisor/Instructor in the Center for Student Success and First-Year Experience*
Mariana earned her B.S. in psychology from Lipscomb University in 2010, M.Ed. in counseling for the University of Mississippi in 2012, and recently completed her doctorate in higher education administration at Ole Miss.

Kyle Ellis, *Director of the Center for Student Success and First-Year Experience*
Kyle came to the University of Mississippi in 2004 as an academic advisor. He received his B.S. in health and human performance and M.S. in education for the University of Tennessee at Martin. He earned his Ph.D. in higher education in 2011 from the University of Mississippi.

Jennifer Fos, *Assistant Director for the Center for Student Success and First-Year Experience*
Jennifer received her B.A. in English, M.A. in higher education, and Ph.D. in higher education from the University of Mississippi. In her spare time she likes to read.

Travis Hitchcock, *Assistant Director for the Center for Student Success and First-Year Experience*
Travis received his B.S. in family and consumer sciences, his M.A. in higher education, and his Ph.D. in higher education from the University of Mississippi.

Beth Whittington, *Assistant to the Dean of Undergraduate Programs in the School of Business*
Beth earned her B.S. in secondary education with an emphasis in Spanish from Mississippi State University in 2008 and her M.A. in higher education from the University of Mississippi in 2012.

CHAPTER 16

MAKE A DIFFERENCE
Get Involved!

By Bradley Baker

Getting involved is different for everyone. More often than not, how many organizations you are a part of is how student involvement is quantified. Thinking that way only scratches the surface of campus or community involvement. Registered Student Organizations (RSOs) are just one of the many resources the University and surrounding community provide to students. Your activities outside the classroom can help you develop and prepare for the profession that awaits you after your college experience. Create your involvement so that you not only enjoy what you are doing but also build on what you learn in the classroom. **The term for this is co-curricular activities**.

Be intentional about your activities outside the classroom. Find the things that you enjoy doing. You will put more effort into activities and subjects that you enjoy and appeal to you. Do not choose your involvement for the wrong reasons such as social pressure or others' ideals. This chapter attempts to outline resources and opportunities on campus and in the Oxford community. It is up to you to take advantage of these offerings to increase your portfolio and skills, while enhancing your college experience. These skills and experiences will be with you long after you graduate.

Find out what being involved means to you: whether it is a Registered Student Organization, a campus job, Ole Miss Outdoors, or a community organization such as Leap Frog, your niche exists.

- **Become a part of the community:** Get involved on campus and connect with other students, faculty, and staff. It will not take long for you to be comfortable and feel at home.

- **Make new friends:** If you limit yourself to the classroom, a residence hall, or an apartment complex to meet people, you miss the chance to participate in the diverse campus opportunities around you. Join organizations and meet people with similar interests or discover new interests to counter the homesickness many new students experience.

Campus involvement helps you develop relationships.

- **Leadership and teamwork skills:** In today's workforce, teamwork is a critical skill for success. Participating in student organizations where you have the opportunity to learn, grow, and reach your full potential is vital to your future success.

- **Life skills you cannot get behind a desk:** Involvement in campus activities builds confidence and provides opportunities to perform in situations that are similar to those you may experience beyond college. College involvement is a great way to discover your interests, strengths, and abilities.

- **Have fun:** Yes, the primary goal while at Ole Miss is to learn through studying, going to class, and reading your course materials, but it is also important to find interests and areas where you can enjoy yourself and relax.

- **Learn to manage your time:** Campus involvement certainly keeps you busy, but it also helps you to be productive with your time. Students who are involved waste much less time than those who choose not to be involved.

- **Build relationships:** Networking, networking, networking. Being involved in campus activities gives you the chance to fine tune your skills in making contacts and developing relationships.

Brief History of Registered Student Organizations

The University of Mississippi was chartered in 1844, and most likely the next day, students started forming groups and organizations of common interests and goals. College students have always looked for peers of like mind and involvement. Today, students gather in the coffee shop in the Library, at picnic tables in The Grove, and the lobby of the Union to discuss various topics and enjoy each other's company.

Some of the first formal organizations were literary societies that met in secrecy. The first two literary societies were the Hermaean Society (1849–1946) and Phi Sigma Society (1849–1934).

Most literary societies' activities consisted of formal debates on topical issues of the day, but literary activity could include original essays, poetry, and music. As a part of their literary work, many also collected and maintained their own libraries for the use of the society's members. College societies were the training grounds for men in public affairs in the nineteenth century (Harding, 2008).

These societies were the precursors to the modern Greek system. Delta Kappa Epsilon was founded in 1850 as the University's first fraternity. Chi Omega was founded in 1899 as the first sorority. Ole Miss's first traditionally African-American fraternity, Omega Psi Phi, was founded in 1973 (Sansing, 1999). The Greek system at the University is still strong today; approximately 40 percent of undergraduate students are Greek.

Soon after the Civil War, the University of Mississippi began to publish *The M-Book*, which is published online today. *The M-Book* served as a guide to activities on campus. In the 1890s *The M-Book* was the first glimpse into student activity that did not include the literary societies or Greek organizations. The students were just as involved then as they are today with many different types of clubs and organizations. Honor societies and social clubs such as The Stag Club, composed of seven members per class of the Law School, were prominent. Academic clubs such as the Press Club, Science Club, and Teachers Club, kept students focused on their academic interests. Recreational clubs such as YMCA, Glee Club, and Racket Club were all outlets for students to have fun (Sansing, 1999). The Ole Miss chapter of the Black Student Union (BSU) began in 1968 as a lobbying organization for African-American students. Today, the BSU is one of the largest organizations on campus.

In the early 1900s, Chancellor Kincannon created the Student Honor Council, and in 1917, it became the Associated Student Body (ASB). Over the years, ASB has been integral in instituting change. In 1946, ASB ordered an investigation into outdated food services and regulations governing women (Sansing, 1999). As a result, the University lessened the regulations on women and improved the food services.

Role of Registered Student Organizations on campus

Registered Student Organizations (RSOs) serve many roles at the University of Mississippi. RSOs provide the opportunity to develop interests, build community, serve others, prepare for life after college, and provide a voice on current issues. Since the very beginning of the University of Mississippi, students have been finding ways to institute change and develop groups of similar interests. RSOs play a vital role in the growth of the University and you as an individual and responsible community member.

Types of student organizations

> **"Don't be too quick to tell people about your high school honors. They are all very commendable, but college students don't appreciate them so much as your home-town acquaintances did."**
>
> 1928–29
> The M-Book

The University of Mississippi has more than 400 student organizations registered with the Student Union Office. As a University, we place these organizations in categories so that it is easier for students to find organizations that meet their interests. RSOs can be tied to departments, colleges, specific majors, or just a group of students with a similar interest. You will be hard pressed not to find an RSO with which to get involved. If you have a cause, service project, or interest that is not represented at the University of Mississippi, you can work with the Student Union Office to launch a new RSO.

- **Academic/Professional:** Organizations designed for students interested in a particular career or academic field of study who want to establish networks and further develop their skills in that area.

- **Creative**: Organizations committed to creative expression through various mediums—art, film, music writing, and craft.

- **Cultural/Multicultural:** Organizations focused on providing support and fostering community within various cultures, races, religions, and orientations represented among the student body.

- **Fraternity/Sorority:** Organizations represented by the National Panhellenic Conference (CPH), Inter-Fraternity Council (IFC), and National Pan-Hellenic Council (NPHC). These organizations are advised by Fraternal Leadership and Learning.

- **Graduate School:** Organizations designed specifically to support the unique needs of students who are members of various graduate study programs.

- **Health/Wellness:** Organizations focused on the improvement and betterment of all University members.

- **Honors Society:** Organizations, both local and national, that provide service and leadership opportunities as a well as recognition for students with academic honors.

- **Leadership:** Organizations that are committed to enhancing students' capacity to develop as leaders both on campus and beyond.

- **Military & Intelligence:** Organizations affiliated or associated with the armed services and intelligence industry.

- **Political:** Organizations that encourage expressions, debate, and support of political issues, views, and/or candidates.

- **Religious/Spiritual:** Organizations that provide spiritual and/or religious development and support.

- **Service/Philanthropic:** Organizations that provide volunteer or service opportunities for civic minded students eager to serve the campus and/or community.

- **Special Interest:** Organizations that exist to enhance campus life and provide support to students through a variety of programs and events.

- **Sponsored:** Organizations that have a designated and acknowledged partnership with a University, academic, or administrative unit.

- **Sport Clubs:** Organizations sponsored through the Department of Campus Recreation that serve students, faculty, and staff members in different sports and recreational activities.

- **Student Governance:** Organizations designed to support and represent University students.

- **Women's Interests:** Organizations that have an interest in supporting women and women's issues both on campus and throughout the world.

The Forum

To get involved on campus or in any of our Registered Student Organizations, log-in to The Forum (olemiss.edu/forum) using your Ole Miss username and password. The Forum is the hub of all campus involvement. This web-based platform streamlines communication and helps build a stronger campus community. Not only can you find a profile for each RSO, but there is also a calendar of events and a newsfeed to keep you up-to-date with campus events and opportunities to get involved.

Getting involved outside of registered student organizations

The University, city of Oxford, and Lafayette County offer many ways to get involved in the community. Getting involved can often mean more than joining a club or RSO. It can mean getting out of your comfort zone and trying something different. Maybe you have never attended a theatre production or been to an art exhibit. During your time at Ole Miss, experience everything the area has to offer. If you are looking for opportunities in Oxford and Lafayette County, read the local paper or contact the Chamber of Commerce.

Involvement opportunities on campus

Take advantage of campus departments to develop skills or get guidance. There are so many offices that are dedicated to giving you a great experience at the University and to help you develop as a person. If you are interested in how to get an internship, develop a resume, or improve your interviewing skills, go to the Career Center. The Gertrude C. Ford Ole Miss Student Union office offers student involvement consultations with Leadership & Engagement ambassadors, leadership development programs, student activities, and employment opportunities. Visit the Center for Inclusion and Cross-Cultural Engagement to develop your multicultural competencies. The Study Abroad Office is a place on campus that provides cultural opportunities both in and out of the country in formats that range from full semesters abroad to experiences that last for just a few weeks. Develop your personal health and wellness at Campus Recreation, become an Ole Miss Ambassador or Orientation Leader through the Office of Admissions, or become an International Student Ambassador in the Office of International Programs. These are all ways that you can get involved and take advantage of leadership opportunities on campus.

To find something to do on campus, you do not have to look any further than the Ole Miss Student Union.

Inside J.D. Williams Library is the largest blues archive in the world with thousands of recordings, videos, photographs, and more.

Included within the archive is B.B. King's personal record collection, among other musical treasures. Throughout the year, the Department of Art sponsors exhibitions of both undergraduate and graduate student work in Gallery 130 of Meek Hall. The exhibitions also include work by visiting professional artists. The University Museum, located on the edge of campus, is home to several collections such as the Mississippi Folk Art Collection and Millington-Barnard Collection of Scientific Instruments. In addition to existing collections, the museum hosts several traveling exhibitions year-round.

And there is more! The University offers several entertainment options throughout the fall and spring semesters. The Student Activities Association (SAA), for example, sponsors more than 125 events each year. From Welcome Week, concerts and movies in The Grove to the Miss University Pageant and the Parade of Beauties pageant, the SAA offers students opportunities to get involved with an organization or simply enjoy an event. The Gertrude C. Ford Center for the Performing Arts also serves as a premier entertainment venue in North Mississippi, featuring Broadway shows, concerts, and ballet, to name just a few. Built in 2003, the Ford Center has hosted Morgan Freeman, Marty Stuart, James Earl Jones, and even the 2008 Presidential Debate. The University's Music Department provides opportunities for entertainment through visiting performers as well as faculty, staff, and student performances. Likewise, Ole Miss Theatre features student productions throughout the academic year that provide entertainment as well as artistic training for the students participating in the productions. Last, Ole Miss Outdoors (OMOD) provides students with once-in-a-lifetime opportunities to experience the outdoors across the southeast of the U.S. and beyond.

Previous OMOD trips have included fly-fishing in Arkansas, white water rafting in Colorado, and dog sledding in Canada.

Involvement opportunities in Oxford

The Oxford area has a rich history in both the literary and musical arts. For example, Nobel Peace Prize winner, William Faulkner, made Oxford his home in the early 1900s. Faulkner is best known for penning popular novels including *As I Lay Dying* and *Absalom, Absalom!* Rowan Oak, home to Faulkner and his family for more than 40 years, is located just outside of our main campus. Faulkner's presence in Oxford attracts visitors each year to the Oxford Conference for the Book and the Faulkner and Yoknapatawpha Conference held on campus and at Rowan Oak. Thacker Mountain Radio is a free show held on the Square every Thursday night that features musical performances as well as author readings. The popular show is recorded and broadcast across the state on Saturday nights on Mississippi Public Radio. The area also offers a chance to take in the artistic abilities of others with Southside Gallery,

Powerhouse Community Arts Center, and Taylor Arts in nearby Taylor. If you are looking for something to do outdoors, the City of Oxford sponsors the LOU Pathways project with walking and biking paths throughout the city. Additionally, the University has mountain biking trails that are free and open to the public.

Volunteer opportunities on campus and in the community

RSOs do not provide the only means for service opportunities within the community. There are several groups both on and off campus that provide students with a chance to get involved by volunteering. For example, The Big Event is held in the spring each year. The event is the University's largest student-led volunteer effort and a means for students to say thank you to the Lafayette, Oxford, and University communities through service to local residents. Outside of the University, activities such as popular after-school programs at the Boys and Girls Club and Leapfrog afford students the chance to mentor school-age children from both Oxford and Lafayette County schools. Other service opportunities include the 9/11 Week of Services and Remembrance, Make a Difference Day, Martin Luther King, Jr. Day of Service, National Volunteer Week, and RebelTHON.

Student involvement

The concept of getting involved while at Ole Miss differs from student to student as each person has unique aspirations and goals. Getting involved means being intentional about your time at the University of Mississippi by taking advantage of the opportunities outside the classroom to gain experience, network, build your resume, and develop skills necessary to be successful when you jump into the real world. Whether you join a RSO, participate in volunteer work on or off campus, develop a relationship with a particular University office, or find an organization in the Oxford/Lafayette community, make your involvement your own and have a purpose. College is a fun time; make the most of your experience at the University of Mississippi.

INVOLVEMENT ONLINE RESOURCES

- **Associated Student Body:**
  http://olemissasb.org

- **Career Center:**
  https://career.olemiss.edu/

- **Campus Recreation:**
  https://campusrec.olemiss.edu/

- **Ford Center:**
  https://fordcenter.org/

- **Fraternity & Sorority Life:**
  http://greeks.olemiss.edu

- **Gallery 130:**
  https://art.olemiss.edu/
  facilities-gallery-130/

- **Ole Miss Outdoors:**
  https://campusrec.olemiss.
  edu/omod/

- **Ole Miss Student Union:**
  https://union.olemiss.edu/

- **Rowan Oak:**
  https://www.rowanoak.com/

- **Student Activities Association:**
  https://saa.olemiss.edu/

- **Study Abroad:**
  https://studyabroad.olemiss.edu/

- **Thacker Mountain Radio:**
  http://thackermountain.com/

- **The Big Event:**
  https://bigevent.olemiss.edu/

- **The Forum:**
  http://olemiss.edu/forum

- **UM Music Department:**
  https://music.olemiss.edu/

- **UM Theatre Department:**
  http://theatreandfilm.olemiss.edu/

- **United Way of Oxford and Lafayette County:**
  https://www.unitedwayox-
  fordms.org/volunteer

- **University Museum:**
  https://museum.olemiss.edu/

- **Visit Oxford:**
  https://visitoxfordms.com/

- **Volunteer Oxford:**
  https://www.unitedwayox-
  fordms.org/volunteer

ABOUT THE AUTHOR

Bradley Baker, *Director of the Ole Miss Student Union*

Bradley Baker has been a staff member with the University since 2005 after receiving his Bachelor of Arts in English. He received his Master of Arts in higher education/student personnel degree from the University in 2011, and is currently pursuing a Doctor of Education. In his role on campus, he manages the daily operations of the Student Union and oversees the areas of student activities, leadership programing, and student organization management. Baker's office advises student organizations such as the Student Activities Association, RebelTHON, Ole Miss Big Event, and the Associated Student Body as well as coordinates leadership programs such as the M-Power Extended Orientation and and StrengthsFinder on campus. Additionally, the student involvement platform, The Forum, is housed within the Gertrude C. Ford Ole Miss Student Union office.

OVERVIEW OF ROBERT'S RULES OF ORDER

This is a condensed version of Robert's Rules of Order. It is intended to provide a basic background in parliamentary procedure to conduct business in as efficient and orderly a manner as possible.

Addressing the chair

All meetings should be conducted from the "chair" (usually president). Members addressing the chair should refer to the presiding officer as "Brother President."

Obtaining the floor

Before a member may make a motion or speak in debate, he or she must obtain the "floor." To claim the floor, a member raises his or her hand and waits to be "recognized" by the chair. The chair will recognize the member by announcing his or her name or title. This member then has the floor and can stand and speak until yielding the floor by sitting down. While a motion is open to debate, there are three situations where the floor should be assigned to a person who may not have been the first to rise and address the chair. These situations:

If the member who made the motion claims the floor and has not already spoken on the question, he or she is entitled to be recognized in preference to other members.

No one is entitled to the floor a second time as long as any other member who has not yet spoken to the pending motion requests the floor.

The chair should attempt to alternate opposing opinions on a question if he or she is aware of members requesting the floor who have opposing views.

Making a motion

First, a member makes a motion. Though he or she makes a motion, the member uses the word "move" to make the motion (for example: "I move to allocate...").

Another member seconds the motion by saying, "I second it" or simply, "Second." It should be noted that a second by a member merely implies that the motion should come before the meeting and not that he or she necessarily favors the motion. A member may second a motion because he or she would like to see the assembly go on record as rejecting the proposal, if the member believes a vote on the motion would have such a result.

The chair then states the "question" on the motion. Neither the making nor the seconding of a motion places it before the council; only the chair can do that by this step (stating the question). When the chair has stated the question, the motion is pending and is then open to debate (providing it is a debatable motion). If the organization decides to do what a motion proposes, it adopts a motion or it is carried. If it decides against the motion, it is rejected or lost.

Amending a motion

The motion to amend is a motion to modify the wording (within certain limits) of a pending motion before it is acted upon. An amendment must be germane; that is, it must be closely related to or have some bearing on the subject of the motion to be amended.

A motion to amend is handled the same way as a main motion and requires a second to be considered. An amendment is adopted by a majority vote even in cases where the motion to be amended requires a 2/3 vote for adoption.

Point of order

When a member thinks that the rules of the meeting are being violated, he or she may make a "point of order," calling upon the chair to make a ruling and enforce the regular rules. A point of order: can be applied to any breach of the meeting's rules; is in order when another has the floor; does not require a second; and is

not debatable unless the chair, being in doubt, submits the point to a vote of the meeting, in which case the rules governing its debate-ability are the same as for an appeal.

Previous question

The previous question is the motion used to bring the meeting to an immediate vote on one or more pending questions. The motion for the previous question: takes precedence over all debatable or amendable motions to which it is applied; can be applied to any immediately pending debatable or amendable motion; is out of order when another has the floor; must be seconded; is not debatable; is not amendable; and requires a 2/3 vote.

Postpone indefinitely

A motion to postpone indefinitely is a motion that the assembly declines to take a position on the main question. Its adoption kills the main motion, at least for the duration of the session, and avoids a direct vote on the question. It is useful in disposing of a badly chosen main motion that cannot be either adopted or expressly rejected without possibly undesirable consequences. The motion to postpone indefinitely: is out of order when another has the floor; must be seconded; is debatable; is not amendable; and requires a majority vote.

Adjourn

To adjourn means to close the meeting. The motion to adjourn is a motion to close the meeting immediately, made under conditions where some other provision for another meeting exists and where no time for adjourning the present meeting has already been set. The motion to adjourn: is not applied to any motion and no motion can be applied to it; is out of order when another has the floor; does not need to be seconded; is not amendable; and requires a majority vote.

STUDENT PROFILE:
MORGAN ATKINS

HOMETOWN:
OLIVE BRANCH, MS
MAJORS:
PUBLIC POLICY AND LEADERSHIP

How do I get involved?

There are so many ways to get involved at the University of Mississippi! Following organizations you are interested in on social media is a great way to keep up with applications timelines and opportunities for involvement. Additionally, we have the ForUM, which is an online catalog of our over 400 registered student organizations. Here you can find everything from the Gardening Club to Milk and Cookies Club. This portal is a huge asset for anyone looking to connect with a student group. It also helps to reach out to older students at the University to ask what involvements they have enjoyed the most. My older friends were able to give me a lot of personal advice that was extremely helpful in making my decisions about applications and involvement.

How soon should I get involved?

Everyone's college experience is vastly different, so you should get involved as soon as you feel comfortable. The adjustment to college life can be very difficult, so do not feel like you need to dive head first into involving yourself with every organization you come across. Take a step back and evaluate what matters most to you. Do you want to do philanthropic work? Do you want to be in social organizations? Do you want to advocate for change? These questions and many more helped me make my involvement decisions, and knowing why you want to be involved makes figuring out what you want to be involved in so much easier.

What are the benefits of being involved?

One of the most beneficial aspects of being involved is plugging you into a group of like-minded people. College can be very isolating and lonely at times, so having a space where you can meet with others who share similar passions is invaluable to your personal and social growth. I have met some of my best friends through our on campus organizations, and I would not trade the experiences I have shared serving with them for anything.

285

How has getting involved helped you as a student and prepared you for your career?

Being involved has helped me learn how to budget my time. Being involved in ASB and other organizations, taking classes, and working on campus are all commitments, so I have had to balance my schedule. I also have learned how to build relationships with those around me, especially those who might not share the same beliefs as me. Most importantly, I think being involved has helped me learn that determination is the key to success. Without perseverance and determination, it is so easy to get overwhelmed and feel like you cannot enact the change you want to see. All of these skills will help me greatly in my career, especially with wanting to go into work in the nonprofit sector.

What has been your favorite moment or experience you have had by getting involved on campus, in the Oxford community, or with a national opportunity?

My favorite moment being involved on campus was being able to attend the meeting of the Institutions of Higher Learning where the relocation of the Confederate Statue on campus was finally approved. The plan for relocation originated my freshman year at the University, so I was proud to be a part of the group that saw it through. It was a monumental step toward change that benefits all students of our community.

Is there such a thing as being too involved?

There is absolutely such a thing as being too involved. While you think involvement is joining as many organizations you can, involvement is so much more centered around investing your time into a few key organizations. Being overly involved can lead to burnout, which will keep you from wanting to stay involved for your entire college career. Learning to say no to involvement opportunities is difficult, but you have to learn how to do it for your mental and academic well being. Just remember that you get to live your own unique college experience, so prioritize involvement in what you care about most and not the most you can be involved in.

THE UNIVERSITY OF MISSISSIPPI
MUSEUM AND HISTORIC HOUSES

University of Mississippi students and faculty have free admission during the Museum's open hours of Tuesday to Saturday, 10AM to 6PM – and during frequent evening events, receptions, and special programs (no ID required). When visiting the Museum, Visitor Parking is at no cost in the designated visitor spaces. Admission is also free to student and faculty visitors at William Faulkner's Rowan Oak (with ID). For more information about Exhibitions and Programs, please go to: https://museum.olemiss.edu/

The University of Mississippi Museum has its origins as the City of Oxford's Mary Buie Museum, built in 1939 as a WPA Federal Art Center, one of two in the state of Mississippi. Upon its transfer to the University in 1974, the construction of a large addition permitted departmental collections from across the campus to be consolidated in the new "University Museum" when it opened in February 1977. The Museum's collection holdings total over 20,000 artworks and cultural heritage artifacts, representing multiple continents and millennia. The Museum is steward of the largest collection of Greek and Roman Antiquities in the southern United States and also manages Rowan Oak, the National Historic Landmark home of novelist William Faulkner, and the Walton-Young House, home of novelist, playwright, and drama critic Stark Young.

Rowan Oak is the Oxford, Mississippi, home where William Faulkner lived from 1930 until his death in 1962. He wrote most of his major works here and also used the home and grounds as a setting for many of his stories and novels. He named the place for two trees: the Rowan tree, thought to ward off evil spirits, and the Live Oak, known for strength and solitude. A National Historic Landmark and a National Literary Landmark, Rowan Oak is now a house museum for visitors interested in Faulkner's life.

The **Walton-Young House** is a registered State of Mississippi Landmark and a typical middle class home of the Victorian era. Horace H. Walton, who owned a hardware store on the Oxford Square, built the house in 1880. Stark Young is widely recognized to be the most famous resident of the Walton-Young house. The University purchased the house in 1974, and it originally housed the Center for the Study of Southern Culture and the Honors College. The house became a part of the University Museum in 1997, and is located at the corner of University Avenue and Fifth Street, adjacent to the University Museum.

The house is currently closed to the public.

COLLECTIONS:

Millington-Barnard Collection of Scientific Instruments

Approximately 500 19th century scientific instruments, used by John Millington and Frederick A.P. Barnard to teach University students from 1848 to 1861, are preserved in the University Museum's collections. Included are telescopes, models of large machines, and demonstration devices for the teaching of natural philosophy, physics, and astronomy.

David M. Robinson Collection of Greek and Roman Antiquities

The David M. Robinson Collection of Greek and Roman Antiquities is one of the finest university collections of its kind in the United States. Covering the period from 1500 B.C. to 300 A.D., the collection contains Greek and Roman sculpture, Greek decorated pottery, architectural fragments, small artifacts in terracotta and bronze, and Greek and Roman coins. Portions of this collection are on display at all times.

The Seymour Lawrence Collection of American Art

In 1998, editor and publisher Seymour Lawrence gave much of his personal art collection to the museum and funded the construction of the Seymour Lawrence Gallery of American Art. Included in this collection are works by Georgia O'Keefe, Kurt Vonnegut, Man Ray, Russell Chatham, Morris Graves, Marsden Hartley, Mark Tobey, John Marin, Arthur G. Dove, among others.

Theora Hamblett Collection

Paintings by Mississippian Theora Hamblett are the core of the Museum's folk art collection. In over 200 works of art, Miss Hamblett recorded her childhood memories, religious visions, and the joys and sorrows of a vanished way of life. Selections from this collection are on exhibition at all times.

The Mary Buie and Kate Skipwith Collections

Mary Buie, a talented artist, bequeathed the funds to build her museum as a gift to the city of Oxford, Mississippi. Her sister Kate Skipwith oversaw the building construction. In 1939, the Mary Buie Museum opened with a collection of art and historic memorabilia collected by them.

For more information about the collections, go to *museum.olemiss.edu/collections/*

CHAPTER 17

SUSTAINABILITY

AT THE

University of Mississippi

By Lindsey Abernathy, Jade Chalkley
and Kendall McDonald

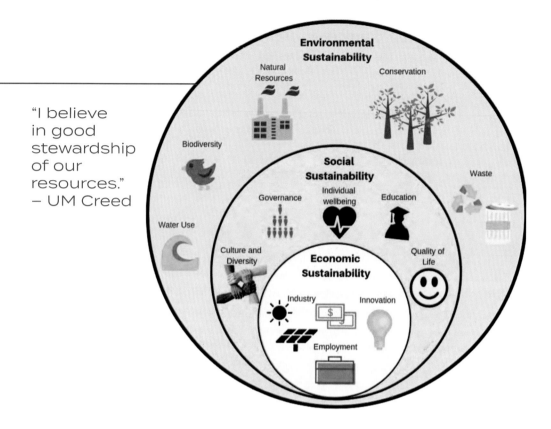

"I believe in good stewardship of our resources."
— UM Creed

Introduction to Sustainability

All living things have needs, and humans are no exception. We need shelter, nutritious food, drinking water and safety. We also have many complex needs, like a need for community, social support, and infrastructure. Resources meet our needs. Resources include things like minerals, air and clean water.

Some resources are renewable, which means that they can be replenished. Some resources are non-renewable, which means they are finite in their availability to us. Sustainability seeks to balance our needs with what resources are available to us.

As the University of Mississippi Office of Sustainability defines it, sustainability is a multi-disciplinary, problem-solving approach to creating a social system that meets the needs of the present generation without compromising the needs of future generations or the needs of the ecological systems in which humans exist.

Right now, the ability of future generations and our ecological systems to meet their needs is compromised by our rate of consumption and waste generation. This is what it means for a system to be unsustainable. When a system is unsustainable, it can lead to drastic changes in the health of our environment, including climate change—the sudden shift in predictable patterns of weather over time, often producing frequent extreme weather events (like wildfires, hurricanes and flooding).

Climate refers to the weather conditions (including temperatures, precipitation, air pressure, humidity, sunshine and winds) prevailing in an area over time. Climate differs from weather in that climate refers to weather patterns over large stretches of time in a particular area. When we discuss the weather, we are referring to conditions in a particular moment in time. Weather in a place (like Oxford, for example) can change frequently and still remain in a normal range for our area. However, the climate for a given area generally shows a stable pattern over hundreds of years. Climate can change over time, but it typically stays within a reliable range unless something else is introduced into our atmosphere that changes the balance of the system.

Internationally, a scientific consensus has been reached that human activity is contributing to changes in global climate trends. Scientific consensus refers to the collective judgment, position, and opinion of the community of scientists in a particular field of study (Greenfacts). Currently, humans produce large amounts of harmful greenhouse gas emissions through unsustainable means of food and commodity production, consumption, transportation and waste generation. Greenhouse gases are those that get trapped in our atmosphere and prevent the heat generated by our sun from escaping.

In our region, National Climate Assessment Reports predict that rising temperatures will cause sea level rises, more frequent hurricanes and tornadoes, greater susceptibility to certain diseases like malaria, extreme heat and decreased water availability, all of which will dramatically impact human health and the economy within our lifetimes. Ecosystems that have evolved to particular climates are also at risk as those climates change.

Agents of Change

The good news is that we have agency over our own actions. There are lots of things we can do to live a more resource-conscious lifestyle. We are not alone as we work toward a more sustainable future.

On a university-wide level, campus planners are prioritizing tenets of sustainability, such as creating infrastructure to support active transportation, preserving natural spaces and working to achieve utility efficiencies. Researchers are collaborating to change lives in the state of Mississippi and beyond through community wellbeing and disaster resilience work. UM is also a signatory of the American College and University Presidents Carbon Commitment, meaning that the university has publicly recognized higher education's unique responsibility to play a leadership role in addressing climate change.

Students are uniquely well equipped to be change agents. A change agent is a leader, whether formally or informally, who desires to use their talents to facilitate positive change. Anyone can be a change agent. Your voice is particularly important in advocating for better resource stewardship in our university community and among your friends and families.

If you decide to be a change agent for sustainability, you will be joining a very strong community. Student interest in sustainability work is at an all-time high, with hundreds of volunteers engaged in sustainability projects on and off campus, record applicant numbers to student sustainability leadership opportunities and an estimated 1,200-plus student hours spent on sustainability projects last year.

This chapter will equip you with the knowledge to be good stewards of our resources and to join us as we advance sustainability on our campus.

Waste Reduction

We are living in an unprecedented period of waste generation. Did you know that a plastic water bottle tossed in the trash ends up in a landfill, where it does not begin to decompose for 700 years? Or that Americans throw away 2.5 million plastic bottles every hour?

According to the Environmental Protection Agency, the average American produces 4.3 pounds of waste daily—that would be more than 15 tons of trash generated by residents of Stockard and Martin Halls in one week. Because the majority of this waste ends up in landfills, it is important to take steps to reduce our waste contributions as individuals and as a university community. Three options to consider are reducing, reusing, and recycling.

Reducing and Reusing

Though recycling gets much attention as a strategy to decrease landfill waste, the most effective way to do so is to avoid waste in the first place. You can reduce landfill waste by avoiding disposable items intended only for one use. You can refill reusable water bottles at any of the many hydration station water dispensers on campus. You can also bring reusable coffee cups to campus Starbucks and Einsteins locations (and often receive a discount), and use the reusable to-go boxes at Rebel Market. You can always refuse items as well, such as a plastic bag at the grocery store or a plastic drink straw if it is not needed.

Recycling

A simple way to reduce the waste you do generate is to recycle. Bins are located in all academic buildings, residence hall lobbies, and the J.D. Williams Library. Off campus, you can sign up for curbside recycling through the City of Oxford, or drop off your recycling at any of the locations listed on their website, www.oxfordms.net/departments/recycling.

On campus and in Oxford, you can recycle:
- Paper (including newspapers, notebook paper, magazines, and junk mail)
- Cardboard
- Plastics #1 and #2 (look on the bottom of the container for the number)
- Aluminum
- Printer ink and toner cartridges (in select bins labeled "e-waste")

The Office of Sustainability has put together an extensive guide to recycling on campus and in Oxford. View the guide at https://sustain.olemiss.edu/recycle/ If you would like to get more involved in recycling efforts, volunteer for the Green Grove Gameday Recycling Program. Green Grove facilitates recycling in the Grove on home football gamedays. Green Grove volunteers help educate tailgaters about what is recyclable and how to recycle in the Grove, and also help sort recycling.

Composting

Composting is similar to recycling in that it gives waste a chance to be used in a different way.

Composting takes food waste and turns it to a nutrient-rich soil amendment that can be used to grow more food. Finished compost is great for plants, the environment and the wallets of farmers and gardeners, as it offers a more cost effective and low-impact alternative to synthetic fertilizers. Additionally, composting food waste reduces the amount of food that breaks down in landfill. Food in a landfill does not have access to oxygen, causing it to produce harmful methane pollution as a byproduct.

If you have eaten food prepared at Rebel Market and other residential dining locations, you have indirectly contributed to the UM Compost Program. The program composts pre-consumer food waste from these dining facilities, converting eggshells, banana peels, and other kitchen scraps into soil for campus and community gardens. Since the program's creation in 2013, the compost program has diverted about

100,000 pounds of food waste from the landfill—more than 50 tons! The program was proposed by a student through the UM Green Fund, and is operated by the Office of Sustainability. The UM Compost Program offers at least one volunteer opportunity per semester.

Sustainable Transportation

Oxford is a compact community. On average, most people who commute to the university live less than three miles from campus. As a student at Ole Miss, you do not need a car to get around campus and Oxford. With the increasing mileage of bike lanes, sidewalks, and bus routes, UM students, faculty and staff are finding new ways to commute.

Biking on Campus and in Oxford

UM has been designated a Bicycle Friendly University at the bronze level by the League of American Bicyclists. Biking is a great way to be active, save money on fuel expenses and avoid searching for a parking spot. There are several ways to bike on campus:

Semester Bike Rentals - Through the UM Bike Shop, the university offers affordable bike rentals by the semester. The UM Bike Shop also offers maintenance services and is located across from the Turner Center.

Short-Term Bike Rentals - Parking and Transportation also provides students with the easy and affordable option of utilizing our campus bikeshare program. Download the Social Bicycles app on your phone, register your account, and find one of the many bikeshare stations on campus. Students receive up to two hours of riding free per day! Be sure to review the safety information included with each bike.

Bring your personal bike - You can bring your personal bike to campus. The UM Bike Shop provides maintenance services to personal bikes at steeply discounted prices. According to UM policy, students living on campus may also keep their bikes in their rooms over long breaks. If you do bring a bike to campus, make sure to register it at the UM Bike Shop. Use a secure U-lock and park it only at the university's many available bike racks.

The City of Oxford is a Bicycle Friendly Community and has many miles of bike lanes and mountain bike trails. Ride solo or join the UM Cycling Club on their group rides on the trails.

The O.U.T. Bus System

The Oxford University Transit (O.U.T.) bus system is an easy way to get around campus and the city. It is free to UM students—just make sure to show your student ID. Every O.U.T. bus is equipped with a bike rack so you can split your commute between bus and bike. The O.U.T. system is wheelchair accessible.

Car Rentals and Rideshares

Discounted short-term car rentals are offered through the University's partnership with Zipcar. Apply for your student membership online at https://www.zipcar.com/universities/university-of-mississippi to begin driving. The university also offers membership to Zimride, a service that helps students, faculty and staff coordinate carpools either for everyday use or for special trips, like to the airport. If you commute to campus from Batesville, Water Valley or another surrounding area, you may also be interested in Zimride's vanpool program. Sign up for Zimride's services at https://new.zimride.com/olemiss.

For complete information about transportation on the UM campus, visit parking.olemiss.edu.

Energy Conservation

Did you know that when you go to class and leave your cell phone charger plugged into the outlet, it is still using energy? An easy way to avoid this "vampire energy" use is to plug your electronics into a power strip, and flip it off when you are not using them. When purchasing electronics, look for ENERGY STAR-certified products. If you have a lamp in your room, be sure to use energy efficient bulbs such as LEDs or compact fluorescent bulbs (CFL). CFLs are 13 times more efficient than standard incandescent light bulbs. Finally, be sure to turn off or unplug lights, speakers, televisions, and other electronics when you leave your room for long periods of time, especially over holiday breaks. This small action can have a big impact.

Sustainable Food Systems

Seventy percent of the average American's diet is made up of processed foods—that is, foods that are not in their true form or contain artificial ingredients. The term "real food" means eating local, fresh, and non-artificial foods. Real food is healthier for your body, and it is often better for the land on which the food is grown.

According to the *Huffington Post*, if all Americans ate vegetable-based meals for just one day, the U.S. would save 70 million gallons of gas and 100 billion gallons of water. Check out https://sustain.olemiss.edu/ for a guide to vegan and vegetarian meals on campus.

If you are looking to have an even more direct impact with the food you are eating you can learn how to grow your own produce by joining the UM Garden Club. The garden, which is located behind Residential College South, acts as an educational tool for all levels of interested gardeners. Members grow produce for themselves and the UM Food Bank. Email the Garden Club at umgarden@olemiss.edu for more information on getting involved. No prior experience is necessary.

When grocery shopping in Oxford, visit the Oxford Community Market, MidTown Farmer's Market or Chicory Market, a farmstand offering local goods. Visit sustain.olemiss.edu/food for more information.

Grove Grocery

Lack of access to food and resources to fulfill other basic needs is a reality for many college students across the United States and on the University of Mississippi campus. The UM Food Bank is a confidential service open to all UM students who need food or toiletry items. The hours of the Food Bank change each semester, so be sure to check https://foodbank.olemiss.edu/ before your visit. The Food Bank is located in 213 Kinard Hall.

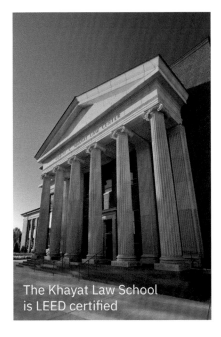

The Khayat Law School is LEED certified

Green Buildings on Campus

There are several buildings on campus you can visit to see sustainable design in action. The Center for Manufacturing Excellence (CME) is home to the state's largest roof-mounted solar power complex, with 414 photovoltaic solar panels on the roof. This building generates enough electricity to run the lights and air conditioning for the entire building.

CME is one of multiple buildings on campus to receive a Leadership in Energy and Environmental Design (LEED) certification by the U.S. Green Building Council, along with others including the Khayat Law Center and the School of Pharmacy's Medicinal Plant Garden.

Biodiversity

The University of Mississippi is located in a diverse region of plants, animals, and insects. This region is a highly-developed and farmed landscape in which pollinator species are integral to the agricultural systems. In addition, the region acts as a migration route for many species of insects and birds. It is important to foster native and beneficial habitats for pollinators in order to support their migrations, species survival, and human agricultural systems.

In fall 2019, UM became a designated affiliate of Bee Campus USA, an organization that ensures the protection, advocacy, and fostering of pollinator habitats. Bee Campus serves as an institutional commitment to protecting bees and other important native species. The University of Mississippi has several pollinator gardens that you can visit. These gardens facilitate the conservation and protection of pollinator species and are installed and maintained by Landscape Services, prioritizing ethical and safe practices. Learn more at sustain.olemiss.edu/pollinatorgardens.

The UM Green Fund

The University works to support student sustainability projects through the UM Green Fund. Since its launch, the Green Fund has financed projects like the UM Compost Program, the installation of hydration stations in UM buildings and efforts to increase recycling opportunities in residence halls.

Any UM student, organization or class can propose a project. In addition to a baseline donation from the University, the UM Green Fund relies on donations from students, faculty, and staff. Students can donate through myOleMiss.

SEVEN WAYS TO GET INVOLVED IN SUSTAINABILITY

Take a Class - UM offers two interdisciplinary minors that are focused on sustainability. These include the Environmental Studies minor and Disaster Sciences, both which are applicable to all majors.

Volunteer - Almost all volunteer work supports the principles of sustainability, whether you are working at the UM Food Bank or the Oxford Recycling Center. Visit sustain.olemiss.edu or check out UM Today for volunteer opportunities.

Join a Student Group – The UM Garden Club, Magnolia Grove Campus Audubon Chapter, and UM Beekeepers Club are directly sustainability-related student organizations.

Attend an Event – Attending an event on campus is a great way to learn about new topics and issues. UM hosts events including Food Day in the fall and Green Week in the spring.

Serve in a Leadership Role – The Associated Student Body Sustainability Committee, UM Green Fund Committee and Green Grove Team Leaders Program are all opportunities for students to play a larger role in UM sustainability efforts.

Intern – The Office of Sustainability's Green Student Intern Program provides opportunities for students to gain professional experience working on topics ranging from waste reduction to sustainable transportation.

Submit a Green Fund proposal – Do you have an idea for making the University more sustainable? Write a Green Fund proposal! The Office of Sustainability can guide you through this process.

AN OLE MISS STUDENT'S
PERSPECTIVE

By Anish Bista

"No one will protect what they don't care about, and no one will care about what they have never experienced."
— Sir David Atteborough

This famous quote by Sir David Attenborough has been crucial in my understanding of the concept of "sustainability" and how I went on to make it an inseparable part of my life. My name is Anish Bista and I am a mechanical engineering undergraduate at the University of Mississippi. As an engineering major, I wasn't intuitively engaged in sustainability but I learned through my friends about the Green Grove Gameday Recycling Program, the UM Compost Program, and the campus vegetable garden. It was after I visited the Office of Sustainability's table during an outreach event that I learned more about the sustainability programs like waste reduction, recycling, and sustainable transportation that were ongoing in the university. Having been never exposed to this aspect of experiential learning I quickly decided to learn more and applied to the Office of Sustainability's Green Student Intern Program.

The internship with the Office of Sustainability helped me learn more about sustainability. The first thing that intrigued me was that sustainability didn't just include the environment but is actually a delicate balance of environmental, social and economic aspects. Unknowingly, I had always been contributing to sustainability. Back in my home country Nepal, I used to make earthworm compost using the organic waste from my house with my dad. We would then use the compost in our small kitchen garden to fertilize the vegetables. I recall that my mom would empty and clean the plastic bags from the local grocery store and ask me to return them so they could be reused.

As a data collection and analysis intern in the Office of Sustainability, I helped visualize sustainability efforts by creating graphs. This helped us identify and investigate the results of our efforts so that we could make targeted improvements in selected areas. I wanted people like me to understand the true meaning of sustainability, to experience it and to care about it. This was especially true for engineering students like me. I thought that we (future engineers) are the next generation of product developers and infrastructure designers and that we must know to build our products and infrastructure with environmental effects in mind. This led me to develop and give a presentation on "Sustainability and Engineering" to a civil engineering class in fall 2019.

Outside of the office, I attended a birding trip, volunteered with Strawberry Plains Audubon Center's Hummingbird Migration and Nature Celebration and also joined Magnolia Grove, the campus chapter of the National Audubon Society. Joining my partner on our weekly compost shift was one of my favorite parts of my internship. Apart from that, volunteering during the university's annual Food Day Festival and Farmers Market on campus helped me learn about healthy options on campus while getting a chance to see some interesting plants. These experiences led me to persuade my friends to actually be a part of such a program, which I guess indirectly promoted sustainability efforts on campus.

Being a part of the Office of Sustainability, its amazing team, and working to advance sustainability in general helped me not only understand the concept of sustainability better, but also experience it. Now that I have experienced it, I believe I have started caring about it even more. Ole Miss provides this great opportunity for everyone to experience sustainability efforts as I did and I hope it will result in more people caring, as Sir Attenborough said.

ABOUT THE AUTHORS

Lindsey Abernathy, *Associate Director, Office of Sustainability*

Lindsey Abernathy joined the Office of Sustainability in 2014. Lindsey leads campus sustainability data collection efforts including UM's greenhouse gas inventory, works to institutionalize sustainable practices at the university and is involved in all Office of Sustainability projects and initiatives. Lindsey holds a bachelor's degree in journalism and an MBA from UM.

Jade Chalkley, *Sustainability Fellow*

Jade joined the Office of Sustainability in August 2018. As the Sustainability Fellow, Jade serves as a mentor for interns and students, leads projects and data collection within the office, and works to develop a variety of other programs. Jade also manages the Office of Sustainability's social media projects and other outreach initiatives. Jade graduated from Florida Gulf Coast University and holds a bachelor's degree in environmental studies. She is currently pursuing her M.A. in higher education at UM.

Kendall McDonald, *Project Manager, Office of Sustainability*

Kendall McDonald joined the Office of Sustainability in 2015 as Sustainability Fellow and assumed the role of project manager in fall 2017. Kendall works extensively with the Green Student Intern Program, the UM Compost Program and the Green Grove Gameday Recycling Program. She also facilitates programming like Food Day and Green Week. She holds a bachelor's degree in public policy leadership with minors in environmental studies and English.

CHAPTER 18

HEALTHY RELATIONSHIPS
AND Sexual Wellness

By Marc Showalter,
Updated By Erin Cromeans, Sierra Elston, and Jazmine Kelley

Much of our success in college has to do with the quality of our relationships. Whether it's the new relationships we develop once we get to campus or hanging onto the relationships we had when we left home, relationships have a huge impact on our level of contentment and satisfaction with life.

While every relationship, platonic or romantic, is different and has its own unique set of concerns, there are same characteristics that are typically part of any healthy relationship.

Respect

Mutual respect is essential for any healthy relationship. This begins with respect for yourself and extends to respect for the other person. It means having respect for the relationship and believing that what you want in a relationship matters. It also means respecting that the other person's thoughts and feelings are important.

People in healthy relationships have respect for the differences someone else brings to the relationship and are open to learning about the other person and their life experiences. Respect means not trying to control or coerce the other person to be and do what we want. Respect for your boundaries and the boundaries of the other person shows that you understand that without care and respect, the relationship is in jeopardy.

Trust

When we trust the other person, both people feel safe to share their thoughts and feelings without fear of rejection, judgment, or ridicule. Trusting yourself and feeling free to be yourself, and allowing the other person to do the same, is another indication of a healthy relationship.

Trust means being reliable and consistent in your actions and doing what you say you will do. It means demonstrating that you will not intentionally hurt the other person and having confidence that they will not intentionally hurt you.

Setting boundaries and knowing that it is okay to say "no" is another example that there is trust in the relationship. We build trust by giving the other person the benefit of the doubt and believing that we are all doing the best we can at the time.

Open and Honest Communication

Telling the truth. Speaking up, even if your voice is shaking. Saying what you are feeling instead of holding onto it. Being honest about what you want and need. These are all examples of open and honest communication. We should not expect the other person to be able to guess what we are thinking, nor should we decide what the other person thinks, feels, or meant without first listening and trying to understand what happened. Ask. Be clear. Deal with conflicts as soon as possible. Do not expect things to get better on their own. Most people do not like conflicts, but part of becoming a mature person is developing the ability to face challenges rather than avoid them. Try to understand where the other person is coming from before you try to make your point. Try to see things from the other's perspective. Be willing to set boundaries honestly and openly even when it is scary. Brené Brown said it very well, "Daring to set boundaries is about having the courage to love ourselves, even when we risk disappointing others. We can't base our own worthiness on others' approval. Only when we believe, deep down, that we are enough can we say 'Enough!'"

Characteristics of a Healthy Relationship

Think about these characteristics and decide how they apply to you. This can be a great topic of conversation with that special person in your life.

- Respect for each other
- Free to be yourself
- Honest and open communication—primarily face to face

- Best friends
- Don't abuse alcohol or drugs
- Don't control or manipulate
- Feel secure, safe, and comfortable
- Trust—don't cheat
- Resolve conflicts effectively
- No violence
- Have fun together—enjoy the same things
- Maintain separate interests and activities—each supports the other's separate pursuits
- No pressure for sex
- Proud of each other
- Friends and family are happy about the relationship
- More good times than bad
- Have close friends outside the relationship
- Share values

Unfortunately, many students end up in relationships that are not good for them. When you are in the middle of a poor relationship, it can be difficult to see things objectively. On the next page is a list to consider if you or a friend is in an unhealthy relationship. Do you see anything that looks familiar?

Characteristics of an Unhealthy Relationship

- Controlled or manipulated
- Makes you feel bad about yourself
- Abuses alcohol or drugs
- Criticizes you and puts you down
- Physically abusive
- Doesn't have other friends
- Not trustworthy—cheats
- Pressure for sex
- You and the relationship aren't a priority
- Doesn't listen—interrupts
- Friends and family are unhappy about the relationship
- Feel scared or uncomfortable
- Afraid of his or her temper
- Unhappy most of the time
- Tries to distance you from other friends, relationships (family), or activities

If you think you or a friend might be in an unhealthy relationship, here are a few suggestions for what you can do. It can be hard to acknowledge that this might be going on, and you might even be in denial. No matter what, please consider these things:

1. Realize that you deserve better.

2. Ask for help from family and friends.

3. Do not keep secrets.

4. End a relationship you feel is unhealthy or wrong for you.

5. If you feel the relationship is unhealthy, but you feel unable or scared to end it, seek support from the Violence Intervention and Prevention office, the University Counseling Center, or other support services on campus or at home. If you are worried about a friend, get help from any of these places. It may be the most loving thing you can do.

S-E-X is a mysterious three-letter word that we are all curious about at some point in our lives. Sex talks with college students focus on a variety of topics including communication and consent, reproductive health, abstinence, and much more. The truth is, when people learn the facts, they act with confidence rather than fear and are better prepared to make informed choices about their health, safety, and relationships. Before we get started in this section on sex and sexuality, take a minute to think about three things:

1. Where did you first learn about sex? What did you learn?

2. In your life, who talked with you about sex? Was the overarching message positive or negative?

3. What questions do you have about sex? Write them down and see if you find the answers by the end of this chapter.

College Culture

In each part of the world, there are social norms that help shape the customs and actions of the people living there. Sex does not escape this phenomenon. When thinking about how you learned about sex or who in your life has talked with you about sex, it probably comes down to the culture, religion, and values of your family. It is important for you to remember who you are and the family culture you come from as we begin to explore the college culture. Please recognize that there may be vast differences, and we each experience the culture in our own way. If you ask students across campus what the following terms mean, we guarantee you'll get different answers: dating, hooking up, hanging out with, and talking to. However, even with our differing interpretations of culture, experience, and language, there are a few things we need to be clear about before we can move on.

Let's be clear

Let's be clear... good sex is not something to research in the magazine aisle at the grocery store but is a healthy part of many relationships. It is natural and perfectly okay to be attracted to other people. These are biologically and physiologically-based feelings. Let's be clear on one more thing: good sex requires mutual consent. For more information on consent, what it is, how to get it, how to give it, and what to do with a "yes" or "no," see the Communication section.

What is sexual wellness?

There are multiple aspects that we can think of as defining the word sex. Sex can mean the biological characteristics that define humans as male or female, but often times, sex is used when referencing sexual activity. According to the World Health Organization (WHO), sexual wellness is defined as:

- A state of physical, emotional, mental, and social well-being in relation to sexuality

- Not merely the absence of disease, dysfunction, or infirmity

- Positive and respectful approach to sexuality and sexual relationships

- Ability to have pleasurable and safe sexual experiences free of coercion, discrimination, and violence

- All persons must be respected, protected, and fulfilled

While it is important to understand what sex and sexual wellness are, it is also necessary to understand what is not sex. Kissing, hugging, cuddling, snuggling, feeling, and touching are not considered sex. Individuals can enjoy all of these activities without having sex.

What's not sex? Who's having sex? Perception on college campuses

Often times, people believe that everyone in college is having sex. However, perception is often much different than reality. According to the American College Health Association—National College Health Assessment in 2018—approximately 76 percent of college students reported having 0–1 sexual partners in the past 12 months. That data busts the myth that college students are engaging in sexual activity every night or are on a quest to have sex with as many partners as possible during their college career.

Abstinence

Now that we understand that not everyone is having sex during college, let's consider abstinence and what it means. Abstinence is always a healthy choice, even if you have previously had sex. In its purest form, abstinence is the act of refraining from some kind of action. In this chapter, we are referring to refraining from some or all forms of sexual activity. It does not matter what others are doing, what they think about you, or what they might say about you. You should make choices that make you feel comfortable. Additionally, there are benefits to abstinence as it prevents pregnancy and reduces the risk for disease contraction.

Safe Sexual Wellness practices

Sexually Transmitted Infections (STIs) are infections that are passed from one person to another during sexual contact. Many STIs are asymptomatic, meaning they have no symptoms. There are many types of STIs, and they are very common and easily spreadable. Remember that when you have sex with someone, you are potentially exposing yourself not only to STIs they might have, but the STIs their previous partners and their previous partner's partners may also have carried. This means that even though you may have had unprotected sex with only one person, if they had unprotected sex with multiple partners who also had unprotected sex with others, you could still be indirectly exposing yourself to the STIs of dozens of other individuals. Practicing safer sex enables individuals to reduce their risk of getting an infection. Before we go into further detail, note that there are more than 20 types of STIs; however, we are going to discuss the most common infections: chlamydia, gonorrhea, syphilis, genital herpes, HPV (genital warts) and HIV.

BACTERIAL	CONTRACTED	SYMPTOMS	HEALTH RISKS
Chlamydia	Unprotected vaginal sex Unprotected anal sex Unprotected oral sex	"Silent disease" **Women** may have a slight vaginal discharge, pain during urination, pain during sex,frequent urination. **Men** may have discharge or itchy feeling, mild pain on urination, infection of anus or throat.	**Women** may have infertility, infected cervix, pelvic pain, Pelvic Inflammatory Disease, ectopic pregnancy, arthritis. Can be passed to infant during labor/delivery. **Men** may have infertility,arthritis, eye infections, urinary infections.
Gonorrhea	Unprotected vaginal sex Unprotected anal sex Unprotected oral sex Mother to unborn	**Women** may have vaginal discharge, pain during urination, increase in urination. **Men** may have thick yellow/green discharge from penis, pain on urination, pain in penis. **Both men and women** may have rectal bleeding and discharge.	Infection of genital area; lip, mouth, or anus of both men and women. Pelvis Inflammatory Disease, problems with pregnancy and infertility.
Syphilis	Unprotected vaginal sex Unprotected anal sex Unprotected oral sex Direct touch Close body contact Kissing Mother to unborn	**Both men and women** may have painless sores, swollen glands, skin rashes, flu-like symptoms, brain infection.	Skin, bone, heart disease, dementia, blindness if left untreated, fatal if left untreated.
Genital Herpes	Unprotected vaginal sex Unprotected anal sex Unprotected oral sex Direct contact Skin to skin	**Both men and women** may have fatigue and fever, painful blisters, itching, red skin formed into groups of sores; sores may vrust and heal with scarring.	Virus hides in nerve endings and reoccurs.
HPV (Genital Warts)	Unprotected vaginal sex Unprotected anal sex Unprotected oral sex	**Both men and women** may have soft, moist, pink growths either on penis or in female genitals and around anus; growths may be cauliflower in shape.	Invasive cervical cancer and bladder cancers.
HIV	Unprotected vaginal sex Unprotected anal sex Unprotected oral sex Sharing needles	**Both men and women** may have swollen glands, flu-like symptoms.	Damages body's immune system, AIDS, can be fatal.

Vaccinations

Vaccinations are available for a few STIs including Hepatitis A and B and HPV. Hepatitis A is most frequently transmitted through sexual contact, particularly among men who have sex with men. Exposure to Hepatitis B may be common in certain high-risk groups, including heterosexuals with multiple partners and men who have sex with men. HPV vaccinations are used to prevent the most common strands of the virus; however, being vaccinated for HPV does not mean that an individual will not contract the disease. It is still possible to contract HPV with viral strands not included in the immunization.

Contraception

During sexual activity, skin-to-skin contact and bodily fluids are exchanged that can pass infections from one person to another. The body fluids by which infections can pass are blood, semen, pre-ejaculation, vaginal fluids and sometimes breast milk. Using contraception can help stop the spread of sexually transmitted infections and reduce the risk of pregnancy. Contraception is a method of preventing 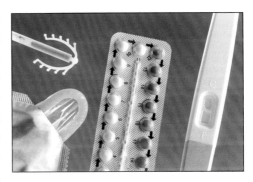 pregnancy; it is any method or procedure that prevents fertilization. There are three types of contraception:

1. **Intrauterine contraception**
   a. Device inserted in the uterus to prevent pregnancy
   b. May be kept in place five to ten years

2. **Hormonal methods**
   a. Implant
      i. A thin rod (device) placed under skin
      ii. Can last up to three years
   b. Shots
   c. Patch, vaginal ring, progestin pill, combined estrogen/progestin, emergency contraception

3. **Barrier methods**
   a. Male Condom (most common)
   b. Female Condom
   c. Diaphragm/Cervical Cap

A closer look

Using a condom is a simple and effective way to protect you and your partner when having sex. Women and men typically like condoms because they are inexpensive and easy to use. When using condoms, check to make sure that the packaging is not damaged and the condom is not expired. They help prevent pregnancy and sexually transmitted infections, unlike hormonal and intrauterine methods that protect only against pregnancy. Condoms do not require a prescription, and they can be used with other forms of birth control methods, except with another condom. (You cannot use a male and female condom at the same time.) Condoms also have no side effects unless you are allergic to latex, in which case you can use non-latex condoms.

Communication

A whole book could be written on the importance of communication, both verbal and nonverbal, within the context of sexual relationships. However, for brevity, we'll look at three things in particular:

1. **Determine what you want** (or don't want) from sex and communicate those wants and needs effectively. Sure, that sounds easy enough, but in the moment, how do you do it? Our advice: don't wait until "the moment"—have the conversation well before that time. Sex does not happen automatically once you start kissing, touching, or drinking. Each individual is constantly communicating; pay attention to your partner's words, actions, and body language. Ask questions, provide clear responses, and respect both your and your partner's boundaries.

2. **Communicate consent.** Sexual wellness can be achieved only when clear communication and consent are part of the equation. Consent is an enthusiastic, sober, verbal, mutually understood "yes." The absence of a "no" does not mean "yes." You should always make an effort to understand how your partner is feeling and what he or she wants before engaging in sexual activity. Remember, consent is free of coercion, understood, and changeable, meaning both partners are equally free to stop at any time when engaging in activity. Consent empowers people, and failure to get consent has serious consequences. If your partner is drunk, high, or in a mental state caused by a substance that would in any way affect their ability to make a decision, he or she cannot give consent. It can be confusing or hard to tell sometimes if someone can give consent. If you have to think about it, then you should wait before having sex. Coercing someone or pressuring someone to have sex is never consent. (See Violence Prevention chapter for more information on this topic.)

3. **Negotiate the use of contraceptives** or disease prevention techniques. To some, this may seem like a no-brainer, but it's not always the woman's responsibility to take a pill and the man's responsibility to bring a condom. The responsibility, conversation, and negotiation belong to anyone wishing to have sex. Ask these questions: "What would you like us to do for birth control?" and "How about disease prevention?" There are many reasons people give for not wanting to use preventive measures such as condoms. Listen to your partner's concerns and work out any possible alternatives, but in the end make the healthiest decision for both of you, and that might mean not having sex.

Talking about using condoms

Communication about the use of condoms with your partner is important. Though you may be nervous, telling your partner about an STI or unexpected pregnancy will be far more difficult. Practice what you might say beforehand, then choose the right time to talk. Don't be shy; be direct and honest about what you want and don't want. If you cannot talk to your partner about sex, it may not be the right time to become sexually active with this person. Planned Parenthood has some great examples of ways to start the conversation with your partner.

If Your Partner Says: It doesn't feel as good with a condom.
You Can Say: I'll feel more relaxed. If I'm more relaxed, it will be better for both of us.

If Your Partner Says: Don't you trust me?
You Can Say: Trust isn't the point. People can carry sexually transmitted infections without knowing it.

If Your Partner Says: I'll pull out in time.
You Can Say: I want to feel relaxed and enjoy this and pulling out is just too risky. There's a chance I could get pregnant, or we might get too excited to stop. And pulling out won't prevent sexually transmitted infections.

If Your Partner Says: Putting it on interrupts everything.
You Can Say: Not if I help put it on.

If Your Partner Says: But I love you.
You Can Say: Then you'll help me protect myself.

If Your Partner Says: I guess you don't really love me.

You Can Say: I'm not going to "prove my love" by risking my health. If you really love me, you would want me to feel safe.

It may help to talk to someone you trust and who cares about you when you need to make such a decision.

Campus and Community Resources

After all this information you still may have questions that have not been answered. For a deeper discussion on any of these topics, you should talk with your physician or nurse practitioner at the Student Health Center, Lafayette County Health Department, or Planned Parenthood. These agencies also provide STI testing for all sexually transmitted infections. It is important to remember to get tested if you engage in sexual activity. We encourage you to get tested every three to six months if you have multiple partners, and if you have one partner, we encourage you to get tested every six months to a year.

More information about testing centers is below:

Testing Centers

Student Health Center
662-915-7274
V.B. Harrison Health Center
Mon.–Thurs.: 8 a.m.–5 p.m., Fri.: 9 a.m.–5 p.m.

Lafayette Co. Health Dept.
662-234-5231
101 Veterans Dr., Oxford, MS
Open Mon.–Fri.: 8 a.m.–5 p.m

Planned Parenthood
901-725-1717
2430 Poplar Ave. Ste. 100, Memphis, TN 38112
Mon., Tues., Thurs.: 9 a.m.–6 p.m., Wed., Fri.: 8 a.m.–4 p.m., Sat.: 8 a.m.–noon

---

ABOUT THE AUTHORS

Marc Showalter, former Clinical Assistant Professor in Leadership and Counselor Education

Marc Showalter recently retired from the University.

Erin Cromeans, Assistant Director of Wellness Education, William Magee Center for AOD and Wellness Education

Erin Cromeans is currently pursuing a doctorate in health and kinesiology with a focus in health behavior. She received a Master of Science in nutrition and hospitality management degree at the University of Mississippi in 2011, a Master of Science in health promotion at the University of Mississippi in 2009, and a Bachelor of Science in exercise science at the University of Mississippi in 2007. Ms. Cromeans is a Certified Health Education Specialist (CHES) through the National Commission for Health Education and Credentialing. Ms. Cromeans has been a part of the Ole Miss Family for more than ten years and loves Oxford more and more each day. Hotty Toddy!

Sierra Elston, Coordinator for Wellness Education, William Magee Center for AOD and Wellness Education

Sierra is from Montgomery, Alabama, and attended the University of North Alabama in Florence to complete her B.S. in therapeutic nutrition and her M.S. in wellness and health promotion. While completing her master's degree she had the opportunity to design and support a university wellness program, and she enjoys developing solutions for the unique challenges that campus health programming presents. She is excited to bring her passion for wellness to Oxford, and aims to serve and inspire by providing learning opportunities to students that will empower them to live healthier, happier lives. Sierra enjoys spending her free time hiking, painting, cooking, or simply relaxing at home with her cat Stella.

ABOUT THE AUTHORS

Jazmine Kelley, *Coordinator of Wellness Education, William Magee Center for AOD and Wellness Education*

Jazmine is from Memphis, Tennessee. She received her B.S. in biochemistry and molecular biology as well as her M.S. in food science, nutrition, and health promotion from Mississippi State University in Starkville, Mississippi. While completing her degrees, she discovered her passion for rural health, student well-being, and health promotion in higher education. Jazmine is currently a Certified Health Education Specialist, Clinical Health Promotion and Wellness Coach, Certified Wellness Practitioner, and Certified Physical Trainer. She aspires to enhance the overall health and well-being of populations through the lens of community structures and health promotion practices. During her free time, Jazmine enjoys reading, journaling, and hanging out with her family and friends.

CHAPTER 19

HEALTH CARE IN A College Setting

By Alex Langhart

Your Health Care is Vital to Academic Success

In college, it is advantageous to actively participate in your education to be successful. Sometimes, it isn't accidentally hitting the snooze button too many times that keeps you from class, studying, or an extracurricular activity. Colds, stomach bugs, flu, sprains, and other nagging ailments can negatively impact your ability to fully engage. It is important to be a good steward of your health and well-being.

Taking preventive health measures and seeking health services when sick will ensure that you are positioned for success as you navigate your college experience. This chapter will help break down the intricate world of the US health care system and give you some guidance on how to take a proactive role in your health.

Health Literacy

As complicated as health care is today, it is vital to have a solid foundation when it comes to obtaining, processing, and understanding basic health information and services needed to make appropriate health decisions (1). This is called health literacy.

Health literacy affects people's ability to:

- Navigate the health care system, including filling out complex forms and locating providers and services.

- Share personal information, such as health history, with providers.

- Engage in self-care and chronic disease management.

- Understand mathematical concepts such as probability and risk.

Let's look at the most common financial terms when dealing with payment:

Deductible- a deductible is the amount you pay for health care services before your health insurance begins to pay.

For example: Check to see what your current plan's deductible is. In this scenario, it is $1,000. That means you will be responsible for 100% of your medical bills until the amount you pay reaches $1,000. After that, your insurance plan should start covering a share of the costs.

Copay- a copay is a fixed amount you pay at the time of service. This amount can vary by the type of service and insurance plan. Some plans require a copay for prescriptions too.

For example: your insurance plan may state that a physician office visit might have a copay of $25. When you check in for your appointment, this payment will be expected before receiving health services. Make sure that you pay close attention to the copay amounts because an emergency room copay may be significantly more than a physician office visit.

Coinsurance- coinsurance is your share of the costs of a health care service calculated as a percentage. You start paying coinsurance after you've paid your plan's deductible.

For example: let's say you need a shot. Currently, you have reached your $1,000 deductible. However, you have a coinsurance percentage of 20%. This means that your plan will cover 80% of the cost of your shot. You will be responsible for the other 20 percent - your coinsurance. If your shot costs $50, your plan will pay $40 and you will pay $10.

Now that we have covered some of the common payment terms, let's look at pricing and costs. After you have received care and have elected for the health facility to bill your insurance, you will receive an **Explanation of Benefits (EOB).** This paper or electronic form notifies you of claims submitted to your insurance. It gives you details about what your insurance will pay for and what you are responsible for paying. Remember, an EOB is not a bill. Anything that you do owe, you will receive as a bill from the provider or health facility where you were seen. However, an EOB is important when determining if you are being fully covered according to your policy and if the correct amount from the provider or health facility is being charged. **HealthSmart** has a good example of an EOB broken down:

SCAN ME

You may notice the terms **amount billed** and **allowed amount** when scanning over an EOB. **Amount billed:** refers to the amount the provider or health facility charges for a particular service. **Allowed amount:** refers to an agreed upon amount that your health insurance will actually pay the provider or health facility for a particular service.

This can get confusing. Every provider or health facility sets a chargemaster that lists the costs of each service they offer. If you do not have health insurance or want to pay in cash, this is the charge or amount billed that you would owe. However, providers that accept certain health insurance products have payment contracts that negotiate payment on the patient's behalf. The provider or health facility will charge the normal price for a service, however, if that health insurance product has negotiated a lower rate, that is the allowed amount and can decrease the amount a patient owes.

Let's look at an example:

You have become ill and decide to visit your primary care physician. The physician does an exam, orders some labs, fills a prescription, and sends you on your way. When your EOB arrives, you notice the amount billed versus the allowed amount. Your physician has billed your insurance $125 for your visit. This is the amount billed. However, your insurance has negotiated with your physician what they will pay for that particular visit. In this case, they will only pay $80 – the allowed amount. This can have quite the impact on your total costs depending on the status of your deductible. Review the two scenarios in the table below using the information from above:

Maura's Health Insurance Plan: $500 Deductible					
Maura filing health insurance (Has not met deductible)			Maura not filing health insurance (Paying out of pocket)		
Billed Amount	Allowed Amount	Maura will pay	Billed Amount	Allowed Amount	Maura will pay
$125	$80	$80	$125	Does not apply	$125

Now, this is a very simplified example, but negotiated rates through a health insurance product can greatly impact the costs you incur.

Here is another twist affecting cost – **in-network** versus **out-of-network**. You may also see this as **preferred provider** and **non-preferred provider**. Your health insurance will have a network of providers and hospitals it considers **in-network** due to contracts with them. As we saw previously, those providers and health facilities should be your first choice when seeking care. You will get the best rate and coverage with in-network providers compared to out-of-network providers. If you must choose an **out-of-network** provider, be prepared to potentially pay more out-of-pocket. This is due to the fact that your health insurance has not negotiated a rate with that provider. Your insurance may cover very little or nothing at all of the service, making you responsible for the rest of the bill. To find out who is in-network, it is always a good idea to call your health insurance or check their website before you schedule an appointment.

Health care finance can be overwhelming. This is why it is so important to familiarize yourself with your health insurance and know what services are covered. Never be afraid to ask questions especially when considering costs. The current landscape is demanding more transparency in health care, which can only benefit us as patients. Stay sharp on your health literacy.

Patient Rights

Some of the hottest topics in health care revolve around patient rights, privacy, and security. Health care professionals take privacy and security very seriously. Access to care, confidentiality, and consent to treatment are some examples that fall under this category. Did you know that according to the **Emergency Medical Treatment and Active Labor Act (EMTALA)**, no patient can be turned away from an emergency room no matter their financial situation before receiving a screening exam? This is important when thinking about access to care.

When it comes to confidentiality, you want to ensure that your sensitive medical information is not easily accessible by those you would not grant access. The **Health Insurance Portability and Accountability Act (HIPAA)** was signed in 1996. It was created to stipulate how personal information is maintained and protected and to address some gaps in insurance coverage. There are two rules within HIPAA that you should know. The Privacy Rule, a Federal law, gives you rights over your health information and sets rules and limits on who can look at and receive your health information. The Privacy Rule applies to all forms of individuals' protected health information, whether electronic, written, or oral. The Security Rule is a Federal law that requires security for health information in electronic form (2). To learn more about HIPAA, check this out:

Health plans, most health care providers, and health care clearinghouses are considered covered entities and must follow these laws. The contents of your medical record, billing information, and anything relating to your care are protected. Covered entities must have procedures and policies in place to secure your information. This is why if you ever request to have your medical records sent somewhere, the covered entity will require you to sign an authorization to release this information.

Informed consent is your patient right to receive information and actively engage providers with questions about treatments so that you can make a well-informed decision about your health care. Honesty and transparency are crucial to this process. You as the patient must understand the relevant medical information and implications of the recommended treatment because you may choose an alternate plan of care once presented with the facts.

Privacy and security are of paramount importance when it comes to managing your health information. You have a right to know who has access to it and can choose who may receive it.

UM Student Health Service

Now that we have talked through the technical world of health care, we will look at what is offered here at the university. Our Student Health Service is located at **400 Rebel Drive** across from George Hall and behind Meek Auditorium. We are staffed with 4 board certified physicians, 2 nurse practitioners, 5 registered nurses, 1 certified lab technician, and 1 certified x-ray technician. Our providers are specialized in internal medicine, sports medicine, pediatric medicine, and psychiatric medicine.

Here are a few of the services we provide:

Acute Care: Illness, minor injuries	Wellness
X-Ray	LGBTQ+ Care
Immunizations	Physicals
Labs	Nutrition Services
Allergy Shots	Pharmacy On-site
Physical Therapy	Travel Clinic

Who is eligible for services?

All enrolled students can receive care at Student Health.

What insurance do you accept?

We take and file any insurance you have as a courtesy (except Medicare, Medicaid, and state or federally funded plans). However, we are currently only in-network with Blue Cross Blue Shield and Student Aetna. If you do not have either of those insurances, it will be filed as out-of-network so please ask our business staff about potential costs.

Can I still be seen without insurance?

Yes! However, you will be responsible for any charges from that visit.

How much does it cost, and how do I pay?

There is NO Office Visit fee no matter if you have insurance or not. That means we will not collect a copay or deductible. You will only be charged for ancillary services such as lab, x-ray, supplies, injections, etc. If you have insurance, we will bill that first, and anything left over will be placed on your bursar account. We strive to be the most affordable option in town.

Do you take walk-ins?

Absolutely! We do encourage students to call and make an appointment because our walk-in spots are limited throughout the day due to demand. Call 662-915-7274.

When are you open?

Hours: Monday – Thursday, 8:00 a.m. – 5:00 p.m.,
Friday, 9:00 a.m. – 5:00 p.m.

Want to learn more about our services? Visit our website:

Urgent Care Clinics and Hospital

What happens when Student Health is closed? Luckily, there are urgent care clinics in town with extended hours and weekend coverage. If you are in need of emergency services, call 911. Baptist Memorial Hospital is located less than 3 miles from campus and offers a 24/7 emergency room.

Health Care Survival Tips

Hopefully, this crash course in the complicated world of health care is beneficial and helps you make well-informed decisions concerning your health and well-being. Below are some health care tips to remember while navigating through college.

- Familiarize yourself with health care financial terms and EOBs.

- Find out what your health insurance covers and considers in-network. Know your patient rights.

- Be proactive in your health care.

ABOUT THE AUTHORS

Alex Langhart, *Director of Student Health Services*

Alex received his undergraduate and graduate degrees from the University of Mississippi. He became the Director for Student Health Services in 2019.

CHAPTER 20

ACHIEVING MENTAL Wellness

By Bud Edwards and Rachel McClain

C oming to college can be one of the most exciting times in a person's life. Social events, athletic events, new people, and new experiences combined with academic pressures, financial concerns, and adjustment issues can also make coming to college one of the more stressful times in a person's life. Establishing and maintaining your overall wellness, including mental wellness, is an important component in an overall strategy to being successful in college. Here at Ole Miss we are encouraging students to learn or improve their skills in balancing a busy lifestyle, managing stress on a regular and an acute basis, and creating and implementing a wellness management routine for the physical, emotional, mental, sexual, financial, social, intellectual, spiritual, and environmental aspects of their lives.

STRESS

What is the first thought that comes to your mind? Perhaps it was something physical (stomach-ache) or mental (memory lapses) or emotional (fear or sadness) or some other unpleasant response. You may have a negative perception of stress but at its essence, stress is your mind and/or your body giving you feedback about your reflection on past events, your encounter with present events, or your anticipation/ anxiety about future events. Stress can have a productive effect (motivation to study for a test) or an unproductive effect (so much anxiety about taking the test that you struggle to focus) and needs to be successfully managed to do well in college and in life as a whole. Failure to successfully manage stress well can lead to a decline in mental wellness and, if not addressed, certain mental health conditions.

Stress affects each of us differently and it is crucial to know yourself well enough to identify the impact of stress in your life, place it on a scale at an appropriate place of intensity, and have a variety of strategies to manage that stress on a routine and on an immediate basis. The graph below outlines some of the ways that stress can affect each of us.

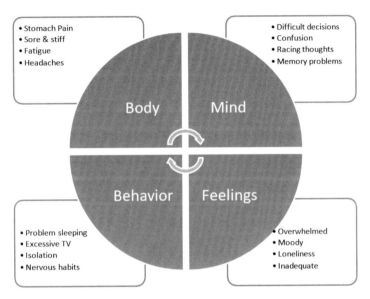

Take another look at the graph and identify where you are likely to experience stress in your life. Think of both really challenging and difficult times as well as daily activities/events that affect you. There may be ways that you respond that are not listed so be sure to jot those down for future use. Now use the gauge to place the impact of each of those events on your functioning at the time that event occurs. This gives you a template for the types of interventions that you need to have to success-fully manage the stress in your life.

Self-Care	Mind	Social	Spirit
• Eat well • Regular exercise • Make time for fun • Healthy rewards • Manage time	• Perspective • Accept limits • Counter negative thoughts • Establish doable goals • Be proactive	• Positive relationships • Communicate • Assert boundaries • Reach out to others	• Clarify values • Identify strengths / weaknesses • Positive life philosophy • Live up to commitments

Suicide: A Preventable Condition

Every fall I participate in a number of campus welcoming events as we celebrate the arrival of new students, and each spring I attend other celebration ceremonies to mark the completion of the college experience, graduation. In between those events is a year where students face a great of deal stress that can lead to a variety of mental health issues. One of those issues is suicide. Suicide is an extreme response to life circumstances that includes a variety of contributing factors. These factors manifest themselves differently in different people and may have been present over a long period of time or arise in a short period of time with a high level of intensity. Suicide as a singular act is difficult to predict, but the good news is that it is preventable.

Suicide prevention is rooted in several domains. One domain is an accepting community that cares for its members and wants the best for each other within that community. This type of community is reflected in The Creed, where we pledge to respect the dignity of each other and to treat each other with fairness and civility. Another domain is for that community to be knowledgeable about good mental health and to practice good mental health by promoting self-care with ourselves and with each other. It is important to know all of the resources on campus that support good physical and mental health and to use those resources appropriately. A third domain is to connect with each other and to value those relationships enough to have productive conversations about good mental health. In other words, our relationships are important enough to speak to each other if/when we see something wrong. We care enough about each other to accept that a community member may be struggling, to address our concerns with that person, to direct him or her to the appropriate resources, and to provide support while he or she works to get to a better, healthier place.

THE NUMBERS:

Among all suicides, **33.4%** of those deaths involved alcohol; **23.8%** tested positive for antidepressants; **20%** involved opiates, both legal and illegal forms.

Among high school students who were surveyed, **17%** had seriously considered attempting suicide. Female students in this sub-population were twice as likely to seriously consider suicide (22.4% to 11.6%).

Among adults age 18–22 in college who were surveyed, **8%** had suicidal thoughts and **2.4%** made a suicide plan. *cdc.gov/violenceprevention/*

A national survey of university/college students reported in the last 12 months:

- **46.4%** of respondents reported feeling hopeless

- **32.6%** of respondents reported feeling so depressed that it was difficult to function

- **6.4%** had intentionally harmed themselves

- **8.1%** had seriously considered suicide

- **1.3%** had attempted suicide

At Ole Miss we enjoy a sense of family that is the essence of the University. As family, we hold each other close and lift each other up during our time here on campus and after we graduate and move on to the next chapter of our lives. Please review the following information and allow this moment to be the start of our commitment. While we are here, join me in pledging to make our campus suicide free. Let's demonstrate our dedication to The Creed by applying its principles daily to meet this goal of no suicides in our community.

Tips for talking with someone who might be considering suicide:

- **Be honest and direct about your concerns.** People may feel isolated and hopeless, and letting them know that you care can be helpful.

- **Ask if they are thinking of harming themselves.** This can be done directly (Have you had thoughts of killing yourself?) or indirectly (Have you had thoughts of hurting yourself?). Either way is valid and may depend on your comfort level and/or your relationship with the other person. It is important to ask this question. If you cannot ask this question, please find someone who can.

- **Remind them that they are not alone and that there is plenty of help** for them on campus; something can be done to help them feel better. Again, try to decrease the feelings of isolation and/or hopelessness.

- **Make a connection with one of the campus resources.** Help them talk about their concerns with the University Counseling Center (UCC); an advisor; or someone in Student Affairs, such as a Housing staff member, a physician, or nurse practitioner at Student Health Services; a UPD officer; or some other trusted professional. The goal is to get them to the UCC to speak with a clinical staff member. Reaching out to any of the above individuals can help achieve that goal.

- **Suicide is preventable.** For most people, there is a window of vulnerability that we can intervene in and work to help them make a different choice. Do not underestimate your ability to help save a life.

Warning Signs

According to the National Institute for Mental Health, there are several warning signs that may indicate someone might be considering suicide:

Talking about wanting to die or to kill oneself

Talking about feeling hopeless or having no reason to live

Looking for a way to kill oneself, such as searching online or buying a gun

Talking about being a burden to others and that others would be better off if one was gone

Talking about feeling trapped or in unbearable pain

Showing rage or talking about seeking revenge

Withdrawing or feeling isolated

Increasing the use of alcohol, drugs, or both

Giving away prized possessions

Acting anxious or agitated; behaving recklessly

Sleeping too little or too much

Displaying extreme mood swings

ABOUT THE AUTHORS

Bud Edwards, *Director of the Counseling Center*

Bud is originally from Mississippi and came back home to give back to the university, Oxford, and the state of Mississippi. His experience and expertise includes working with students with anxiety, depression, developmental issues, and trauma.

Rachel McClain, *Graduate Assistant in the Counseling Center*

CHAPTER
21
FINANCIAL
Literacy

By Laura Diven-Brown and Nataša Novićević

Many new college students are challenged with the balancing act of independence and responsibilities. This is not an easy task, and many students feel overwhelmed, especially when it comes to managing their finances.

This chapter is about smart money management. As you read it, you will see why financial literacy has become an important topic on college campuses, both inside and outside the classroom.

We understand that talking about money isn't too fun, but maybe you have noticed how the cost of a cup of coffee or soda a day adds up, right? If you get in the habit of thinking about your spending now, it will help you in the long run when you are making bigger decisions than whether to buy coffee.

So, we will cover a few topics that are useful right now but also later in life:

- The cost of college
- Understanding financial aid
- Living within a budget
- A few thoughts about credit/debit cards and debt
- Having fun in college without overspending
- The power of education and saving
- Planning for financial emergencies

You're still not convinced that this chapter is relevant to you? That could be because you are not too worried about money at this moment. You may not have many (if any) monthly bills this year – and for some of you, your parents may be taking care of all your educational expenses. But this won't be the case forever. If you live in an apartment now or plan to move off campus as soon as next year, you need to budget for rent, utilities, and trips to the grocery store. You can't plan on Internet being provided, and streaming services aren't free either. These are all monthly expenses. Even if your parents help you, it is a good idea to understand what they have to do to manage these costs.

Your participation in the following exercises will help you learn about personal finance. We want you to be aware of your college expenses, to talk with your family about how you are paying for college, and to be knowledgeable about your financing options. Knowing this information is the first step toward creating a budget and learning to live within your means.

THE **COST** OF COLLEGE

What is your budget? It is the estimated cost of attending college for one academic year. Realistically, it is not just about tuition - it is a lot more. Your budget includes both direct costs (the charges you see on your Bursar bill such as tuition and fees, on-campus housing, and meal plan) and indirect costs (not charged to your Bursar account, but things that must be paid for nonetheless: books, gas for your car, trips back home, and other personal expenses). FYI - The terms "budget" and "cost of attendance" can be used interchangeably.

So, how much do you think your first year at Ole Miss costs? After you have taken a few minutes to add things up, look at the numbers below.

ESTIMATED STUDENT BUDGET
Based on the 2020-21 Academic Year
(Also known as your Cost of Attendance)

EXPENSE	UNDERGRADUATE
Tuition	$8,718
Capital Improvements Fee	$100
On-campus Housing	$6,264
Food	$4,470
Books/Supplies	$1,100
Personal/Travel	$5,100
Total for Residents	**$25,752**
Additional Fee for Nonresidents	*$16,272*
Total for Nonresidents	**$42,024**

Were you close? Or are you thousands of dollars off in your calculations? How are you or your parents paying for this? (And did you even consider things such as football tickets, eating out, or fees for extracurricular activities?)

Have you ever thought about how much just one three-credit class costs? If you are a Mississippi resident, it is approximately $1,090, and, if you are a nonresident, the cost is $3,124. This may put things in perspective when you decide to sleep instead of attending class. Each time you miss a Tuesday/Thursday class, that comes to about $36 for Mississippi residents, or $102 for nonresidents! Think about it. Thirty-five dollars is about three pizzas or a tank of gas! Skipping class is like buying an expensive concert ticket and then choosing to take a nap instead. You have paid for the class — go!

This is a perfect example of what you should begin noticing. So, even if you do not personally feel the direct effect of spending money on your education (either because of financial aid awards or because your family is helping you), we hope you learn how important it is to be aware of the flow of money.

UNDERSTANDING **FINANCIAL AID**

We encourage all of you to read this section, even if you do not use financial aid – and even if you are quick to say "my parents handle this stuff." Did you know that 87% of our freshmen receive some form of financial assistance?

So, what exactly is "financial aid"? It is any money that can help you pay for college – scholarships, grants, loans, and work opportunities. This money can come from the U.S. Department of Education, the state where you live, outside organizations, or from Ole Miss.

What is on your award letter? Here are a few terms to understand.

Grants and Scholarships: Grants and scholarships are considered "gift aid" because they do not have to be repaid. Grants are typically need-based (meaning that you have to demonstrate financial need based on a processed Free Application for Federal Student Aid – FAFSA - to qualify), and the funds usually come from governmental sources. Scholarships are typically merit-based. Ole Miss offers many institutional scholarships, particularly to entering freshmen and community college transfer students, but there are private scholarship dollars available as well. Never turn down a grant or scholarship unless you cannot comply with the award requirements. It is free money!

Loans: Institutional, federal, and private educational loans are awards that must be repaid. Some are need-based, some are not, and they usually have a set annual loan limit.

Work-Study: The Federal Work-Study program is a need-based employment opportunity on campus. If you are eligible, it is your responsibility to contact prospective supervisors and interview for a position. The Office of Financial Aid can provide job leads.

Estimated awards: These awards are indicators of what you may be eligible for depending on requirements and/or appropriate applications submitted. They are not guaranteed.

Before you accept anything and everything that has been offered to you on your financial aid award letter, stop and question what it is you are being offered. Does it have to be paid back later? What do you have to do to keep receiving the award? Or, is the award amount for only one or two semesters?

Where do I start? Federal aid is the largest single source of funding for students. To qualify, students must complete the Free Application for Federal Student Aid (FAFSA). This application also is used to determine eligibility for state and institutional need-based awards. It must be submitted every year. This is the first step you should take. Remember these two things: file your FAFSA early and provide accurate information.

The FAFSA application for the upcoming school year goes live October 1.

Here are some reasons to file early:

To receive your aid on the earliest date: Some applications are selected for "verification" by the U.S. Department of Education. This is a process to confirm the accuracy of the information submitted on the FAFSA. During peak season (typically June through September), processing can take three or more weeks. Make sure you check your processed FAFSA (or contact the Office of Financial Aid), to find out if you have been selected for verification.

To gain access to better loans and other aid: Funding is often available in limited allocations, so some need-based student loans and aid programs such as Federal Work-Study are awarded on a first-come, first- served basis. The earlier you file, the more likely you are to receive them, if eligible.

To avoid penalties for late fees: You know that fall semester bill that was due mid-August? If you still have not paid it by the end of October, the balance starts to accrue interest (1.5% per month). This may not seem like much, but if you wait until the end of the semester, you could wind up paying an additional several hundred dollars in interest. There are better things to do with that money! That's why you should ideally have your financial aid package and financial plan in place before you arrive for school.

After you have filed your FAFSA, you need to be diligent and FOLLOW UP. Do not wait for someone to contact you about the next steps; find out if the Office of Financial Aid needs additional information from you. Always read the e-mails you receive through your go.olemiss.edu e-mail address because that is how Financial Aid attempts to reach you.

If you receive an e-mail and are not sure what it is telling you to do, SCHEDULE AN APPOINTMENT TO VISIT THE OFFICE. You will find that taking care of these

kinds of matters is considerably easier when you are proactive. There are advisors on duty at the front desk in the lobby who are happy to assist you. Or, if you prefer to speak to an advisor in private, this can easily be arranged with an appointment. Get to know the staff member who helps you, so later you can follow up with questions directly if needed – without having to tell your story again.

NEVER STOP LOOKING for financial aid options. While it is true that much of the scholarship aid available through the University of Mississippi is offered to incoming freshmen only, these scholarships are certainly not the only ones out there. All students should consult their academic departments for major-specific scholarship opportunities. Participating in University-related activities or organizations, may sometimes yield scholarships as well. Examples include band, choirs, or ROTC (we have Army, Navy, and Airforce at University of Mississippi.

Another often overlooked place to hunt for scholarship aid is in your local community. A few potential sources are civic organizations, churches, alumni association chapters, and parent employers. You also can visit national scholarship search engines such as https://www.fastweb.com/ and https://bigfuture.collegeboard.org/.

If you have already secured scholarships, be sure that you are aware of the terms and conditions to keep them. If, for some reason, you find yourself in the unfortunate situation of failing to meet those terms (or if you are concerned that you won't), you should always check with the scholarship provider or the Office of Financial Aid. In many cases, you will have the opportunity to appeal the loss of your scholarship and continue to receive it under probationary status until you are back in good standing.

Mississippi residents also should remember to apply for state grants every year. Do not pass up this opportunity. The application deadline for the Mississippi Tuition Assistance Grant (MTAG) and Mississippi Eminent Scholars Grant (MESG) is September 15 each year, and the deadline for the Higher Education Legislative Plan for Needy Students (HELP Grant) is March 1 each year.

WHAT'S MY PART IN KEEPING MY AWARDS?

There are enrollment and GPA requirements for your awards. That's where you come in.

Scholarships – For most awards, maintain full-time enrollment and a 3.0 resident (UM credits) GPA to stay eligible. Many scholarships require that you agree to certain terms and conditions. If you have any questions about your scholarship requirements, visit the Office of Financial Aid.

Federal aid – Must be meeting the three Satisfactory Academic Progress Standards to stay eligible:

• Have a Federal GPA of at least 2.0 (which still includes any forgiven or excluded course grades)

• Be passing 2/3 of all attempted credit hours at UM

• Not exceed a certain amount of attempted credit hours (i.e. For a Bachelor's Degree, you can't exceed more than 180 attempted hours from all institutions attended.)

Go to class: If you miss class and get behind, you might not be able to keep up with your grades. And please know that for federal aid purposes, your attendance must be confirmed in each class by the Mandatory Drop Date of each term.

Understand student loans: Although everyone wants grants and scholarships – and we understand why – there is not enough of them to go around. More than 50% of our undergraduates use loans to fill the gap in funding.

It is important to remember that borrowing loans is a serious financial decision. These loans are typically the first credit you will have in your own name, and this obligation will most likely play a role in your life for years after college.

When borrowing is necessary, here are some important questions to ask:

What kind of a loan should I borrow first? Borrow Federal Direct Student Loans first before turning to private loans. Federal loans typically have better terms and conditions.

Which loan is better? A subsidized loan has more favorable terms than an unsubsidized loan. The interest that accrues on a subsidized loan while you are in school is paid by the government (and not by you!). The interest on the unsubsidized loans begins to accrue from the very first disbursement and you are responsible when the time comes to repay. We suggest that you at least make payments on the interest that is accruing on these loans while still in school. It may not be much per month, but it will make a huge difference after a few years, saving you hundreds of dollars in the long run.

How much assistance do I need? Do not accept the maximum offered to you if you don't need it. Remember that loans are DEBT. You must pay them back. Do not saddle yourself with a heavy burden that will cause you real financial pain later. Instead, strategize when you will use this money. For example, you may want to use loan funds during a year when you have especially difficult classes and won't be able to maintain a job. Or, you may opt to save some of your annual loan eligibility for summer classes when funding is limited.

When do I have to start repaying these loans? Most federal and institutional loans have grace periods, which are set periods of time after you graduate (or drop below half-time enrollment) when payment is not yet due. For Federal Direct Loans, for example, the grace period is six months. The idea is to give you the opportunity to get a job before payments begin.

Who is the lender of my loans and how much have I borrowed so far? You can request your loan history from the Financial Aid Office or check out the U.S. Department of Education's Informed Borrower Tool for all your borrowed federal loans. If you have borrowed a private loan, make sure you know who the lender is and how to get in touch.

Do I have the option to postpone making payments after graduation? In some cases, yes – based on your circumstances. A deferment is a period of time when your payments are postponed and any interest accrued on a subsidized loan is paid by the government. A forbearance is a period of time when your payments are either postponed or reduced, but interest continues to accrue on both subsidized and unsubsidized loans. It is important to be aware of these options, particularly if you are experiencing financial hardships. You do not want to find yourself with overdue payments and no way to get caught up. In either case, your lender can advise you. No one wants to see you default – it is in everyone's best interest for you to pay back the loan funds.

Will my first salary make it possible for me to start paying back my loans? This is a smart question. Definitely research this further, but below are some figures to get you started and also consult the UM Career Center— they are here to help you. See the next chapter on Finding Your Way.

Borrow Wisely!
A good rule: Don't borrow more than your annual starting salary.

The national average monthly student loan payment is $393 (studentloanhero.com/student-loan-debt-statistics/). At the University of Mississippi, students who began as freshmen and took loans for school, graduated with about $31,000 debt.

MEAN NATIONAL STARTING SALARIES BY MAJOR

Academic Major	Mean Salary	Academic Major	Mean Salary
Accounting	$54,056	International Business	$56,778
Advertising	$52,909	Industrial/Manu. Engineering	$68,619
Aeronautical Eng.	$69, 507	Info. Sciences & Systems	$66,705
Area & Gender Studies	$57,400	Journalism	$52,333
Business Admin./Mngmt	$57,133	Liberal Arts / Gen. Studies	$55,444
Biological Sciences	$61,136	Logistics/Supply Chain	$57,060
Communications	$51,412	Management Info. Systems	$61,697
Computer Science	$68,103	Marketing	$56,186
Chemical Engineering	$72,889	Mathematics/Statistics	$62,823
Chemistry	$57,429	Mechanical Engineering	$70,329
Civil Engineering	$65,977	Philosophy	$57,400
Economics	$59,480	Physics	$66,718
Environmental Science	$61,667	Psychology	$57,000
Finance	$58,464	Public Relations	$51,929
Hospitality Management	$55,000	Social Work	$54,900
History	$55,714	Sociology	$55,813
Geological Sciences	$62, 250	Software Applications	$67,691
Human Resources	$54,295	Visual & Performing Arts	$57,000

Source: NACE Salary Survey Winter 2019

We hope this information has made you a little more comfortable with your cost of attendance, award letter, and your understanding of student loans. Let's move on to managing your daily budget.

Let's now consider **good debt versus bad debt**. The main difference is the long-term value that you may or may not gain from these debts. For example, if you choose to go on a shopping spree and buy $300 worth of clothes, this would not be considered good debt because this purchase is setting you back financially and is not going to increase in value in the future. Borrowing loans for your educational expenses, however, is considered a good debt because you are investing in your education and in your long term success. Be careful, though, because loan debt can also be bad debt if you borrow for the wrong reasons. This is why we warned against borrowing the maximum loans offered to you; be sure you have a reason to borrow.

LOAN REPAYMENT CHART

Amount Borrowed	# of Payments	Monthly Payment	annual payment
$10,000	120	$106	$1,272
$20,000	120	$212	$2,544
$30,000	120	$318	$3,816
$40,000	120	$424	$5,088
$50,000	120	$530	$6,360
$60,000	120	$636	$7,632

Based on 5% interest

LIVING WITHIN A **BUDGET**

Basically, you must get in the habit of tracking where your money goes and making sure you do not overspend. This means learning to differentiate between what is truly necessary and what is not (acknowledging your **"needs"** versus **"wants"**). It is also a matter of examining your expenses and knowing which are "fixed" (the same amount each month, such as rent) and which are "variable" (varying from month to month, such as groceries).

Budgeting can be frustrating. It is almost impossible for every week to be the same, so holding yourself to a budget takes time and work each week. When unexpected expenses occur, such as a visit to the doctor or a higher than expected electricity bill, many people just give up. But, this is exactly when you need to stick to it because that is how you learn to plan for these challenges. Getting a head start now will make you more comfortable later when budgeting is even more important to you and your family.

We know that some students come to college with a new car and new clothes, and do not have to worry about money. Other students rely on their financial aid disbursement to pay for books and tuition and are looking for a job to cover other costs. Each person is different, and every budget plan is different. But, unless your money grows on trees, you need a budget.

According to the U.S. Department of Education, creating and following a budget helps you plan ahead for purchasing textbooks, buying a laptop, as well as paying off student loans after graduation and saving for an emergency fund. When you know where your money is going, you can find ways to reduce spending and minimize debt. See Activities Two and Three of your text to get started, and refer to the Glossary and Resources page at the end of this chapter for more reading on budgeting.

Reality Check: Do you actually know if your semester bill has been paid in full? If not, then this should be the first conversation you have with your parents or with a financial aid advisor. It is important to have a financial plan in place for each

BUDGET APPS

Need an easy way to keep up with your budget? There are plenty of apps for smart phones that do just that: you can input your expenses, create categories with set expense amounts, and track how much you are spending on all the aspects of your college life.

MINT (iPhone and Android): free, syncs with bank account

ACE BUDGET 3 (iPhone): $1.99 (with a Lite version available for free)

MY WEEKLY BUDGET (iPhone): $0.99

FINANCISTO PERSONAL FINANCE TRACKER (Android): free

semester (and summer!) and be aware of payment deadlines. Any unpaid balance means a hold on your account that could prevent you from registering for upcoming terms. To help you continually monitor the status of your Bursar bill, remember that you can view it online through myOleMiss, 24/7, and you can authorize your parent to access this information, too.

In addition to being aware of the things you need to do to keep your awards, you may want to consider finding a part-time job to earn money to contribute to your financial plan. That could be a huge help (and it will give you an opportunity to make more connections on campus or in Oxford)! Most employers in Oxford will work around your class schedule because they know you have academic obligations. Jobs to consider: pizza delivery, babysitting, campus office work, lifeguarding, library assistant, or residence hall Community Assistant. Once you start earning your own money, you will find that you think more about how you spend it.

REAL EXAMPLES OF WORK-STUDY JOBS

- Tutoring local K-9th grade students (contact the Financial Aid Office for more information)
- Biology Lab Assistant
- Student Worker for Campus Recreation
- Game Day Operations
- Equipment Manager for Theatre Arts

ACTIVITY ONE – Your Costs and Financial Aid

Now let's try out this activity to connect your costs and financial aid awards to your budget:

Determine individual costs associated with going to school. Check your Bursar bill to include the direct components we mentioned earlier: tuition, nonresident fee (if applicable), course fees, residence hall rent, and meal plan. Then add text books, athletic tickets, school supplies, organizational dues (fraternity, sorority, sport clubs), gas, laundry, going out with friends, grocery shopping, parking pass, and any other costs you can think to include.

Find out how much you receive in financial aid (grants, scholarships, work-study, and loans). Once you know your total award package for the semester, subtract that figure from your costs. If you get all of this information from myOleMiss, that is fine, but remember that a financial aid advisor may know about additional money for which you are eligible.

Determine the amount of money you have to pay for the semester, and talk with your family or financial aid advisor about how you will cover for these expenses. Here are some possible conversation starters to have with your parents:

"I'm reading this chapter about financial literacy for my class. I found out how much it costs to go here, and compared it with the amount of financial aid I am getting. I have determined that college costs $____per semester. I got that figure by adding the fixed costs and personal expenses and then subtracting my financial aid. Do my figures sound about right to you?"

"How are you/we paying for this? Do I have a lump sum of money to manage this semester for my personal spending money, or will I get a monthly allotment in my checking account?"

"At this rate, it looks like I will owe $____in loans when I graduate, and I know that repaying them is my responsibility. I wonder if there might be another way to pay for college that doesn't put the burden on me later. What do you think about me getting a part-time job to help with these expenses?"

"I planned on being Greek (or participating on a club sports team). I found out it costs about $____per month for about nine months a year. I also hear there are other costs for pictures, t-shirts, travel, formals, etc. Are you okay with these costs?"

Following this assignment, you should feel differently about your financial situation. You now have a working knowledge of the financial capital it will take to get you through college, and you are ready to assess your daily financial habits.

ACTIVITY TWO – Track Your Spending

Keep track of your daily spending beginning on a Friday. At the end of the week, it will be interesting to look back and see how you feel about your spending habits. List all purchases you made (or bills you paid) during this period. Be sure to include Ole Miss Express charges, too. Although it seems like they are "free" when all you have to do is swipe your ID card, there really is an associated cost! If you used your meal plan, estimate $8.00 per meal, and do the same for any meals you had at a Greek house.

Date	What was Purchased?	Fixed Cost or Variable Cost	Need or Want	Amount	Reason – If this purchase was a "want," why did you buy it?
FRIDAY					
SATURDAY					
SUNDAY					
MONDAY					
TUESDAY					
WEDNESDAY					
THURSDAY					
TOTAL					

So, how did you do? Did you spend money the way you thought you would? If not, that is ok! Things can and will get in the way sometimes. Remember: as important as it is to budget, it is just as important to forgive yourself if you happen to spend too much in one week. Dwelling on it will only discourage your efforts. Of course, do not make a habit of over-spending every week!

ACTIVITY THREE – Cash Budget

Take a plain envelope and place $50 inside (or a reasonable amount that you decide). That is your budget for the weekend. Once you run out of money in your envelope, stop buying things. Report back, and let your classmates know how this activity went. Did you stay within your budget? Did you secretly add to the envelope as the weekend went on? Or say, "whatever!" – and use plastic instead? For some people, this is the best way to see just how quickly money can go when you do not plan ahead.

ACTIVITY FOUR – Apartment Living

Break into small groups. In this exercise, you are going to be roommates next year. Find out how much you would spend each month on rent, utilities, and personal expenses living off-campus in an apartment complex assigned to you by your instructor. Consider the following costs: rent, cable, internet, electricity, gas, cell phone, laundry, and gas for your car. Do some research around town on the prices offered from different companies, and try to come up with the best deals. For electricity and gas costs, you could talk to a manager of the apartment complex for monthly estimates. Be prepared to share your findings with the class. Each group member may be asked to turn in an individual reflection paper about his or her experience.

A FEW THOUGHTS ABOUT
CREDIT/DEBIT CARDS AND CHECKS

Some people buy everything with credit cards, while others stay as far away from them as possible.

You will decide the best approach for you. It is not necessarily the case that you need to avoid using them, but you do need to be careful.

It's important to shop around when applying for credit cards. The Federal Trade Commission, which is the nation's consumer protection agency, has some helpful hints on what to look for when selecting a credit card.

What is the annual percentage rate (APR) that was offered to you? The APR is a measure of the cost of credit, expressed as a yearly interest rate. It must be disclosed to you prior to your account being activated and is a good way for you to compare the credit card offers that you are considering. Remember - if you don't pay your bill on time or in full when it's due, you will owe a charge in addition to the amount of your purchase. Be careful, because credit card rates tend to be high —typically more than student loans.

Is there an annual fee or an individual transaction fee? There could be a fee just for having the card, and you should also know if an additional fee will be tacked on to each purchase you make.

- Is there a fee for late payments?
- Can you call customer service 24/7?
- What happens if the card is stolen?
- Does the card have a "cash back" feature?

Every time you make a purchase with a credit card, you should be prepared to make payments on the balance right away to prevent the monthly interest from accruing for too long. If you are able to do this, and you continue to make payments until your balance is down to zero again, it is a great way to start building your credit history. You will be glad for it later in life when you make bigger purchasing decisions such as renting an apartment, buying a car, borrowing a credit-based loan, or even buying a home.

There are three primary organizations, or credit bureaus, that compile this information for consumers – Equifax, Experian, and TransUnion - and they look for trends in your financial activity to create what is called your credit report. According to Experian, factors such as on-time bill payments, how much debt there is to your name, and the length of time you have managed your credit accounts are taken into consideration. In other words, this is a report card on how you handle your finances. And, it's very important because it is the basis for your credit score, which is used to predict a borrower's ability to repay a debt and may have a big impact on every future financial decision.

Reviewing your credit report regularly is a good way to stay aware and catch any fraudulent or inaccurate activity on your accounts that may negatively impact your credit score. Did you know that you can get your credit report for free once every 12 months from each of above-mentioned credit reporting companies? Visit https://www.annualcreditreport.com/index.action for more information.

Bottom line: If you do not have a reliable income and cannot discipline yourself to pay for your purchases as you go, a credit card will lead to economic disaster. If possible, avoid using your student loans and credit cards for clothing, spring break trips, going out, car payments, or Greek dues. It can be dangerous to become accustomed to a standard of living that you really cannot sustain without going heavily into debt. Trust us, it is not fun to graduate and be stuck with having to pay on debt with your first paycheck!

DEBIT CARDS

A Debit card doubles as an ATM card and an automatic checkbook, enabling you to get cash and make purchases from your checking account quickly and easily. Using a debit card is the most convenient way to shop, but you should take some precautions.

KEEP YOUR RECEIPTS: It is easy to forget how much you have spent, and if you do not use your receipts to keep track of the amount of money in your account, you may quickly become overdrawn. If you overdraw your account (meaning you have spent more money than you have), the bank charges you hefty fees (usually $20 to $30 for every purchase made after your balance hits zero).

PROTECT YOUR CARD: If someone steals your debit card, he or she could spend all the money in your account before you realize the card is gone. Check with your bank to see if you are liable for fraud ulent charges.

RESERVATIONS: Be careful when using a debit card to reserve a car or a hotel room. Many companies charge the full amount to your card up front or even charge an excess amount for incidentals (such as room service). These charges could freeze your assets for the duration of your stay, leaving you without available cash. For hotels and car rentals, use a credit card if you have one.

MANAGING A CHECKING ACCOUNT

Although most students use debit cards, there are times when writing a check is necessary. Landlords may insist that rent be paid with checks, and some small businesses may not take cards or may charge a small fee for processing a card.

1. Keep a careful record of your checks to prevent overdrawing your account.
2. Do not sign a check until you are sure the information is correct and complete. Void a check that is not usable. An altered check looks suspicious and might not be cashed. Notify your bank as soon as you discover that your checks have been lost or stolen to avoid the risk of forgery.
3. Always use a pen to make out a check. Never use a pencil.
4. Immediately deposit or cash checks you receive, since checks held too long may be refused.
5. If you mail a check for deposit, write "for deposit only" immediately above your signature endorsement on the back of the check. Then, no one can cash it.
6. Periodically, you will receive a statement of your account. It is important that your checkbook and the bank statement agree. Remember that the actual amount of money remaining in your account may be less than that shown on the account statement if some checks you have written have not yet been cashed, or if you have made recent debit card transactions.

HAVING FUN IN COLLEGE **WITHOUT OVERSPENDING**

In this section, we want to share some advice with you about how to be a smart consumer.

Some easy ways to save on every day pick-me-ups: In a typical day, you might purchase a small café mocha (about $4), peanut M&M's from a vending machine ($1.25), an Ole Miss sweatshirt from the campus bookstore (about $65 with tax), and Tylenol (about $4 for a bottle of 24 capsules). So, in one day you just spent $74. Is there a way to spend less?

Consider this: a cup of coffee brewed in your room (same caffeine, a lot less money), a bag of M&M's you stashed after a grocery store run (you can buy in bulk), a sweatshirt bought from a store that sells more than just Ole Miss apparel, and generic brand headache medicine. You can save a bundle by planning ahead.

"We buy things we don't need with the money we don't have to impress people we don't like."
– Dave Ramsey

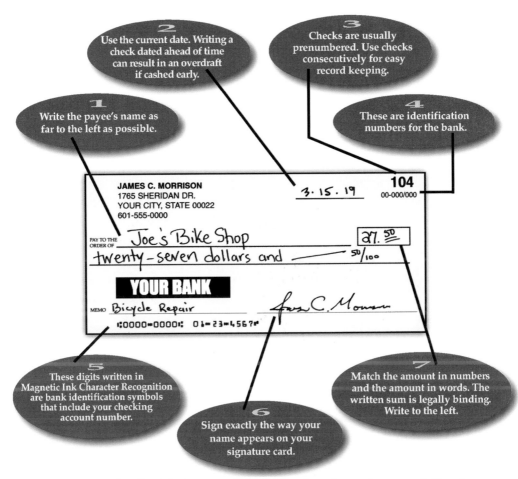

2 Use the current date. Writing a check dated ahead of time can result in an overdraft if cashed early.

3 Checks are usually prenumbered. Use checks consecutively for easy record keeping.

1 Write the payee's name as far to the left as possible.

4 These are identification numbers for the bank.

5 These digits written in Magnetic Ink Character Recognition are bank identification symbols that include your checking account number.

6 Sign exactly the way your name appears on your signature card.

7 Match the amount in numbers and the amount in words. The written sum is legally binding. Write to the left.

Learn to say "no": This is a tough one for a lot of people, especially when you find yourself in a new setting where it is important to make friends and feel like you belong. Standing out or not being included is a common fear of new students. There are ways to be included even if you do not participate in every single event. If someone asks, "Do you want to go hang out with us?" think before you say yes. Hanging out typically means spending money. If you are not in a position to go out, but you do not feel like telling your friends the reason why every time, consider some of these polite answers that were proposed by past EDHE students. The question was, "Hey, we're going to Wendy's. Want to come along?"

Thanks, but I am not hungry right now; maybe next time.

Thanks, but I just ate a little while ago. I don't mind going and keeping you company, though. Oh, man, I just don't like Wendy's, but you guys have fun.

I would love to, but I'm trying to cut back on fast food.

I'm really tired right now, but please ask me next time.

No, I have to study for a test right now. Y'all have fun.

No thanks, but I appreciate it.

All these responses are perfectly fine. You may even have a better way of answering. But just know that it is OK to say "no" because you should not need to spend money to buy friendship.

It is sometimes harder, though, to say no to yourself. Next time you come across something that costs

$40 or more, make a deal with yourself. If you are still thinking about that item the next day, go back and buy it. But you might find that once you are out of the store, the item is forgotten.

If you are better prepared for the kinds of spending opportunities that have caught you off guard in the past, you can choose responsibly and save yourself a lot of worry. Of course, you can always remember that something simply is not in your budget for that week and maybe that will encourage you to save up for next time.

Top Tips from fellow Ole Miss Students:

- Create a budget!
- Never go shopping for groceries, clothes, etc., without a list.
- Always buy necessities first, such as food, gas, toiletries, and school supplies.
- Think twice before using a credit card! Do not carry it with you if you might be tempted.
- Save money for emergencies.
- Find free or low-cost, "things to do" in Oxford, just go to visitoxfordms.com.
- Don't spend impulsively...if you know you don't need it, don't buy it.
- Get a part time job...in addition to earning money, it's a great way to get involved and meet people.

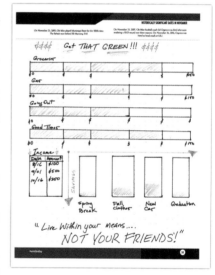

- Track your debit card expenses online to see how much you're spending and where you're spending it.
- We all have different financial situations. Live within YOUR means, not your friends'.
- Set a cap on the number of times you eat off campus per week or month.
- Use OUT public transit to get around town! It's free for students and saves gas money...and parking ticket fees when you return and are un able to find a legal spot.

REAL LIFE REASONS TO MANAGE YOUR MONEY AT OLE MISS

- You can't have just one pair of Nike shorts...or rain boots.
- So you won't be sitting at home while your friends are at the beach for Spring Break.
- To avoid angry phone calls from your parents!
- To prevent a heart attack when you realize you can't register for the upcoming semester because you owe money (that you don't have) for parking tickets.
- You may not purchase a meal plan for every year you're here...but you will never stop wanting to buy chicken on a stick.
- Concerts at The Lyric aren't free.
- Because there's a t-shirt for everything, and you need ALL OF THEM.

HOW THE LITTLE THINGS ADD UP

1 Venti Caramel Frappuccino per week:
$4.95 x 15 weeks = $74.25

3 Tall Lattes per week:
$2.95 (x3) x 15 weeks = $132.75

5 Tall regular coffees per week:
$1.95 (x5) x 15 weeks = $146.25

THE POWER OF EDUCATION AND SAVING

Your education is critical to your future financial strength and saving opportunities. The higher the educational level, the higher income earned over time. So, stay in school and get your degree.

Let's talk about Fred. For 36 years, Fred put $300 into his savings account that yielded an annual interest rate of 3%, and he started doing this at age 30. So, from age 30 to 65, he managed to gain a net amount of $8,752. (The amount in his savings account at age 65 minus the total amount of money he invested during those 36 years.) What Fred didn't know is that had he started saving earlier in life, at age 19 for example, he would have gained more money over the same number of years. Take a look at this comparison – had Fred started putting $300 into his savings at age 19 and did that for 36 years, he would have had a net gain of $16,265. That is almost twice as much as he gained by starting at age 30.

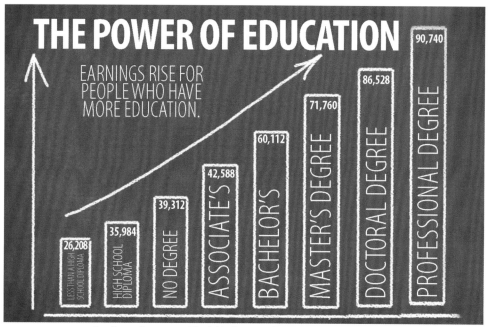

Note: Data are for persons age 25 and older. Earnings are for full-time wage and salary workers.
Source: U.S. Bureau of Labor Statistics, Current Population Survey 2016.

Also consider list example of starting to save and invest earlier rather than later in life.

Think of a snowball rolling downhill - the earlier it starts to roll, the bigger it gets. Do not wait until middle age! Believe it or not, you could start saving right after college - or maybe even start now.

Age	SCENARIO ONE Fred Invests Later From Age 30 - 65 (36 Years)		SCENARIO TWO Fred Invests Early From Age 19-54 (36 years)	
19	$0	$0	$300	$309
20	$0	$0	$300	$627
21	$0	$0	$300	$955
22	$0	$0	$300	$1,293
23	$0	$0	$300	$1,641
24	$0	$0	$300	$1,999
25	$0	$0	$300	$2,368
26	$0	$0	$300	$2,748
27	$0	$0	$300	$3,139
28	$0	$0	$300	$3,542
29	$0	$0	$300	$3,958
30	$300	$309	$300	$4,385
31	$300	$627	$300	$4,826
32	$300	$955	$300	$5,280
33	$300	$1,293	$300	$5,747
34	$300	$1,641	$300	$6,228
35	$300	$1,999	$300	$6,724
36	$300	$2,368	$300	$7,235
37	$300	$2,748	$300	$7,761
38	$300	$3,139	$300	$8,303
39	$300	$3,542	$300	$8,861
40	$300	$3,958	$300	$9,436
41	$300	$4,385	$300	$10,028
42	$300	$4,826	$300	$10,638
43	$300	$5,280	$300	$11,266
44	$300	$5,747	$300	$11,913
45	$300	$6,228	$300	$12,579
46	$300	$6,724	$300	$13,266
47	$300	$7,235	$300	$13,973
48	$300	$7,761	$300	$14,701
49	$300	$8,303	$300	$15,451
50	$300	$8,861	$300	$16,223
51	$300	$9,436	$300	$17,019
52	$300	$10,028	$300	$17,839
53	$300	$10,638	$300	$18,683
54	$300	$11,266	$300	$19,552
55	$300	$11,913	$-	$20,139
56	$300	$12,579	$-	$20,743
57	$300	$13,266	$-	$21,365
58	$300	$13,973	$-	$22,006
59	$300	$14,701	$-	$22,666
60	$300	$15,451	$-	$23,346
61	$300	$16,223	$-	$24,047
62	$300	$17,019	$-	$24,768
63	$300	$17,839	$-	$25,511
64	$300	$18,683	$-	$26,277
65	$300	$19,552	$-	$27,065
	$10,800		$10,800	

PLANNING FOR FINANCIAL EMERGENCIES

The COVID-19 (Coronavirus) pandemic that we have experienced in the year 2020 and into 2021 has impacted lives around the world. Some people could not work, schools and universities closed buildings and moved learning to online platforms, many businesses closed their doors for good, and many people lost loved ones to the virus. This has been a sad and scary as well as unpredictable time for us all – it still is.

All of these changes bring unexpected financial hardships, and it has brought to our attention the importance of being prepared. What would you do if you could not work for the next year? What if your parents lost their jobs tomorrow? What if you unexpectedly have many medical bills? These are very stressful scenarios, but we can sometimes lessen their impact if we plan ahead.

As we discussed in this chapter, one way to plan ahead is to submit your FAFSA each year that you are in school because you just do not know how it may help you down the road. For example, in order to receive many scholarships, grants, and loans, a FAFSA is required. It is also required for most emergency student funding that Ole Miss offers. You just never know when you may need some assistance, so preparing for it now in order to have some peace of mind later is worth it.

IT IS UP TO YOU

We hope the information in this chapter, along with the activities, has given you a better understanding of your finances. Financial literacy will continue to be an important part of your college education because this is the perfect time to strengthen your independence and form healthy financial habits.

Remember, there are many things you can do to manage your money. You can budget and plan. You can think about situations before they occur and act rather than react. You can learn to say no. You can save and earn. You've got this!

ABOUT THE AUTHORS

Laura Diven-Brown, *Director of Financial Aid*

Laura Diven-Brown is originally from the Chicago suburbs but now calls Oxford her home. She earned a B.S. in psychology from the University of Illinois, and a M.Ed. in higher education from the University of Mississippi. In her role as the Director of Financial Aid, she oversees management of student financial assistance programs totaling $300 million annually. She also served as an EDHE 105 instructor for four years.

Nataša Novićević, *Assistant Director of Financial Aid*

Originally from Belgrade, Serbia, Nataša Novićević has lived in the U.S. since 1993. She earned both a B.A. degree in business and marketing and a M.A. in higher education from the University of Mississippi, and is currently pursuing an Ed.D. in higher education. She taught EDHE 105 while serving as a graduate assistant in the Office of Financial Aid.

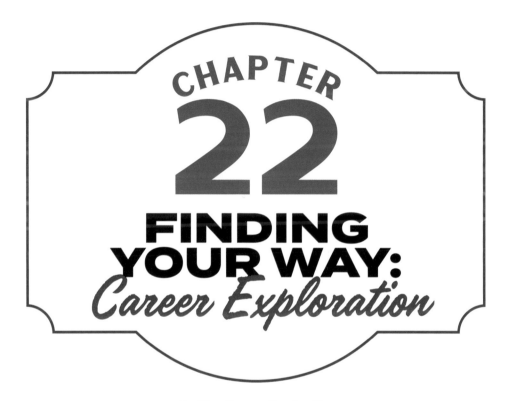

CHAPTER

22

FINDING
YOUR WAY:
Career Exploration

By The Career Center Team

You may be thinking, "Why do I have to think about the job search and careers now? Graduation is such a long time away! I just got here, and I want to enjoy my first year at The University of Mississippi!"

Yes, you do have a lot going on right now. You have classes, extracurricular activities, hanging out with friends, and, of course, cheering on the Rebs! But you should squeeze in a little time to make yourself an attractive candidate for your first job, an internship, or graduate program. And you want to start now.

Don't get overwhelmed. Preparing for your career is not that difficult if you start early. By participating in activities such as internships, campus organizations, community service, and job shadowing, you will not only develop important skills that look great on your resume, but you will understand more about whether a job is the right fit for you. Also, you will gain experiences which will make you much more competitive than the friend who took naps between classes.

The best part is you don't have to figure out any of this stuff on your own. The Career Center is available as a resource to help you—from deciding what you want to do all the way to securing that first job. We can help you choose a major and find part time employment while in school. We can also assist you in developing your resume and interview skills so that you can secure internships and jobs. The most successful students are the ones who visit us early and often. Be one of those students.

Make an appointment today.
The University of Mississippi Career Center
303 Martindale | Student Services | 662-915-7174
Hours: Monday–Friday | 8 a.m.–5 p.m. | career.olemiss.edu

Choosing A Major

The first step to a dream career is finding your dream major. Some students may know exactly what they want to study when they get to the university, while others may not be so sure. However, even the students who seem most confident may change their minds. And by the way, it is OK not to know exactly what you want to do the minute you set foot on campus. College is a time to explore and to allow yourself to grow. Choosing a major is a part of that growth.

We understand that committing at 19 or 20 or even 25 to what you want to do for the rest of your life can be intimidating. How do you know if you will still like the career path you choose now when you are 35? At the Career Center, we have advisors to guide you through the process and to help you make a choice that fits you.

Getting help choosing a major is easy. All you need to do is make an appointment with a career advisor. During the appointment, your advisor helps you begin the process of selecting a major by asking you a few career and academic questions. Your advisor also may ask you exploratory questions that are similar to the ones located in the box below. These questions are aimed at digging deeper into your passions and interests. Remember that all answers you share with your advisor remain confidential.

Depending on what you and the advisor discuss, he or she might suggest that you take the Strong Interest Inventory, Myers-Briggs Type Indicator (MBTI), or TypeFocus. These are career assessments that find out your values, interests, personality, and skills to determine how they fit into a major or career. Read on to see how the Strong Interest Inventory, MBTI, and TypeFocus can help you discover your dream major!

EXPLORATORY QUESTIONS

- Who were the people you admired when you were growing up? (Keep in mind that role models can be either real persons or fictional characters.) How are you like each person? How are you different from each person?

- What magazines do you read regularly? What do you like about these magazines? What television shows do you watch regularly? What do you like about these shows? What websites do you visit regularly? What do you like about these websites? What keeps drawing you back to these?

- What is your all-time favorite story, either from a book or movie? What do you like about this story?

- What do you like to do with your free time? What are your hobbies? What do you enjoy about these hobbies?

- What were your three favorite subjects in middle or high school? What three subjects did you hate? Why did you love or hate these subjects?

Strong Interest Inventory

You are going to spend much of your adult life working, so wouldn't you like to choose a major and career that you find interesting? That is what the Strong Interest Inventory is all about: determining your career interests. This career assessment compares your interests to various occupations to determine what you might find to be the most appealing. The assessment gives you an in-depth list of occupations and majors that might be a match for you. Once you take the assessment and have your list, you and your advisor will discuss which options seem like the best fit and what steps to take next.

How does the Strong Interest Inventory work? The results work something like this: Imagine you walk into a room full of people. You notice that these people are split into six different groups, and each group is discussing a different topic (see box below). Naturally you are interested in certain topics more than others, so you are more drawn to those groups. Which group do you go to first? Second? Third? Believe it or not, the groups to which you are naturally drawn are a good indication of your career interests. The career advisor at the Career Center uses these interest areas to help you in selecting an academic major that excites you. For more information about the different categories, visit discoveryourpersonality.com/aboutstrong.html.

TypeFocus and the Myers-Briggs Type Indicator

TypeFocus is another tool available to you through the Career Center that may help you in making career decisions. Like the Strong Interest Inventory, the results of your TypeFocus inventory serve as a guide to your interests but on a more limited level. This assessment also allows you to learn about your workplace values and personality type and how they relate to choosing an academic major and career. Unlike the Strong Interest Inventory, you can take Typefocus without making an appointment with the Career Center.

To access the TypeFocus assessment, just login to your Career Center Handshake account (olemiss.joinhandshake.com/login). Click on the Resources link under the Career Center section to find the TypleFocus assessment. Username: Ole Miss email address; Password: Student ID number.

Additionally, the Myers-Briggs Type Indicator (MBTI) may help you in making career decisions.

With this assessment, you will learn your natural preferences. Your MBTI results serve as a guide to your interests and your personality to provide insight into how you receive, organize, and act on information. After taking the assessment, you will meet with an advisor to discuss your results and career options.

The Strong Interest Inventory, MBTI, and TypeFocus are great tools to help you get started in the career and major search, but the only way to truly know what is the right fit for you is to get out there and explore! There are several ways to do this.

Strong Interest Inventory

Realistic: participating in intramural sports at the Turner Center; working on the latest Habitat for Humanity project.

Investigative: attending open house at Kennon Observatory; assisting a professor in a research lab.

Artistic: going to the Buie-Skipwith Museum or the Gertrude C. Ford Center; performing in a theatre group; photographing various sites on the Ole Miss campus.

Social: volunteering for The Big Event or other campus organization; organizing activities for Greek Recruitment.

Enterprising: running for president or a leadership position in a campus organization; competing in an entrepreneur contest.

Conventional: keeping the books for Associated Student Body; building model airplanes.

EXPLORING YOUR MAJOR

Classes and Campus Involvement

As a new student, you have a lot of classes ahead of you during your time at the University of Mississippi. Why not use these classes to help you choose a potential major and career? You can "try on" majors before committing to them by selecting electives based on your interests. Another way to use your time wisely is to get involved on campus. The university has over 400 different student organizations that are looking for you to join! Educating yourself on all the opportunities that are available by taking a variety of classes and investing time into organizations on campus are both effective approaches to finding your career path at the university.

"Before I began working in the Career Center, I was not aware of the extensive resources that were offered, but I've since utilized them to grow professionally. I've been able to find the right major for me, gain internships, upgrade my resume, and I've been accepted into law school. My advice to students would be to go early and often during your collegiate career. You won't be disappointed!"

–Casey Hardaway, Business Administration in Marketing and Corporate Relations
Sharon, Mississippi, May 2019

Job Shadowing

Would you like to do a quick test drive of a profession before committing to it? Of course, you would, who wouldn't? Why commit to something when you are not really sure you will enjoy it?

Job shadowing is a great way to gain access to a career without having to be hired into it. While a job shadowing experience is not as in-depth as an internship, you get some exposure to a field which helps you determine if that is the direction for you. Also, job shadowing experience is something you want on your resume because it shows you took the initiative to find out more about your future profession.

In a job shadowing experience, you learn what someone does on a day-to-day basis. You are exposed to some of the challenges, trends, and rewards of the field. If you are interested in shadowing, do not be afraid to reach out! Think of professionals you admire and ask to follow them for a short period of time. Most professionals love talking to students. If you are still nervous about contacting someone for job shadowing, come by the Career Center, and we will help you develop a strategy for reaching out.

Volunteering

You will learn about the value of volunteering in another chapter of the text, but have you ever considered how volunteering can help you choose a major? When you volunteer you are not only helping the community but also experiencing activities that can potentially turn into a career.

Volunteering also expands your experience section of your resume. If you volunteer, you are taking on responsibilities that transfer into job skills. Think about it: communication, leadership, and teamwork, just to name a few. You are picking up all these skills as a volunteer. You also can volunteer in a professional setting. For example, if you are a journalism major with a public relations emphasis, you could volunteer to do press releases and campaigns for a community organization. This type of volunteer experience helps you have examples of your work to discuss and showcase when you are searching for a job. Employers do not care if the experience is paid or unpaid. Experience is experience, whether it is a volunteer or paid internship.

Informational Interviewing

If you are choosing a major or entering the workforce, informational interviewing can help you find the right career. Informational interviewing is an informal conversation you can have with someone working in an area of interest to you. It is an effective research tool and is best done after preliminary online research. It can help you discover the "hot" issues in your chosen field, learn the lingo, and find out what people value in job applicants.

Keep in touch with the person you interview, especially if you had a particularly nice interaction; let them know that you followed up on their advice and the outcome. This person could become an important part of your network!

It is not a job interview, and the objective is not to find job openings. Armed with information gained from your interview(s), you can polish your resume to highlight your competence in areas prospective employers find most valuable. You may feel awkward reaching out to people you don't know. However, most people actually enjoy taking a few moments out of their day to reflect on their professional life and give advice to someone with an interest in the field.

Follow these few steps to conduct a successful (and fun) informational interview:

1. Schedule an appointment with the person.

2. Choose either professional or business casual attire.

3. Arrive on time.

4. You direct the interview. Have some questions prepared that you would like to ask.

5. Thank the interviewee.

6. Send a thank you note.

7. Stay in touch with the interviewee in the future. You are developing a strong network base.

Internships

Did you know that today employers not only like to see one, but multiple, internships on your resume? Interning is one of the most effective ways to show that you have taken initiative outside of the classroom to get experience in a potential career. Through interning you learn if this type of work is a good match for you while simultaneously developing networking contacts and getting to add experience to your resume.

You can start interning as early as the summer after your freshman year. If you are going to spend your summers interning, then you want something good, right? In that case, you need to come see us as early as this fall. Yes, that means now. The most competitive internships have early deadlines from November through February. We can help you find internships to apply for, prepare your application materials, and practice your interview skills.

Getting any internship is not terribly hard, but being offered a great internship is a little more difficult. Here are a few tips to follow:

- **Start early.** Freshmen may not qualify for some of the internship opportunities available; however, it is never too early to gain knowledge about what is to come in the next year. By seeing what opportunities are available and the criteria for selection, you will know what you need to do to be selected.

- **Do your research.** A great candidate does more than just look over the company website. A smart candidate does a simple Google search to also find recent press releases, company reviews, and industry journals. You want to know how the company is performing as well as identify their competitors. You will be an informed candidate by also knowing their recent successes and what is unique about the company. You will be successful if you not only know the company product but use it and are passionate about the product. Find the answers to all of the above to be the most informed (and most attractive) candidate (Bridges, 2012).

- **Stand out.** Do something that helps you stand out from your competition. The harsh reality is your high school accomplishments are what got you to college. However, the moment you become a college student, those achievements start to fade. You have to replace them with new achievements. It is time to get involved with an organization you love, and do not be afraid to be a leader. Volunteer in the community. Excel in your classes. There are a variety of ways to stand out, so choose a few that fit you so you have something to put on your college resume when the time comes to apply for internships.

Resources

You can find internships in a lot of different places from networking to websites. Some of our favorite and most effective are:

- https://olemiss.joinhandshake.com/login

- https://www.linkedin.com/

- Vault Career Library at https://www.vault.com/

- https://www.idealist.org/en/ (for internships in the non-profit sector)

- https://www.mediabistro.com/ (for social media internships)

- https://www.internqueen.com/

- https://www.usajobs.gov/

Consider these resources and next steps if you are ready to apply for an internship. Remember to start looking as early as possible to avoid missing deadlines!

Other ideas: Career Center and School of Business Internship Fair (usually held in the fall). Make an appointment with an advisor at the Career Center.

You have taken the assessments which gave you an idea of which career options to explore. You researched these options by job shadowing, conducting informational interviews, gaining experience through interning, and taking a variety of classes. You have a great amount of information to help you commit to a major you love. You are on your way to your dream career! Your relationship with the Career Center does not stop now; we have more work to do to turn you into a competitive candidate. This work starts now.

What You Can Do Now

By participating in the exploratory activities we have discussed, you are well

"I came to Ole Miss with my whole future planned out, but it didn't take long to realize I was not happy with my career path and the classes it required. With the help of the Career Center, I was able to receive career counseling and take a test that introduced me to three different majors that fit my interests. After meeting with the department heads for those majors, I found the program that was perfect for me. The Career Center put me on the right track and showed me special opportunities I didn't know existed."

–Davis Roberts, Bachelor of Science in Integrated Marketing Communication (IMC) and with an emphasis in Public Relations Grenada, Mississippi, May 2019

on your way to becoming a competitive candidate for employers and graduate schools. Although it is a little more work now, you will be glad you did it rather than wait until later to start gaining experience. There are other ways to begin putting yourself ahead of the pack.

Information Sessions

One way to gain valuable career information is to attend employer and graduate school information sessions in the Career Center. The Career Center hosts several employers from a variety of fields every semester to speak on the different opportunities offered. While you may not be applying for these jobs or graduate admissions right away, you can get information on what they are looking for in a candidate so you will be ready when the time comes for you to apply. If you wait until your senior year to attend these sessions you may not have time to pick up the needed qualifications. Go to the information sessions often and start now.

Career Fairs

You also can understand what employers and graduate schools are looking for in candidates by attending career fairs early in your college experience. The Career Center hosts several fairs every semester. These fairs include events for all majors, internships, and specialty major fairs. You can attend these fairs to talk to employers and admission officers for after graduation or even secure an internship for next summer. The career fairs are a helpful way to gain an understanding of what you should do now to prepare for future opportunities. For updated information on registered participants, log in to olemiss.joinhandshake.com where events are updated in real time.

Networking

College life is designed for networking. There are activities and events going on every day of the week. So many activities, in fact, that you have to choose which ones you go to and which ones you have to miss. All of these events allow you to meet other college students, faculty, staff, alumni, professionals, and community members. Each interaction holds the possibility of being a contact that can help you in the future. Remember to keep in touch with people over the years. Once you meet a good contact or acquaintance, make sure to reach out to the person at least once per semester.

A caution about social media—use Facebook, Instagram, Twitter, LinkedIn, and other platforms appropriately! Google is your new resume. While these sites are a convenient way to keep in touch with all of your new contacts, remember that future employers, professors, and staff can see your profiles, so keep them PG. And trust me, you will be "Googled." Simple rule to follow—if you would not want your family to know something then it probably should not be on the Internet. If you stay close to that rule, you can enjoy the sites without endangering your future professional chances.

Career development—a life-long process

So, you have everything figured out—the perfect career path and the perfect academic major—to support your decision. Your work is done, right? If only it were that simple. Your professional development is a lifelong process.

Once you commit to an academic major and move through your education at the University, you are well on your way to launching your career. However, that is not enough. Developing your career and yourself as a professional is a process, meaning you work on it most of your life. Do not be discouraged by this, however. Attending to your career development can be exciting and rewarding. Continual career development may take you places professionally you have only dreamed of going.

Dream Job Questionnaire

Though the Career Center has several assessments that can assist you in making smart career choices, there are always more questions to ask to help you make the best decision. After you have identified some possible career choices, ask:

- What would I be doing on a daily basis?
- What would be my main responsibilities?
- Do I naturally gravitate to shows, books, or activities that are related to my career option?
- Do I find people already in my chosen field to be interesting?
- Have I taken courses in this field? If so, is the material engaging to me?
- Do I know where the majority of jobs are located geographically?
- What are the typical salaries?

From an Intern's Perspective
by Reagan Bintz – Cypress, Texas

Reagan Bintz is a recent graduate from the University of Mississippi who earned a Bachelor of Business Administration degree in Management with an emphasis in Human Resources and a Minor in Entrepreneurship. Reagan now works for BP in Houston, Texas, as part of their Graduate Development Program. She shares her internship experience below:

Where did you do your internship? I was a Structuring Intern at MP2 Energy LLC, a Wholly Owned Subsidiary of Shell Energy North America, in The Woodlands, Texas.

Why did you decide to do an internship? I decided to do an internship because I wanted an experience that would help me better understand what I was looking for in a lifelong career. Having an internship allowed me to see different functions of the business world and helped me decide what sector interested me most. I also knew by having an internship and real-world work experience on my resume, it would help me post-graduation in finding a permanent position.

How did you find the internship? LinkedIn. If you haven't already created a profile or if you haven't updated it in a while, I highly recommend doing so. I started the process of looking for an internship around November before the summer I went to work (Note: This is when most companies are looking for interns.) I set aside time every few days to search, and I applied to any and all that were of interest. I got rejected by some, never heard from others, and was asked for an interview from very few. But remember, it only takes one!

Describe the duties you had as an intern. I analyzed historical demand data to forecast pricing for potential sales through the use of Excel and proprietary software with up to 20 deals a day and turn arounds as quick as two days. I supported the credit department in managing risk protocols to ensure counterparty credit worthiness and the minimization of bad debt. I generated competitive pricing in the ERCOT and PJM deregulated energy markets based on load shape, usage, and forward power curves for broker partners in order to achieve sales quotas.

How did your internship differ from your expectations? I thought going in as an "intern" I would be given small administrative projects and mainly shadow people for a few months. While that was partially true, to my surprise, within just a couple weeks of training I was being given deals of my own to value. I enjoyed being treated like any other employee and it made it super enjoyable going into work every day knowing I was making an impact and contributing to the business.

How did it help you decide what to do next in your career? I had no idea what kind of career in business I wanted, or even what industry or department interested me. The internship, however, gave me a great deal of clarity into one of those questions; I knew I wanted to be in the Energy Industry. The internship also allowed me to gain knowledge and understanding of the fundamentals of a business sector not taught in classes; however, the mathematics, economics, and business skills taught in classes were critical for me to succeed on the projects I was assigned. By the end of the summer I didn't want to leave!

What tips do you have for students who will be interns?

- Ask questions. You're an intern so they don't expect you to know everything when you start; Find a mentor and set aside time to meet with him or her on a regular basis;

- Never let yourself be bored. Seek out projects and assignments if you think you can take on more; use your internship as an opportunity to network and build relationships... you never know when connections might help you down the road;

- Be open to learning and showing people you are eager to learn as well; and have an idea of what you want to get out of the internship and let people know what you are thinking.

What would you say to students who are just starting out at Ole Miss and considering an internship? Go for it! You'll be glad when graduation comes around and you have internship experience that puts you ahead of others. Plus, internships are an opportunity for you to explore your future before having to make long-term decisions. So make sure your resume is up to date and you are practicing your interview skills (both of which the Career Center at the University can help you with)!

"The Career Center has helped me immensely throughout my college career. From helping me with my resume to staging mock interviews, I would not know how to conduct myself in a business setting without their guidance. I can remember numerous times when I called, emailed, or met with people from the Career Center for help with my resume and cover letter. I have also done a mock interview that taught me how to market myself in a way that was both honest and appealing to possible employers. The Career Center is an extremely important asset to students on campus. Without it, a lot of students would not have the resources to create a strong resume and cover letter, and students would also not have the opportunity to experience what a job interview may be like.

.–JT Vinson, Business Administration in Business Management
Oxford, MIssissippi, May 2020

MY PERSONAL CAREER BUILDING CHECKLIST

❑ I have taken the Strong Interest Inventory.

❑ I have taken the MBTI.

❑ I have worked with a career professional at the Ole Miss Career Center.

❑ I have spoken with the internship specialist at the Ole Miss Career Center.

❑ I have shadowed someone who is working in an occupational field in which I am interested.

❑ I have spoken to my professors to learn more about careers in their areas of expertise.

❑ I have attended one or more information sessions at the Ole Miss Career Center.

❑ I have attended an Ole Miss Career Fair.

❑ I have formulated short- and long-term goals for my future.

ABOUT THE AUTHORS

The **Career Center Team**'s mission is to collaborate with the university community to provide services, resources, and professional networking opportunities. We educate students in the exploration of occupational pathways and in the development of career readiness skills that prepare students to compete in the global market. Come visit us in the Career Center in 303 Martindale!

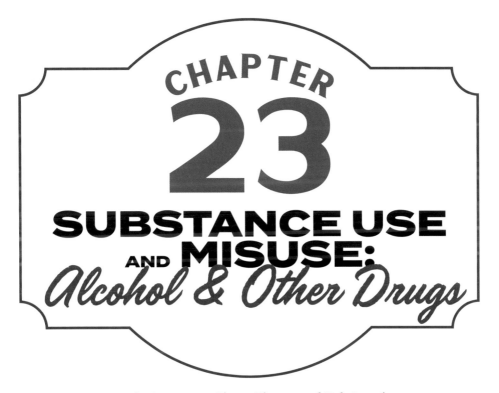

CHAPTER 23

SUBSTANCE USE AND MISUSE:
Alcohol & Other Drugs

By Erin Cromeans, Sierra Elston, and Kyle Loggins

"Some people get in so deep in college they can never get out of it," I told him. "I've seen it happen too many times. Be careful."— David Magee

August 28, 2016 For Ole Miss freshmen: My son William's story. A new freshman class started at Ole Miss this week and I wish I could tell them all this story. It's about my oldest son, William, who was a freshman in 2008. He would gladly tell them himself, if only he were alive.

With a quick wit and a big, friendly smile, William was an A student in the Honors College and Croft Institute at Ole Miss. He was fluent in Spanish, a member of Sigma Nu fraternity, and ran track for the Rebels his freshman and sophomore years.

The 400 hurdles is considered by many one of the most difficult in sports, and William had the courage to walk on and do it in the SEC. He lettered at Ole Miss his sophomore year and was rewarded by participation in the SEC Outdoor Track and Field Championships in 2010. The Ole Miss letterman's jacket he earned is one of our most prized possessions. That and the plaque he received for making the SEC's all-academic team in 2010. It was quite an achievement considering he managed the Honors College, Croft Institute, fraternity, and track at the same time and came out on top.

"Making any kind of all-SEC team is a big deal," I told him the year he worked to excel in track and academics for the Rebels. "It will be an achievement that will always mark who you are and what you can do."

I still remember the pride in his voice the night he called me after receiving the plaque for the SEC academic honor on the floor of Ole Miss' Tad Smith Coliseum during halftime of a Rebel basketball game.

"I was out there with the football players," he said. "It was so cool." William met a beautiful, smart girl at Ole Miss who became his girlfriend for four years in college that we loved, and hoped that he would one day marry. He had friends who shared his joy of music and laughter and traveling the world. He was the same sweet, smart competitive young man who sang in the church choir and camped at Alpine in summers during his youth.

In college those first two years he appeared to be all-everything, and track practice kept him in check most weekdays his freshman and sophomore years. The season ran both fall and spring semesters with early morning weightlifting and afternoon workouts.

Enough to keep anybody straight. On the weekends, when the music cranked up and the lights turned low, he partied, with so many other students.

It was all contextualized into a good collegiate reason as opposed to abuse or a problem. It's the fraternity Christmas party, it's Double Decker, it's the night before the Alabama game, the Grove, a music festival. It was alcohol, it was ecstasy, marijuana, and Xanax, lots of Xanax.

We had talked before his freshman year at Ole Miss about the perils of viewing alcohol abuse and recreational drug use as something of a rite of passage in college.

"Some people get in so deep in college they can never get out of it," I told him. "I've seen it happen too many times. Be careful."

William suffered from anxiety and low self-esteem. He tried to medicate with alcohol and drugs, like so many others. He was comforted that substances like alcohol brought him closer to the conversation in social situations.

He was considered a square more than a partier, and William hid his habit from many friends, but privately drawing the line was hard and one drug led to another over time as so often happens, sometimes by accident.

I had warned him that drug dealers can't be trusted, that drug dealers know tricks, like mixing heroin with cocaine to make it doubly addictive before a user knows what hit them. And it is easier to succumb when the dealer is a fraternity brother or the guy down the hall at the dorm who looks a lot like you.

"I know," he said, brushing off my warning. "Everybody knows that."

William was a senior at Ole Miss by the time we recognized the depths of his troubles. He graduated, another proud moment, but he was frail. He had wanted to go to law school but instead checked into rehabilitation once he realized the addiction had advanced to the point that he was no longer the person he once was.

William was scared. The drugs had taken over. Dropping our firstborn off at a rehabilitation facility that cool fall day wasn't easy. We hoped the 30-day stay in an inpatient treatment center would get this problem under control and his life back on track, then we could all get back to normal.

We were naïve, or maybe just hopeful, as parents tend to be. William bounced between several rehabilitation facilities around the country for the next year. He was kicked out of one in Colorado because he purchased a bottle of cough syrup from a drugstore and drank it to get high. He was kicked out of another because he and a friend found a way to purchase one pain killer pill each from the outside world. They took it, for old times sake, and William confessed the misdeed to the counselor, asking for another chance, thinking his admission might make a difference.

"You were right," William told me. "My plan was to graduate (from Ole Miss) and quit. But it's harder (to quit) than I thought. I'm not sure how to get out of this."

We got William back into a rehab facility in Nashville, and finally, progress. He graduated to a halfway house. With a college degree, he got a job at a Mac computer store. They put him in charge of training. His coworkers bragged about his sales skills and said he was a joy to work with.

"Sweetest young man," they said. Yes, and so very smart.

I quit my job and took another to be closer to him, visiting weekly and having daily phone conversations, anything to try and help. So, I was alarmed one Friday night when I kept calling and he did not answer. By the next morning, when he still did not answer, I knew. The drive to Nashville took two hours but it felt like 22. I could not feel my hands on the wheel and my stomach churned. Once there, I found him dead from an accidental drug overdose.

William had gotten off work that Friday and gone to a Widespread Panic concert, where he ingested alcohol and most every drug imaginable for hours. When he got home from the concert he texted a dealer and bought more drugs.

That cocaine, ingested just before midnight, combined with the other drugs in his system and took his life. The body can only take so much, after all. Eventually, it shuts down.

Three years plus a few months later we have made peace with William's addiction and tragic death, as much as parents can. We were blessed beyond measure to have been given this son to have in our lives for 23 years. Blessed beyond measure. And that is enough. We have memories of laughter and warm hugs, plus a hard-earned letter jacket from Ole Miss and so much more to cling to. But we don't want other students to suffer like he did, or other families to suffer like we have. That's why I wish I could reach out and touch every freshman to tell them William's story, to tell them that alcohol and drug binging and abuse isn't a collegiate rite of passage, or a contextual excuse.

It can be a dangerous if not deadly path that is hard to escape.

David Magee former Publisher of *The Oxford Eagle*

U.S. Dept. of Health and Human Services Centers for Disease Control and Prevention

ALCOHOL

Drinking too much alcohol can contribute to many negative consequences. It is responsible for 88,000 deaths in the United States and costs the economy $224 billion each year (CDC, 2014). Drinking too much alcohol can be defined in many ways. Overall, the CDC will classify drinking too much as excessive drinking. Excessive drinking includes binge drinking, underage drinking, heavy drinking, and pregnant drinking. College is a time when many students experiment with excessive drinking but often don't understand how their bodies will respond to alcohol. Research indicates that people who drink moderately may be less likely to experience dependency.

According to the Center for Disease Control (CDC) moderate means:

FOR MEN: No more than 2 standard drinks per day
FOR WOMEN: No more than 1 standard drinks per day

What is a standard drink? The amount of liquid in your can, bottle, or glass does not reflect the amount of alcohol you are consuming. In fact, different types of drinks can have varying amounts of alcohol.

Even though they come in different sizes, the drinks below are examples of ONE standard drink:

WHAT IS CONSIDERED A "DRINK"?
U.S. STANDARD DRINK SIZES

12 OUNCES OF 5% BEER

8 OUNCES OF 7% MALT LIQUOR

5 OUNCES OF 12% WINE

1.5 OUNCES OF 40% (80-PROOF) DISTILLED SPIRITS OR LIQUOR (Examples: gin, rum, vodka, whiskey)

U.S. Dept. of Health and Human Services Centers for Disease Control and Prevention

Binge Drinking

It is responsible for 88,000 deaths in the United States, and costs the economy $224 billion each year (CDC, 2014). Drinking too alcohol can contribute to many negative consequences. Binge drinking affects the entire campus and community, and is responsible for:

- 1,825 alcohol-related unintentional injuries and motor vehicle related deaths in college students between the ages of 18 and 24.

- 696,000 assaults caused by students who have been drinking

- 97,000 sexual assaults or date rapes caused by students who have been drinking (NIAAA, 2020)

According to the CDC, binge drinking is defined as:
FOR MEN: 5 or more standard drinks during a two-hour period
FOR WOMEN: 4 or more standard drinks a two-hour period.

Frequent binge drinking is a cause for concern, and can indicate the development of habits of alcohol addiction and abuse. Some students may binge drink in social settings in an attempt to relax, not realizing that recurring repeated binge drinking sessions put them at greater risk for future substance abuse disorders. While there are many things to look out for when someone is abusing alcohol, we want to highlight some prominent signs that you may see.

If you see someone experiencing one or more of these signs, do not hesitate to reach out for help.

Signs/Symptoms:

- Temporary blackouts or memory loss
- Recurrent arguments or fights with family members or friends as well as irritability, depression, or mood swings
- Continuing use of alcohol to relax, to cheer up, to sleep, to deal with problems, or to feel "normal." Headache, anxiety, insomnia, nausea, or other unpleasant symptoms when a person stops drinking
- Flushed skin and broken capillaries on the face; a husky voice; trembling hands; bloody or black/tarry stools or vomiting blood; chronic diarrhea
- Drinking alone, in the mornings, or in secret

Zero Tolerance Law

Understanding Laws: If you choose to consume alcohol, there are a couple of important things to remember. Those who are under the age of 21 are not permitted to use alcohol according to the law. In the state of Mississippi, if an individual is driving with a Blood Alcohol Content (BAC) level at or above 0.02, the individual will receive a DUI. It is important to realize that for many students, this could mean just one drink.

The legal limit for individuals who are 21 years and older is a BAC level at or above 0.08, and that is probably the most common number you have heard. Regardless if you are of legal drinking age or not, you should make responsible and healthy choices to protect yourself and others if you choose to use.

Critical Thinking: What are the immediate and long-term consequences of breaking the law for both under aged and legal consumers?

Protective Behaviors

There are many things you can do to reduce your risk for negative consequences around substance use. Try incorporating these actions if you choose to drink:

- Plan ahead and set limits (decide how much you will drink and do not drink (pre-game) before going out. Avoid drinking games as they encourage irresponsible behavior – getting drunk fast and drinking too much. Stay with the same group of friends all night.
- Use bystander intervention strategies to monitor how much you have consumed.
- Keep track of time and pace of consumption.
- Stay hydrated with water. Alternate non-alcoholic beverages and alcoholic.
- Include food in your night. (Don't drink on an empty stomach.)
- Know your NO. In the event you are offered a drink when you do not want one, have a polite and convincing "no thanks" ready.

Bystander Intervention Techniques

What is a bystander? A bystander is someone who is present but not involved; an onlooker.

What is bystander intervention? An intervention is when those around an individual or group who are engaging in risky or dangerous behavior step up and intervene in an attempt to prevent harm.

What barriers prevent bystanders from acting?

Social Impact: being influenced by others in a social situation.

Fear of Embarrassment: not wanting to call attention to yourself or be singled out by speaking up.

Diffusion of Responsibility: believing that someone else will do something.

Retaliation Anxiety: being afraid of emotional or physical harm as a result of intervening.

Pluralistic Ignorance: thinking you must be the only one feeling this way.

What does bystander intervention look like?

- **Notice the problem.**
  Problem or emergency?

- **Assume responsibility.**
  Thoughts to overcome:
  "I am scared of what might happen," or

"No one else is doing anything, it must not be a problem," or "It's not my job, someone else will do it."

- **Know how to help.**

- **Take action.**

NOTE: The University of Mississippi's Medical Amnesty policy states that amnesty will be granted for anyone who seeks medical attention for another person or themselves when in need of medical attention. This means that any student or student organization who seeks emergency assistance on behalf of him- or herself, another community member, or a friend experiencing an alcohol or drug related emergency will not be subject to disciplinary action under the University Code of Conduct.

CLASS DISCUSSION: Discuss potential scenarios and work through the bystander intervention barriers and techniques.

When the above strategies and techniques are not used, risky behavior occurs. Typically, on our campus, we see the following negative consequences:

Negative Consequences of Risky Student Drinking

We have mentioned that there are negative consequences that can happen if you do not choose to use responsible behaviors while drinking. These consequences can touch multiple parts of your life: social, physical, academic, financial, sexual, and even harm to others. Though not limited to the list below, here are some of the more common negative outcomes from risky drinking in college.

Social
1. Arguments and fights
2. Embarrassment of own behavior*
3. Regretting own behavior
4. Waking or disturbing roommate
5. Damaging property
6. Trouble with police and University authorities

*In our world of widespread social media, let's remember that everything we do and say can easily be seen by thousands with the click of a button.

Physical
1. Hangover
2. Blackout/memory loss
3. Nausea/vomiting
4. Physical injury

Academic

1. Missing class or work
2. Performing poorly on a test or assignment
3. Getting behind.

Sexual

1. Unwanted sexual experience
2. Sexual aggression
3. Sexually Transmitted Infections

Drunk Driving

1. Riding with a driver who has been drinking
2. Driving after drinking
3. DUI, DWI arrest
4. Seriously injuring or killing yourself or someone else.

Avoid these negative consequences by practicing the protective behaviors listed previously.

PRESCRIPTION DRUGS

Higher education is currently faced with an epidemic of prescription drug abuse by college age students. Nearly 41 percent of surveyed teens agreed that prescription drugs are safer to use than illegal drugs, even if a doctor does not prescribe them. (drugfree.org retrieved Jan. 2015) Also, about one-third of teens believe that there is "nothing wrong" with using prescription drugs without a prescription "once in a while." (theantidrug.com, retrieved Jan. 2015)

Why do college students sometimes choose to misuse or abuse prescription drugs? Research has discovered some common reasons include:

- Attempting to cope with stress
- Getting high
- Using prescription drugs to study
- Attempting to fit in with other students
- Self-treating a condition (theantidrug.com, retrieved Jan. 2015)

This risky behavior is dangerous, and the consequences can be deadly. In fact, about 100 people die every day in the U.S. from unintentional drug overdoses. This equates to about one death every 15 minutes. Also, every year more people die from prescription painkiller overdoses than from those due to heroin or cocaine combined – and the rate of overdose death from prescription painkillers has more than tripled since 1999. (CDC, 2015).

Stimulants

While the abuse of several kinds of prescription medications is seen on college campuses, one class of medications – stimulants – has been on the rise. Stimulants such as Adderall ® are used to treat Attention Deficit Hyperactivity Disorder (ADHD) and also are known to have addictive potential, especially when they are being used without medical supervision.

ADHD is a complex behavioral disorder characterized by symptoms such as difficulty paying attention, hyperactivity, and/or impulsivity that are distractive and inappropriate for one's developmental level. ADHD is a chronic condition characterized by significant impairment at school, work, or in social functioning. In 2009, the Substance Abuse and Mental Health Services Administration (SAMSHA) reported that the non-medical use of Adderall ® among 18-22 year olds was twice as high for full-time college students than for non-students. This is an alarming statistic, but unfortunately, few students are surprised to hear that college students are more prone to misusing these so-called "cognitive enhancers."

Students that use prescription stimulants such as Adderall ®, but do not have ADHD or conditions that justify the prescription may be doing themselves more harm than good. Research has shown that unprescribed prescription stimulants do not improve academic performance. Students may perceive an improvement in their academic ability based upon their perceptions of how they think the drug works, but that is not the case in reality. Students that abstain from prescription stimulants are more likely to experience an increase in GPA over the course of their college enrollment.

A recent study at The Ohio State University found a vast disparity (approximately eightfold) between self-reported non-medical use of prescription stimulants and perceptions of what other students were doing. This inaccurate assessment of the social norm on college campuses can create a feeling that "everyone is doing it," when they actually are not. Students may use this perception as a rationalization for their experimentation with prescription stimulants, or it may provide an impetus to do so.

Here are some healthy alternatives:

Do not skip class! This is one of the biggest mistakes students make in terms of academic success.

Stay current with class material and review a little every day.

Establish good study habits and a regular study schedule. Set aside extra time before important tests or deadlines.

Use healthier "stimulants" – snacks, exercise, light, and even caffeine in moderation.

Use your available resources (TAs, professors, tutors, friends, etc.) to get help when needed.

Establish a study group to reinforce your learning.

Other Drugs

College students across the country frequently use drugs such as marijuana, cocaine, and hallucinogens. The following is a chart of illegal drugs that may be found on college campuses with a brief description of some of their effects and health risks.

Substances	Intoxication Effects	Health Risks
Marijuana/Hashish	Increased appetite, impaired learning, distorted sensory perception, panic attacks	Respiratory infections, possible mental health decline
Stimulants (Cocaine, Amphetamine, and Methamphetamine)	Increased energy, reduced appetite, anxiety, paranoia	Seizure, stroke, cardiovascular complications, insomnia
MDMA (Ecstasy, Molly)	Chills, sweating, muscle cramping, mild hallucinogenic effects	Sleep disturbance, depression, impaired memory
GHB (Date rape drug)	Drowsiness, disorientation, loss of memory, loss of coordination	Unconsciousness, seizures, coma
Hallucinogens (LSD, Acid, Mushrooms)	Panic, nervousness, paranoia, impulsive behavior, sleeplessness, increased heart rate	Hallucinogen persisting perception disorder, flashbacks
Inhalants (Dust it, Whip Its)	Headache, wheezing, slurred speech, loss of moto coordination	Memory impairment, unconsciousness, sudden death
DXM (Robo, Triple C, found in some cough and cold medications)	Confusion, dizziness, distorted visual perceptions	Anxiety, numbness, tremors, memory loss, nausea
Synthetic Cannabinoids (Spice, K2)	Extreme anxiety, paranoia, hallucinations	Rapid heart rate, vomiting, agitation, increased blood pressure
Steroids	No intoxication effects	Blood clotting and cholesterol changes, hepatitis, hypertension, hostility, aggression, acne
Opioids (Opium, Heroin)	Euphoria, nausea, sedation, slowed or arrested breathing	Constipation, endocarditis, HIV, fatal overdose

Risk Factors and Addiction

It is not uncommon to associate risky behavior with being in college, but what risk factors do you think specifically relate to the misuse and abuse of prescription medications in the 18-25 year old population? Perhaps one of the biggest factors is that you have grown up in a drug-infused society. In the United States, we use more medications than any other country. We are one of only two countries (United States and New Zealand) that allows direct-to-consumer advertising of prescription drugs. We expect "quick fixes," and all of this may normalize the use of medications.

It also is possible for students who abuse alcohol or drugs to become dependent on those substances. Dependence may be physical, psychological, or both. Dependence often is accompanied by tolerance, or the need to use more of a substance to receive the same effect. Dependence and increased tolerance may lead to addiction.

Some risk factors associated with addiction include: genetic predisposition, use of substances at an early age, psychological factors such as depression, environmental influences such as history of addiction in the family, and substance use among peers (CASA, 2013). Susceptibility to addiction differs with each individual, and no single factor determines whether a person will develop an addiction.

Among prescription drugs, illicit drugs, alcohol, nicotine, and countless others, there are many addictive substances in the world today. Many students are unaware of the symptoms of addiction, or may not know how to recognize signs of addiction in friends, family, and peers. If you or someone you know is dealing with an addiction, you should be familiar with the following signs and symptoms.

If you see one or more of these signs reach out for help!

Loss of Control: Drinking or drugging more than a person wants to or intended

Neglecting Other Activities: Spending less time on activities that used to be important, or a drop in attendance and performance at work or school.

Risk Taking: More likely to take serious risks to obtain the drug of choice.

Relationship Issues: People struggling with addiction are known to act out against those closest to them, particularly if someone is attempting to address their substance problems; complaints from co-workers, supervisors, teachers, or classmates.

Secrecy: Going out of the way to hide the amount of drugs or alcohol consumed

Changing Appearance: Serious changes or deterioration in hygiene or physical appearance.

Family History: A family history of addiction can dramatically increase predisposition to substance abuse Tolerance: Over time, a person's body adapts to a substance to the point that he or she needs more and more of it to have the same reaction.

Withdrawal: As the effect of the alcohol or drugs wears off the person may experience symptoms such as anxiety or jumpiness, shakiness or trembling, sweating, nausea, vomiting, insomnia, depression, irritability, fatigue, loss of appetite, and headaches.

Continued Use Despite Negative Consequences: Even though it is causing problems (work, school, relationships, health), a person continues drinking and drugging. (National Council on Alcoholism and Drug Dependence, 2016)

Recognizing the signs and symptoms of substance abuse early is important to help prevent dependence and serious life-threatening consequences.

Who to contact:
Emergency: (911), University Counseling Center (662-915-3784) William Magee Center for AOD and Wellness Education (662-915-6543)
University Police Department (662-915-7234)
Community Assistant (Residence Halls)
House Mother, Chapter President (Greek Life) or Friends and Family

When a student is ready to enter or resume college life in recovery, it can be extremely challenging. For UM students, the best resource is our Collegiate Recovery Community. The Collegiate Recovery Community at the University of Mississippi was established to help students in recovery achieve their academic goals. Academic and social support are provided through a network of peers, faculty, and staff who understand the unique challenges recovering students face in a collegiate environment. The benefits of student involvement in the Collegiate Recovery Community are sober events and activities, volunteer opportunities, scholarships, and peer-led meetings on campus where students can support each other in their journey of recovery.
For more information about the Collegiate Recovery Community, visit magee.olemiss.edu or recovery@olemiss.edu.

Tobacco Use and Campus Policy
Nicotine and Addiction
In its pure form, nicotine (the additive chemical in tobacco) is a poison, an insecticide. In fact, in 1988, the Surgeon General asserted that nicotine is more addictive than heroin (U.S. department of Health and Human Services, 1988.) "Whether they are smoking cigarettes or chewing tobacco, most users quickly develop a tolerance for nicotine and need greater amounts to produce desired effects. When you consider a pack-a-day smoker takes 200-300 hits of nicotine daily, it is no surprise that addiction occurs" (Human Relations Media 2002). Regardless of whether you ingest or inhale the nicotine in consumable products, they are deliberately designed

by manufacturers to be highly addictive. This applies to cigarettes, vapes, chewing tobacco, or any other number of products available on the market today. As with any addiction, when tobacco users try quitting, they often suffer withdrawal symptoms. Many of the physical symptoms of dependency are a major reason why quitting tobacco is considered difficult.

The University of Mississippi adopted a Smoke Free and Tobacco Free Campus Policy in December 2020.

Policy Details

The University of Mississippi is a smoke-free/tobacco-free/electronic smoking device-free environment. This policy applies to all campuses of the university. Smoking, vaping (the use of an electronic smoking device, or ESD) and/or the use of smokeless tobacco shall not be permitted in any university facilities, on any university property or in any university vehicles. This policy applies to all students, faculty, staff, visitors, contractors and vendors on campus, regardless of the purpose of their visit. Exemptions to this policy are not allowed.

Important Definitions

Electronic Smoking Device (or ESD) — means any product containing or delivering nicotine or any other substance intended for human consumption that can be used by a person in any manner for the purpose of inhaling vapor or aerosol ("vaping") from the product. The term includes any such device, whether manufactured, distributed, marketed or sold as an e-cigarette, e-cigar, e-pipe, e-hookah or vape pen, or under any other product name or descriptor.

Vaping — using an ESD.

Smokeless Tobacco — products such as snuff, snus, chewing tobacco or dipping tobacco derived from the tobacco plant or other plant and designed to be used in a manner other than by smoking, such as by placing in the mouth, chewing or sucking.

Smoking — means inhaling, exhaling, burning or carrying any lighted or heated cigar, cigarette, pipe, hookah, or any other lighted or heated tobacco or plant product intended for inhalation, including marijuana, whether natural or synthetic, in any manner or in any form. Smoking also includes the use of an ESD, which creates an aerosol or vapor, in any manner or in any form, or the use of any oral smoking device to circumvent the prohibition of smoking in this policy.

Tobacco Products — products derived from tobacco, such as cigarettes, cigars, pipe tobacco, chewing tobacco, snuff, snus, dipping tobacco and ESDs, and the fluids or juices designed to be used in those devices.

Hookah — a water pipe and any associated products and devices that are used to produce fumes, smoke and/or vapor from the burning of material including, but not limited to, tobacco, shisha or other plant matter.

The success of this policy depends on the consideration and cooperation of smokers and nonsmokers. All members of the university community share in the responsibility of adhering to and enforcing this policy. Any complaints should be brought to the attention of the University of Mississippi Police Department, and anyone who files a complaint about a violation of this policy shall be protected against retaliation. The University of Mississippi has the authority to enforce this policy. Visitors, contractors and other individuals temporarily on campus should be reminded of the policy and asked to comply. Those individuals refusing to cooperate may be asked to leave a facility, event or the campus, and repeated violations may result in the individual(s) being issued a "no trespassing notice" from UPD. Students who violate this policy will be referred to Conflict Resolution and Student Conduct and subject to sanctions, including fines. Employees who violate this policy may face employment-related discipline and/or fines. Questions or comments about this policy may be referred to the assistant vice chancellor for student affairs for wellness and student success.

Overwhelming use of Vapes on College Campuses

Many students have the misconception that vaping causes minimal harm, and that vapes are a safe way to consume nicotine. In 2015, the US Surgeon General reported e-cigarette use among high school students had increased 900% over the last four years (CDC, 2019). The reality is that e-cigarettes expose them to many of the same carcinogens and toxic substances that they would encounter while smoking a traditional cigarette. Vapes, also known as e-cigarettes, function by heating e-liquid and converting it to a vapor which is then inhaled. Many students who vape enjoy this aspect of vape use, as it gives them the ability to choose from the thousands of eliquid flavors available for purchase today, but they do not realize that vaping exposes them to rarely discussed risks. In 2019, the CDC identified a new lung disease referred to as e-cigarette or vaping product use associated lung injury (EVALI). As of 2020, CDC has confirmed thousands have been hospitalized due to EVALI with 60 individuals dying from this new disease (CDC, 2020).

E-cigarette companies have confessed that they do not fully understand what chemical reactions occur when e-liquid is vaporized, but research has shown that there are few "safe" chemicals involved in the process. One study comparing e-cigarettes to traditional cigarettes found that the contents of e-liquid are composed of numerous heavy metals and other pollutants (Samburova, et al., 2018). A government study determined that e-cigarette users were being exposed to the metals contained in the heating element of the vape, which is generally a coil located near the mouthpiece of the vape. Heating coils were found to have imparted aluminum, nickel, titanium, uranium, copper, and zinc into the e-liquid during the heat vaporization process (Ween, Thredgold, Reynolds, & Hodge, 2019). In addition to exposing their airways and other tissues to harmful chemicals, there is the added risk of the device potential overheating, and potentially even leading to a lethal explosion. There is no safe way to vape, but vape use, and the accompanying nicotine addiction can be overcome using the same practices used during traditional smoking cessation.

Quitting

If you or someone you know has tried to quit smoking, then you know that it is a challenge. Most people make more than one attempt to quit; you may have to try many times before quitting for good, but with each effort you learn more about yourself and your addiction. Your chances of quitting increase simply by getting help rather than attempting to quit on your own. According to the U.S. Department of Health and Human Services (2000), there are five keys to help you make a successful quit attempt: 1. Get ready. Set a quit date and change your environment. 2. Get support and encouragement. You have a better chance of being successful if you have help. 3. Learn new skills and behaviors. Practice stress reduction techniques, watch your diet, and drink plenty of water. 4. Get medication, and use it correctly. Ask your heath care provider for advice about which options are best for you. Some examples of medications that could help your chances of quitting for good include Chantix and Nicotine gum/inhaler/nasal spray/patch. Some are available by prescription, while others you can buy over-the counter. 5. Be prepared for relapse or difficult situations. Many tobacco users relapse; do not be discouraged. Remember, it may take several attempts before you finally quit. Some difficult situations to watch out for include alcohol, other smokers, weight gain, and depression. If you are having problems with any of these situations, talk to your doctor before you start smoking again.

Tobacco Cessation Programs

The William Magee Center for Alcohol and Other Drugs and Wellness Education has a tobacco cessation specialist on staff. WMC has partnered with University Health Services to create a robust tobacco cessation program and offers a range of smoking cessation and support for any member of the university community who desires to quit the use of tobacco products. Individuals who want to quit smoking may be eligible for free counseling, over-the-counter nicotine replacement therapy and smoking cessation prescriptions. For information about these resources, please visit magee.olemiss.edu.

Project Free

WMC provides Project Free as a robust educational tool to create healthy changes in one's tobacco use. This program will provide educational modules, cued reminders and opportunities to access nicotine replacement modalities from University Health Services.

Scan this QR code to join our educational tool.

Wellness Consultation

WMC provides opportunities for one-on-one health consulting on select topics. This one-time session will provide you an opportunity to hear from our wellness education coordinators regarding risks of tobacco use. Our goal is to provide you with information and resources to make an informed decision regarding your personal use. Registration for wellness consultations can be found on our website at magee. olemiss.edu.

William Magee Center Tobacco Quit Text Service

Prefer a more hands-off approach, or maybe not ready to make a change yet? This text-based service will provide you cues to action and reminders, and cheer you on as you navigate changing your tobacco use.

Simply text QUIT to 662-915-6543 to opt in.

Need more?

University Health Services' pharmacy can provide nicotine replacement therapy to students, faculty and staff at the University of Mississippi. For more information about NRT, please call 662-915-7274.

What is Nicotine Replacement Therapy?

Nicotine replacement therapy is the most common form of smoking cessation medications. NRT releases small doses of nicotine into the body without the other harmful chemicals that can be found in cigarettes and other smoking devices.

Nicotine replacement therapy is most beneficial in relieving most physical symptoms of withdrawal so the user can focus on maintaining the psychological symptoms of withdrawal.

Some of the most common types of NRT include:

- Patches
- Gum
- Nasal spray
- Inhaler
- Lozenges

CAMPUS RESOURCES

William Magee Center for AOD and Wellness Education
Phone: 662-915-6543
E-mail: wellnessedu@olemiss.edu
magee.olemiss.edu

University Police Department
Kinard Hall, Wing C
Non-emergency number: 662-915-7234 E-mail: upd@olemiss.edu
upd.olemiss.edu
Community safety, emergency response, and outreach

University Counseling Center
Lester Hall
Phone: 662-915-3784
counseling.olemiss.edu
Confidential individual and group counseling

Collegiate Recovery Community (William Magee Center for AOD and Wellness Education
Phone: 662-915-6543
E-mail: recovery.olemiss.edu
magee.olemiss.edu

ABOUT THE AUTHORS

Erin Cromeans, *Assistant Director of Wellness Education, William Magee Center for Wellness Education*

Erin Cromeans is currently pursuing a doctorate in health and kinesiology with a focus in Health Behavior. She received a master of science in nutrition and hospitality management degree at the University of Mississippi in 2011, a master of science in health promotion at the University of Mississippi in 2009, and a bachelor of science in exercise science at the University of Mississippi in 2007. Ms. Cromeans is a certified health education specialist (CHES) through the National Commission for Health Education and Credentialing. Ms. Cromeans has been a part of the Ole Miss Family for more than ten years and loves Oxford more and more each day. Hotty Toddy!

Sierra Elston, *Coordinator for Wellness Education, William Magee Center* for Wellness Education

Sierra is from Montgomery, Alabama, and attended the University of North Alabama in Florence to complete her B.S. in therapeutic nutrition and her M.S. in wellness and health promotion. While completing her master's degree she had the opportunity to design and support a university wellness program, and she enjoys developing solutions for the unique challenges that campus health programming presents. She is excited to bring her passion for wellness to Oxford, and aims to serve and inspire by providing learning opportunities to students that will empower them to live healthier, happier lives. Sierra enjoys spending her free time hiking, painting, cooking, or simply relaxing at home with her cat Stella.

Kyle Loggins, *Certified Prevention Specialist, William Magee Center for AOD and Wellness Education*

Kyle Loggins grew up in Olive Branch, MS. Currently, he is a 4th year doctoral student in the Health Education and Promotion program at The University of Alabama (UA). He earned a master's degree in counselor education at Mississippi State University (MSU) focused specifically on clinical mental health counseling and graduated magna cum laude at MSU with a bachelor's in psychology. Before becoming the certified prevention specialist at the William Magee Center (WMC), Kyle was a substance abuse counselor at Indian Rivers Mental Health Center and a Community Director at UA. These experiences shaped his foundation for helping others by providing a holistic approach to health and wellness to ensure individuals can become the best versions of themselves. Kyle is excited to bring his skillset to the Ole Miss community and be part of the WMC team.

CHAPTER 24

PHYSICAL *Fitness*

By Shannon Richardson

"He who has health, has hope; and he who has hope, has everything."
— Thomas Carlyle

P hysical fitness is a term used to describe an individual ability to perform physical activity; physical fitness is an important dimension of wellness, and it is the most visible indication of overall health.

You already know that going to class, making notes, studying, and earning good grades are essential to receive your diploma, but did you know there are other things vital to your education? To enjoy a healthy life as a college student, you must consider all dimensions of wellness, including physical fitness.

While being a good student is critical to your success in college, you also must take care of your body. This chapter provides you with the knowledge and resources you need to achieve a top level of physical fitness while you are an Ole Miss student and to maintain a healthy lifestyle after you graduate.

What is Physical Fitness?

The American College of Sports Medicine (ACSM) defines physical fitness as "a set of attributes or characteristics that people have or achieve that relates to the ability to perform physical activity" (American College of Sports Medicine, 2010, p. 2). In layman's terms, physical fitness is a task-specific term used to describe an individual's ability to perform physical activity. What makes it task specific?

Let's look at two former Ole Miss athletes to find the answer. First consider Sam Kendricks, U.S.A., NCAA, and SEC pole vault champion of 2014, and the first person in school history to win the U.S.A. pole vault title as well as an Olympic medal for that event. Kendricks is 6'1" and 170 pounds.

Now consider Marquis Haynes, the 2017 starting defensive end for the football team who is the Rebels' modern-era sacks leader (since 1983) with 32 and holds the modern-era career tackles for loss record with 47.5. Haynes is 6'3" and weighs 230 pounds. His strength, power, and agility make him fit for his position on the football team, but he would not be successful at the pole vault in which Kendricks competes. Conversely, Kendricks probably would not fare very well as an offensive lineman on the football team. Both athletes are fit, but that fitness is specific to their tasks.

Fitness as a Part of Total Wellness

Not everyone is going to be a collegiate or professional athlete. For those who are not, physical fitness sometimes is not as high on the priority list as maybe it should be. Adjusting to the collegiate lifestyle, balancing academic assignments, studying, employment, and a social life can leave little room for exercise, which is purposeful, structured physical activity designed to improve physical fitness. Nevertheless, physical fitness is no more or less important than any other aspect of wellness, and neglecting physical fitness in college can lead to potential health problems in the future, and can negatively impact your collegiate experience. With that in mind, here are a few tips to assist in maximizing the benefits of your exercise and physical activity. It is important to note that physical activity and exercise are often used interchangeably, but by definition, there is a difference so each term is used separately in this section.

To Improve Fitness, You Have to Exercise

The overload principle states that a body must be subjected to a stimulus that requires effort outside its current capacity to elicit adaptation. In this case, the stimulus is physical activity or exercise, and the desired adaptation is improved fitness. Whether it is running, biking, swimming, or resistance training, if it feels easy to you, you likely are not getting enough change-causing stimuli to elicit adaptation. At best, you are just burning calories, but that is better than doing nothing.

Resistance Training is Important

A common myth about resistance training is that if women lift weights they will get "big." Not true.

Unless women use performance enhancing substances, they have a much different hormonal profile than men and do not get as big as men from resistance training. The way an individual performs resistance training can affect muscle size as well (see Strength vs. Hypertrophy vs. Endurance).

There are too many benefits to resistance training for women not to lift weights. Some of these benefits include increased metabolism, more favorable body composition, improved performance in physical activity, and protection against the development of osteoporosis. Adding resistance training exercises to your workout two to three days per week will help you realize thesebenefits.

Strength vs. Hypertrophy vs. Endurance

Lifting weights to improve muscular strength, muscular endurance, and muscle size is similar, but there are a few differences. Those differences most easily are seen in the variations of the number of sets performed for each exercise, the number of repetitions performed in each set, and the rest periods between exercise sets. Use the chart below as a guide. The take home point is that you do not have to be big to be strong, and the biggest person in the gym is not always the strongest.

TRAINING SPECIFICITY

Training Goal	% 1RM	# of Sets	Rep Range	Rest b/w Sets
Muscular Endurance	<70	1-3	12-20	20-30 seconds
Hypertrophy	70-80	1-6	8-12	30-120 seconds
Muscular Strength	80-100	1-8	1-5+	2-5 minutes

(American Council on Exercise, 2003, p. 268)

Doing Anything is Better Than Doing Nothing

Thirty minutes of accumulated physical activity per day at a moderate intensity has significant health benefits (American College of Sports Medicine, 2010). This does not have to be vigorous exercise; physical activity such as walking the dog, gardening, or throwing a Frisbee in the Grove can be beneficial. Exercise does not have to be 30 continuous minutes to make a difference in your health. As long as at least 30 minutes of physical activity are accumulated throughout the day, health benefits are present.

Listen to Your Body

Recovery from exercise is just as important, if not more important than performing the actual exercise. Exercise creates micro tears in muscle fibers, and recovery time between workouts is when the fibers repair themselves, becoming stronger in the process. It is common for people to drastically increase their exercise volume as a result of a New Year's resolution or an attempt to get the perfect "beach body" for Spring Break. This commonly leads to fatigue and burnout, and a lack of results. Reaching physical fitness goals requires a long-term outlook and specific plan. You do not need to crash diet or starve to achieve results; consistency is the key to success.

Always listen to what your body is trying to tell you. If you are thirsty, drink water. Reserve sports drinks for vigorous and extended activities; water is sufficient for a 20-minute run. Dehydration negatively affects a person's ability to exercise; combat this by regularly drinking water throughout the day, not just when you feel thirsty. Six to eight ounces of water every 15–20 minutes during exercise is recommended; longer exercise periods require more fluids. Let hunger tell you when to eat. Use food to fuel exercise and activity; match food intake to activity levels. Freshmen often are concerned about additional weight gain during the first year, but fad diets and severely reducing caloric intake are not healthy or viable options.

Focus on eating a variety of nutrient-dense, whole foods and maintaining a consistent, structured exercise routine for a physically fit first year at Ole Miss.

The Department of Campus Recreation

Campus Recreation provides facilities, equipment, and programs for physical activity and wellness. Campus Recreation operates two facilities: the Turner Center and the South Campus Recreation Center (SCRC). The Turner Center is located on the main campus, just west of the Pavilion, and the SCRC is located on the periphery of campus on Chucky Mullins Drive, just south of Highway 6. Campus Recreation is composed of five program areas, each designed to  meet the recreational and wellness needs of students: Aquatics, Facility Operations, Fitness, Intramural Sports and Sport Clubs, and Outdoors.

Fitness

The Turner Center fitness center is a 9,000 square foot facility located on the third floor, and is home to cardiovascular, strength, and specialty training equipment. The SCRC offers 25,000 square feet of fitness space throughout the building, including a 6,000 square foot indoor/outdoor functional training area. In addition to the fitness equipment, over 50 group fitness classes are offered each week at both facilities; students can find a class suitable for any fitness level and abilities.

Classes include: TRX, Suspension Training, HIIT Fitcamp, Cardio Kickboxing, and more. Mind/body classes are offered in four different formats with yoga relax, yoga flow, and power yoga. Classes are free during the first week of each semester and then cost $20 for unlimited classes during the semester.

Students have the opportunity to hire a personal trainer or purchase small group training sessions for a more focused and instructional fitness program.

Intramural Sports and Sport Clubs

For students who prefer team sports and competitive activities, Intramural Sports and Sport Clubs may be the perfect way to help you stay fit. Flag football, sand volleyball, basketball, and softball are just some of the standard sports offered. More adventurous students can register for some of the unique tournaments such as: Battleship (in canoes!), spikeball, dodgeball, wheelchair basketball, or inner tube water polo. Sport Clubs are a more competitive option and often compete against other schools within and outside of Mississippi. These include badminton, baseball, soccer, rugby, lacrosse, and ice hockey. With 28 sport clubs and a constantly increasing number of intramural sports, there are options for everyone to be active and fit through sport.

Informal Recreation

Campus Recreation also offers opportunities to engage in less formal sports competition. Turner Center offers four basketball courts for pick-up games, and these courts can also accommodate badminton or volleyball. Racquetball and squash courts can be found on the first floor as well as a game room and study lounge. The South Campus Recreation Center offers two basketball courts, a multi-activity court, and an indoor track. Any equipment needed for activities can be checked-out or purchased from the front desk.

Ole Miss Outdoors

Ole Miss Outdoors, affectionately called OMOD (oh-mod), is located at the South Campus Recreation Center. OMOD is not a club but rather an inclusive program open to all students, faculty, staff, and community members—and for people of all abilities. OMOD offers a variety of organized outdoor trips each year including kayaking, rafting, rock climbing, backpacking, skiing, caving, and more. Students lead these adventure trips after completing an academic course and becoming certified Wilderness First Responders. The price of these trips includes gear rentals necessary to outfit these trips, including tents, sleeping bags, backpacks, stoves, canoes, and kayaks. OMOD also oversees a 35-foot atrium climbing wall, and a 70-linear-foot bouldering wall. Additionally, OMOD operates the Rebel Challenge Course, a high and low ropes course located near the intramural fields. The challenge course is designed for groups to foster team building, increase communication skills, and sharpen their problem-solving abilities. Groups can reserve the challenge course online. OMOD also supervises the South Campus Rail Trail, which is a beautiful, rustic nature trail open to the Oxford and Ole Miss communities located across from the SCRC. You can walk, jog, and bike on this trail—check it out, take a friend, or walk your dog.

Aquatics

The Olympic-size natatorium is located on the first floor of the Turner Center. During the hours the pool is open, at least one section is open for lap swim. The natatorium hosts events throughout the year, including swimming lessons, swim meets, and triathlons. Aquatics also hosts a variety of events and resources, including a Master's swim program, water aerobics, and a free swim lesson program for students called Swim to Live. Visit the aquatics office to register for any of these events or to get more information.

Student Employment

In addition to numerous opportunities for recreation, Campus Recreation is the largest employer of students on campus, with the number of student employees reaching 250+ during fall and spring semesters. Students are hired to work a variety of positions including customer service representatives, facility managers, fitness supervisors, life-guards, personal trainers, trip leaders, climbing wall attendants, challenge course facilitators, and intramural officials. Please visit the website for more information: https://campusrec.olemiss.edu/.

Active Class Options for Instructors:

Book a private group fitness session for your class; you may request a variety of disciplines including Yoga, TRX, and Cardio Kickboxing; oftentimes instructors are able to accommodate you during your class meeting time. E-mail campusrec@ olemiss.edu to set up a time with the Fitness professionals.

Reserve the Rebel Challenge Course or indoor climbing wall; the trained facilitators will create a fun experience that incorporates fitness with team-building and communication as students traverse the elements or challenge themselves to climb the tower. Visit https://campusrec.olemiss.edu/, then click Rebel Challenge Course or Climbing Wall to reserve the course or wall.

Teach class while following one of the UM Walking Paths on campus or along the South Campus Rail Trail; review this chapter on physical fitness while you get some fresh air and physical activity. Visit https://rebelwell.olemiss.edu/walkatwork/ to view the walking paths.

THE DEPARTMENT OF CAMPUS RECREATION FACILITIES AND AMENITIES

Turner Center - 106,000 sq. ft. facility located across from the Pavilion

- **Gymnasium:** 4 basketball courts; accommodates 2 volleyball and 3 badminton courts

- **Track:** elevated track around perimeter of gymnasium: 8.5 laps = 1 mile

- **Fitness Center:** 9,000 sq. ft. facility with cardiovascular and resistance equipment

- **Studio 305:** accommodates a variety of group fitness classes

- **Group Fitness Studios 125 and 125 Cycle:** TRX, Yoga, and cycle classes

- **Natatorium:** two (25 yard), 8-lane swim areas and shallow area; pool depth is 3.5-13 ft.

- **Racquet Courts:** one Squash Court; three Racquetball Courts (two can host Wallyball)

- **The Tank:** a re-purposed racquetball court with functional training equipment

- **The Vault:** a re-purposed racquetball court with various circuit equipment

- **Game Room:** table tennis, X-Box, and lounge

- **Locker Rooms:** men's, women's, and universal

- **The Well:** quiet, restful space overlooking the pool

- **Intramural Sports and Sport Clubs Office:** registration and information

- **Tennis Courts:** four courts located behind the Turner Center

South Campus Recreation Center (SCRC) - 98,000 sq. ft. facility off Chucky Mullins Drive

- **Gymnasium:** two basketball courts & one Multi-Activity Court (MAC)

- **Track:** elevated jogging/walking track on upper level: 9 laps = 1 mile

- **Fitness Floor:** 25,000 sq. ft. facility with cardiovascular, strength, and specialty equipment

- **Group Fitness Studios:** three studios accommodating mind/body, cardio, and more

William Magee Center for Wellness Education

- **Locker Rooms:** men's, women's, and universal

- **Ole Miss Outdoors Office:** trip registration, gear rentals, climbing gear, and merchandise

- **Climbing Wall:** 35 foot, 360 degree, top rope and lead climbing

- **Bouldering wall:** 70 linear feet and teaching area

- **South Campus Rail Trail:** five-mile loop nature trail across from SCRC

- **South Campus Recreation Fields:** two full-size fields for sport clubs and intramurals

Outdoor Sports Complex: 10 acres located along Insight Park Drive

- **Intramural Sports and Sport Clubs Fields**

- **Disc Golf Course:** 23 holes

- **FitRig:** outdoor gym equipment

- **Rebel Challenge Course:** high and low ropes course

ABOUT THE AUTHOR

__Shannon Richardson__, Assistant Director of Campus Recreation

Shannon Richardson has 20 years of experience in campus recreation and student affairs. She holds a bachelor's degree in exercise physiology from North Georgia University, a master's degree in public administration from Georgia State University, and a doctorate in higher education administration from the University of Mississippi. Dr. Richardson resides in Oxford with her husband, Hunter, and their daughters, Emma and Meg.

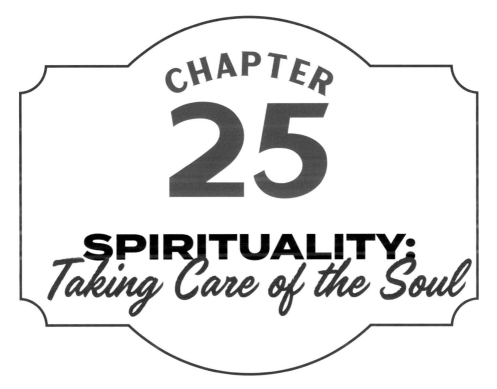

CHAPTER 25

SPIRITUALITY:
Taking Care of the Soul

By Reverend Ollie V. Rencher

The Paris-Yates Chapel provides a spiritual home on our campus where members of the Ole Miss family may seek peace, guidance, trust, and wisdom.

At the core of every human being lives a beautiful and sacred center that historically benefits and grows best when it is nurtured. And so, it is with young adult women and men who enter the new life of higher education at The University of Mississippi. Amidst University life essentials (studying, eating and drinking for nourishment, sleeping, working, building relationships), non-stop adjustments, and the challenges that come with the freshman experience, individual wellness includes taking care of the soul. To take care of the soul is to focus on spirituality, something that every human being possesses. The essence of spirituality is the search by an individual to know her or his true self, to tap into the Holy which lives at the sacred center.

For five years, I had the privilege to serve as one of several campus ministers at the University. It was powerful and humbling to experience the intentional involvement of freshmen in the nourishment of their spiritual lives. (I wish I had been so intentional when I was a freshman more than twenty years ago at a small liberal arts college in Mississippi!)

Daily, weekly, term after term, it was both joyful and encouraging to witness and hear about the rewards experienced by a variety of students who sought advice and settings that would help them take care of their souls. From their energy, I too increasingly improved my spiritual quest and practices, which included going away for retreats, reading, engaging holy conversation, and more to take care of my soul. Such focused choices were then – and are today – central to the wellness promoted for freshmen, as well as all members of the university community. As I reflect fondly and gratefully on my time at Ole Miss, I offer to all who might listen: to take care of the soul is to get the most from and bring good balance to the freshman experience.

Thanks to the intentional offerings and programs of the Student Religious Organizations at The University of Mississippi, an environment for spiritual growth and development is provided for those who might wish to go deeper – individually and in community with others. Not limited to the three Abrahamic religions (Judaism, Christianity, Islam) about which our local society tends to hear and know the most, spirituality reminds us that the Holy existed long before any religion evolved. Nonetheless, these and other religions, philosophies and practices, in one way or another, can benefit the care of the soul, namely when the individual approaches the quest with intention and openness. And if you are wondering about the possibility of having additional organizations, associations, or circles to nurture your spirit while enrolled at the University, consult with the Office of the Dean of Students for help.

Recently, during a rich and insightful conversation with an alumna of the University, I was asked what advice I would give to current students at the University – especially freshmen who were entering such a new and rich experience. After long contemplation of what I learned during my years in Oxford, I responded with the following four opportunities that can assist an individual with caring for her or his soul.

Embrace nature. Take a moment each day simply to look, hear, touch, and even smell the mystery and beauty of creation and of all that lives and grows in it; maybe even find time to be still, move slowly from place to place, or exercise in whatever way might allow some time in nature. It can be as easy as opening or looking out from a window or door, finding a non-climate-controlled space that feels different from your normal environment, listening to the rain or staring at the sky. Give thanks for any and all of it as a gift. Worship and take care of it. Remember that nature, like us, is sacred.

Observe silence. Take at least five minutes at the start of each day to be still, quiet, and removed from the countless noises, sounds, gadgets, things, and even people that often distract us from necessary moments to hear and know the sacred center living within us. Depending on where you live, this may take some creativity. Use this time simply to wake up, give thanks for life and its endless blessings, process problems, clear the mind, open the heart, and provide some clarity to make for a better day ahead. If it does not happen at the start of the day, find a moment between or after classes.

Take a moment each day to enter any kind of conversation with the sacred center.

Pray. Take a moment each day to enter any kind of conversation with the sacred center; with or without words, with eyes open or closed, with hands clasped or palms open, by standing, kneeling, sitting, or even stretching. Be still and try to raise all that is on your mind and in your heart that might need processing, releasing, answers, and ultimately peace; maybe even do so by journaling. Find a faith community in which to pray and worship with others or a setting where spiritual things can be discussed and practiced. Daily and weekly spiritual practices typically make for better days and weeks. If you don't know how to pray or worship, you're not alone; ask someone, find a book about either, show up where others are gathered.

Serve. Take advantage of the community service and volunteer opportunities organized by the University, local non-profits, or faith-based organizations as ways to extend your sacred center and gifts to others; spirituality helps us to know the true self by looking inward as well as by outwardly engaging others who, like us, are sacred. When we serve others, especially the poor, sick, needy, and lonely, it never fails that we too are served and rewarded. The Oxford-University community has an impressive variety of ways to serve, to bless, and be blessed by others.

These four opportunities (embrace nature, observe silence, pray, serve) through good intention and work can deepen the journey to discover the nature of our inner-most essence – and search for the Holy within whom we "live and move and have our being." Through such practices, I personally have learned and heard from countless others that the inner life becomes increasingly developed. And most often, the individual is led to an experience of connectedness with the larger core reality, yielding a more comprehensive self – a better self, a balanced self.

Not limited to the three Abrahamic religions (Judaism, Christianity, Islam) about which our local society tends to hear and know the most, spirituality reminds us that the Holy existed long before any religion evolved.

As the realities and challenges of university life unfold, may you stay in touch with your sacred center and keep its care as a priority – don't ignore it, nourish it – and most of all, celebrate it. Your wellness includes taking care of the soul, which is to focus on your spirituality. May your freshman experience be extraordinary and become increasingly better through your encounter with the Holy.

ABOUT THE AUTHORS

Rev. Ollie Rencher, *Rector of Grace-St. Luke's Episcopal Church in Memphis, Tennessee*

The Rev. Ollie V. Rencher served the University of Mississippi from 2003 until 2008 as campus minister for The Episcopal Church at Ole Miss (ECOM) and Assistant Rector of St. Peter's Episcopal Church, Oxford. Passionate about ministry that cares for and connects people more deeply to God and one another, he serves in a variety of ways in his local community. A native of Clarksdale, alumnus of Millsaps College and The General Theological Seminary of the Episcopal Church (Manhattan), Rencher deeply enjoys his ministry.

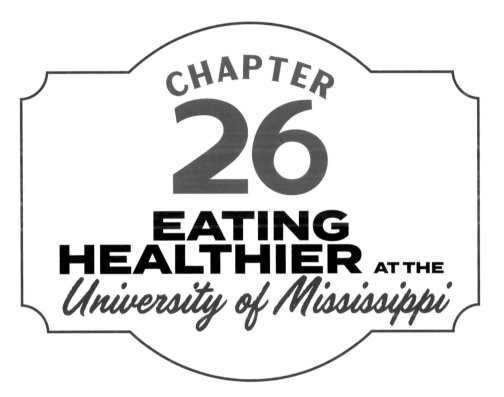

CHAPTER

26

EATING HEALTHIER AT THE

University of Mississippi

By Mariana A. Jurss

Eating Healthy During College

While college life introduces exciting new experiences, there are also challenges. Eating healthy can be one of those challenges. You may find yourself in stressful situations, eating on the run, bogged down with late night study sessions, and navigating all-you-can-eat dining facilities. These situations, along with tight budgets, lack of (or limited) cooking supplies, and hectic schedules make it difficult to make healthy eating choices. It takes time to adjust and adapt to new habits in your new environment, but it is important to know that it is possible to follow a healthy diet on campus with the right tools and motivation.

This chapter is a guide to help you make the healthiest food choices in the college environment. The key is balance, not perfection. Healthy eating does not mean starving yourself, being unrealistically thin, or eliminating foods you love. Instead, it is about feeling energized, finding balance, and feeling good about your body. Do not deprive yourself, or you are likely to overeat later. Make simple goals and work toward those goals to achieve healthier eating habits, keeping in mind that healthy eating takes planning and practice.

Nutrition Basics and Building a Healthy Meal

Once you understand the fundamentals of nutrition, it is easier to comprehend the "why" and the "how" of healthy eating. We need food to provide us with energy and nutrients that our bodies require to function and keep us alive. There are six classes of *essential nutrients:*

- Carbohydrates
- Lipids (fats)
- Proteins
- Vitamins
- Minerals
- Water

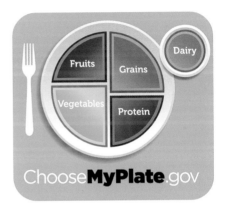

These nutrients come from the food we eat. Each food group contains a key nutrient that is fundamental for good health and body function. Our food is divided into *five main food groups:*

- Proteins
- Grains
- Vegetables
- Fruits
- Dairy

In 2011, the U.S. Department of Agriculture (USDA) launched MyPlate, an educational tool designed to help U.S. consumers create healthy, balanced meals. MyPlate focuses on providing a visual portion guide without having to measure food from the five main food groups to create a balanced meal. To get your personalized MyPlate Plan, check out the link below. Just click start to get started! https://www.choosemyplate.gov/resources/MyPlatePlan

To create a balanced meal, **begin by filling half of your plate with fruits and vegetables**. Key nutrients in vegetables and fruits are vitamins and minerals. Each vitamin and mineral has a specific role and is required for healthy skin, hair, nails, immune system, and overall proper function. Your goal when selecting fruits and vegetables is variety. You want to obtain a range of vitamins and minerals. Choose red, orange, and dark leafy greens such as tomatoes, sweet potatoes, and spinach. These protect our bodies from chronic disease, and most are low in fat, sodium, and calories.

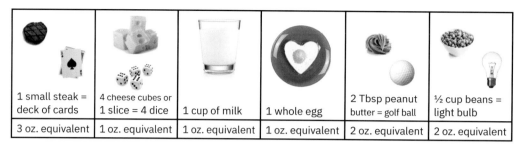

1 small steak = deck of cards	4 cheese cubes or 1 slice = 4 dice	1 cup of milk	1 whole egg	2 Tbsp peanut butter = golf ball	½ cup beans = light bulb
3 oz. equivalent	1 oz. equivalent	1 oz. equivalent	1 oz. equivalent	2 oz. equivalent	2 oz. equivalent

Next, fill a fourth of your plate with a **lean protein**, such as fish, poultry without skin, beans, tofu, nuts, and seeds. The key nutrient in this food group is protein. Protein provides the body with energy, and it helps maintain muscle and replace hormones, blood cells, and other essential components in the body. Most people consume enough protein, so the goal is to choose leaner options and vary your choices to maximize nutrient intake and health benefits. For example, choose cooked seafood as your protein choice at least twice per week. Also, limit your intake of processed meats such as sausages, pepperoni, hot dogs, and even chicken nuggets as these are usually high in fat and sodium.

Fill the last fourth of your plate with **grains**. The key nutrient in this food group is carbohydrates. Carbohydrates are the primary energy source for our body, particularly our brain and muscles; therefore, we need carbohydrates to have the energy to move and to think. The grain food group includes bread, pasta, rice, oatmeal, grits, crackers, cereals, popcorn, and tortillas. There are two types of grains, whole grains and refined grains. Whole grains provide you with more nutrients and fiber compared to the refined grains. Choose whole grains at least 50% of the time. Whole grains include oats, whole wheat bread, brown rice, and whole grain cereals.

Dairy is separated from the plate to emphasize that dairy does not need to be part of every meal, and your needs are dependent on your age. The key nutrient in this food group is the mineral calcium, which is the primary mineral of our bones and plays a role in muscle contraction and blood clotting. The dairy group is made up of milk products that retain their calcium content, such as milk, cheese, and yogurt. For those who do not consume dairy, calcium rich food sources include calcium-fortified plant based milk alternatives (soymilk, almond milk, rice milk, etc.), leafy greens, and canned fish. When choosing dairy products make sure you select the non-fat or low-fat dairy varieties of milk, cheese, and yogurt.

What about **fats**? The human body requires fat for optimal health. A well-balanced diet requires at least some fat; however, getting enough fat is typically not a concern. Most of us get enough oil/fat in the foods we eat regularly, such as cooking oil, fish, nuts, salad dressings, meats, and dairy. There are different types of dietary fats, these include saturated fats, trans fats, and unsaturated fats. Saturated fats and trans fats are characterized by being solid at room temperature, such as butter and coconut oil. Unsaturated fats are characterized by being liquid at room temperature, such as vegetable cooking oil. Saturated and trans fats can raise your bad cholesterol levels. Thus, be sure to read food labels and choose foods that are low in these types of fats. Keep in mind that people are more likely to over-consume fat versus not getting enough. Therefore, the general recommendation is to limit fat intake.

Lastly, another key ingredient to making healthy choices is to know what is in your food by reading food labels. Learn more about reading food labels from the supplemental handout "What is in your food? Read the label." Food labels can provide you with the information to make informed and healthy choices. At the top of the Nutrition Facts label, you will find the total number of servings in the container and the food or drink's serving size. The serving size on the label is based on the amount of food that people typically eat at one time and is not a recommendation of how much to eat. Learn more about "What's On The Nutrition Facts Label" by checking this out: https://www.fda.gov/food/food-labeling nutrition.

Also, did you know that there is a new and improved nutrition food label? Check this out to know the key changes. https://www.fda.gov/media/99331/download

With this information in mind, MyPlate can serve as a guide to help you design balanced meals. Having a healthy understanding of what should go on your plate will assist you in making healthy choices.

The Busy College Student

You have probably heard the phrase "You are what you eat." This phrase reminds us that the food we choose to eat does something in our bodies. Food provides us with nutrients that help us stay alive, and depending on what foods we choose to eat, our bodies will feel energized and strong (healthy) or tired and sluggish (less healthy). Most of us want to feel good, and what we choose to eat plays a big role. Right now, you are probably thinking "Healthy? Whatever, pass me the pizza and wings!" However, the habits you  create in your college years will likely transfer to lifelong habits. Having unhealthy eating habits can lead to weight gain or the "freshman 15." Gaining weight is uncomfortable for anyone; even a few pounds can make your clothing fit tighter and lead to uncomfortable aches and pain. In addition, there is increased risk to develop high blood pressure, diabetes, cardiovascular disease, and certain forms of cancer associated with being overweight. However, having a good plan and creating a routine will help you make healthier food choices and develop healthy meal patterns that work for you. Maintaining a healthy lifestyle should be one of your goals in college.

General Healthy Eating Habits, Creating Structure, and Having a Plan

Healthy eating habits require planning. The first weeks of college are chaotic and perhaps even overwhelming, but once you get used to your class schedule you can figure out a routine that allows you to eat healthy. Your meal times may vary from day to day depending on your classes, but creating a plan or routine helps you avoid eating on the run or skipping meals. Here are some tips to get started:

-  **Make time for meals a priority, especially breakfast.** This may be the first time you are on your own and planning your meals. Making scheduled meals a priority helps you avoid making unhealthy food selections on the run or skipping meals all together, especially breakfast. You probably have heard the phrase "Breakfast is the most important meal of the day." This is because breakfast, along with sleeping and exercise, provides you the energy you need to get through the day. If you are interested in doing well on an exam, eat a healthy breakfast. Research shows that eating a healthy breakfast improves brain function, attention span, and concentration. Particularly, it improves memory and recall, which are key to absorbing new information and utilizing it later during an exam. If you are concerned about your weight, start eating breakfast! Research shows that those who skip breakfast tend to weigh more compared to breakfast eaters. In addition, eating breakfast helps you make healthier food choices throughout the day. Aim to have three meals per day, plus one or two snacks between meals if you get hungry. Need ideas on how to improve your breakfast? Check out this video! https://youtu.be/cKeuCuBQjcU

- **Know your food options.** Know all of your food options. If you are on a meal plan, The University of Mississippi has three main dining facilities, the Rebel Market, The Marketplace at the RC, and The Grill at 1810, in addition to multiple P.O.D. locations (Grab and Go food options) and restaurants located at the Union and other locations across campus. Lenoir Dining, a restaurant on campus run exclusively by the Department of Nutrition and Hospitality Management students, is also a great option. The dining facilities have a variety of healthy food options such as grilled chicken, soups, a salad bar, and a fruit bar. In addition, for those with a gluten allergy or intolerance, the Rebel Market has a gluten free station. Check out the menu options at the various dining facilities and restaurants on campus. https://olemiss.campus-dish.com/

■ **Find healthy options you enjoy.** With so many on-campus dining options to choose from, it can be hard to differentiate between what is healthy from what is not. Most dining facilities on-campus display nutrition information next to each food item. Take the time to read this information  to know what is in your food! Make sure you survey all the stations at the dining facility to see your options. You can also download the CampusDish app to access nutrition information for the dining facilities at University of Mississippi. Fast-food restaurants such as Chick-fil-A or Panda Express make nutrition information available online. To select healthy options, remember to use MyPlate as a guide. It is important to be conscious of what you are putting in your body. This does not mean you can never have fried items or dessert; it just means you know the nutrition content of the food, which will make you more aware of what you are putting in your body. It is okay to occasionally have empty calorie food items such as cookies and ice cream; the key is being conscious of the portion and how often you are eating it. Remember that healthy eating is about balance—enjoying your food while taking care of your body.

■ **Select healthy food options most of the time.** Once you have found healthy options you enjoy, you can select those healthy choices most of the time. Having a plan keeps you on a healthy track. If you focus on making healthy choices most of the time, enjoying an occasional treat can easily fit into a healthy lifestyle. Make sure you add only one or two treats occasionally. For some, it may help to create a routine for treats. For example, if you like fried food, you can make "Fried Fridays" the day you select the fried item you enjoy. Alternatively, maybe Saturday is the day you enjoy a frozen yogurt or other sweet treat. You have to create a system that works for you; remember that we are all different, with different preferences, with different circumstances. The goal is to find what will work for you!

HEALTHY FOOD CHOICES AT OLE MISS

Navigating the Dining Facilities

To make healthy choices at the dining hall we are going to go back to the basics, MyPlate. If you recall, the goal of my plate is to fill half the plate with vegetables and/or fruit, one-fourth with a grain, one-fourth with a protein, and don't forget your dairy. We are going to use MyPlate and other tips to make healthy choices at the dining facilities.

Plan and know what you are eating.

- Look at the menu before hitting the dining facilities. Planning your meals is a smart way to make healthy, balanced choices. You are more likely to splurge and choose unhealthy options at the last minute when you are hungry or in a rush, so plan.
- Read the posted nutrition information. Remember that The University of Mississippi dining facilities post nutrition information at most locations and/or online.

Make half of your plate fruits and vegetables.

- Select fruit and low-fat yogurt for a quick grab-and-go breakfast.
- Start with salad or vegetable soup a few days a week.
- Choose a cooked vegetable or salad as a side.
- Hit the fruit bar for dessert.

Pick a lean protein.

- An omelet is a great choice for breakfast. Add veggies to your omelet and pair it with whole wheat bread for a balanced meal.
- Grilled chicken and fish are good protein choices.
- Add bean, eggs, tofu, cottage cheese, or seeds to your salad.
- Decode the menu, and look for proteins that are labeled baked, grilled, roasted, sautéed, or in stews. These are usually significantly lower in fat compared to proteins labeled fried, crispy, crunchy, crusted, tempura, breaded, and battered.

Make half of your grains whole grains.

- Choose oatmeal for breakfast.
- Select whole wheat bread for sandwiches. Create a balanced meal by adding a slice of low-fat cheese, veggies, and a lean protein to your sandwich.
- Choose whole grain pasta at the pasta bar.
- Select 100% whole grains when available, such as whole-wheat bread, whole-grain cereals, oatmeal, whole-grain pasta, brown rice, whole-grain tortillas, and quinoa.

Remember to enjoy your food, but eat less.

- Resist the temptation of eating too much at the all-you-can-eat dining facilities. Make sure you survey each station, and select food that you really want to eat. If available, choose smaller plates/bowls or stick to single food servings to help with portion control. Do not worry about going hungry; you can always go back for more.
- Be mindful of your hunger cues. Wait at least 20 minutes before you go back for seconds. If you are still hungry, then your body needs a little more.
- Do not linger! Enjoy eating with friends, but avoid staying for long periods at the dining facilities to reduce the temptation to continue eating.

Make it your own. Do not be afraid to mix and match plates.

- Be proactive and creative when it comes to creating your meals. Take advantage of the "make it your own" stations. Dining facilities are on a cycle menu meaning that options repeat, and you can easily become bored.

Slow down on sauces.

- Sauces, gravies, and dressings tend to be high in fat and sodium.
- Entrees with teriyaki, BBQ, glazed, and honey sauces are higher in sugar.
- Watch out for foods prepared with a lot of oil, butter, or topped with heavy condiments such as mayonnaise, cream, or cheese.
- You do not have to do away with sauces and condiments altogether; just ask for less or put them on the side. Reducing extras helps you control how much fat, sugar, and sodium you put in your body.

Be on your guard at the Salad Bar.

- Salads are a great way to add vegetables to your meals, but not all salads are healthy! Most veggies get the green light, as they are filled with nutrients and most are naturally low in calories—romaine lettuce, spinach, tomato, cucumber, carrots, bell peppers, broccoli, red onion, mushrooms, etc.
- Be cautious of foods high in fat and sodium—olives, bacon bits, fried noodles, croutons, and pastas and potato salad made with mayonnaise and oil.

- Ask for dressing on the side, stick to one serving, and choose dressings that are light, low-fat, or fat free. Balsamic vinaigrette and Lite Italian dressing are low-calorie options offered on campus.

Make dessert and fried food special occasion treats.

- Save dessert for the weekend or for special occasions. If you cannot resist, choose a nutrient-rich option such as fruit or yogurt parfait.
- Skip the fried food on most days—save it for Fried Fridays! If you cannot resist, have one small piece or small side of the fried item and add a salad or a side vegetable.

Rethink your drink.

- Americans drink about 400 calories every day. Consider how often you drink sugary beverages such as sweet tea, sodas, sports drinks, energy drinks, fruit juices, and coffee beverages with sugar. A 20-ounce soda contains about 250 calories.
- Choose water, unsweetened tea with a splash of sweet tea, or infused water which are available at all the dining facilities on campus. Check out this video to learn how you can drink smarter! https://youtu.be/zNuWUyb6TGI

Make sure you know the operation hours. Some campus dining facilities close or open earlier than others. Thus, make sure you know the operating hours for different dining facilities so that you do not have to go hungry or have limited food options to choose from. The University of Mississippi dining facilities hours can be viewed here: https://olemiss.campusdish.com/

Need more ideas on how to improve your meals? Check out this video: https://youtu.be/ArSnyWaOAmQ

We realize that dining facilities may not always be ideal, so if you are a vegan or vegetarian, have food allergies or intolerances, do not be afraid to speak up. Dining staff and a dietitian are available to help and give you information on ingredients and options available to you. We want you to have the best experience at the University of Mississippi, and we are working hard to offer healthy options tailored to your needs. We are here to serve you!

Keeping it Healthy while Eating Out

When eating out, follow the same MyPlate principles previously discussed – one-half plate of vegetables and/or fruit, one-fourth grains, one-fourth protein, and dairy. In addition, make sure you limit fried items and sugary beverages. Fast-food restaurants are convenient and can easily become an unhealthy habit. Be sure to make smart choices if you eat out more than once a week. Plan ahead, and check out the nutrition information online before you arrive. Similarly to eating on campus, if you plan, it is less likely that you will splurge and make last minute unhealthy selections.

Here are some tips to help you make healthy choices when eating out:

- Look over the menu carefully. Some restaurants have sections for "Healthy" or "Light" choices.

- Look for words that may mean lower calorie or healthy cooking preparation: baked, braised, broiled, grilled, lightly sautéed, poached, roasted, and steamed.

- Also look for words that indicate more added fat: batter-fried, pan-fried, buttered, creamed, crispy, and breaded. Choose these food options less often.

- Order the small or child-sized portion if possible. Many restaurants serve more food than one person needs at one meal. If smaller portions are not available, or if it is more economical to get a main dish, split it with a friend or take half home.

- It is OK to make special requests; just keep them simple. For example, ask for a side salad or baked potato instead of French fries; no mayonnaise or bacon on your sandwich; salad dressing or other sauces on the side.

- As a beverage choice, choose water with lemon for added flavor, unsweetened tea, or other drinks without added sugar.

- Avoid having an appetizer and dessert in addition to your main course. If you want to get a dessert or appetizer, order one for the table to share.

- At fast-food restaurants, anything that says super, big, or double adds a lot of calories and fat to your meal. If you are selecting a value meal at a fast-food restaurant, make sure that you keep your sides small and you choose a non-sugary beverage. A large order of fries and sugary beverage alone can add around 800—950 calories to your meal. Choose wisely!

- Do not allow yourself to get overly hungry: Starving before going to dine out may compromise your ability to order healthier food options. For example, you might end up ordering higher calorie foods or eating larger portions than you normally would. Thus, if you are hungry before going to a restaurant, have a healthy snack such as piece of fruit.

- For healthy eating options: https://rebelwell.olemiss.edu/video-library-nutrition/

Snacks to Keep in your Room, Apartment, or Mini Fridge

Snacks can be an important part of a nutritious eating plan if the foods you choose are healthy and contribute to a well-balanced diet. You want to choose nutrient-dense foods, and keep away from processed foods with added sugar and fat. Also, if you are watching your calorie intake, remember that snack calories count in your total calories for the day, so make sure to pick healthy, low-calorie snacks, and skip junk food and unhealthy vending machine options.

So how can we make our snack choices healthy? Think about whole foods in their natural form. If you are looking for something crunchy, grab a handful of almonds instead of reaching for a bag of chips. Nuts are rich in heart-healthy fats and are a good source of protein and fiber. If you are craving something sweet and salty, make some homemade trail mix (seeds, dried fruit, nuts, and whole-grain cereals) and portion it out for the rest of the week. You can also include two food groups in your snacks. For example, an apple and string cheese, celery sticks with peanut butter, light yogurt with fresh berries, or carrots with hummus. These are all easy grab-and-go options that fit into a well-balanced diet. Below are simple snack ideas, you can also check out this video – https://youtu.be/srJXLmrmp7s

Snack ideas:

- **Fruits**, such as apples, bananas, pears, grapes, and peaches all are healthy snacks. You can select fresh, frozen, canned, and dried fruit. Just make sure you watch out for varieties with added sugar or syrup.

- **Vegetables**, such as baby carrots, celery, broccoli florets, grape tomatoes, and bell peppers are all great options. Pre-washed and pre-cut veggies are convenient, and you can pair them with a healthy dip, such as salsa, hummus, nut butters, or enjoy them by themselves. Broth-based vegetable soups are also a great option; make sure you select low-sodium versions.

- **Dairy**, such as low-fat yogurt, yogurt parfaits, low-fat string cheese, low-fat cottage cheese, low-fat milk.

- **Grains**, such as unsalted pretzels, brown rice cakes, oatmeal packets, whole grain crackers, whole-wheat bread, granola bars (make sure these have less than 10 grams of sugar, and more than 3 grams of fiber.)

- **Protein**, such as nuts (almonds, peanuts, etc.) and nut butters, roasted chickpeas, eggs, tuna pouches, canned chicken, pre-cooked chicken.

- **Water:** keep water handy! Invest in a water filter pitcher; it is a convenient and economical way to store water in your room or apartment.

Stay Hydrated

Hydration is important year-round, especially during the summer and fall when temperatures are high. Your body depends on water to survive, from the lubrication of joints, to cell development, to removing waste. We get water from the food and beverages that we eat and drink, such as fruits, vegetables, soups, juices, and milk. However, drinking water is the best source of fluid for the body. The

recommended daily fluid intake is about 91 ounces for females and 125 ounces for males. Generally, 20 percent of fluids come from food, therefore aim to have about 9 cups of fluids for women and 13 cups of fluids for men. It is important to listen to your body to keep adequately hydrated, i.e. your sense of thirst. Follow these tips to help you stay hydrated throughout the day:

1. Start your day by drinking a glass of water.

2. Keep a bottle of water with you during the day and refill it throughout the day. Take advantage of the various Hotty Toddy hydration stations located throughout campus. To get a complete list of all the locations where you can find a hydration station, visit the Office of Sustainability website at green. olemiss.edu/hydration-station

3. If you do not care for the taste of plain water, add lemon, lime, or berries to add flavor to your water.

4. Drink a glass of water with all of your meals.

5. Drink water before, during, and after exercise.

6. Keep track of hydration. You might even set a timer on your phone to remind yourself to drink water throughout the day.

7. Listen to your body and drink water when you are thirsty.

Also, do not let beverages with the word "water" fool you. Check the nutrition label and ingredients if you are buying flavored water. Tonic water contains calories, sugar, and more sodium compared to sparkling and seltzer water, which are calorie-free and contain small amounts of sodium. Let water be your go-to beverage because it is calorie-free, sugar-free, sodium-free, and low cost.

Drink Responsibly

Drinking has become a part of many social events in college, from parties to sporting events. Nutritionally, alcoholic beverages are one of the top contributors to caloric intake with minimal nutrition value. If you are of legal drinking age, drink in moderation if you decide to drink. Moderate alcohol intake is one drink per day for women and two drinks per day for men.

What counts as one drink?

Drink	Calories
12 ounces beer	150 calories
5 ounces table wine	100 calories
1.5 ounces 80% proof liquor	100 calories

When choosing to consume alcohol, alternate your alcoholic beverages with water to keep your calorie count down and stay hydrated. Also, never drink on an empty stomach. Be sure to eat food if you are planning to drink, as skipping meals is dangerous - especially when alcohol is involved.

It may be a good idea to prepare a healthy late-night snack (ex: carrots and hummus, peanut butter and apple slices) before going out with friends so that when you return home, you will have something to eat on hand. This way you will not be tempted to make unhealthy late-night food choices like ordering a whole pizza for yourself.

Outsmart Emotional Eating

College life is full of emotions, and many times, we turn to food to soothe our feelings. When feeling anxious, stressed, homesick, or tired, make sure you ask yourself if you are truly hungry before you reach for that extra snack. Pay attention to what you are eating when you are stressed. Having a regular meal schedule can prevent emotional eating. Also, be sure you get enough sleep as a lack of sleep can directly affect your weight, eating habits, and stress level. When you are studying for an exam or working late on a project, keep healthy snacks available if you need an energy boost. If you realize you are not hungry, have a list of three things you can do to prevent overeating, such as playing a short game on your phone, painting your nails, drinking a glass of water, taking a shower, or doing a few stretch exercises. To prevent emotional eating, you need to find an alternative to food to satisfy yourself emotionally. Recognizing that you turn to food to soothe your emotions is the first step, now you need to plan an alternative activity that will soothe those emotions.

Here is a list of activities that can help with emotional management:

- **If you are depressed, lonely, or homesick,** call a friend or someone who always makes you feel better, play with your dog or cat, or look into joining a club/organization on campus.

- **If you are anxious,** expend your nervous energy doing your favorite exercise routine, dancing to your favorite song, squeezing a stress ball, or taking a brisk walk.

- **If you are exhausted,** treat yourself with a hot cup of tea, warm shower, or nap.

- **If you are bored,** read a good book, watch a comedy show, explore the outdoors, or turn to an activity you enjoy (playing an instrument, shooting hoops, scrapbooking, etc.)

  *Adapted and excerpt from the HELPGUIDE.ORG – Emotional Eating – How to recognize and Stop Emotional Eating.

Still have nutrition questions?

This chapter includes only a few of many helpful tips for healthy eating in college. With all the nutrition information you read online or see on TV, it may seem like eating right is impossible. Claims that promote the new power food that will slim you down or easy solutions to your dietary needs may seem like good solutions; however, your best bet is a personalized visit with a registered dietitian. If you want to address your food intolerances, find healthy options on campus, eat for performance, or simply eat healthier; a registered dietitian can help you decipher all of the confusing information and provide you with nutrition advice that is catered to your goals. A registered dietitian is a food and nutrition expert who has gone through extensive nutrition training and education in addition to passing the examination requirements set forth by the Commission on Dietetic Registration. The Student Health Center offers individual nutrition appointments at no cost to enrolled students. To make an appointment, contact the Student Health Center.

ABOUT THE AUTHOR

Mariana A. Jurss, *Registered Dietitian*

Mariana A. Jurss joined Ole Miss in July 2014. Prior to moving to Oxford, Mariana worked for a pediatric weight management program at a Children's Hospital in California working to prevent and treat childhood obesity and related illnesses, such as diabetes, heart disease, and high blood pressure. She is a registered dietitian and holds a master's degree in public health from the University of California, Berkeley.

CHAPTER 27

VIOLENCE PREVENTION AND *Campus Safety*

By Shelli Poole

The first year of college is filled with excitement, change, and inevitably some degree of stress. It's a time when students are learning how to live on their own for the first time, how to do laundry, eat balanced meals (or even eat at all), plug in socially, and succeed academically. There is so much change at once that students are at the highest risk of sexual violence in their first semester of college. National statistics are that 1 in 5 women will be victim-survivors of sexual assault, 1 in 16 men will experience sexual violence, and we know our LGBTQ+ community and people of color are at even higher risk during their college career. When we are talking about violence in this chapter, we are referring to three specific areas: sexual assault, intimate partner violence, and stalking. The underlying thread in all types of sexual violence is power and control. It is one person exerting power and control over another person. The Violence Intervention and Prevention Services area, along with RASA (Rallying Against Sexual Assault), exists to raise awareness of sexual violence at the University of Mississippi, educate the campus on prevention, and provide an immediate, supportive response to any student who experiences gender-based violence. We want you to know you are not alone and there are resources in place to support you if anything happens.

Sexual Assault

Sexual assault is defined as any nonconsensual sexual contact that occurs and includes when someone is incapable of giving consent. Consent can be given either verbally or non-verbally, but it must be given, never assumed, and it can be withdrawn at any time.

According to the National Sexual Violence Resource Center (NSVRC):

- 20% - 25% of college women and 15% of college men are victims of forced sex during their time in college.

- A 2002 study revealed that 63.3% of men at one university who self-reported acts qualifying as rape or attempted rape admitted to committing repeat rapes.

- More than 90% of sexual assault victims on college campuses do not report the assault.

- 27% of college women have experienced some form of unwanted sexual contact.

- Nearly two thirds of college students experience sexual harassment.

The underlying theme of all gender-based violence is power and control. It is one person exerting power and control over another person through sexual violence. According to the Office for Victims of Crime (OVC), hate crimes occur more often towards people of color. Furthermore, 80% of the sexual assaults that are reported, are reported by white women. Most anti-sexual violence education is based on Feminist theory and programming focuses more on White middle-class women. PoC advocates are few and far between, so it's important for all advocates to be aware of resources, local based services, and the needs of all communities. Sexual violence also occurs at higher rates in the LGBTQ+ communities.

According to the NSVRC, acts of sexual assault may be the mechanism for carrying out hate violence against a particular group of individuals, often based on sexual orientation, gender identify, or other demographic factors, such as race. Experiences of violence vary even within marginalized communities; for example, transgender women of color experience a national crisis of deadly violence. In 2014, at least 12 transgender people of color were killed. In 2015, 24 hate violence-related homicides were committed or reported as such; 54 percent of the victims were transgender women of color.

To prevent sexual violence on a college campus, every individual needs to be educated. Understanding the impact on a societal level is important as it can impact groups of people, particularly marginalized groups more, when used as a tool of oppression. On an individual level it's essential to understand the communication needed to ensure the sexual activity is consensual, safe, and healthy.

Consent is the most important aspect of sexual activity. You must have consent for every single activity. Consent is not a one-time conversation and it is essential in any relationship – it doesn't pertain to just sexual activity. It sounds like it might be awkward to gain consent, and have an agreement before activity, but you can make it sound comfortable! Consent can be fun, and it doesn't have to "ruin the mood." It allows both people to express what they're comfortable with as well as what they want. You can say, "Does this feel good?"

- According to the One Love Foundation, this is what consent is not:
- When someone says "no"
- The absence of a "no"
- Saying yes while you are intoxicated or otherwise incapable of giving consent
- Not saying anything
- Repeatedly asking someone to say yes, or pressuring them to say yes until they do

The best way to gain consent is to ask and have the other person enthusiastically say, "Yes!" Let's say you are in the middle of a make out session and the person starts to pull away and their body language indicates they are uncomfortable. This is a good time to check in and ask how the other person is doing. It's a good idea to check in throughout the session to see how the other person is feeling and certainly before engaging in a new sexual act. Of course, consent can also be withdrawn at any time, so just because someone says yes to one act does not mean they want to engage in another act.

What makes someone incapable of giving consent? A person who is mentally or physically incapacitated can not give consent. If a person is under the influence of alcohol or drugs they are unable to give consent. Some indications that a person is under the influence of alcohol or drugs are slurred speech, stumbling, unable to walk or stand alone, vomiting, or being partially or totally unconscious.

Intimate Partner Violence

Intimate Partner Violence (IPV) is defined as a pattern of abusive or aggressive behavior in a close relationship, according to the Center for Disease Control. According to the NSVRC, most sexual assaults occur in the context of an intimate partner relationship, and more education is needed around IPV. Intimate partner sexual violence (IPSV) is then defined as any unwanted sexual contact or activity by an intimate partner forced on the other partner through fear, threats, violence, or other forms of control. Love is such an important part of life and we spend so little time learning about it. People in the age range of 18-24 people are at their highest risk of intimate partner violence, and the ideal approach for prevention is to recognize the red flags in the beginning of the relationship. However, this can be more challenging than it seems as potential abusers are often manipulative and convincing. As the relationship progresses it becomes more and more difficult to recognize the dynamics and end the relationship. Ideally, we want people to learn what a healthy and unhealthy relationship is, be empowered to prevent and end an abusive relationship, as well as learn to love even better! The One Love Foundation created 10 Signs of an Unhealthy Relationship and 10 Signs of a Healthy Relationship to help educate people on what to look for in relationships!

10 Signs of Healthy Relationship

Healthy relationships bring out the best in you and make you feel good about yourself. A healthy relationship does not mean a "perfect" relationship, and no one is healthy 100% of the time, but the signs below are behaviors you should strive for in all of your relationships.

Healthy relationships manifest themselves as healthy communication, but in order to have a healthy relationship, you need to love yourself first. Here are some characteristics and behaviors of a healthy relationship.

Comfortable Pace
The relationship moves at a speed that feels enjoyable for each person.

Trust
Confidence that your partner won't do anything to hurt you or ruin the relationship.

Honesty
You can be truthful and candid without fearing how the other person will respond.

Independence
You have space to be yourself outside of the relationship.

Respect
You value one another's beliefs and opinions, and love one another for who you are as a person.

Equality
The relationship feels balanced and everyone puts the same effort into the success of the relationship.

Kindness
You are caring and empathetic to one another, and provide comfort and support.

Taking Responsibility
Owning your own actions and words.

Healthy Conflict
Openly and respectfully discussing issues and confronting disagreements non-judgmentally.

Fun
You enjoy spending time together and bring out the best in each other.

Learn more at joinonelove.org

10 Signs of Unhealthy Relationship

While everyone does unhealthy things sometimes, we can all learn to love better by recognizing unhealthy signs and shifting to healthy behaviors. If you are seeing unhealthy signs in your relationship, it's important to not ignore them and understand they can escalate to abuse. If you think you are in a dangerous situation, trust your gut and get help.

Intensity
When someone expresses very extreme feelings and over-the top behavior that feels overwhelming.

Possessiveness
When someone is jealous to a point where they try to control who you spend time with and what you do.

Manipulation
When someone tries to control your decisions, actions or emotions.

Isolation
When someone keeps you away from friends, family, or other people.

Sabotage
When someone purposely ruins your reputation, achievements, or success.

Belittling
When someone does and says things to make you feel bad about yourself.

Guilting
When someone makes you feel responsible for their actions or makes you feel like it's your job to keep them happy.

Volatility
When someone has a really strong, unpredictable reaction that makes you feel scared, confused or intimidated.

Deflecting Responsibility
When someone repeatedly makes excuses for their unhealthy behavior.

Betrayal
When someone is disloyal or acts in an intentionally dishonest way.

Learn more at joinonelove.org

It's helpful to review these before you're in a relationship to recognize warning signs, as well as during a relationship, to evaluate the relationship. Relationships exist on a continuum from healthy, to unhealthy, to abusive. If it's unhealthy at times, it's a good time to reach out and talk to someone. If you can tell your friend is in an unhealthy or abusive relationship, it's okay to reach out to talk to someone about that too. Friends should avoid demonizing the other person but look for opportunities to check in and see how their friend is feeling about the relationship. The reason the age range of people from 18-24 are at highest risk of IPV is because often it's a person's first serious relationship. During college, students are living on their own for the first time and aren't with family and friends who have known them their entire lives and would recognize behavior changes. Almost all relationships start off in the honeymoon phase when there is great chemistry, connection, and conversation. The person often feels seen and cared about for the first time in a romantic relationship. Quickly after this phase there is the period of isolation when the abusive person starts isolating the other person from their friends, family, and even their co-workers and academic connections.

According to the CDC, protective factors for sexual violence are having solid friendships and a healthy support system. On a community level, protective factors include having social connectedness within neighborhoods as well as robust resources and cross agency collaboration. The NSVRC suggests the socio-ecological prevention model which means the individual, community, and society need to be educated on sexual violence, it's impact on survivors, and how to connect survivors to resources if there is an incident.

Stalking

Stalking, according to the Stalking Resource Center, is any course of conduct directed at a person that would create fear in a reasonable person. Oftentimes, stalking is done through technology and called cyber-stalking. Even if stalking isn't done in person it can be scary, and it's okay to be scared. Some examples of stalking include someone showing up uninvited at a person's home, school, or place of employment. The person stalking can give the victim-survivor unwanted gifts, letters, phone calls, and texts. People stalking often look up information using public records, social media, and even family, friends and neighbors to learn unwanted information about the victim-survivor. Each of these behaviors may not seem dangerous but it is important to reach out for support before they escalate. Stalking is a serious crime and can quickly escalate to sexual assault and violent behavior. If someone has the slightest concern, it's okay to reach out and ask for support and consider options.

Bystander Intervention

Bystander Intervention is considered the number one, evidence based, way to prevent sexual violence on college campuses. The idea is that everyone is responsible for creating a safe environment, and we all have a responsibility for creating a campus free of harm and violence. Intervening can be challenging because of human nature most people hope that someone else will intervene. It's easy to dismiss concerning behavior and think we are over reacting, but we're asking each of you to stand up and stop potentially problematic or violent behavior.

There are three recommended ways to intervene if you see a potentially concerning situation developing.

Direct: You can go up to your friend and ask if they are "okay?" It's okay to approach someone and just ask how they are doing. If you are concerned about the potential perpetrator it's also a direct intervention to approach the person and call it out. You can say, "Hey, I don't think this is a good idea." Sometimes if you're concerned about how much your friends have been drinking or drugs they have consumed, you can say, "Hey, you've consumed quite a bit and they have too. I don't think this is a good idea."

Distraction: If you aren't comfortable approaching the person then distraction is a favorite method of intervention. You can approach your friend and ask them if they need to go to the bathroom or go get food. Maybe you could say another friend just arrived and you think you should both go say "hi." Distraction can occur in a myriad of ways and is a simple way to intervene if you're concerned about a friend.

Delegate: If you aren't comfortable approaching either person it's always okay to delegate to someone else to intervene. You can ask a friend to check in, and if you don't know the person you could find their friends and ask them to check in on the situation. If you don't feel safe then you can call a CA or UPD.

The important part is to know ahead of time that you will witness situations that you know may lead to a concerning or even violent incident and it's everyone's responsibility to attempt to intervene and keep each other safe. Don't stand by – step up! Also, remember if something does happen you can connect your friend to resources to help them heal. Remember to never tell them what you think they should do, but support them by listening, and help them connect to resources.

Impact of Campus Sexual Violence

One form of prevention is for members of the campus community to understand the impact of sexual violence. Often victim-survivors of sexual violence experience long-term impacts. All too often, survivors blame themselves as a way to gain back control. They say they shouldn't have been drinking or should not have gone with the other person. A consequence of any of these actions should never be sexual violence. It is never the survivor's fault to be a victim-survivor of sexual violence. Survivors experience an increased risk for post-traumatic stress disorder, substance abuse, and depression, according the NSVRC. Furthermore, research suggests that campuses need to move beyond a one program, annual awareness event, to creating a campus culture that is safe for all students, faculty and staff. The NSVRC suggests each student, faculty member and staff member should be educated and trained on what sexual violence is, how many people are affected by sexual violence, the impact, as well as resources to support someone following an incident. A combination of awareness activities, risk-reduction strategies to recognize warning signs, a trauma-informed response to a survivor, and then prevention that goes beyond raising awareness to engage the campus community in creating long-term solutions to social issues are all needed to address sexual violence on college campuses. It is a community wide effort to be knowledgeable, informed, and know how to address sexual violence. Below is a copy of the different reporting options for someone who may have experienced sexual assault, intimate partner violence, or stalking. There are confidential resources, as well as information on how to receive medical care, and reporting to Title IX and law enforcement. We want you to know you're not alone and it's okay to reach out.

I May Have Experienced Sexual Assault, Intimate Partner Violence, or Stalking and...

I NEED MEDICAL ATTENTION:	I WANT A CONFIDENTIAL CONVERSATION:	I WANT TO MAKE A REPORT:
For immediate 24-hour help call:	Shelli Poole, Advocate Violence Intervention and Prevention Services sapoole@olemiss.edu 662-915-1059	On Campus:
Off Campus -911 On Campus - 4911		Title IX Office 662-915-7045 hbussery@olemiss.edu
For Medical Care:	Counseling Center 320 Lester Hall 662-915-3784	University of Mississippi Police 662-915-7234
Student Health Center M-F, 8-5 662-915-7274	Student Health Center M-F, 8-5 662-915-7274	Off Campus: 911 Oxford Police Department 662-234-2400
Baptist Memorial Hospital 24-hour care 662-636-1000	*Unlike most UM faculty and staff, these offices are NOT required to report incidents of sexual harassment or assault to the Title IX Coordinator*	Lafayette County Sheriff 662-234-6421

Reporting a sexual assault does not mean you have to pursue an investigation. There are people to help. Visit umsafe.olemiss.edu to review options and resources.

Violence Intervention and Prevention Services exists to support students who may have experienced sexual assault, intimate partner violence, or stalking. There is a confidential advocate to listen, be supportive, and explore next steps in a safe, non-judgmental environment. Some services provided in VIPS are academic accommodations (help with classes), safety planning and risk assessment, safe housing, accompaniment to the Student Health Center or the hospital, no-contact directives with people of concern, scholarship retention, financial aid advocacy, as well as support through conduct and legal systems as needed. The advocate also provides referrals for counseling on and off campus and ongoing support if situations arise throughout the student's time at the University of Mississippi. The VIPS confidential advocate hopes to support students reach their personal and academic goals from a trauma-informed, caring perspective.

CAMPUS SAFETY ACTIVE SHOOTER

University of Mississippi Police and Campus Safety

The rate of violent crimes on college campuses, especially campus shootings, is increasing in America. Recently, national attention has focused on incidents of shootings/mass murders on college and university campuses. Higher education institutions across the country have struggled with violent and disruptive behavior for years, and it seems difficult to find a solution to this ever-growing threat that hinders academic life (Baker & Boland, 2011).

With heightened national attention on college campuses as a result of an increase in shootings, the image of colleges and universities as safe and secure environments has been impacted. The need for college campus to prioritize their commitment to campus safety and security in light of recent campus shooting is increasingly clear. Recent unfortunate shooting tragedies throughout the United States serve as a reminder of this need. Discussing these incidents, as well as preparing students in advance of potential incidence is critical.

The University of Mississippi is committed to the health and safety of all constituents, in the case of an active shooter, the University Police Department (UPD) recommends the Avoid, Deny, and Defend strategy for managing an active shooter.

Avoid
- Plan and practice egress routes.
- Routinely inspect the routes for obstacles.
- Designate a gathering place away from the building.

About Fleeing:
If it is possible to flee the area safely and avoid danger, do so. If it is safe to do so, consider:
- Escaping out of the other side of the building.
- Moving to a central and secure area within the building.

In case you must flee, do not go to the normal gathering site for your building. Instead, get far away from the shooting scene and contact the Police Department to advise them of your location. Do not attempt to flee if the shooter is between you and your escape. If you are unsure, do not attempt to flee.

Deny
- Designate multiple safe rooms in your building.
- Routinely inspect locks, lights, flashlights, and fire extinguishers.
- Make sure all windows have blinds or are covered.

About Hiding in Place:

- Go dark. Turn off all the lights. Use the flashlight app on your smart phone. Lock all windows and doors and secure yourself in your safe room.
- If the door does not lock, barricade the room with tables, chairs, etc.
- Windows and doors must lock from the inside and the shooter must not be able to see into the room.
- Get everyone down on the floor or under a desk and out of the line of fire and remain silent.
- Make sure there is a fire extinguisher readily available and working.
- You will need telephone or cell phone communication with UPD in your safe room. However, ringers must be silenced or placed on vibrate.

Defend

- Consider taking a self-defense course.
- Discuss the plan with others.
- Assign duties to everyone.

If the shooter enters your room:

- No one procedure can be recommended in this situation.
- Attempting to negotiate with the individual may be very dangerous.
- Taking the shooter by force should only be tried as a last resort. But, again, DO SOMETHING!

About notifying others:

- Attempt to get the word out to others in your building or nearby if possible.
- From an on-campus phone, dial 4-9-1-1 or from a non-campus phone, dial 662-915-4911 to notify police and give your location.
- DO NOT pull the fire alarm.

"All-Clear?"

Wait for the "all-clear" instruction given by a known voice. If the staff or students do not recognize the voice that is giving the instruction, they should not change their status.

- Unknown or unfamiliar voices may be giving false assurances.
- Remember, there may be more than one active shooter.

After a valid "All-Clear":

- Follow the direction of Police Officers as you leave the building.
- Police may direct you to one collection point.
- When encountering Police Officers, keep your hands on your head or open in front of you. Officers are trained to be aware of all possible dangers and

need to see quickly that you are not a threat.

- Be careful not to make any changes to the scene of the incident since law enforcement authorities need to investigate the area better.

REFERENCES

Baker, K., & Boland, K. (2011). Assessing safety: A campus wide initiative. College Student Journal, 45(4), 683-699

ABOUT THE AUTHORS

Shellie Poole, *Assistant Director Violence Intervention/Prevention*

Shelli Poole has served as an advocate for survivors of sexual assault and intimate partner violence for over ten years. Prior to moving to Oxford in 2011, Shelli worked for the Boulder County Rape Crisis team and the Rape Assistance and Awareness Program providing education and prevention in schools and law enforcement agencies, advocating for survivors, and co-facilitating psychotherapy groups. Shelli had completed coursework for her Psy.D. from the University of Denver.

University of Mississippi Police and Campus Safety, upd@olemiss.edu

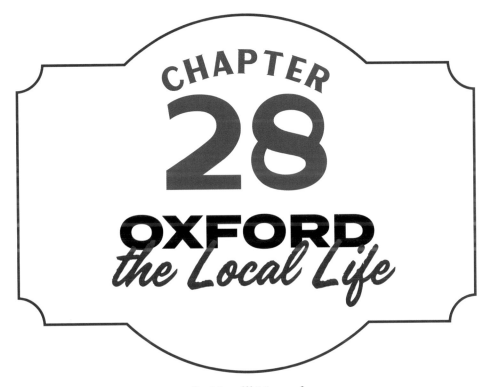

CHAPTER
28

OXFORD
the Local Life

By Merrill Magruder

"To understand the world, you must first understand a place like Mississippi."
–William Faulkner

T he Velvet Ditch, The Little Easy, and the Cultural Mecca of the South are all monikers for your new home, Oxford. Whether you are taking a stroll through the Square, enjoying a concert at the Lyric, or find yourself drawn to the waters of Sardis Lake – you will soon find your niche. This chapter is a resource to take advantage of all that Oxford and the Hill Country of North Mississippi have to offer, in addition to living like a local.

"Locals" as you will hear around town, are the residents of Oxford who are here when students go   home for holidays and breaks. They are permanent residents. The best way to embody being a local is to narrow down to a few traits:

- The ability to drive on the Square and to navigate roundabouts
- Driving responsibly (i.e., no drinking, texting, snapchatting)
- Treating your neighbors with respect
- Being a good steward of Oxford's resources
- Trying something new or out of your comfort zone.

Driving in Oxford

There is an unspoken rule to assume the speed limit is 35 mph everywhere in the city of Oxford (barring the neighboring highways). If in doubt, just lower your speed.

One thing Oxford city planners favor are roundabouts. These are designed to make intersections safer and more efficient for drivers, pedestrians, and cyclists. **There are a few key things to remember about driving roundabouts:**

- Do not stop in the roundabout
- Yield to drivers in the roundabout
- Stay in your lane; do not change lanes
- Avoid driving next to oversize vehicles

Located in the heart of Oxford is the historic Oxford Square, locally known as "The Square." With a variety of restaurants, museums, art galleries, clothing boutiques, specialty shops, and more, The Square offers students, tourists, and locals a place to congregate, people-watch, shop, and experience Oxford.

Whether it is good food, art, live local music, or specialty items – you will have an experience you will not forget.

Navigating the Square can be challenging.

- One of the key tricks in knowing when to yield is following this simple order of people and vehicles:

- Pedestrians always have the right-of-way (first)

- Vehicles going around the center lane (circling the large, white courthouse) are next in line for the right of way (inside, second)

- Drivers circling the largest section of the square lining the shops yield to all other vehicles (outside, last).

Be a Good Neighbor and Informed Citizen

Living off campus in Oxford or the surrounding Lafayette County is an opportunity coveted by many and one that will suit your need for independence and privacy. It is also a choice that comes with increased responsibility to be a respectful member of the neighborhood and community in which you choose to live. Living in a new community is exciting, but it also can be daunting, especially when nobody tells you the rules. Accordingly, the information provided here will help you be an informed citizen and good neighbor of the Oxford-Lafayette County community.

Roommates

If you are renting with one or more roommates, you are each liable for all of the obligations in your lease, unless your lease specifically states otherwise. This means that if your roommate does not pay his or her share of the rent, then the property owner can look to you to collect it. You and your roommates should come to some understanding about how your apartment is to be used and who is responsible for certain expenses. You may even want to have a written agreement with your roommate so that if a dispute occurs, you can turn to the written proof to amicably resolve your disagreement.

Utilities

Unless your lease states that your property owner is responsible for utilities, you are responsible for opening and maintaining your own utility accounts. Please be aware that in some cases certain utilities such as cable and Internet services may be included in the rental price, particularly if you are renting in an apartment complex. Make sure that you consider this when comparing the overall price among different living options. In addition, in most cases, you will be required to make an initial deposit to have your utilities connected, unless they are included in your rental package. The person in whose name a utility account is opened is the person responsible to the utility company for payment of the bill. If you have roommates, it might be good for each of you to be responsible for a particular utility account. For instance, one of you could be responsible for the electric bill, one for the cable bill, etc. This way, each roommate can limit to that utility the risk that he or she will have to take in possibly paying for a roommate's share of the bill.

If you have any questions about your utilities, your landlord can tell you which entities provide your electricity, water, natural gas, garbage pickup, cable and internet service, and whether or not you live in the city limits of Oxford or in the county.

Meet your neighbors and learn their names as soon as possible. Many Ole Miss students have found good friends in their neighbors, even though they are often at different stages in life. The connections you make with your neighbors can provide friendships, safety, security, and sometimes even job leads.

Maintain your yard if you are responsible for this in your lease. If your landlord is responsible, make sure that your yard is mowed regularly. Always pick up litter in your yard and on the nearby street.

Always respect your neighbor's property. Remind your friends that when they come to a party or to study at your house, the neighbor's property and parking area are off limits. Moreover, if someone happens to accidentally block your neighbor's driveway, you will be happy that you introduced yourself earlier, so the first call likely will be to you rather than the police.

Keep the noise down. Be courteous and considerate of your neighbors around you. If you can hear the music coming from inside your house while standing outside your house, it is probably too loud. The city of Oxford has specific ordinances dealing with the regulation of excessive noise in the city.

Park cars and motorcycles in the driveway or next to the curb in the street, not in the yard. Do not park in restricted zones, or your vehicle will be towed. It is against the law in the city of Oxford to use a premise for the open storage of abandoned or junked vehicles or appliances.

If you own a pet (or pets), follow all local ordinances regarding its care and supervision, especially regarding leash laws. Oxford's ordinance states that no dog shall be allowed to run at large, and it shall be unlawful for any person who shall own, keep, or harbor any dog to allow or permit such dog to run or be at large at any time within the city. It also is unlawful to allow your pet to be on someone else's property without that person's permission; and it shall be the duty of each dog owner or person having custody, care, or control of a dog to promptly remove any feces deposited by the dog on someone else's property or any sidewalk, gutter, street, or other public walkway within the city limits.

Skip the Risk: Be a Responsible Host: Tips for Hosting a Successful Party in your Neighborhood

So, you've moved into your new home; the big football weekend has rolled around, and it's time to host a party. Here are a few things to keep in mind so that your party is safe and successful and does not   disturb your neighbors:

Talk with your neighbors before you have a party. Be sure to tell them the time and date of the party, and give them your telephone number. Encourage them to call you should the party disturb them. Again, it is better to be given a chance to correct the problem before anything escalates.

Invite a reasonable number of people you know and avoid "open" party invitations. Otherwise, you may quickly lose control of the party.

Be aware of all local ordinances involving noise and alcohol consumption. Keep the noise down and remember that it is unlawful for anyone under the age of 21 to consume alcohol in the city of Oxford, and you can be charged criminally if you serve alcohol to anyone under that age.

Students who live outside the city limits in Lafayette County should remember that Lafayette County is "dry" for beer and light wine (less than 5 percent alcohol by weight). Thus, distribution, possession and consumption of beer and light wine are illegal in the county. Liquor is legal in the county for anyone over the age of 21, but it cannot be purchased outside any incorporated area.

Also, remember, it is unlawful for any person to have in his or her possession alcoholic beverages in open containers while on public streets or sidewalks in Oxford.

Have one or more sober hosts at your party. Do not allow your guests to stay on overcrowded decks or porches. Try to serve plenty of food, water, and nonalcoholic drinks at your party.

Be vigilant about encouraging your guests to not drink and drive. Intoxicated guests should be allowed to spend the night, or you can assist them in getting a ride home through a taxi or car service (Uber, Lyft)

Know what to do when one of your guests has had too much to drink. The following situations indicate that a person needs immediate medical assistance:

Mental confusion, stupor, coma, or inability to be roused

Vomiting and Seizures

Slow breathing (fewer than eight breaths per minute) Irregular breathing (10 seconds or more between breaths)

Hypothermia (low body temperature), bluish skin color, paleness

Respect your neighborhood, and clean up your yard as soon as possible after your party, if not that night, then first thing the next morning. Remember, as the host of the party, you can be held responsible for the behavior of your guests, even after they leave your house. If you are permitting underage guests to drink alcohol at your party, you can be held responsible for their actions, injury, or death. The less disruptive your parties are to your neighbors, the easier it will be for you to continue to entertain in your home.

BE SAFE AT HOME:

Here are some suggestions for your personal safety when living off campus: Make sure your apartment or house has new or rekeyed locks. Doors should have dead-bolt locks and one-way security peepholes; windows should have working locks and appropriate coverings (shades, blinds, curtains) to prevent someone from looking into the apartment or house.

Always know who is on the other side of your door before opening it. Keep shrubs and trees trimmed around your house. Also, the outside of your apartment or house should be well-lit at night. Never walk by yourself at night; always walk with others. Lastly try to stay in well-lit places and avoid dark alleys.

When leaving for breaks or weekends, follow these specific tips:

1. Lock all doors and windows; leave your shades and blinds in their usual positions. Take expensive items with you: jewelry, laptops, game systems, etc.

2. Unplug all extension cords.

3. Try to have a friend or neighbor staying in your area during breaks check on your apartment or house from time to time. Make sure he or she has a phone number to contact you.

4. In the colder months, turn down your heat, but to prevent pipes from freezing and bursting, do not turn it completely off.

5. Leave a few lights on inside.

Here are some handy contact numbers for living off campus in Oxford: **Electric** (in the city limits):

Oxford Utilities 662-232-2373 *Please Note: In the City of Oxford, your water, garbage pickup, and sewer utility service all are provided by the Electric Department.*

Electric (outside city limits):

Northeast MS Electric Power Association 662-234-6331 or 1-877-234-6331

Natural Gas Service (city and county):

Centerpoint Energy 800-371-5417

Water and Sewer Services in the county generally are provided by community water associations and are determined by the community in which you live, i.e., Abbeville, Taylor, Yocona, Tula, etc.

Garbage Pickup (outside city limits)

Lafayette County Solid Waste Department 662-236-2535

GETTING AROUND IN OXFORD

Bus System: Oxford University Transit (OUT) is your hassle-free way of getting around Oxford. With constant changes, increasing number of buses and stops coverage, improved bus quality such as free Wi- Fi onboard, OUT strives to better serve the students, residents and visitors of Oxford. The newly designed OUT website allows riders to track their bus, look up fares, routes maps, and schedules and special routes such as Safe Ride and weekend Purple Line. OUT is currently implementing a real-time status system so riders can be up to date with their bus route status. OUT is also collaborating with Google Transit to bring all the routes on Google Maps. With over 15 buses, OUT can transport you throughout Oxford and Lafayette County.

For Pedestrians and Cyclists: The Oxford Pathways Commission seeks to maintain the friendly, small- town feel of Oxford in the face of rapid growth and development. The commission works to keep the town connected by accessible walking and biking paths. It also tries to keep Oxford's citizens and visitors healthy and happy by encouraging them to enjoy all that the community has to offer while traveling under their own power. Visit loupathways.org for information on bike and pedestrian routes.

GET TO KNOW OXFORD

The city of Oxford has been touted as the "Cultural Mecca of the South," thanks in large part to its abundance of musicians, artists, writers, and fine dining establishments. Whether you enjoy shopping, recreation, or arts and entertainment, there is limitless opportunity to engage with your surroundings. Oxford has been named one of the top six college towns in the nation by *USA Today* and has also been included in *The 100 Best Small Towns in America.* Oxford has at one time been home to Nobel Prize- winning author William Faulkner and other authors such as Larry Brown, John Grisham, Barry Hannah, and Willie Morris.

Important Phone Numbers

Any Emergency: 911

Police: 662-232-2400

Sheriff: 662-234-6421

Fire: 662-232-2411

Hospital: 662-232-8100

Health Department: 662-234-5231

Mayor's Office: 662-232-2340

City Clerk: 662-232-1310

Crimestoppers: 662-234-8477

Poison Control: 601-354-7660

Arts and Entertainment

Gertrude C. Ford Center for the Performing Arts: Home to the first Presidential Debate in 2008, the Ford Center for the Performing Arts offers an assortment of Broadway shows, concerts, ballets, and more. Student discounts are available for most performances.

The Lyric Theatre: Situated just off the Square, The Lyric originally opened in 1913 as a silent movie theatre and was renovated to provide premier live music and event space in Oxford and the Southeast. Past musical acts have included the Flaming Lips, the North Mississippi Allstars, Snoop Dogg, and Willie Nelson, among others.

Thacker Mountain Radio: Thacker Mountain Radio is a live radio show featuring weekly author readings and a wide array of musical performances from the Square. The free show is taped and broadcast every Thursday at 6 p.m. during the fall and spring and rebroadcast every Saturday night on Mississippi Public Radio.

The Power House: The community arts center opened in 2006 and features a 140-seat performing arts room, exhibit and classroom space, and Yoknapatawpha Arts Council office. The Power House features eight rotating art exhibits throughout the year that are free to the public and feature Mississippi artists and artists inspired by the South.

ATTRACTIONS

Burns-Belfry Museum and Multicultural Center: The old Burns United Methodist Church was built in 1910 and holds the distinction of being both a state and local landmark because of its many years of service to the African American community. It offers a museum exhibit on African American history from slavery through the Civil Rights era.

L.Q.C. Lamar House Museum: The one-time home of former U.S. Senator and Supreme Court Justice L.Q.C. Lamar has been declared a National Historic Landmark. It houses professionally designed exhibits that tell the story of this Civil War-era politician.

Rowan Oak: Built in 1848, Rowan Oak became William Faulkner's home in 1930 and remained so until his death in 1962. Faulkner wrote masterpieces such as *I Lay Dying, Absalom, Absalom!, Light in August,* and *A Fable* in the home, which is owned by the University and maintained for memorial and educational purposes.

St. Peter's Cemetery: The old Oxford Cemetery is nestled in the rolling hills of a quiet neighborhood just northeast of the Square. It is the final resting place of both William Faulkner and L.Q.C. Lamar. Many students, local residents, and visitors often make the pilgrimage to Faulkner's grave to pay their respects.

Square Books, Off Square Book, Square Books Junior, and Rare Square Books: Square Books, established in 1979, is an award-winning independent bookstore in a two-story building with a café and balcony on the second floor. It is known for its strong selection of literary fiction, books on the American South and by Southern writers. Off Square Books, located just a few doors down, offers books on cooking, gardening, travel, and other lifestyle categories as well as a very large inventory of used books and remainders, which take up half the space of this store. Square Books Junior is the perfect place for kids at heart with children's books and young adult series, and a plethora of children's gifts. Rare Square Books opened in 2019 feature collectible, vintage, first-edition books.

Sardis Lake: Sardis Lake is a 98,520-acre reservoir on the Little Tallahatchie River in Lafayette, Panola, and Marshall counties. Sardis Lake is impounded by Sardis Dam, located twenty miles west of Oxford.

The Sardis Lake Marina services the lake with access to fuel docks, 140 wet slips (both covered and uncovered), a restaurant, and a ship store. They offer rental boats as well as rental skis, tubes, and knee/wake boards.

EVENTS

Double Decker Arts Festival: The annual festival held in April is a celebration of food, music, and the arts. Vendors and patrons from across the South and the entire nation descend on the historic Oxford Square for two days of beautiful weather and a bustling atmosphere.

Faulkner Conference: The annual conference gathers writers, teachers, students, and other lovers of Faulkner's work for five days of lectures and discussions exploring William Faulkner's writing.

Oxford Blues Festival: The annual event is held in July and attracts local and regional blues musicians to perform. Blues enthusiasts from all over the world descend on Oxford for the experience.

Oxford Conference for the Book: Each year in March the Conference brings together fiction and nonfiction writers, journalists, artists, poets, publishers, teachers, students, and literacy advocates for three days of conversation.

Oxford Film Festival: Created in 2003, the annual four-day festival continues to attract quality films and highlight the talents of young filmmakers from all over the world and from right here in North Mississippi.

RECREATION

Running, Walking, and Biking

South Campus Trails: This is a network of single-track trails on the Ole Miss campus. The trails can be accessed from the rail bed at the end of Chucky Mullins Drive and Front Street.

Clear Creek Trail: Located within a 30-minute drive from Oxford near Clear Creek Landing by Sardis Lake, it was selected as the best trail in Mississippi by *Mountain Bike Magazine.*

Camping and Fishing: John W. Kyle State Park and Wall Doxey State Park: Located within relative proximity to Oxford, both parks offer cabins, RV spots, tent spots, and boat launches. Wall Doxey also offers two disc golf courses.

North Mississippi is home to world-class crappie fishing. Popular destinations include Sardis Lake and the Holly Springs National Forest, which is home to more than 30 fishable lakes ranging in size from two acres to 260 acres.

Golf

Oxford boasts two local golf courses that are open to the public. The Ole Miss Golf Course is an 18- hole course that also features a driving range, chipping and putting greens, Pro Shop, and dressing rooms. The Links Oxford is a 9-hole regulation course available for a fee for nonresidents of the Link Apartments.

Where to Eat

Oxford's diverse culinary scene is home to a plethora of restaurant options, including fine dining, local favorites, chain restaurants, and even gas station cuisine. James Beard Award-winning chef John Currence resides in Oxford and owns several popular restaurants in town.

Branch out and try something new! Venture with a new friend to a restaurant that you normally wouldn't try. Try something that sounds intimidating. When else can you say you ate a brain taco or spicy bacon ice cream?

A list of the town's restaurants can be found online:

visitoxfordms.com/what-to-eat/

ABOUT THE AUTHORS

Merrill Magruder, *Coordinator of Special Projects in the Office of the Chancellor and Coordinator of Family Programs for the Office of the Vice Chancellor for Student Affairs*

Merrill has a shared appointment in the Office of the Chancellor and in the Division of Student Affairs. Her primary responsibilities include: planning and coordinating family programs and events through the Ole Miss Family Association.

TRANSFER STUDENT SECTION

CHAPTER
29
MAKING THE
Transition to UM

By Anne Klingen, Alice Myatt, Holly Reynolds,
Rebekah Reysen, and Nancy Wiggers

Every student has different transition experiences during his or her first semester at the University of Mississippi. One recent transfer student focused on the academic challenges by stating that "the most difficult situation was realizing that your study habits must change. I made good grades at community college, but here the classes are harder. Balancing the new things there are to do with the harder classes is difficult, but priorities have to take place." Another transfer student mentioned the social environment challenge: "The most difficult part of being a transfer student is finding a group of friends. Most people have formed their own cliques by junior year, and coming in at that point is sort of difficult." Still others find the move to Oxford brings financial challenges: "Budgeting my money was the most difficult aspect of my transition. I had saved up a great deal of money, knowing that it would cost more to attend a senior college, but I still had trouble budgeting my money. I have yet to have to pay anything for my academic expenses, thanks to scholarships and awards, but the cost of living and the fact that there is more to do in Oxford cost me a lot of money that I didn't have to spend while in community college."

The transition from community college to UM provides you with many opportunities to expand your educational experiences and grow as an individual. You will encounter some things that are familiar and others that might initially make you a bit uncomfortable.

Just like any other new experience, a bit of practice and a few strategies to manage these new experiences will help you adjust and make these experiences your own. This chapter focuses on some academic differences many transfer students see between the community college experience and university setting. We discuss differences in the university classroom, types of faculty, faculty expectations for examinations and writing assignments, communication strategies, and research opportunities for students.

THE CLASSROOM

One new experience you might encounter concerns the sizes of some of the classes in which you enroll. Some community college classes are larger than at UM, and some are smaller. Community college classes may average 25-30 students and take place in what you would consider traditional classrooms. At UM, however, you may have a class that is as small as 15 students who meet in a conference room or as many as 200 students, who meet in an auditorium. For example, College of Liberal Arts classes average 24 students with 84% of the classes having fewer than 35 students. Walking into an auditorium with many students can be intimidating, and trying to concentrate on a professor's lecture can be challenging at first with all of the distractions. The small classroom can be equally intimidating to some students with "no place to hide" and the heightened expectations for active participation. Consider some of the following suggestions to help you anticipate and manage these potentially new experiences.

Keep ID ready. Most of the medium to large classrooms at UM have ID scanners installed on the walls near the doors or on the lecterns. (Faculty are required to take regular attendance in only 100- and 200-level courses; it is optional in advanced courses.) Each professor must enable the scanner to take attendance for his or her class and set a window of time just before class and for the first few minutes of class that will allow the system to record attendance for that particular class. Be sure that you know the window of time set by each instructor. When you scan your ID within the proper window for your class, there is a green message stating the scan was successful and a beep. If you scan you ID outside of that window for your class there is a red message about the scan not being successful and a "negative" buzz sound. In large classes, especially, professors do not take the time to take roll. You must scan your ID to indicate that you are present for the class. If there is a problem with you ID or you do not have your ID, inform the instructor immediately. Do not delay as you have no other proof that you were present that day other than talking with the instructor before or after class. Check the website: attendance.olemiss.edu, which is dedicated to the attendance scanner system. On the right of the screen is a "For Students" button that takes you to your course schedule. If any of your classes use the scanners, there will be a link next to the course that shows the scan window the professor has set and the scan logs for your attendance. You also can access your attendance information through myOleMiss using the tab for "academics" and "absences." Get into the habit of checking that log to verify your attendance.

Location, location, location. Do your best to arrive to class early so that you can sit as close as possible to the front of the large classroom. This allows you to sit in the least distracting location and also allows the professor to see you and become familiar with your name and face. It is hard to miss someone who sits right in front of you several times a week. An added bonus is that sitting near the front of the classroom often equates to higher course grades.

Focus, focus! Faculty who teach in large lecture halls may rely on visual aids such as PowerPoint presentations and occasional group work. Stay engaged and present during class. Look over your notes before class, take good notes during class, review/clean-up your notes as soon as possible (also a proven method for information retention), and create study guides after class is over. Before you know it, you will have put in a few hours of studying each day, which means better time management skills as well as higher grades!

It is all about you. In large classes, you may feel challenged to get noticed, but you should not assume no one wants to notice you. Introduce yourself to your professors and fellow students; speak with them on a regular basis. If you have questions or concerns, do not wait and hope things will just work out. Take action! See your professor during his or her office hours, which are required to be included on all syllabi. If you have a time conflict during the posted office hours, contact your professor for an appointment. Get to know the students who sit next to you in class. More often than not, they want to meet new people, too. Your fellow students are great resources, as they may help you with missed notes and can serve as study partners to review for tests. Additionally, investigate whether there are study groups, such as Supplemental Instruction, associated with your course. This is another way of not only studying, but also getting to know your classmates.

Just say "CLICK." Blackboard (Bb) is associated with most courses on the UM campus. Many professors provide their materials and handouts only online. Your instructors may upload the syllabus and articles to read, create assignments, post announcements and quizzes, as well as record course grades on Blackboard. When you create your weekly and semester schedules for classes and assignments, be sure to include time to check **Bb** every day.

Some professors like to ensure students are engaged in the class by creating activities and quizzes with software that allows students to respond through clickers or even their smart phones. If you are enrolled in such a course, be sure to get the device that is necessary and practice with it before you go to class. In many instances, this is how professors grade participation, and it is always good to earn as many points as possible.

You also may have a choice of online courses. For most online classes, the majority of course content is available through the web, but there might be a required live element. Many online courses require proctored tests. A few even have a required online meeting in a virtual classroom or in a live classroom setting. Online learning is flexible and convenient, but it also more challenging. Below are several strategies for success in online classes.

Persistence. Students who are successful in online courses are those willing to work through technical problems. They seek help and assistance when needed, keep a daily course work schedule, and continue through challenges. To help with persistence and avoid technical problems, confirm technical requirements and test your computer to make sure it works with all the online tools, and that you know how to navigate the technology.

Time management and preparation. Avoid procrastination by developing a plan of action for assignment completion and having a daily "to do" list. Read your course syllabus to create your plan of action and "to do" list. Schedule time for yourself to log in to your course two or three times a week, schedule study times and time for assignments/discussions.

Communicate and connect. Use communication tools built into Blackboard to communicate with your instructor. In the course syllabus, the instructor also provides other ways to contact him or her. In traditional classes, instructors have visual cues and body language to know when a student is struggling. The online environment does not allow for these cues, so reach out. If you do not reach out, your instructor cannot know you need help. The same goes for your fellow classmates. Get to know classmates and create connections with them. The social tools and applications available today make building a learning community relatively easy.

Motivation and independence. To be successful in an online course, a student must be independent, self-motivated, disciplined, responsible, and mature.

Appropriate study environment. No matter the format of the course, whether it is online, hybrid, flipped, or traditional, every student needs a suitable study environment. Create your perfect study environment by locating a quiet space, avoiding games (consider uninstalling games on your computer), turning your phone off, and avoiding surfing the net or social media.

Be active, be present. Time management plans of action and "to do" lists help you be active and present in an online course. Check regularly for discussion posts, course announcements, course materials, and other important information. While checking for updates in your online course, get involved in a discussion and respond to your classmates' postings. This enhances your learning experience and makes you a more active member of that online community.

FACULTY

At UM you will encounter different types of instructors and faculty members. They are generally divided into two groups – instructional faculty and tenure track faculty. No matter what their title or rank, faculty and instructors at UM are open to meet with students. The general expectation is for students to utilize posted office hours. We sometimes hear that one difference between community college instructors and faculty at research-intensive universities is the greater distance between  students and faculty at the universities. It is true that the responsibilities of the faculty, particularly the tenure track faculty, are more varied. That is the reason for posted office hours. While personalities differ among individuals, making some more naturally approachable to students, faculty members are hired because they want to do research AND teach students. Take advantage of those office hours or make an appointment (and keep it) if you have a time conflict with the posted office hours.

Whether you are communicating with faculty and instructor in a face-to-face setting, phone, or electronic format, be mindful of the tone of your communications. Some students wait until they are feeling frustrated about a problem before reaching out for help, and the intensity of their negative feelings can create an unpleasant exchange. Messages with poor grammar and spelling also make a bad impression upon those you may be asking for assistance. Social media and texting have created a casual style of electronic messaging. Do not communicate with faculty members in the same way that you would with your friends. Faculty are in a position of authority and generally care very much that you are developing strong written communication skills. (Earlier in this text email etiquette was discussed.)

EXAMINATIONS

Some transfer students experience shock as a result of their first examinations at the university. Typically, they are moving directly into upper-level courses where faculty members have high expectations about the amount of work necessary before each class period, the amount and type of student writing assignments and projects, and the type of exam questions. These expectations may be different from what was experienced at community college. Students are sometimes shocked to see problems to solve on the exam that they have "never seen before."

A well-design exam has a variety of types of questions with emphasis on those requiring critical thinking skills. You need to be ready to tackle the questions with emphasis on those requiring critical thinking skills. You need to be ready to tackle the questions towards the top of the pyramid. How do you get prepared? The Academic Support Programs in the Center for Student Success and First Year Experience provide resources on topics such as time management, note making, mapping strategy, and test taking. Beyond that, you should meet with your faculty member and ask about his or her expectations on assignments and exams. Create and share with the faculty member your self-test questions (and answers), which are invaluable study tools. He or she can tell you if you are on the right track in preparing for the kinds of questions on the exam.

NAVIGATING ADVANCED WRITING

Many transfer students recognize the more writing-intensive nature of many advanced courses at UM. You will need to make a quick adjustment to faculty writing expectations. The Writing Center can help at all stages of the writing process. Depending on how writing was taught at your prior college, you may encounter these differences in your writing assignments at the University of Mississippi:

Papers are longer. Many transfer students say that they are unaccustomed to writing papers of length. Some have rarely written more than two- or four-page papers before coming to UM, where some courses may require writing projects of 10 to 15 pages (or longer).

Critical thinking is required. Most upper-level courses ask students to assess or judge the quality of one source's evidence in relation to that of another source.

Professors have high standards for conventions and mechanics. Faculty expect students to proof their papers to check for errors, whether typographical, syntactical, or grammatical, before turning in work for a grade. They also expect students to understand and use the documentation and citation style associated with their majors.

Students have the responsibility to turn in their work on time. Faculty provide detailed syllabi, class meeting schedules, detailed assignments, and rubrics to accompany such assignments, and test dates well in advance of the actual exam or due dates. They expect students to read and carefully follow such information – doing so is a path to success. (Do not rely on faculty to remind you of project due dates or exams. That is your job.)

RESEARCH OPPORTUNITIES

Another difference between the community college setting and a research-intensive university is the range of opportunities for students to engage in research/creative activities, both inside and outside of the classroom. This is an important way to maximize your educational experience and to make the most of the opportunities available in your degree program. Our recommendation is to reach beyond the "traditional" classroom or lab or studio as soon as possible. Find what opportunities exist within your home department, the Gertrude C. Ford Student Union (student organizations), Center for Inclusion and Cross-Cultural Engagement, Career Center, or make your own opportunities off campus.

Investigate interests. Most departments list faculty and their research interests/current projects on the department website. Find out what is going on in the research world within the department.

Find fit. Ask yourself which faculty member is doing work in the area that most interests you and matches your career goals. If your interest lies in working with children in a clinical setting, working with rats in a neuroscience lab is a rather poor fit. However, some research experience is better than none. And the truth is, you may not actually know what you wish to do long term, and that is okay, too.

Inquire with inquisitiveness. Approach a faculty member with your enthusiastic interest in joining his or her project or lab. Ask about openings, prerequisites, and expectations. He or she also will be looking at fit and evidence of motivation, reliability, integrity, curiosity, intellect, drive, and the like.

Be brilliant. Note that the two main responsibilities of a professor are to generate new knowledge and to share their knowledge, which aligns with the research and teaching missions of a research university.

CONCLUSION

The bottom line: do not wait. If you have a question, ask it. Be proactive in getting your needs met. Seek assistance from the many faculty and staff who want to help you. Do not wait for someone to reach out to you. No matter who you are or what course you are taking, there is help for you. Each person will face different challenges in the transition to a different institution. There are faculty and staff on the UM campus ready to help students make the most of their educational opportunities. Push yourself to take advantage of the many research and creative opportunities on our campus.

CHAPTER

30

ADVISING AND
Graduation

By Kyle EIlis and Holly Reynolds

A wise University of Mississippi professor once said, "The two most important aspects of college are getting in and getting out," although many valuable learning and growing opportunities occur in between those two key moments. The foundation of your higher education experience is getting admitted to the university, followed by the culmination of earning your degree, and taking the next step in life.

Congratulations! The fact that you are in EDHE 305 and reading this chapter has proven you have mastered the first key component by getting admitted to the University of Mississippi. Now that you are here, you want to efficiently work your way to the next important milestone, graduation. This chapter will assist you in understanding the university's academic advising process, transfer equivalencies, and graduation requirements. As a University of Mississippi student, you are responsible for your education. Be proactive and take ownership of all aspects of earning your college degree. As a commencement speaker said a few years ago in The Grove to the graduates, "I hope you enjoyed the journey, but now it is time to take the next step." Enjoy every minute of your academic journey at Ole Miss, because the next step will be here before you know it.

ADVISING ON THE OXFORD CAMPUS

Academic advising is a valuable resource for students in higher education. Professional and/or faculty advisors at the University of Mississippi work with students on numerous components related to student success and degree completion. Please read Chapter 13 "Academic Advising" to better understand the purpose of advising, advisor and advisee expectations, UM's registration system, calculating GPA, and academic standing. We summarize below the basics of the advising systems for each of the undergraduate colleges/schools. When transfer students come to orientation, they meet with a representative for their degree program. However, their permanent advisor will be assigned as the semester begins. Students with multiple majors or degree programs will have an advisor for each one.

To find your academic advisor:
Log on to your myOleMiss account [my.olemiss.edu]
Click on "Academics" at the top
Click "Advising" on the left

College of Liberal Arts

College of Liberal Arts students are assigned an advisor in their major department. For about half of the departments in the college, the student services staff in the dean's office will assign the student's advisor. Students majoring in psychology, economics, and interdisciplinary studies are advised by academic counselors in the College of Liberal Arts Student Services Office. Students should contact student services (662.915.7177) when they want to declare/change their major and need a new advisor. Students and advisors meet every semester to discuss degree requirements and the class schedule for next semester, and to provide academic mentorship. Advisors also can provide helpful information regarding post-graduate plans. Student Services staff provide support to the departments, process certain student forms, and verify students for graduation. [libarts.olemiss.edu/current-students]

Office of General Studies

The bachelor of multi-disciplinary studies (B.M.D.S) is one of the degree programs offered under the Office of General Studies. Students interested in this degree program must apply to the program detailing the career goal that led to the selection of this degree, the three minors selected for completion, and the rationale for the selection of each minor. The application is available on the Office of General Studies website (generalstudies.olemiss.edu). Once the application has been approved, students are notified through a welcome email, which also contains contact information for the newly assigned academic counselor.

Patterson School of Accountancy

In the Patterson School of Accountancy, there are two staff advisors for all accounting students. Therefore, students must take an active role in advising. Students are assigned to both advisors and may schedule a meeting with either one using an online appointment system. Advising is an in-depth process each semester, and advising expectations for both the advisors and students help keep it running smoothly. Students are expected to schedule and arrive on time for their meeting, have researched possible classes, and be clear about their goals. [accountancy.olemiss.edu/especially-for-students]

School of Applied Sciences

School of Applied Sciences students are assigned an advisor by their major department. Students are expected to be aware of the courses required for graduation, total number of hours needed, and GPA requirements for their degree. Students should come to their advising meeting with a copy of their degree audit and with some idea of what courses they would like to take. Advisors are expected to be a guide to the student, ensuring they take courses in the correct sequence and fulfill requirements. [sas.olemiss.edu/student-help]

School of Business Administration

Students in the School of Business Administration are assigned to multiple professional advisors known as academic counselors, and may choose to meet with any of them, which allows flexibility in scheduling advising appointments. Students must submit to the School of Business website a proposed schedule using the pre-advising form for the upcoming term [business.olemiss.edu/preadvising] to have their advisor hold lifted. They are sent a response to verify receipt of the email and to provide a link to schedule an appointment with an academic counselor, if they wish. Students are provided with a follow up email with suggested/approved courses after an academic counselor has reviewed the student's file. Students are expected to a) be proactive in keeping track of academic progress; b) become knowledgeable about programs, degree requirements, policies, and procedures; c) come prepared to appointments with questions and materials for discussion; d) accept responsibility for their actions or inactions that affect their educational progress and goals. [business.olemiss.edu/current/undergraduate/advising]

School of Education

The School of Education has two full-time professional advisors who are available to meet with students during peak advising times in October and March. Students can use an online appointment system to schedule their advising time. During non-peak times, students may come to the advising office between 8 a.m. and 5 p.m. [safe.education.olemiss.edu/advising]

School of Engineering

School of Engineering students are assigned faculty advisors in their major department. Advisors can lift holds to allow students to register, plan for classes, discuss career paths, and apply for internships. There are high expectations for the advising process. Students should come to meetings well prepared to discuss their academic plans and progress. [engineering.olemiss.edu/advising]

School of Journalism and New Media

The academic advisor in the dean's office advises all freshmen and sophomores, while faculty members advise all other students. Course degree information is readily available in the dean's office and on the school website. Students also are notified periodically through email of important course or degree information. [jnm.olemiss.edu/advising]

School of Pharmacy

The School of Pharmacy requires all students to individually meet with their assigned faculty advisor at least once per semester prior to course registration. [pharmacy.olemiss.edu/studentaffairs/supportservices/academic-support/]

Freshman Studies

Freshman Studies students are assigned a professional advisor in the Center for Student Success and First-Year Experience. Students may remain in Freshman Studies until they have earned 45 credit hours. Students who have more than 45 hours but do not have the required GPA to declare a specific major may stay in Freshman Studies until they meet the needed GPA or declare a different major. Students can make an appointment with their advisor through the appointment link located on the Center's homepage. [cssfy.olemiss.edu/advising/]

TRANSFER EQUIVALENCY

When a transfer student registers for an orientation session, a flag is raised to have the transfer course work evaluated. If the course is not in the transfer database, the dean of the college or school that offers the course determines how the course will transfer, in consultation with the appropriate department chair. For example, a transfer agreement for a mathematics course would be determined through the College of Liberal Arts. A computer science course would be determined through the School of Engineering. The dean of the college or school that offers the student's degree will determine which transfer credits will apply to the degree program. Students ordinarily receive no transfer credit for courses designed specifically for technical and vocational career programs. The status of a student's transfer credits will need to be re-evaluated if a student changes his or her degree program resulting in a change of schools, such as changing from a degree in the School of Business Administration to the School of Engineering.

THE UNIVERSITY OF MISSISSIPPI

Transfer Students

| Academics | Financial Aid | Apply Now | Admissions Requirements | Transfer Equivalencies |

UM Transfer Course Equivalencies
Show validity period | Hide no-credit agreements | Show inactive agreements

- **List All Mississippi Community Colleges**
- **List All Institutions with Equivalency Agreements**

Search Courses
Search for a UM Course:
Writ 101, Writing I   [Search Courses]

Search Schools
Search for an Institution:
Full or Partial Name   [Search Schools]

The university maintains a database of transfer agreements. This database is available at [transfer.olemiss.edu/transferequivalencies/]

The Mississippi Community Colleges (MCC) follow a uniform course numbering system. Any course listed in the uniform course numbering system document will transfer the same way, regardless of the institution at which it is taken. For example, MAT 1313 transfers as Math 121 at the University of Mississippi whether it is taken at Hinds Community College, Itawamba Community College, or Northwest Mississippi Community College. If a course appears in the uniform course numbering system, its transfer agreement can be found under "Mississippi Community Colleges (C999999)" in the Transfer Equivalency Database. If there is a unique course taught at one of the MCC institutions that does not appear in the uniform course numbering system, then its transfer agreement would be listed under the individual school.

C002409 Itawamba Community College	Fulton	MS	US
C002411 Jones County Junior College	Ellisville	MS	US
C002413 Meridian Community College	Meridian	MS	US
C999999 Mississippi Community Colleges	Unknown	MS	US
C002416 Mississippi Delta Community College	Moorhead	MS	US
C002418 Mississippi Gulf Coast Community College	Perkinston	MS	US

Transfer Equivalency Report

Each student can generate a personalized Transfer Equivalency Report that lists all the transfer work that has been transferred to UM. The report can be accessed through the myOleMiss portal at [olemiss.edu/mytransferequivreport]. Just because a course does not appear on the Transfer Equivalency Report does not mean the course does not transfer. It simply means the course has not been previously encountered. Contact the registrar's office to inquire about the status of the decision that needs to be made about this transfer credit.

Holmes Community College

EO Course	Attemp Hrs	EO Course Title	Term	Year	UM Course	UM Attemp	UM Earned	UM Graded	Grade
SOC 2113	3.00	Introduction To Sociology I	Fall Session	2012	Soc 101	3.00	3.00	3.00	A
CHE 1213	3.00	General Chemistry I	Fall Session	2011	Chem 105	3.00	3.00	3.00	B
CHE 1223	3.00	General Chemistry II	Spring Session	2012	Chem 106	3.00	3.00	3.00	D
ENG 1113	3.00	English Composition I	Full Summer	2009	Engl 101	3.00	3.00	3.00	A
MAT 1313	3.00	College Algebra	Full Summer	2011	Math 121	3.00	3.00	3.00	A
MAT 1623	3.00	Calculus II-A	Spring Session	2012	Math 262	3.00	3.00	3.00	A
MFL 1213	3.00	Spanish I	Fall Session	2012	Span 101	3.00	3.00	3.00	A
MUS 1113	3.00	Music Appreciation	Fall Session	2011	Mus 103	3.00	3.00	3.00	B
CHE 1211	1.00	General Chemistry I (Lab)	Fall Session	2011	Chem 115	1.00	1.00	1.00	B
CHE 1221	1.00	General Chemistry II (Lab)	Spring Session	2012	Chem 116	1.00	1.00	1.00	C
MAT 1613	3.00	Calculus I-A	Fall Session	2011	Math 261	3.00	3.00	3.00	A
					Bisc 163	1.00	1.00	1.00	B
BIO 1144	4.00	General Biology II	Spring Session	2012	Bisc 162	3.00	3.00	3.00	B
					Phys 221	1.00	1.00	1.00	A
PHY 2514	4.00	General Physics I-A	Fall Session	2012	Phys 211	3.00	3.00	3.00	A
					Bisc 161	1.00	1.00	1.00	A
BIO 1134	4.00	General Biology I	Fall Session	2011	Bisc 160	3.00	3.00	3.00	A
SPT 1113	3.00	Oral Communications (Prin of Speech)	Spring Session	2012	Spch 102	3.00	3.00	3.00	A
HPR 1551	1.00	Fitness And Conditioning Training I	Fall Session	2011	UM 1XX	1.00	1.00	1.00	A
HPR 1561	1.00	Fitness And Conditioning Training II	Fall Session	2012	UM 1XX	1.00	1.00	1.00	A
LEA 1911	1.00	Lead & Comm Sk I	Spring Session	2012	EDHE 1XX	1.00	1.00	1.00	A
HON 1921	1.00	Honors Forum II-X CAL	Spring Session	2012	UM 1XX	1.00	1.00	1.00	A
ENG 1123	3.00	English Composition II	Fall Session	2012	Writ 102	3.00	3.00	3.00	A

Transfer Work Summary for Holmes Community College

Attempted Hours:51.00	Earned Hours:51.00	Graded Hours: 51.00	Grade Points: 182.00	GPA: 3.56

The following image shows an excerpt from a Transfer Equivalency Report. (Sample for Holmes Community College.)

The Transfer Equivalency Report shows comprehensive information for each transfer course and a summary of the work from each transfer institution. It also shows how courses taken at other institutions can transfer in a variety of ways.

Direct Transfer. If the community college course matches the UM course in content and in the number of credits, the course may transfer directly to a UM course. For example, PHI 2713 from the Mississippi Community Colleges transfers as Phil 103.

PHI 2713	Logic	Phil 103	Logic: Critical Thinking	3

Combination Agreements. Sometimes a combination of courses is required to receive credit for a course at UM. This is often the case when UM offers a combined science lecture/lab course, but the external institution offers separate lecture and lab courses.

BIO 2921	Microbiology (lab)	Bisc 210: Principles of Microbiology	4
BIO 2923	Microbiology		

Departmental Bucket Credit. Academic courses that are within a discipline offered by a department at UM but do not have a direct matching course may be given departmental bucket credit. The number used indicates whether the course is a lower division course at the 100 and 200 level (freshman and sophomore) or an upper division course at the 300 and 400 level (junior and senior). For example, math 1XX could be given to a freshman-level mathematics courses; but AH 3XX could be given to a junior-level art history course. The student's academic dean determines whether departmental bucket credit may be applied to degree requirements.

CRJ 1383	Criminology CJ1XX	Generic 100 Level Criminal Justice	3

Interdisciplinary Courses. The College of Liberal Arts has several courses designed specifically to handle interdisciplinary transfer course work. Each college or school at UM determines how these interdisciplinary courses may be applied toward degree requirements. Prior to the creation of these interdisciplinary courses, the transfer course may very likely have been assigned UM bucket credit. Please contact the College of Liberal Arts if you have an interdisciplinary course equated to UM bucket and would like to request to have it re-evaluated.

UM Bucket Credit. Academic courses that do not match a discipline offered by a department at UM may be given generic bucket credit. This credit will count only as general elective credit. UM 1XX, UM 2XX, UM 3XX, and UM 4XX do not satisfy specific degree requirements but may provide elective hours towards the degree.

EDU 1211	Self-Affirmation	UM1XX	Generic University 100 Level	1

No UM Credit. Students ordinarily receive no transfer credit for courses designed specifically for technical and vocational career programs.

IED 2414   History & Appreciation of the Artcraft   No Credit No UM Credit (UG) 0

Re-evaluation of an Existing Agreement. Courses can change over time, and existing transfer agreements may be reviewed upon request. If a student believes a course on his or her Transfer Equivalency Report should receive more specific credit that departmental bucket credit or UM bucket credit, the student should contact the registrar's office and request that the existing agreement be reviewed. The registrar's office will then contact the appropriate academic unit. A syllabus may be required for review.

Permission to Transfer Credit. Once admitted to UM, a student must obtain written approval from his or her academic dean before taking courses at another institution with the intention of transferring credits towards a UM degree. A student will not receive credit for courses taken at another college or university while simultaneously attending the University of Mississippi unless prior approval is obtained rom the student's academic dean.

The list that follows, although not exhaustive, shows several university regulations that apply to transfer work and graduation requirements.

1. No more than half of the coursework submitted for a degree may be from a community college.
2. No more than 6 of the last 21 hours can be transfer work and/or independent study.
3. Twenty-five percent (25%) of the total hours counted toward the degree must be taken in residence.
4. The colleges and schools may apply additional regulations. For example, in the College of Liberal Arts, twelve (12) hours of the courses applied toward the major must be taken in residence, and six (6) hours of the courses applied toward the minor must be taken in residence.

GRADUATION

Transfer students are closer to graduation and should know the process for applying for graduation in their college or school. While the beginning of the process may differ by school, ultimately each dean's office must approve a graduation plan. It is the dean's office that must clear a student to apply for a diploma. For example, students graduating in May/August have a February deadline to complete the registrar's online diploma application. Well before that date, students and advisors must create a graduation plan and have that plan approved by the dean's office, as described below for each college/school. Finally, each dean's office must double check that students have passed the required courses and earned the required minimum grades after the final semester is complete.

College of Liberal Arts

The student services staff in the office of the dean sends second-semester juniors and seniors an email prompt to pick up the degree application and gives a deadline for submission two semesters prior to graduation. Students finalize the degree application with the advisor and department chair before submitting it to the dean's office for evaluation. Each student receives a formal letter or email stating that the application was correct or that there is a deficiency in the graduation plan. Students would then work directly with the student services staff on any revisions to their graduation plan. Psychology, economics, and interdisciplinary studies majors advised by the academic counselors in student services are not required to submit a degree application. These majors are instead required to submit a letter to their advisor of intent to graduate.

Multi-Disciplinary Studies

Multi-disciplinary studies students are advised each semester on their current degree progress. Once it is determined during advising that a student is eligible to graduate the following semester, the advisor prompts the student to submit a letter of intent to graduate to the Office of General Studies. At the start of what the student has indicated to be his or her final semester, the Office of General Studies reviews the student's schedule to ensure that the courses in which the student is enrolled fulfill the remaining degree requirements. If so, the student receives an email notification that he or she has been authorized to complete an online diploma application. If deficiencies are found in the schedule, the Office of General Studies notifies the student and works with both the student and the academic advisor to try to resolve the issue or create a plan for graduation at a later date.

Patterson School of Accountancy

Accountancy students are advised each semester on their current degree progress. Once it is determined that a student will graduate the following semester, the student is sent an email prompting him or her to submit an online diploma application.

School of Applied Sciences

Students will be asked to complete the intent to graduate form the semester before their anticipated graduation term. The link to the form will be provided by the student's academic advisor during their final advisor meeting. This application will be reviewed by the dean's office for any deficiencies.

School of Business Administration

Each senior must apply for a degree by submitting an intended graduation date in their advising submission to the advising office in the semester preceding the semester in which the student expects to graduate. The advising office will complete a checklist using official transcripts on file to date and will notify students prior to their last term of additional academic requirements that must be completed for the degree. It then becomes the responsibility of the student to complete the remaining requirements by the end of the semester in which the student wishes to graduate.

School of Education

During the semester prior to the anticipated graduation date, the dean's office advising staff conducts a full degree audit for students to notify the student of any discrepancies or issues that could impact his or her anticipated graduation date. This audit is reviewed during the advising session prior to the semester of anticipated graduation.

School of Engineering

Students complete the degree application, which is approved by the advisor and department chair. The dean's office reviews and gives the final approval of the graduation application, using degree audit as a verification tool.

School of Journalism and New Media

Students apply for graduation by submitting an intent to graduate form, and the assistant dean for student services reviews all forms. Students are informed by email of their status, whether they are complete to graduate or if their graduation plan is deficient and if so, in what way(s). Students are prompted to complete the intent to graduate form when they have completed at least 70% of the course work for their degree or at least one year before their intended graduation date to allow advance notice of any issues they need to address.

School of Pharmacy

Pharmacy students are advised each semester on their current degree progress. Once it is determined that a student will graduate the following semester, the student is sent an email prompting him or her to submit an online diploma application.

CONCLUSION

Again, the dean's office is always the final arbiter of whether a student has completed the necessary requirements to earn the degree. You will notice that some kind of application or intent to graduate letter/form is due well before the last semester you plan to be in school. Therefore, you can make sure that your last semester schedule will correctly fulfill the last of your requirements to graduate.

The University is moving towards using the online degree audit to check each student's degree requirements as well as to determine the percentage of the degree that is complete at the end of each semester. This is a valuable advising tool that can help students remain on track to graduate. Go to your myOleMiss account and explore the degree audit. You are even able to set up hypothetical degree audits in case you are contemplating changing your degree program. Take a copy of your degree audit to the meeting with your advisor and use it as the basis of your conversation about what courses you need to register for the next semester.

Whether you have a faculty advisor or a professional staff advisor, the advising process is designed for students to take ownership of their degree progress. Just as there are heightened expectations for your active participation in the learning process in the classroom, the University also expects students to step up in the advising process. The advisor is your academic mentor at UM and can guide you to the wide variety of resources on our campus to help you be successful. When in doubt, ask your advisor.

CHAPTER
31
WHAT'S
Next?

By Laura Antonow, Macey Edmonson, Sovent Taylor,
and Amanda Walker

You are now a University of Mississippi student. What's next? As a transfer student, you should begin thinking about your career and increasing your job marketability. Students are encouraged to gain as much industry-related experience as possible prior to graduation. Increasing your job marketability may include building/refining your resume, getting involved with clubs and organizations, and seeking work experience in your field of study.

Internships: The Key to Gaining Experience and Increasing Job Marketability

Across the United States, an emphasis on student participation in experiential learning opportunities, such as internships or co-ops, has been encouraged by many career professionals. In fact, a recent article in the *Chronicle of Higher Education* states "the days of just having a degree and being able to find a great job are over" (Barrett, 2013). Career development professionals encourage students to participate in as many internships or co-ops as possible because the job market for fulltime positions is highly competitive (Walsh & Cuba, 2009).

What is experiential learning? Experiential learning is often called internships, cooperative experiences (co-ops), practicums, or fieldwork. Experiential learning historically has been an opportunity for students to gain hands-on work experience in their field of study prior to graduation. Internships are essentially one-time experiences in which students work for an employer in his/her field of study to gain work-related experience. Cooperative education (Co-op) offers students opportunities to work with an employer to gain work experience over an extended period. The length of this experience varies. Practicums or field work offer students the opportunity to work in a field of study as part of their academic process. Regardless of the type of experiential education, the purpose is to reinforce theory and take learning from the classroom to a professional employment setting (Newell & Will, 1952).

The first step in beginning your search process for an internship, co-op, practicum, or field work experience is to develop a résumé. Generally, an undergraduate résumé should be one page in length. It should highlight your education (your institution and degree information), previous work experience (volunteer and paid), relevant courses, skills, community involvement or activities (including any leadership positions), and references on a separate page. Typically, recruiters spend about 90 seconds looking over a résumé. It should be free of grammatical errors and have concise statements of experience or activities that make you qualified for the position.

The second step is to develop a cover letter. The cover letter is essential to grab the employer's attention. The cover letter displays your true interest in the position and explains your qualifications. The cover letter also should be limited to one page. Recruiters read only relevant information; be concise. A good tip for cover letters is to include past experiences that directly relate to the job description. For example, if you have worked in a customer service industry, and the employer is asking for someone with   excellent customer service, you might highlight your past year(s) of experience in customer service. You also could provide an experience when you went beyond your normal duties to ensure excellent customer service.

The third step is to begin your search. The University of Mississippi Career Center uses a database known as *Handshake*. *Handshake* allows students to create a profile, upload résumés, transcripts, and references, search for jobs, internships or co-ops, explore city and country guides, and view employers participating in upcoming career fairs. Employers may search students' résumés on file. Students have free access to *Handshake* throughout their college career and as alumni. The database allows employers to post jobs, internships, or co-ops free of charge. Employers who post with *Handshake* are specifically interested in hiring University of Mississippi students.

The University of Mississippi Career Center helps in your search for internships or co-ops. You may schedule an appointment with a career advisor to discuss your search strategy. Additional online search resources such as Internships.com, Internmatch.com, Idealist.org, Indeed.com, USAjobs.gov, HireMSGrads.com, and others are available for students.

Research suggests that students who participate in an internship or co-op experience can increase their starting salary from $2,352-$6,302 per year over other entry-level candidates with no prior experience in their field (Blair & Millea, 2004).

The Career Center also has other industry-specific websites and job board information. The Career Center is active on Facebook, Twitter, and LinkedIn, and advertises all job postings to Twitter (@HireOleMissRebs) and Facebook (University of Mississippi Career Center Page).

The last step in your search process is preparing for the interview. Interviews are your opportunity to sell your skills and abilities to the employer. The Career Center offers mock interviews for students and alumni. In addition, the Career Center has online software, #JH Interview, which allows students to experience the interview process. Once you complete the simulated interview, you may email it to a Career Center professional or send it to a friend for feedback. Visit the Career Center (303 Martindale) for more information.

The Division of Outreach Office of College Programs provides innovative academic opportunities for University of Mississippi students. iStudy, Study USA, and the UM Internship Experiences compose the office, which supports student participation in unique off-campus educational experiences and in professional and academic advancement.

iStudy is a self-paced distance learning option for UM students. More than 65 independent study courses are available in either online or paper-based versions. Courses from many different academic disciplines are available, so students can use iStudy course work to catch up, get ahead, or eliminate scheduling conflicts. Contact the iStudy office for more information at [olemiss.edu/istudy] or (662) 915- 7313.

Study USA offers short-term domestic travel courses during intersessions in which students visit sites relevant to their field of study in locations such as New Orleans, Chicago, Miami, the Mississippi Delta, and Washington, D.C. These courses are offered in many disciplines covering topics such as media ethics, geology of coastal regions, the politics of labor, and hospitality management. Courses are taught by University of Mississippi faculty and provide students the opportunity to see their classroom studies in action. To learn more, visit [olemiss.edu/study@usa] or call (662) 915-6511.

The UM Internship Experiences combine work and study to create a semester of professional and academic experience that prepares students for success after graduation. Students in this program receive internship search support from college programs staff and UM alumni, as well as both pre-departure and on-site orientation activities to create a smooth transition between Oxford and life in a dynamic, fast-paced city. Students live with a cohort of UM students in Atlanta, New York, or D.C. and have the opportunity to create a professional network, gain valuable career skills, and enjoy the cultural aspects of their semester-long location. For more information, visit [olemiss.edu/internships], or call (662) 915-2982. Refer to Appendix A for more details on all of these options.

WORDS OF WISDOM:

From Todd Smitherman, associate professor of psychology:

Students need to have realistic expectations about graduate school. We see so many in psychology who indicate a desire to go to grad school, as if it's a foregone conclusion simply because they "want" to do it—many of these programs are EXTREMELY competitive. Clinical psychology Ph.D. programs, for instance, are harder to get into than medical school because they take fewer people than a large med school class. Our Ph.D. clinical program here, for instance, has about 115 applicants each year and admits seven or eight. Obviously getting off on the wrong foot with one to two bad semesters really crushes the dreams of some students, and I have on many occasions had to inform an advisee that his or her grad school aspirations were simply not realistic.

Apply to multiple programs. One of the biggest predictors of not getting in is applying to only one or two places, t, which students often do when they limit themselves to a certain geographical region. They should apply to several places, preferably across regions, to increase their chances.

For Ph.D. programs, getting experience as an undergraduate working in at least one faculty member's research lab is invaluable. Many students can get course credit for doing this, but beyond that it helps solidify (or change) their interest in the field (what they will be doing in grad school) and is really looked upon very favorably at the application stage. This is particularly true if the student is a co-author on a presentation or publication—the more the better. And they should seek out these opportunities early on in college—not the semester before they apply to grad school.

GRE, LSAT, MCAT. The importance of these tests cannot be overstated. Sure, they are imperfect and biased in some ways, but doing poorly on these can really sink an otherwise strong application.

Letters of recommendation. So many students wait until the last minute to think about this. Most grad schools require three, so getting to know several faculty well early in one's college career will save a lot of hassle in the long run. Making connections with faculty they've had for multiple classes, working in a lab, getting to know your advisor other than just the once-a-semester advising meeting, etc., goes a long way to help faculty get to know you better than they would otherwise—which helps them write a stronger letter.

Is a Fifth Year in your future? When discussing a fifth year of college, most students and parents cringe. When thinking of the fifth year, many may think it is a waste of time and money. However, that is not always true. For some majors, a fifth year is the norm (e.g., engineering). Also, for many transfer students, a fifth year can be beneficial. It gives you more time to decide what career path you want to follow. You have more time to participate in internships, assume leadership roles in one or more organizations, and apply for jobs.

It lightens your semester class load. The transition from community college to the University can be a challenging one. The last thing any student needs is to feel overwhelmed. Making the decision to go a fifth year will allow you to lighten your load, which may lead to better performance and a higher-grade point average. It gives you more time to get involved on campus. Many community college transfers feel like they don't have a chance to get involved. It takes a year or so to get adjusted, and then you are a senior who is about to graduate. At that point you are applying for jobs or graduate and professional schools. Staying a fifth year gives you more time for campus involvement that will enhance your résumé and provide numerous opportunities to make life-long friends.

WORDS OF WISDOM:

From Steven Skultety, associate professor and chair of Department of Philosophy and Religion:

Here are the three basic things we stress:

Money is available for graduate study in the humanities. Many students assume that graduate school always involves taking on debt. In philosophy and religious studies, good M.A. and Ph.D. programs award tuition waivers and stipends.

Take the GRE seriously and prepare for it. Because students from UM will be competing against a vast number of other students, every little thing counts: a high GRE score can really help make your application stand out from the pack.

Try to be a memorably good student, not just a student with high grades. There is a big difference between doing everything you need to do to get an "A" on the one hand, and completely devoting your intellectual powers to the material in your class, on the other. If you are thinking about graduate school in the humanities, try to do the best work of which you are personally capable...not just work that will keep your GPA high. This level of devotion will lead to a better writing sample, and it will also lead to better recommendation letters from your professors.

GRADUATE SCHOOL

Deciding to attend graduate or professional school is exciting! You have determined that you will be most successful by continuing your education and have weighed the pros and cons of delaying your career search. *U.S. News & World Report* ranks most graduate programs and  provides links to program websites and admissions offices [usnews.com/education/best-graduate-schools/top-graduate- schools/applying].

Once you have made your decision to attend graduate school, you should take time to choose a variety of schools to apply for admission. Apply to more than one institution so you can weigh your options and make an informed decision. One school may offer more scholarship money, and another may have a narrower focus that is of interest to you. Also, if you have the resources and time, visit these institutions. It is best to get an in-person impression of your future institution as you will be working with its faculty and other graduate students.

WORDS OF WISDOM:

From Virginia (Ginny) Chavis, professor

We may be a little different in the Art Department, but here are a few things that we do:

Encourage internships--(especially for graphic design--there are opportunities in Oxford, but most students do these in the summer in larger cities). Internships are very important because it gives real-world experience where students can utilize the tools they've learned in the classroom.

Well-designed résumés--Creatives have a specific format to follow that is different from what is explained in the Career Center.

Students develop individualized relationships with advisors – helps in several aspects including: determining a focus in his or her portfolio, choosing a career, applying to graduate school, developing portfolios and presentations, strengthening writing skills, steering to courses to strengthen their portfolio, and writing/collecting recommendation letters. Many students keep in touch with advisors after graduation.

Undergraduate students work alongside graduate students in several classes, so they get to see graduate expectations first hand.

Faculty help students develop a cohesive portfolio (which will be used in the application process).

There are multiple opportunities for students to see professional artists in action through community events, art exhibitions on campus and locally (from our own faculty and students as well as visiting artists), faculty working in their studios on campus, student organizations affiliated with professional chapters, and field trips and workshops outside of Oxford.

Opportunities for students to enter juried competitions to build their résumés.

After choosing the institutions that are the best fit, it is time to start the application process. Ideally, you should begin this process during the latter half of your junior year or the beginning of your senior year so that you have plenty of time to organize all of the documentation needed for your application. Graduate schools may ask for transcripts, test scores, application form, writing sample(s), faculty recommendations, employer recommendations, and an application fee. Applications for each institution are different. Pay close attention to deadlines listed on the program's website, and allow adequate time to complete every part of the application. Tailor your responses to each application, and avoid the use of text icons or abbreviations. Use complete sentences and correct grammar; admissions committees scrutinize every aspect of applications.

Transcripts – Of course, good grades are important. Institutions review your transcripts to determine if you have exhibited the ability to master learning during your undergraduate career. For an official transcript, contact the registrar's office to find out how long it will take to process your request. If you transferred to the

University of Mississippi, contact your previous institution's registrar, too, to ensure that you have a complete set of transcripts. To request transcripts from the University of Mississippi, sign on to myOleMiss and click on the "Academics" tab. There you will see the "Request a Transcript" option.

Test Scores – Most graduate and professional schools require applicants to submit scores from a standardized test as part of the application process. Each school's qualifying score varies, and students should research the schools they wish to attend to determine if a minimum score is required. Once you know what test is required for your graduate program, you may want to find out if there is a test preparatory class that would be beneficial to you. For example, there are many commercial test prep courses, such as KAPLAN (kaptest.com), offered to students who want assistance studying the various courses covered by these exams. Alternatively, you could tailor your senior year's class schedule to take coursework that would be covered on the graduate school admission test.

Application Form – Mark the dates of any deadlines indicated on the program's website and allow for adequate time in the event obstacles arise. Make sure you tailor your responses to each application. Do not try to cut and paste information if it is not relevant to the application question. Also, do not use shorthand. Use complete sentences and correct grammar; institutions will look at these things to determine whether you are a good fit for their program. If possible, print out the application and draft your responses before you submit them. Make sure your responses are relevant and contain enough information for the admissions committee to remember your application.

GRE (Graduate Record Examination) is required by most academic graduate schools. It is also required by veterinary, physical therapy, and some occupational therapy schools. - ets.org/gre/

LSAT (Law School Admission Test) is required by law schools.
- lsac.org/JD/LSAT/about-the-LSAT.asp

GMAT (Graduate Management Admission Test) is required by MBA programs in business schools. - mba.com/

MCAT (Medical College Admission Test) is required by medical schools.
- aamc.org/students/applying/mcat/

DAT (Dental Admission Test) is required by dental schools. - ada.org/dat.aspx

PCAT (Pharmacy College Admission Test) is required by many pharmacy schools (but not California schools). - pcatweb.info

OAT (Optometry Admission Test) is required by most optometry schools.
- ada.org/oat/

Praxis Series Test is required by graduate education programs. - ets.org/praxis

---

If you decide to complete your application online, allow yourself adequate time to carefully proof your work before clicking the "submit" button. It is a good idea to use a computer that is up to date and capable of supporting the software programs used at institutions for their application process. If you decide to complete a paper application, factor mail delivery in your timeline to complete and submit the application.

Personal Statement – Personal statements are an important part of the application process. This is your opportunity to share yourself with the admissions committee, providing a glimpse of who you are beyond grades and test scores. Personal statements are not one-size-fits-all. Research each of your potential programs to determine which of your experiences to highlight in your personal statement. The J.D. Williams Library contains a plethora of reference books and articles to assist you with this task. (Be sure to set your search for more recent titles.) If you need help, ask a reference librarian. University's writing centers, [rhetoric.olemiss.edu/writing-centers/], can help with your writing needs. There is even a quick chat window that you can use to ask questions while writing your statement.

Always check your potential program's personal statement requirements to determine what to include in your statement. Typically, institutions want to know about any research efforts in which you are engaged, major service projects in which you participated, life obstacles that you have overcome, why you want to continue your education, and why the institution would benefit by having you as a student. Focus on your individual characteristics and experiences that will set you apart from other applicants.

Writing Samples – An institution may require that you submit a writing sample with your application. It is best to use a writing sample that has been peer reviewed or edited by a professor. Make sure you submit a clean copy without any marks or editorial comments. The University's writing centers can assist here, too. Ask a writing center consultant to review the paper you plan to submit. If you submit  your writing sample online, use a PDF version, Adobe (adobe.com) to avoid formatting errors that could occur with Microsoft Word or WordPerfect.

Faculty and Employer Recommendations – Most graduate and professional programs require faculty and/or employer recommendations. Do not wait until the last minute to request a recommendation. Faculty members tend to be busy toward the end of a semester, so as soon as you find out when recommendations are due, ask your professor or employer so that he or she has plenty of time to craft your letter.

Always identify the person to whom the letter should be addressed and whether there are certain topics your potential program wants covered in the recommendation. Share this information with your professor or employer and provide a copy of your resumé so that he or she can refer to it when writing your letter. Finally, mark on your calendar the date you should send your professor or employer a friendly reminder of the due date for the recommendation.

Application Fees – Most institutions require a fee to process your application. This is something you need to budget for depending on the number of institutions to which you wish to apply. If you are experiencing an extraordinary financial hardship, some institutions provide a fee waiver.

IMPORTANT POINTS

Get to know your professors during your time at the University of Mississippi. Ask them relevant questions about coursework and volunteer to answer questions in class. This will be helpful later when you approach them for a recommendation. If possible, work with a professor to conduct research. This exhibits that you are serious about your studies and wish to continue your education. You can usually accomplish this by approaching a professor to ask if he or she would consider allowing you to take credit hours for independent research. Ask if your department has internship or co-op opportunities. As a professional courtesy, you should inform the graduate or professional schools of your decision to not attend. This allows them to admit students on their wait list. Take advantage of the University of Mississippi's programs, such as guest lecturers, art exhibits, and workshops. You can use these resources to gain knowledge and start building a network.

Always ask your potential program admissions director about scholarships and graduate student funding. This will help you determine the best program for you while balancing the cost of your education.

THE JOB SEARCH

Are you ready...to start your job search? Too many college students wait until their last semester of school to ponder postgraduate job prospects. This is far too late. Ideally, students should begin exploring academic and skill requirements for their ideal job early in their college career so they can craft a transcript and resumé that are a good fit for their career goals.

Your academic major and minor are important, but so are your choices of elective courses, volunteer work, leadership roles, and even travel, in getting you ready to find success after graduating.

Networking – With resumé and transcripts in hand, you can begin your job search by networking. This process can begin the day you set foot on campus, as your professors are a source of information about your prospective career path. Reach out to professionals in your field of interest. Conduct informational interviews, meetings with individuals who have careers to which you aspire, to learn about their companies and their career trajectories.

Additionally, get involved with the Ole Miss Alumni Association. Our alumni are devoted to the school, and many are willing to help recent graduates get a foot in the door with their first job. In addition to the main organization, the association has local clubs throughout the country. To find one in your new region, visit [olemissalumni.com/clubs].

Job Search Engines – Many resources exist to help with your job search. Job search engines can be a good place to begin your search. Some of these sites require registration, and some even include a paid subscription, but they can be a good investment if they help make your search more efficient. Some popular job search sites are:

Idealist.org	Indeed.com	Monster.com
Handshake	SimplyHired.com	USAjobs.gov

Job boards for specific industries can provide a more focused job search. Examples of these types of sites are:

JournalismJobs.com –newspaper, magazine, television, public relations, etc.

MediaBistro.com –advertising, web development, publishing, new media, etc.

HigherEdJobs.com – faculty, administrator, and executive jobs at colleges and universities

WorkInSports.com – media, marketing, broadcasting, sales, and management in the sports industry

Social Media – LinkedIn is the primary social media source for professionals, and while some may dismiss it, it is effective for developing and maintaining professional contacts. At a recent alumni panel in Nashville, an Ole Miss alumnus and successful professional recounted how an Ole Miss student reached out to him through LinkedIn to inquire about his company and request a casual meeting to learn about his company. The alumnus was impressed with the student's interest and professionalism and actually offered him a job a few weeks later.

LinkedIn offers a way for students to have a professional presence on the web, which can include your educational background, work history, résumé, and skills.

You also can connect with other individuals in your industry. While friending people you don't know on Facebook is risky, on LinkedIn, it is a common practice for people trying to connect on a professional level for work-related purposes. It also is a great way to stay in contact with professionals whom you may meet at conferences or other networking events.

Reserve Facebook and SnapChat for personal and social interactions; however, some companies post job listings on Twitter and Instagram. It may be worth following companies or agencies in which you have an interest. Always be careful in responding via social media; be sure to keep the tone, content, and syntax professional.

Communication – When communicating with prospective employers, always be professional and courteous, informed, and enthusiastic. Grammar, spelling, tone, and accuracy are critically important, whether you are communicating via print, email, or even text message. Attention to detail is important to employers, and it takes only one error to bring into question your abilities. Take time and care with every communication between yourself and a prospective employer, being sure to use formal titles and salutations.

Seal the Deal – Employers respond well to applicants who have in-depth knowledge about their company or agency, so research the mission, structure, and culture of the company by visiting its website prior to sending a cover letter and résumé. If an interview is requested, take the time to review the company's site and even search online to find any current events or issues pertaining to the company, so the prospective employer will know that you keep current with the company's accomplishments.

Send a thank you note after the interview. As they become increasingly uncommon, a handwritten note will be well received. At the very least, send a short email thanking the interviewer for his or her time and reaffirming your interest in the position.

Remember, too, that the interview is a two-way process. You are interviewing the employer as much as he or she is interviewing you. A good fit in both directions makes for a successful employment experience. Consider your own goals and expectations for the job and have some questions for the employer that will help you discover if this workplace will be a positive one for you both personally and professionally.

CHAPTER 32

UM REGIONAL Campuses

By Kyle Ellis and Holly Reynolds

The University of Mississippi has four campuses located in North Mississippi: Booneville, DeSoto, Grenada, and Tupelo. Regional campus students receive the same quality education as their fellow students on the main campus in Oxford. All full-time faculty members hired for these sites are part of Oxford campus departments and schools with collegial relationships. Each regional campus is located on a community college campus. They have a partnership with 2+2 arrangements that provide students with the necessary course work to complete their bachelor's degrees on site. When students complete their associate's degrees at the community college, they may opt to enter Ole Miss as a transfer student. All students at the regional campuses are transfer students because their coursework does not begin until their junior year (after they have completed their associate's degree). A majority of regional campus students are non-traditional students.

To be considered a non-traditional student, a student has one or more of the following attributes:

- Postpones enrollment (does not matriculate directly out of high school)
- Works full-time
- Attends part-time during the academic year (for at least one term)
- Considered financially independent for purposes of financial aid eligibility
- Has dependents other than a spouse (usually children but occasionally elderly parents)

Today's non-traditional students are community members who seek to improve their credentials or are unemployed and seek a new career opportunity. Returning military veterans may have VA benefits to help with the cost of attending college. The University of Mississippi regional campuses offer an array of student services onsite to assist students with their individual needs. Some of these services include personal counseling, career preparation, writing assistance, financial aid, and disability services. Pease refer to the information listed below about each service offered at the regional campuses.

Counseling Centers: As a student transitions to a university, it is a time of substantial personal growth and decision-making regarding values, personal relationships, career, and other life goals, all within a demanding academic environment. Oftentimes, students may experience problems with academics, relationships or family problems, self-identity issues, loneliness, depression, and anxiety. The counseling centers at Tupelo and DeSoto offer services designed to complement the University's academic mission by assisting students with their personal and educational development through a variety of psychological services. Confidential, personal counseling is available by appointment, free of charge, to currently enrolled students at UM Tupelo and UM-= Desoto. Grenada and Booneville students are welcome at each site. To schedule an appointment, please contact the coordinator of student services at each site.

Career Services: The UM Career Center's services and programs are designed to facilitate student's transition from academia to a full-time career. Each spring, UM Tupelo and UM Desoto hold a special week of career preparation events such as resume writing workshops and mock interviews. Students also are invited to attend the regional Career Fair held on the Oxford campus each spring semester. On this day, numerous companies and organizations send representatives to discuss employment opportunities.

Writing Center Services: The UM Tupelo Writing Center and the UM Desoto Writing Center are free services provided by the University to assist students in becoming stronger writers and critical thinkers. Within each Writing Center, you will find a community of writing consultants who are specially trained to work with you on any writing project at any stage of the writing process. To see available hours and appointment times, please visit the Writing Center website at [rhetoric.olemiss.edu/writingcenters]. Booneville and Grenada students have access to an on-line Writing Center to aid them in improving their skills. [rhetoric.olemiss.edu/writingcenters].

Student Disability Services: The University of Mississippi is committed to ensuring equal access to education for enrolled or admitted students who have verified disabilities under Section 504 of the Rehabilitation Act of 1973 and the Americans with Disabilities Act of 1990 (ADA). The Office of Student Disability Services provides reasonable classroom accommodations to verified students with physical and nonphysical disabilities. It is the student's responsibility to seek available assistance form the University by contacting Student Disability Services in a timely manner. A student request for reasonable accommodations and modifications intake form must be completed, and current documentation from a licensed health-care professional must be submitted before eligibility for accommodations can be confirmed. For a copy of this form, please visit the Student Disability Services website at [sds.olemiss.edu]. For assistance at the Tupelo or Desoto campus, contact the coordinator of student services.

Financial Aid: The regional campuses and the UM Office of Financial Aid administer a variety of financial assistance programs designed to help students and their families meet the costs of attending the University. A financial aid advisor is staffed at each campus to help students with their financial needs. Please contact the regional site to make an appointment or come by the office during regular working hours. There are four basic types of student financial assistance: scholarships, grants, loans, and part-time employment.

Additional Resources for Regional Campuses:

Technology: As an Ole Miss student, you will use computers and networks throughout your tenure. You will need to download information from course websites, turn in homework via email, communicate with instructors and fellow students, access library databases and other online resources. The UM IT (Information Technology) department provides the following to help you get connected:

WebID: Acts as a single sign-on for all UM Web applications. This is what you will use to access the University's Online Services/myOleMiss, and your Ole Miss email address. By signing in with your WebID on these sites, you will be able to register for classes, check grades, and view your student information. It is also how you will log on to Blackboard, a Web-based course-management system used by many UM instructors.

Ole Miss email account: This is automatically assigned, and because email is the primary way University faculty and staff contact students, it is really important to check this account frequently. This can be done at go.olemiss.edu.

Easy network access: The regional sites are equipped with wireless internet access. Please contact the main office to inquire about having wireless access for your personal laptop while you are in the building.

Computer Lab: There are computers available for the regional campus students to use at each campus.

Library Services: University of Mississippi students currently enrolled at regional campuses enjoy the same borrowing privileges and access to electronic resources as students enrolled at the main campus. You can search for books, e-books, DVDs, music scores, government documents, and enjoy access to databases with thousands of online full-text articles at libraries.olemiss.edu.

Students can ask UM librarians to find any book or article in the world when we do not have immediate access to the full text of the item. You can create an *Illiad* account to place requests through interlibrary loan by going to the library's home page and clicking interlibrary loans. Physical books are delivered to the regional site, Monday through Thursday, via the UM shuttle. Articles are delivered electronically through your *Illiad* account within 48 hours. For more information and assistance, please contact the head of research and instruction, Melissa Dennis, by email at mdennis@olemiss.edu or by calling 662.915.5861. You may also contact the interlibrary loan office at 662.915.5867 for questions about borrowing items, or the reference desk at 662.915.5855 for help with research.

Other Valuable Information for Regional Students

Classroom Assignments: Students can find their classroom numbers for classes at the regional campuses by reviewing bulletin boards near the front offices. If students are unsure about their classroom location, please visit the front office for assistance.

Testing Center: UM Desoto and UM Tupelo each have a testing center that offers students taking online courses or Istudy courses a location to take proctored exams. Since appointment times are limited, particularly for midterm and final exams, please make your appointment at least 48 hours in advance of the exam.

Student Identification Cards: The University of Mississippi requires all students to have an official University ID. Student ID photo are made during orientation. If you do not have an ID or lose your ID, please contact your regional site to have your ID replaced. A student ID also allows you to check out books and prove your identification as a UM student for other services, such as taking a proctored exam or selling back books at the end of the term.

Compressed Video Classrooms: Oftentimes there are courses that cannot be taught live at the regional sites. The regional campuses use Adobe Connect technology to send a course from one site to another (or all sites).

Vehicle Registration, Parking, and Campus Police: Parking decals are available to students attending regional campuses. Each Tupelo or Desoto student must register his or her vehicle by logging on to myOleMiss. Each vehicle that a student drives to campus must be registered separately. Any student who purchases these decals is allowed to park in an authorized commuter parking space on the regional campus as well as on the Oxford campus. Safe and convenient parking is available, but please park in student parking only. There are specific parking spaces reserved for official vehicles, faculty and staff, and for persons with disabilities. Vehicles parked at the regional campus without a valid parking decal or temporary permit are ticketed by the local community college campus police. The campus police provide a safe environment for students, faculty, staff, and guests. The security officers closely monitor access to the campus, so students should have their University ID with them at all times. The ID helps the police approve your presence. Always remember to report any suspicious activity that you might witness while on campus.

Emergency Closings, Class Cancellations, and Safety Procedures: Instructors are responsible for informing their class of cancellations (usually by email and RebAlert messages). Closings due to weather conditions are announced by local radio and/or television stations. Regional campus closing dates due to weather correspond to the closing dates the University of Mississippi Oxford campus. To inquire about closings of the University of Mississippi (any site) due to weather conditions, call 662.915.1040 or visit olemiss.edu.

Graduation: The regional campus students who are a semester away from graduation should discuss applying for graduation with their academic advisors. Although degrees are awarded through the year, the official commencement ceremonies for University of Mississippi graduates are held in the May in Oxford. A graduation celebration to honor student achievements is held for graduates each spring at the regional campuses. Family and friends of graduates are invited to share in recognizing students at their home campus. Students may order and be fitted for rented caps and gowns at the UM Desoto and UM Tupelo campuses prior to graduation in the spring. These caps and gowns are worn at the commencement exercises in Oxford only and are returned to the supplier there. Diplomas are mailed to students after final grades are posted and all fees and exit paperwork have been completed.

Student Organizations and Campus Involvement: Student organizations can improve personal and professional skills that are invaluable to the well-rounded college student. UM Tupelo and UM Desoto faculty and staff help provide these experiences to the student body by offering training and connections within the local communities that will aid students as they graduate and move into their chosen professions. For a complete list of student organizations, check out the FORUM at https://olemiss.campuslabs.com/engage

Did You Know?

The Lyceum circa 1865

- In 1836, when the first settlers of European descent in Lafayette County were considering a name for the county seat, Thomas Isom suggested Oxford, hoping the name might give the town an edge in persuading the state legislature to locate the state university there. On January 21, 1841, the legislature voted to locate the state university in Oxford. The vote was 58 for Oxford; 57 for Mississippi City (now a part of Gulfport).

- The Lyceum building, with a portico reminiscent of the Grecian Ionic Temple near Athens, originally included recitation and lecture rooms, a laboratory, a library and museum, and several society rooms.

- Albert Taylor Bledsoe was the first professor hired at the University of Mississippi, where he taught mathematics and astronomy. He became the interim president of the University when President Holmes left the campus in the spring of 1849. In 1854, Bledsoe left the University to teach mathematics at the University of Virginia.

- The first class of 80 students at Ole Miss included only freshmen and sophomores. Tuition for the ten-month session was $37, payable in advance. Room and board were $8 per month.

- Barnard Observatory was modeled after the Russian Imperial Observatory and the observatory at Harvard University. It was to have nothing but the best, including a 19-inch telescope (the largest in the world at the time). Although the building itself was completed in 1859, the delivery of some of its equipment was delayed by the Civil War.

The 1893 Ole Miss football team

- The Lyceum bell, built by the Buckeye Bell Foundry of Cincinnati, was probably cast in early 1847 and installed when the building was constructed. It is the oldest bell at a university or college in America.

- Architect William Nichols designed the original campus, laying it out on a circle, which was emblematic of the Greek concept of perfection. Nichols also is well known for having designed the layout of Central Park in New York City.

- James Alexander Ventress was elected to the Mississippi House of Representatives in 1835. In 1840 he introduced a bill to establish the University. He was a member of the first board of trustees. In 1938 he was named "Father of the University" by act of the Mississippi legislature. Ventress Hall is named in his memory.

- Four projects on the Ole Miss campus were built with slave labor. One is a cut through some hills to make a route for railroad tracks. The other three are buildings: the Lyceum, completed in 1848, the same year the university opened; an astrological observatory that was finished in 1859 and now houses the Center for the Study of Southern Culture; and a Georgian-style brick building dating to 1853, now home to international studies.

- Professor Alexander Bondurant organized our first football team in 1893. For the team's uniform colors, he chose the red of Harvard and the blue of Yale. The team recorded a record of 4–1. Its only loss came to a semi-professional New Orleans Athletic Club (whose members included a number of former college stars). University students proclaimed an undefeated inaugural season . . . against other college teams.

- The 1897 football season was cancelled due to an outbreak of yellow fever.

- Our football stadium, Vaught-Hemingway Stadium, is named for Coach John Howard Vaught, our most winning football coach of all time, and Judge William Hemingway, long-time chair of the Athletics Committee.

- In his late teens and twenties, William Faulkner spent a good deal of time at the University. For a number of years, he lived with his parents on the University campus (his father was business manager; his relatives were members of the Board of Trustees; a great aunt was a librarian).

GOVERNOR RUSSELL BURNED IN EFFIGY AT THE UNIVERSITY

Student Body Enraged at Ruling to Limit Dances and Stipulate Hours To Be Observed

UNIVERSITY, Miss., Oct. 28.—Governor Lee M. Russell was burned in effigy on the campus of the University of Mississippi last night, more than 200 members of the student body taking part in the event.

A meeting of the faculty is being held this morning to investigate the affair.

The demonstration was provoked by an order of the general board of trustees of the state educational institutions, of which the Governor is chairman, seeking to regulate dances at the University.

A bonfire was built on the campus by the students, after which a dummy figure representing the Governor was brought out and consigned to the flames.

The regulatory order of the board does not prohibit dancing, but seeks to limit the number of these functions and the hours to be observed. The same order also applies to dances at the A. and M. College.

- In 1920, Mississippi Governor Lee Russell insisted that dances and social events contributed to the moral decay of university students. He required all students to sign a pledge to not join social clubs (including Greek organizations) "by high noon on November 10, 1920." Twenty-five students publicly announced they would not sign the pledge (including William Faulkner and three football stars). A group of students marched across campus and burned an effigy of Governor Russell.

Governor Lee Russell banned dancing on campus in 1920

- A riot ensued after the 1926 football game between Ole Miss and Mississippi State. Student leaders from both schools agreed that a football-shaped trophy should be presented to the winning team in a post-game ceremony in hopes it would prevent future violence. The trophy ended up looking more like an egg than a football.

- In 1928, one day after the inauguration of Governor Theodore Bilbo, legislation was introduced to remove the University of Mississippi from Oxford and relocate it to Jackson. The initiative failed.

- Before 1930, Ole Miss sports teams had no nickname. Newspapers generally referred to the teams as the Mighty Mississippians or the University Boys. A contest was held, and an inaugural nickname was selected—the Mississippi Flood.

- Most newspapers refused to use "the Flood" in reports on the team. So, in 1936, *Mississippian* editor Billy Gates initiated another contest. The committee voted 4–3 for a new nickname, Rebels.

- In 1937, the Ole Miss football team was the first squad to fly en masse on a commercial airline to play a football game.

- The 1943 football season was cancelled due to World War II.

- The J.D. Williams Library was the first building on campus with air conditioning. It was installed in 1951.

- Two Ole Miss students—Mary Ann Mobley and Linda Lee Meade—won back-to-back Miss America competitions in 1959 and 1960.

- The Ole Miss football program won national championships in 1959, 1960, and 1962.

Ole Miss student Mary Ann Mobley passed her Miss America Crown to Ole Miss student Linda Lee Meade in 1960.

- In 1962, Ole Miss was the scene of a riot when mobs tried to prevent James Meredith from enrolling in the university. The National Guard was called in to keep peace and ensure a smooth admission for Mr. Meredith. The campus was in the international media spotlight for days. Hundreds were injured, and two people died.

- University of Mississippi Medical Center surgeons, led by Dr. James Hardy, performed the world's first human lung transplant in 1963, and the world's first animal-to-human heart transplant in 1964.

- Coolidge Ball, a native of Indianola, Mississippi, was the first African American athlete to play any sport at Ole Miss. Ball enrolled in 1970 and played forward for the basketball team. On May 15, 2021, a statue of Ball was unveiled in Pavilion Plaza.

- Ben Williams, from Yazoo City, Mississippi, and James Reed, from Meridian, Mississippi, were in 1971 the first two African Americans recruited to play football at Ole Miss. In 1975, Ben Williams was elected Colonel Rebel (the equivalent to Mr. Ole Miss).

- In 1986, Susan Aiken was selected Miss America, the third Ole Miss student to receive the crown.

- Robert Khayat (B.A. education '61, J.D. '66) chancellor emeritus of UM, has quite a list of accomplishments. He was an Academic All-American football player and was chosen as an All-SEC catcher for the 1959 and 1960 SEC champion baseball teams. He was an All-Pro kicker for the Washington Redskins. Most recently, he received a silver medal from the 2014 Independent Publisher Book Awards for his memoir, *The Education of a Lifetime*.

- Under Khayat's leadership, the university started the Barksdale Honors College, received a charter from Phi Beta Kappa, and hosted the first presidential debate in 2008 between Barack Obama and John McCain.

- The university partnered with the state of Mississippi and Toyota Motor Company to establish a one-of-a- kind Center for Manufacturing Excellence, which provides skilled workers for industries that locate in north Mississippi.

- After a five-year, national search, the authors of the 2010 book, *Higher Education? How Colleges Are Wasting Our Money and Failing Our Kids—and What We Can Do About It*, ranked Ole Miss as the best value in higher education in the United States.

- The Mississippi community colleges that send the most students to UM are Northwest CC, Itawamba CC, Northeast CC, and Holmes CC.

- For the first time in the show's 28-year history, ESPN's *College GameDay* came to the campus of UM in October 2014. The show was broadcast from the Grove stage, and the nation watched as Rebel fans became fired up for GameDay. This was one of the biggest weekends in Ole Miss football history as the Rebels defeated the No.1-ranked Alabama Crimson Tide.

Katy Perry dropped in on Gameday during their stop in Oxford in 2014

- The University of Mississippi's online MBA program is ranked in the *U.S. News & World Report*'s 2015 list of 25 Best Online MBA Programs.

- The average ACT score of the 2017 freshman class was 25.2 and overall high school GPA was 3.59—both the highest in University of Mississippi history.

- Virtually 100 percent of our accountancy master's graduates are placed in well-paying jobs, and many students have employment offers as early as 15 months before they graduate.

- The Patterson School of Accountancy has been nationally ranked in the Public Accounting Report (the primary national accounting ranking) every year since 2005, achieving top-20 rankings each year since 2008.

- Each spring, Ole Miss students contribute thousands of hours of volunteer work to the Oxford and Lafayette County communities, thanks to the student-organized Big Event.

- The Center for Inclusion and Cross-Cultural Engagement provides programs and services that encourage cross-cultural interactions and provides a physical space that is both nurturing and welcoming for students from diverse backgrounds.

- With over 60,000 sound recordings in most audio formats; over 20,000 photographs; more than 1,000 videos; and over 6,000 books, periodicals, and newsletters, the Blues Archive at Ole Miss houses one of the largest collections of blues recordings, publications, and memorabilia in the world.

- The College Corps student leadership group in the College of Liberal Arts seeks to alleviate community poverty by placing student volunteers committed to long-term service with nonprofit organizations and schools in Lafayette County. Members serve 10 hours per week with a goal of 300 hours during the school year and receive a Segal Education Award at the year's end.

- A five-week fellowship in bioethics designed for juniors and seniors in the College of Liberal Arts offers a collaboration between the Medical Center and the Department of Philosophy and Religion. The program introduces students to real-world ethical issues that face medical professionals and allows them to engage with medical students in Jackson.

- UM offers the state's only degree program in Mandarin Chinese, and the Department of Defense selected Ole Miss as one of four universities to train cadets and midshipmen as part of its ROTC Language and Culture Program.

- The Medical Center, with Tougaloo College and Jackson State University, is conducting the Jackson Heart Study, the world's largest study of heart disease risk factors in African-Americans.

- The speed limit on campus is 18 miles per hour. The jersey number 18 was worn by legendary Ole Miss quarterback Archie Manning, and it is in his honor that the speed limit is set.

- For several years, ESPN has had at least one summer intern from the School of Journalism and New Media, which also has had interns in New York at CBS News, NBC News, and Fox.

- Ole Miss students raised more than $250,000 for Blair E. Batson Children's Hospital in Jackson with RebelTHON.

- Students who staff the S. Gale Denley Student Media Center are consistent recipients of the Grand Prize (Sweepstakes) at the Southeast Journalism Conference and consistently win individual prizes.

- The University of Mississippi Robert C. Khayat School of Law is the fourth-oldest state-supported law school in the nation.

- Library hours can vary, so daily hours for the J.D. Williams and Science libraries are posted on the website, along with the hours for Starbucks. The libraries are open 24 hours the week before and week of final exams each fall and spring.

- Journalism students produce magazines and documentaries on current topics that are widely distributed. In recent years, they have won the Robert F. Kennedy Prize for College Journalism twice. (One is given per year in the national competition.)

- Over the past decade, the health care sector has added many new jobs. Roughly one in ten college graduates now gets a health-related degree. Former Chancellor Dan Jones challenged students to consider a health profession. "The most important reason to consider: the personal fulfillment. It provides, in my view, the most tangible way for someone to live a life of service."

- Students can and do start businesses. The School of Business Administration's Gillespie Business Plan Competition and Insight Park, a high-tech research and business center, provides support and infrastructure to startup companies.

- Allen Clark, assistant professor of modern languages, is responsible for the state of Mississippi's Arabic Language Flagship Program. The program has brought national recognition to the University and offers a summer study abroad experience that immerses students into Arabic culture.

- Since 2009, UM's Lazarus Project, led by Gregory Heyworth, associate professor of English, has restored and deciphered ancient works using a portable multispectral lab. "Texts we once wrote off as lost forever, or that were never known, are once again legible. And UM students are getting the first glimpses."

- The School of Pharmacy maintains the longest-running National Institutes of Health contract in the country, the Marijuana Project. Working under a competitive contract with the National Institute on Drug Abuse, the school supplies high-quality marijuana to the NIDA Drug Supply Program to allow researchers to study both harmful and beneficial effects. This is the only federally funded facility of its kind.

- The UM School of Pharmacy has been a leader in professional education for many years, and nearly 100 percent of Doctor of Pharmacy graduates pass the national licensure exam on their first attempt. Also, the vast majority of graduates have job offers before they graduate or are employed within weeks of commencement.

- The university funds 18 (men's and women's) intercollegiate athletic teams.

- Throughout the 115-year history of Ole Miss football, the Rebels have won six Southeastern Conference titles (1947, 1954, 1955, 1960, 1962, and 1963) and claim three national championships (1959, 1960, 1962).

Matt Corral and John Rhys Plumlee
produced some impressive statistics in
2019 and 2020.

- Ole Miss baseball team has played in the College World Series five times, most recently in 2014. The 2020 season was cancelled after 17 games. Ole Miss's record was 16-1—one of the best starts in school history.

- The Ole Miss basketball team has played in eight NCAA Tournaments; the team has won five Western Division Championships.

- The Ole Miss women's basketball team has appeared in the NCAA Division I Women's Basketball Championship tournament seventeen times. They have reached the Sweet Sixteen eight times and the Elite Eight five times.

- The Ole Miss women's softball team has appeared in the NCAA Regional Tournament the last four years; they advanced to the Super Regional Tournament in 2017 and 2019.

- The Ole Miss tennis team has won the SEC title five times. It has reached the Elite Eight in the NCAA tournament nine times. In 2009, Ole Miss freshman Devin Briton made history becoming the first Rebel to reach the NCAA men's singles championship match and becoming the first Rebel to ever win a NCAA men's singles championship.

- The University of Mississippi has produced 27 Rhodes Scholars, the highest total in the SEC. Only six other public universities in the United States have produced more. Arielle Hudson became the University of Mississippi's 27th Rhodes Scholar in 2019, making her UM's first African American female to be selected for the prestigious international scholarship program.

- During the 2019 football season, freshman quarterback John Rhys Plumlee rushed for 1,023 yards and 12 touchdowns. He set Ole Miss records for rushing yards, rushing touchdowns and total touchdowns by a freshman and the most rushing yards in a season by a quarterback.

- During the 2020 football season, quarterback Matt Corral set an Ole Miss single-game record (against South Carolina) with 513 passing yards. He led the Ole Miss offense, which averaged 555.9 yards per game (all against SEC opponents). It is the highest average in SEC history.

- Aimee Nezhukumatathil, a professor in the Ole Miss English Department, wrote the *New York Times* bestselling book, *World of Wonder.* The book was also selected as the Ole Miss common read.

- Ole Miss student Asya Branch was crowned Miss USA 2020 and made history as the first Black Miss Mississippi and the first Miss Mississippi to win the crown.

- Patrick Willis, one of the most decorated college and NFL linebackers, delivered the commencement address in May 2021.

- In 2020, the university renamed the student services center from Martindale to Martindale-Cole Student Services Center. The change was requested by Larry Martindale (for whom the building was originally named) to honor

- Donald R. Cole, a former student activist who returned to Ole Miss as a caring mentor and administrator.

Ole Miss student Asya Branch won the 2020 Miss USA contest

■In the summer of 2020, for the fourth year in a row, University of Mississippi students were named the state's best at finding employment and keeping it, according to data from the U.S. Department of Education.

■Notable Ole Miss alumni include Bill Parsons, former director of NASA; John Grisham, one of the world's bestselling authors (a graduate of the Ole Miss law school); Jim Barksdale, the founder of Netscape (the first internet browser); John Palmer, ambassador to Spain; Shephard Smith, former Fox News anchor; and Eli Manning, two-time Superbowl Most Valuable Player.

CAMPUS RESOURCES
Quick Reference Guide Student Support Resources at Ole Miss

Career Center
career.olemiss.edu • 303 Martindale • 662-915-7174

The Career Center assists students in making a successful transition from college life to the professional world. The Center provides educational services and activities that support the career development needs of students from the first year of college through graduation and be- yond, including one-on-one career counseling and assessment. The Center offers two career courses for academic elective credit (EDHE 201 and EDHE 301).

Center for Excellence in Teaching and Learning
olemiss.edu/depts/cetl/ • 105 Hill Hall • 662-915-1391

The purpose of this unit is to promote exemplary teaching and effective learning at the University of Mississippi. The Center provides Academic Success Training (AST) workshops for students: olemiss.edu/depts/cetl/AST.html.

Center for Inclusion and Cross-Cultural Engagement
inclusion.olemiss.edu/ • Suite F101/Student Union • 662-915-1689

The Center emphasizes inclusion and broad cultural educational opportunities for all students and provides programs and services that encourage cross-cultural interactions among Ole Miss community members. The Center is a physical space that is both nurturing and welcoming for students with diverse backgrounds.

Center for Student Success and First-Year Experience (CSSFYE)
cssfye.olemiss.edu • 350 Martindale • 662-915-5970

The Center for Student Success and First-Year Experience (CSSFYE) assists a wide variety of students through five primary units: Academic Advising, First-Year Experience, Student Retention, Academic Support Programs, and Veteran and Military Services. Professional academic advisors work with students who have yet to declare a major and freshmen in the Schools of Accountancy, Applied Sciences, Business Administration, and Engineering, and several departments in the College of Liberal Arts. First-year experience (including this course), academic support programs and classes, and student retention initiatives that support student success and persistence are housed in the CSSFYE. Additionally, the Center is home to Veteran and Military Services.

Clinic for Outreach and Personal Enrichment (COPE)

mailto:cope@olemiss.edu • South Oxford Center (SOC) • 662-915-7197

The UM Counselor Education Clinic for Outreach and Personal Enrichment (COPE) provides counseling services to children, adolescents, college students, and adults. Services are provided by UM faculty members and graduate students enrolled in a counselor education program at the University of Mississippi.

Department of Campus Recreation

campusrec.olemiss.edu • South Campus Recreation Center • 662-915-5591

The University of Mississippi Department of Campus Recreation provides outstanding services, inclusive programs, and educational opportunities to empower the University of Mississippi community in the pursuit of lifelong well-being. Campus Rec is the largest student employer on campus made up of over 250 student employees. The South Campus Recreation Center and the Turner Center serve as transformational spaces to provide students a premiere collegiate experience.

Department of Parking and Transportation

olemiss.edu/parking/ • South Campus Recreation Center • 662-915-7235

The Department of Parking and Transportation provides accessible parking, transit, and travel to students, faculty/staff, and visitors to the Ole Miss campus. The Department oversees day-to-day operations, parking enforcement, and other transportation-related programs and needs. Staff members strive to enforce regulations in a fair and consistent manner.

Equal Opportunity and Regulatory Compliance (EORC)

eorc.olemiss.edu/affirmative-action-plan • 217 Martindale • 662-915-7735

The mission of this office is to ensure the University's compliance with federal regulations regarding fair treatment of faculty, staff, and students; to ensure equal employment opportunity, and to ensure equal access to a quality education for students. EORC is also responsible for investigating complaints of discrimination including any complaints of discrimination filed under Title IX and serves as a liaison between the University and federal enforcement agencies concerned with equal opportunity and non-discrimination. The University of Mississippi is an EEO/AA/TITLE VI/TITLE IX/SECTION 504/ADA/ADEA employer.

ID Center

https://idcenter.olemiss.edu/ • Johnson Commons • 662-915-7423

The Ole Miss ID Center produces identification cards for University of Mississippi students, faculty, staff, and community members. The Center's website has information about the Ole Miss One Card, the University of Mississippi's official identification card. There is also a link to the Ole Miss Express home page at olemissexpress.ugrydnetwork.com/.

IT Helpdesk

olemiss.edu/helpdesk • Weir Hall • 662-915-5222

IT (Information Technology) supports e-mail, web pages, and other applications that run on the University's campus-wide systems. Staff at the Helpdesk are available to assist students regarding software, hardware, and networking.

J.D. Williams Library

libraries.olemiss.edu • 1 Library Loop • 662-915-5858

This is the main and centrally located library on campus. Click ASK LIBRARIAN on the library home page to IM with a librarian about any questions you have regarding research topics, subject guides, or library databases.

Office of the Bursar

olemiss.edu/depts/bursar/ • 202 Martindale • 800-891-4596

The Bursar acts as the University's banker. Responsibilities include receipting and depositing University funds; assessing student tuition and other charges; preparing, mailing, and safe-keeping student loan promissory notes; and disbursing student financial aid refund direct deposits and checks.

Office of Campus Sustainability and Ole Miss Green Initiative

sustain.olemiss.edu • 700 Hathorn Road • 662-915-2074

The Office integrates sustainability principles throughout the University and collaborates with sustainability education and research programs across the campus. Contact the Office to learn about volunteer and internship opportunities.

Office of Conflict Resolution and Student Conduct

conflictresolution.olemiss.edu • Somerville Hall • 662-915-1387

The Office of Conflict Resolution and Student Conduct provides a comprehensive array of approaches to support the University of Mississippi values of civility, respect for human dignity, and the honoring of community standards. Our purpose is to: • Support students as they overcome mistakes • Engage in character development with an emphasis on ethical decision-making and integrity • Resolve conflict at the lowest level possible through education, facilitation, support, and foster a safe and welcoming community.

Office of Financial Aid

finaid.olemiss.edu • 257 Martindale • 1-800-891-4596

The Office of Financial Aid is committed to helping students and their families obtain all available resources for financing the costs of attending the University. These resources include four basic types of student financial aid: scholarships, grants, loans, and part-time employment.

Office of Fraternity and Sorority Life

greeks.olemiss.edu • Suite D101 Student Union • 662-915-7609

With nearly 6,800 affiliated students, representing individuals from across the country and around the world, we are a robust community of engaged scholars, leaders and community servants. Comprising 33 organizations within the Interfraternity Council, National Pan-Hellenic Council, and College Panhellenic Association, we are proud to offer a variety of membership opportunities and a transformative experience for our members.

Fraternity and Sorority Life provides services that culminate in comprehensive support for our members, alumni, advisers, organizations, and councils. In addition to administration and planning, community member and council development, and leadership education, Fraternity and Sorority Life provides advising to all three governing councils and three auxiliary organizations, house director support and training, chapter adviser support, intentional educational programming, and recruitment and intake management.

Office of International Programs (OIP)

international.olemiss.edu • 331 Martindale • 662-915-7404

The OIP offers a wide variety of services to international students, faculty, researchers, and staff. This office provides specific information about admissions, financial aid, international document processing, and health insurance. The OIP presents a wide variety of events that introduce Ole Miss students to the richness and diversity of our international community.

Office of the Registrar

registrar.olemiss.edu • 104 Martindale • 662-915-7792

The Office of the Registrar is the academic record-keeper for the University. The Registrar can provide students copies of their transcripts, proof of enrollment, and letters of good standing.

Office of Student Disability Services

sds.olemiss.edu • 234 Martindale • 662-915-7128

Various services and materials are provided to eligible students for the purpose of allowing equal access to education. Eligible students must complete an intake process for verification at least two weeks prior to the first day of classes.

Office of the Vice Chancellor for Student Affairs

studentaffairs.olemiss.edu • 233 Lyceum • 662-915-7705

The Division of Student Affairs works to create and maintain a living-learning environment that promotes leadership development, academic achievement, and responsible and engaged citizenry. The Division complements and enhances the academic mission of the University by providing facilities, services, and programs to support students in their intellectual, personal, and vocational growth.

Ole Miss Dining and Meal Plans

campusdish.com/en-US/CSS/OleMiss/MealPlans/

Johnson Commons • 662-915-1467

This site provides a wealth of information and a map showing the various locations on campus for student dining. There is additional information describing meal plans offered to students.

Ole Miss Student Union

union.olemiss.edu • Suite H301 Student Union • 662-915-1044

The Ole Miss Student Union serves as the center of student life on campus, while striving to support the educational mission of the University by enhancing the collegiate experience with quality programs, facilities, and services through an inclusive environment. The department aims to ensure that students are successful at Ole Miss, while also providing opportunities to gain valuable experience participating in Registered Student Organizations (RSO). Students can visit the office to talk to a staff member about support for student success. Staff members within the department also serve as advisors for the Associated Student Body, Ole Miss Big Event, RebelTHON, and the Student Activities Association. Each organization offers various ways for students to participate in events and activities, as well as hold leadership roles within the organization.

Psychological Services Center

psc.olemiss.edu • Kinard Hall, Wing G, 382 • 662-915-7385

This center provides diagnostic services such as evaluation of learning difficulties, attention problems, emotional problems, developmental delay, and impairment following brain surgery. Client fees are based on a sliding scale.

Student Disability Services (SDS) Testing Center

sds.olemiss.edu/sds-testing-center/ • Kinard Hall • 662-915-2524

The SDS Testing Center provides a centralized testing location for those with verified test taking accommodations.

Student Housing

studenthousing.olemiss.edu • Minor Hall • 662-915-7328

Student Housing serves the on-campus housing needs of students. They also offer academic tutoring (olemiss.edu/depts/stu_housing/ed_support.html) in Martin/Stockard Halls.

Student Media Center

smc.olemiss.edu • 201 Bishop Hall • 662-915-5503

All students, regardless of major or classification, are invited to participate in multiple platform journalism at the S. Gale Denley Student Media Center. Many paid positions are offered in managing websites, social media, producing a daily newspaper, television newscast, staffing a 5,000-watt radio station, and producing the Ole Miss yearbook.

UMatter: Student Support and Advocacy

UMatter.olemiss.edu • Suite H 301 Student Union • 662-915-7248

UMatter serves the University community by coordinating support efforts both on and off campus to assist students facing challenges or crisis, including sexual assault, in order to promote personal and academic success.

Violence Prevention Program

Violenceprevention.olemiss.edu • 309 Longstreet • 662-915-1059

The Violence Prevention Program promotes awareness of the realities of sexual assault, relationship violence and stalking. The office also provides education and training for students, faculty and staff concerning these topics. The office serves as a confidential advocate to assist survivors of these incidents and as a liaison between the University and local resource groups.

UM Box Office

olemissboxoffice.com • Ford Center for Performing Arts • 662-915-7411

The University of Mississippi Box Office is located in the Ford Center and provides ticketing services for non-athletic productions and events held on campus.

Grove Grocery (formerly UM Food Bank)

foodbank.olemiss.edu • Kinard Hall • 662-915-2074

Grove Grocery seeks to end campus hunger and alleviate poverty by discreetly providing nutritious food products and hygiene products free of charge to students and employees in the Ole Miss community. All UM students and employees are welcome to utilize the Food Bank (Kinard 213). Patrons will have free, discreet access to whatever they need.

University Counseling Center

counseling.olemiss.edu • Lester Hall • 662-915-3784

The University Counseling Center assists students, faculty, and staff with many types of life stressors that interrupt day-to-day functioning. Professional services include crisis intervention, individual psychological counseling, support groups, meditation groups, substance abuse counseling, and wellness programs. Student services are free and confidential.

University Health Services

healthcenter.olemiss.edu • V.B Harrison Health Center • 662-915-7274

The Student Health Center is staffed by Family Practice and Internal Medicine physicians and Family Nurse Practitioners. The Center provides acute care for students.

University Museum
https://museum.olemiss.edu/ • 662-915-7073

The University of Mississippi Museum and Historic Houses complex serves as a cultural center for the University community and beyond. Among its holdings are Southern folk art, Greek and Roman antiquities, 19th century scientific instruments, and American fine art. Part of the museum complex is Rowan Oak, a historic literary legacy that was once the home of William Faulkner, Nobel and Pulitzer Prize-winning author. Rowan Oak was renovated and reopened to the public in 2001 and continues to draw international visitors each year. The Museum also owns the Walton-Young Historic House – once home to critic and satirist Stark Young.

University Police Department (UPD)
upd.olemiss.edu • Kinard Hall, Wing C, 322 • 662-915-7234

The five divisions that compose the University Police Department—patrol, investigation, crime prevention, security staff, and traffic support—are an integrated team striving to achieve excellence in police protection and to ensure a high quality of student-faculty life by promoting a tranquil, safe atmosphere conducive to the objectives of the University.

William Magee Center for Wellness Education
campusrec.olemiss.edu/wellness/

South Campus Recreation Center • 662-915-6543

The mission of the William Magee Center for Wellness Education is to advocate for well-informed, healthful choices and encourage students to strive for wellness in a positive, empowering, open, and inclusive environment.

Writing Center
rhetoric.olemiss.edu • Lamar Hall • 662-915-7689

The Writing Center is part of the Department of Writing and Rhetoric and employs more than 30 student consultants to read and critique students' written assignments. The consultants also offer workshops and provide assistance with word processing and other software programs.

REFERENCES

A Comprehensive time-line: isc.temple.edu/neighbor/ds/disabilityrightstimeline.htm

Addiction? Retrieved from: www.casacolumbia.org/addiction/addiction-risk-factors. National Institute on Drug Abuse. (2011, October). Commonly Abused Prescription Drug Chart.

A Global Education Toolbox. *100 People: A World Portrait*. Retrieved from www.100people.org/statistics_100stats.php. Accessed 2/6/2012

American College of Sports Medicine. (2010). ACSM's guidelines for exercise testing and prescription (8th ed.). Philadelphia, PA: Wolters Kluwer Health/Lippincott Williams & Wilkins.

American Council on Exercise. (2003). ACE personal trainer manual (3rd ed.). San Diego, CA: American Council on Exercise

American Psychiatric Association. (2013). Diagnostic and Statistical Manual of Mental Disorders (5th ed.). Arlington, VA: American Psychiatric Publishing.

American Religious Identification Survey (ARIS). Retrieved from www.americanreligionsurvey-aris.org/2010/02/

American Society of Addiction Medicine. (2011, April). Public Policy Statement: Definition of Addiction. Retrieved from: www.asam.org/for-the-public/definition-of-addiction.

American Sociological Association. *Statement of the American Sociological Association on the Importance of Collecting Data and Doing Social Scientific Research on Race.* Retrieved from www2.asanet.org/governance/racestmt.html. Accessed 2/13/2012.

Anderson, J. (1998). *Plagiarism, Copyright Violation and Other Thefts of Intellectual Property: An Annotated Bibliography with a Lengthy Introduction.* Jefferson, NC: McFarland & Company.

Anti-Defamation League. www.adl.org/hate-patrol/racism.asp.

Association of American Colleges and Universities. (2013). It Takes More than a Major: Employer Priorities for College Learning and Student Success. Washington, D.C.: Hart Research Associates.

Association of American Colleges and Universities. Retrieved from aacu.org/leap/index.cfm

Baldwin, Amy. The First-Generation College Experience. Boston: Pearson Education, Inc., 2012. 193-197. Print.

Blum, S. D. (2009). *My Word! Plagiarism and College Culture*. Ithaca, NY: Cornell University Press.

Bridges, F. (2012). *How to get an awesome internship.* Forbes. Retrieved from Forbes.com/sites/francesbridges/2012/05/31/ how-to-get-am-awesome-internship/#5bfdd1494378

Brown, B., (2014) Brene Brown: 3 Ways to Set Boundaries. Retrieve from oprah.com/spirit/how-to-set-boundaries-brene-browns-advice

Cappex. The University of Mississippi. Retrieved from www.cappex.com/colleges/University-of-Mississippi-Main-Campus-176017

Centers for Disease Control, (2014). Smoking and Tobacco Use: Disease to Death Fact Sheet. Retrieved from: www.cdc.gov/tobacco/data_statistics/fact_sheets/fast_facts/index.htm

Cirillo, Francesco.(n.d.) The Pomodoro Technique. Retrieved from https://francescocirillo.com/pages/pomodoro-technique

CNN.com. Georgia school shooting: Antoinette Tuff hailed as hero. (2013, August 22). Retrieved February 26, 2015, from http://www.cnn.com/2013/08/22/us/georgia-school-shooting-hero

CNN.com. She survived a standoff with a gunman - could you? (2014, February 22). Retrieved February 26, 2015, from http://www.cnn.com/2014/02/22/us/tuff-survivor-gunman

College Prowler. The University of Mississippi – Diversity. Retrieved from www.collegeprowler.com/university-of-mississippi/diversity

Cullen, M. (2008). 35 Dumb Things Well-Intended People Say: Surprising Things We Say That Widen the Diversity Gap. Garden City, NY: Morgan James Publishing.

Cuseo, J., Fecas, V.S., & Thompson, A. (2007). Thriving in college & beyond: Research-based strategies for academic success and personal development. Dubuque, IA: Kendall/Hunt.

Dealing with Homesickness. (2020). Retrieved from https://www.settogo.org/dealing-with-homesickness

Doran, G. T. (1981). There's a S.M.A.R.T. way to write management's goals and objectives. Management Review (AMA FORUM), 70(11), 35–36.

Drucker, P. (1954). The Practice of Management. HarperCollins Publishers. ESPN (Producer). (2014). It's Time [TV Show].

drugfree.org/wp-content/uploads/2011/04/Full-Report-FINAL-PATS-Teens-2008_updated.pdf (Retrieved Jan, 2015)

Dweck, C. S. (2006). Mindset: The new psychology of success. New York: Random House.

Dwyer, B. (2006). Framing the effect of multiculturalism on diversity outcomes among students at historically black colleges and universities. *Educational Foundations*, 37-59.

Erickson, B. L.; Peters, C. B.; & Strommer, D. W. (2009). Teaching First-Year College Students: Revised and Expanded Edition of Teaching College Freshmen. San Francisco, CA: Jossey Bass.

For more reading on budgeting: Federal Student Aid, U.S. Department of Education. Budgeting. Retrieved from: studentaid.ed.gov/sa/prepare-for-college/budgeting.

For more reading on credit, identity theft, and buying a car – and how they can impact your personal finances:Federal Trade Commission. (2013). Focus on finances: Preparing for your future. Retrieved from: consumer.ftc.gov/articles/pdf-0054-focus-on-finances.pdf

Fulfilling the American Dream: Liberal Education and the Future of Work. 2018. American Association of Colleges and Universities. Job Outlook 2019. National Association of Colleges and Employers.

Garavalia, L., Olson, E., Russell, E., Christensen, L. (2007). How do students cheat? In: E. M. Anderman, & T. B. Murdock (Eds.), *Psychology of Academic Cheating* (pp. 33-55). San Francisco, CA: Elsevier.

Generation Rx: How Prescription Drugs are Altering American Lives, Minds, and Bodies (2005, New York: Houghton Mifflin Co.
National Center on Addiction and Substance Abuse. (2013, November). Who Develops Addiction? Retrieved from: www.casacolumbia.org/addiction/addiction-risk-factors.

Gibson, C., & Jung, K. Historical Census Statistics on Population Totals by Race, 1790 to 1990, and by Hispanic Origin, 1970-1990, for the United States, Regions, Divisions, and States. U.S. Census Bureau. Retrieved from www.census.gov/population/www/documentation/twps0056/tabA-26.pdf

Gierdowski, Dana C. EDUCAUSE Center for Analysis and Research (ECAR) Research Hub ECAR Interactive Graphics and Infographics Research Report Survey Instruments Retrieved from educause.edu/ecar.

Giles, R.M. et al. (1982). Recall of lecture information: A question of what, when, and where. Medical Education, 16(5), 264-268. Lipsky, S.A. (2008). College study: The essential ingredients. Upper Saddle River, NJ: Pearson Education.

Gilmore, B. (2008). *Plagiarism: Why it Happens, How to Prevent it*. Portsmouth, NH: Heinemann.

gladstone.uoregon.edu/~asuomca/diversityinit/definition.html

Grace, S., & Gravestock, P. (2009). *Inclusion and Diversity: Meeting the Needs of All Students*. Routledge, New York.

Hacker, D. (2009). *A Writer's Reference*, 6th ed. Boston, MA: Bedford/St. Martin's.

Honor Code at UVa. (2010). Retrieved from scps.virginia.edu/honor_code.htm

Horacek, D. (2009). Academic Integrity and Intellectual Autonomy. In: T. Twomey, H. White, & K. Sagendorf (Eds.), *Pedagogy, not Policing: Positive Approaches to Academic Integrity at the University* (pp.7-17). Syracuse, NY: The Graduate School Press of Syracuse University.

Howard, R. M. (1999). Standing in the Shadow of Giants: Plagiarists, Authors, Collaborators. Stamford, CT: Ablex Publishing Corporation.

https://health.gov/communication/literacy/quickguide/quickguide.pdf

https://www.hhs.gov/hipaa/for-individuals/guidance-materials-for-consumers/index.html

Hurtado, S., Milem, J.F., Clayton-Pederson, A.R., & Allen, W.R. (1998). Enhancing campus climates for racial/ethnic diversity: Educational policy and practice. The Review of Higher Education, *21*(3), 279-302.

Institute of Education Sciences: ies.ed.gov/Income and Poverty in the United States 2014, retrieved from census.gov

Intimate Partner Violence (2020) Retrieved from http://onelovefoundation.org

Iverson, S.V. (2007). Camouflaging power and privilege: A critical race analysis of university diversity policies. *Educational Administration Quarterly, 43*(5), 586-611.

Iverson, A. C. & Iverson, S. V. (2009). Addressing the structure of power and privilege: Implications for diversity efforts at PWIs. *The Voice.* Retrieved from: www.myacpa.org/comm/social/Newsletter0309/newsletter_0309_power.cfm

Jones. R. A. (2005). Race and revisability. *Journal of Black Studies.* 35(5). 612-632.

King Jr., M. L. Remaining Awake Through a Great Revolution. Speech. March 31, 1968. The Martin Luther King, Jr. Research and Education Institute. Retrieved from mlk-kpp01.stanford.edu/ index.php/kingpapers/article/remaining_awake_through_a_great_revolution/

Komarraju, M., Musulkin, S., & Bhattacharya, G. (2010). Role of student-faculty interactions in developing college students' academic self-concept, motivation, and achievement. Journal of College Student Development 51(3), 332-342. doi:10.1353/csd/0/0137.

Lipson, C. (2006). Cite Right: A Quick Guide to Citation Styles – MLA, APA, Chicago, the Sciences, Professions, and More. Chicago, IL: University of Chicago Press.

Lives Worth Living PBS Documentary pbs.org/independents/lives-worth-living/

Lynn, K. (2011). Eight steps for strong time management for college students. Retrieved from collegelife.about.com/od/academiclife/a/timemanagement.htm?p=1

Maher, F.A. & Tetreault, M.K. (2009). Diversity and privilege: We need to understand how privilege works before we can make diversity work. *Academe, 95*(1), pp. 17-20.

Martin, Megan. U.S. Census Definition of Race. Retrieved from www.ehow.com/facts_5589095_u_s_census-definition-race.html. Accessed 2/13/2012.

Martindale, G. (2010, November 5). Time management tips for college students. Retrieved from stateuniversity.com/blog/permalink/Time-Management-Tips.html

Merriam Webster Online. Retrieved April 6, 2015 from http://www.merriam-webster.com/.

Multi-Health Systems. (2011). Emotional quotient inventory 2.0 (EQ-i 2.0) user's handbook. Toronto, Ontario: Multi-Health Systems.

National Association of Colleges and Employers. (2015). Job Outlook 2015. Retrieved from naceweb.org/Research/Job_Outlook/Job_Outlook.aspx

National Careers Service. What are the 'soft skills' employers want? Retrieved February 26, 2015, from https://nationalcareersservice.direct.gov.uk/aboutus/newsarticles/Pages/Spotlight-SoftSkills.aspx

National Endowment for the Arts (2007). To Read or Not to Read: A Question of National Consequence.

National Institute on Drug Abuse. (2010, August). Drugs, Brains, and Behavior: The Science of Addiction. Retrieved from: www.drugabuse.gov/publications/drugs-brains-behavior-science-addiction/drug-abuse-addiction

National Institute on Drug Abuse. (2011, October). Commonly Abused Prescription Drug Chart. Retrieved from: www.drugabuse.gov/drugs-abuse/commonly-abused-drugs/commonly-abused-prescription-drugs-chart ncadd.org/learn-about-drugs/signs-and-symptoms, (Retrieved Jan, 2015)

Nielson, K. E. (2012). A Disability History of the United States (Revising American History). Boston, Massachusetts: Beacon Press.

Nittle, Nadra Kareem. Race Relations. *What is Race?* Retrieved from: racerelations.about.com/od/understandingrac1/a/WhatIsRac.htm. Acessed 2/13/2012.

Nittle, Nadra Kareem. Race Relations. *What is Race? Debunking the Ideas Behind this Construct.* Retrieved from racerelations.about.com/od/understandingrac1/a/WhatIsRace.htm. Accessed 2/13/2012.

Office of Institutional Research & Assessment. Retrieved from www.olemiss.edu/depts/university_planning/

O'Hare, F., & Kline, E. A. (1996). *The Modern Writer's Handbook*, 4th ed. Boston, MA: Allyn and Bacon.

Overdeep, M. (2019). WATCH: Mama was right! Study shows student learn better when they take handwritten notes. Southern Living 21 February 2019.

Photos of Kendricks and Haynes taken by UM Communications Photography.

Quintero, G., Peterson, J., and Young, B. (2006). An exploratory study of socio-cultural factors contributing to prescription drug misuse among college students. Journal of Drug Abuse, 22, 903-926.

Racial Equity Tools Glossary. Retrieved from racialequitytools.org/glossary

Recovery Research Institute. (2014) Seeking Recovery. Retrieved from:www.recoveryanswers.org/who-are-you/seeking-recovery/

Rennels, M. R. & Chaudhari, R.B. (1988). Eye contact and grade distribution. Perceptual and Motor Skills, 67(October), 627-632.

Research Help Tutorial: Plagiarism and Academic Honesty. (2010). Retrieved from olemiss.edu/depts/general_library/instruction/resources/plagiarism_ac_honest/plagiarism_academic_
honesty.html

Research Shows Building This Trait Will Help You Outperform Natural Genius. Retrieved April 6, 2015, from http://riskology.co/outperform-genius/

Roberts, E. Independent Living USA, retrieved from ilusa.com/links/022301ed_roberts.htm

Roberts, J. & Reysen, R. Academic Skills for College. 1st Edition. University of Mississippi, University, MS. 2019.

Roget's II. (1995). *The New Thesaurus*. 3rd Ed. Boston: Houghton-Mifflin.

Samburova, V., Bhattarai, C., Strickland, M., Darrow, L., Angermann, J., Son, Y., & Khlystov, A. (2018). Aldehydes in Exhaled Breath during E-Cigarette Vaping: Pilot Study Results. Toxics, 6(3), 46. doi: 10.3390/toxics6030046

samhsa.gov/data/2k9/adderall/adderall.pdf, (Retrieved Jan, 2015) samhsa.gov/data/nsduh/2k10NSDUH/tabs/Sect1peTabs1to46.htm (Retrieved Jan, 2015)

samhsa.gov/data/2k9/adderall/adderall.pdf (Retrieved Jan, 2015)

Sansing, D. (1999). *The University of Mississippi: A Sesquicentennial History*. Jackson: University Press of Mississippi.

Savickas, M. L. & Hartung, P. J. (2012). The Career Construction Interview. Retrieved February 7, 2016 from http://www.vocopher.com/CSI/CCI.pdf

Schweik, S. M. (2009). The Ugly Laws: Disability in Public. New York and London: NYU Press.

Scott, E. (2016). Stress in College: Common Causes of Stress in College. Retrieved from http://stress.about.com/od/studentstress/a/stress_college.htm

Sexual Assault, (2020) Retrieved from http://nsvrc.org and cdc.gov/violenceprevention

Sexual transmitted infections. National Institute of Health (NIH): National Institute of Allergy and Infectious Diseases retrieved on 01.24.14 from www.nlm.nih.gov/medlineplus/sexuallytransmitteddiseases.html

Sparkman, L., Maulding, W., Roberts, J., (2012). Non-Cognitive Predictors of Student Success in College. College Student Journal, 46 (3), 642-652.

Staley, Constance. "Test Taking." Focus on College Success. Second Edition. University of Colorado, Colorado Springs. Wadsworth Cengage Learning. 2011. 208-239.

Stalking (2020) Retrieved from http://victimsofcrime.org

Stein, S., & Book, H. (2011). The EQ edge: Emotional Intelligence and your success. Ontario, ON: Wiley.

Strategy Driven. Diversity and Inclusion. Retrieved from www.strategydriven.com/2010/07/300/diversity-and-inclusion-what-is-diversity-and-inclusion/

Strong Interest Inventory Career Assessment - Psychometrics. Retrieved February 7, 2016 from https://www.psychometrics.com/assessments/strong-interest-inventory/

Student Academic Conduct and Discipline (ACA.AR.600.001). (2010). Retrieved from secure4.olemiss.edu/umpolicyopen/ShowDetails.jsp?istatPara=1&policyObjidPara=10817696

Substance abuse and Mental Health Services Administration (SAMHSA, 2009), Office of Applied Studies. (February 5, 2009). The NSDUH report: Trends in Nonmedical Use of Prescription Pain Relievers: 2002 to 2007. Rockville, MD. Retrieved from www.oas.samhsa.gov/2k9/painRelievers/nonmedicalTrends.pdf

Substance Abuse and Mental Health Services Administration. (2012). Working Definition of Recovery. Retrieved from: store.samhsa.gov/shin/content//PEP12-RECDEF/PEP12-RECDEF.pdf

Sue, Derald (2010). Micro-aggressions: More than just race. Psychology Today. Retrieved at psychologytoday.com/blog/microaggressions-in-everyday-life/201011/microaggressions-more-just-race.

Sufka, K. J. (2011). The A Game: Nine Steps to Better Grades. Nautilus Publishing Company: Oxford, MS.

Surowiecki, J. (2010, October 11). What we can learn from procrastination. The New Yorker. Retrieved from newyorker.com/arts/critics/books/2010/10/11/101011crbo_books_surowiecki

Talking about condoms. Planned Parenthood. Retrieved on 01.24.14 from plannedparenthood.org/health-topics/sex-101/understanding-sexual-activity-23973.htm

Talking to your partner. Retrieved on 01.24.14 from plannedparenthood.org/health-topics/sex-101/understanding-sexual-activity-23973.htm

Talking about using a condom. Retrieved on 01.24.14 from plannedparenthood.org/health-topics/sex-101/understanding-sexual-activity-23973.htm

Test Anxiety. Sharon Mitchell. University at Buffalo. 8 February 2012. ub-counseling.buffalo.edu/stresstestanxiety.php

theantidrug.com/pdfs/TEENS_AND_PRESCRIPTION_DRUGS.pdf (Retrieved Jan, 2015)

theantidrug.com/pdfs/prescription_report.pdf (Retrieved Jan, 2015)

The Oxford English Dictionary. Retrieved from www.oxforddictionaries.com

The University of Mississippi's Center for Student Success and First-Year Experience. (n.d.) Academic Support Programs. Retrieved from http://cssfye.olemiss.edu/student-support-programs/.

The White House. Office of Management and Budget. Standards for the Classification of Federal Data on Race and Ethnicity. Retrieved from www.whitehouse.gov/omb/fedreg_race-ethnicity

Time management. Retrieved frompennstatelearning.psu.edu/time-management

Time management for college students. Retrieved from timemangementhelp.com/college.htm University Learning Center.

True Grit – 2013 AP Annual Conference Keynote by Dr. Angela Duckworth. Retrieved April 4, 2015, from https://www.youtube.com/watch?v=BrkwrHSfsMY

Types of Plagiarism. (2010, November). Retrieved from plagiarism.org/plag_article_types_of_plagiarism.html

United Spinal Association. "Disability Etiquette: tips on Interacting with People with Disabilities," retrieved from unitedspinal.org

United States Census 1990. Your Guide for the 1990 US Census Form. Retrieved from www.census.gov/prod/1/90dec/cph4/appdxe.pdf

United States Census 2010. Explore the Form. Retrieved from 2010.census.gov/2010census/about/interactive-form.php

United States Census Bureau. 2009 American Community Survey. Retrieved from www.census.gov/acs/www/

United States Department of Labor. (2015, December 17). Occupational Outlook Handbook Homepage. Retrieved from http://www.bls.gov/ooh/

U.S. Constitution Online. *I Have A Dream Speech.* Retrieved from www.usconstitution.net/dream.html

University Creed. (2010). Retrieved from olemiss.edu/info/creed.html

Van Blerkom, Dianna L."Preparing for Final Exams." Orientation to College Learning. 4th ed. Wadsworth Publishing Co.2004. 323-340.

Van Eerde, W., & Klingsieck, K. B. (2018). Overcoming procrastination? A meta-analysis of intervention studies. Educational Research Review, 25, 73-85. doi:10.1016/j.edurey.2018.09.002 Washington, 2007. Retrieved from nea.gov/research/toread.pdf

VonSchrader, S. L. and Lee, C. G. (2015). Disability Statistics from the Current Population Survey (CPS). Ithaca, NY: Cornell University Employment and Disability Institute (EDI). Retrieved from disabilitystatistics.org

Ween, M., Thredgold, L., Reynolds, P., & Hodge, S. (2019). Device, Flavour, And Coil Temperature In An E-Cigarette All Contribute To Viability Of Primary Bronchial Epithelial Cells And Efferocytosis Of Apoptotic Bronchial Cells By Macrophages. Respirology, 24(S2), 11–11. doi: 10.1111/resp.13699_24

What is Plagiarism? (2010, November). Retrieved from plagiarism.org

World Diversity Patterns. Retrieved from www.anthro.palomar.edu/ethnicity/ethnic_5.htm

World Health Organization (WHO) retrieved 01.24.2014 from who.int/reproductivehealth/topics/sexual_health/sh_definitions/en/ 390

www.cdc.gov/Features/VitalSigns/PainkillerOverdoses/ (Retrieved Jan, 2015)

Xhelo, Gerta (Producer). (2013, April). Angela Lee Duckworth: The Key to Success? Grit. Ted Talks Education. Podcast retrieved from: http://www.ted.com/talks/angela_lee_duckworth_the_key_to_success_gri

GLOSSARY

Academic Dean: Chief Academic Officer over a specific school or college; ex: Dean of the College of Liberal Arts, Dean of the School of Education, etc.

Academic Discipline: a field of study or branch of knowledge, such as history, business management, chemistry, etc.

Acceptance: The Oxford English Dictionary defines acceptance as the agreement with or belief in an idea, opinion, or explanation. It also means recognizing and showing appreciation for our differences.

Add-Drop Period: time at the beginning of each semester when students can add or drop courses without financial aid or academic repercussions. Check academic calendar for specific dates.

Adjunct: part-time instructors.

Advisors and Counselors: there are multiple types of advisors and counselors available to assist you at the University. Academic Advisors help you plan your academic path towards a degree. Financial Aid Advisors help you identify and manage financial resources to fund your education and living expenses as a student. Career counselors help you develop a plan to reach your vocational goals.

Affirmative action: Policies that take factors including race, color, religion, sex, or national origin into consideration in order to benefit an underrepresented group in areas of employment, education, and business.

AIDS: Acquired Immune Deficiency Syndrome, a disease.

Allowed Amount: refers to an agreed upon amount that your health insurance will actually pay the provider or health facility for a particular service.

Alma Mater: *Use 1*: Alma Mater is a beautiful song with great meaning and sentiment written specifcally for UM and played at special events; *Use 2*: an individual's college or university from which he or she graduates is called alma mater. Alma Mater is a Latin phrase meaning Nourishing Mother.

Amount Billed: refers to the amount the provider or health facility charges for a particular service.

Analytical skills: ability to separate an object or an idea into constituent parts to classify and understand it, draw conclusions, or solve problems.

Anti-racist: An anti-racist is someone who makes a conscious choice and persistent effort to challenge white supremacy, including her/his own white privilege, and to actively oppose forms of discrimination against people of color.*

ASB: The Associated Student Body is the student government of the University which represents all students; located in Suite J301 of the Student Union.

Asexual: an individual who experiences little or no sexual attraction to any gender. Those who consciously abstain or are celibate are not considered to be asexual.

BAC: Blood Alcohol Content or Blood Alcohol Concentration.

Bisexual: an individual who is sexually oriented towards individuals of both genders.

Bias: A prejudice or unreasonable judgment, view, or outlook drawn before gathering all the facts.

Bid: a formal invitation to join a Greek-letter organization.

Bigotry: The Oxford English Dictionary defines bigotry as intolerance towards those who hold different opinions from oneself.

Bisexual: an individual who is sexually oriented towards individuals of two genders.

Blackboard: a web-based learning management system used by UM instructors to share important class information, assignments, and grades (blackboard.olemiss.edu).

Blue Book: a blank lined book, with a blue cover, used for written exams; can be purchased at bookstores both on and off campus.

Bursar's Office: manages student accounts, assesses tuition and fees, provides monthly billing statements, and processes payments and refunds. At many colleges and universities, this function is the responsibility of the business office; at Ole Miss we do not have a business office, rather we have a Bursar's Office.

Calorie: (food energy) a measure of the energy used by the body and of the energy that foods supply to the body.

Carbohydrates: essential nutrients that are the body's main source of energy. These are found in breads, cereals, and rice.

Career Fair: a networking event on specific days set aside each semester where students have the opportunity to meet with potential employers and learn about career paths and employment opportunities.

Career Professional: a person skilled in collaborating with and assisting students in determining a career path and selecting an academic major to support the chosen career path. Career professionals are skilled, also, in coaching students for upcoming interviews and in providing job search resources.

Census: The Oxford English Dictionary defines census as an official, periodic count or survey of a population, typically recording various details of individuals.

Chancellor: the Chief Executive Officer of the University; at many universities the Chief Executive Officer is known as the president.

Chancellor Robert Fulton: His most lasting and endearing contribution to the geography, spirit, and aesthetics of the University was preserving the wooded area in the center of the campus that would later become known to generations of University students and alumni as "The Grove."

Chapter: a membership unit of a national or international fraternal organization.

Closed Class: the limit on the number of students allowed in a specific section/course has been reached.

College and Schools: within the University, there are smaller academic units that are separated by subject or content area, for example: College of Liberal Arts, School of Engineering, School of Pharmacy, etc.; a student chooses a major that is housed within a specific college or school.

Coinsurance: coinsurance is your share of the costs of a health care service calculated as a percentage. You start paying coinsurance after you've paid your plan's deductible.

Complex Carbohydrates: carbohydrates such as whole-grain breads and cereals, starchy vegetables, and legumes. Many of the complex carbohydrates are good sources of fiber.

Copay - a copay is a fixed amount you pay at the time of service. This amount can vary by the type of service and insurance plan. Some plans require a copay for prescriptions too.

Commencement: the ceremony when degrees are conferred by the University; also known as graduation; it is held annually at the end of the spring semester.

Community Advisor (CAs): students who work for Student Housing and are responsible for residents of a specific floor or area of a residence hall or on-campus apartment complex.

Comprehensive Test: a test that includes information covered throughout the entire course/semester.

Conditionally Booked: student is temporarily booked in a course and will be automatically added to the course if he or she satisfactorily meets the course prerequisite.

Copay: a copay is a fixed amount you pay at the time of service. This amount can vary by the type of service and insurance plan. Some plans require a copay for prescriptions too.

Counseling Center: serves students, faculty, and staff. At the University Counseling Center you will find a team of dedicated professionals who strive to offer the best care possible in an atmosphere of caring respect. All services are offered in accordance with the legal limits of confidentiality.

Course Number: identifies the course with an abbreviation of the department and number.

Credit Hour: typically referred to as an "hour;" the equivalent of one hour of class per week in a regular 16 week course/semester.

Creed of the University of Mississippi: also known as the Ole Miss Creed, it is a statement of shared values of the University community.

Critical thinking skills: skills that allow one to reason well, including the abilities to clarify goals, values, and assumptions; evaluate evidence; and determine outcomes based on that evidence.

Dean of Students: unlike an academic dean, this individual has responsibility for non-academic areas such as leadership, Greek affairs, campus organizations, etc.

Deductible: a deductible is the amount you pay for health care services before your health insurance begins to pay.

Dehydration: condition of having less than optimum level of body water.

Department: a smaller academic unit that is housed under a college or school, for example: under the School of Education at Ole Miss there is a Department of Teacher Education and a Department of Leadership and Counselor Education.

Department Chair: typically an academic department chair is a faculty member of the department who reports to the Academic Dean and is assigned to manage the department.

Dependence: A strong need to continue using a particular substance.

Discrimination: The Oxford English Dictionary defines discrimination as the unjust or prejudicial treatment of different categories of people or things, especially on the grounds of race, age, or sex.

Diversity: The Oxford English Dictionary defines diversity as the state of being diverse, variety. Diverse, as showing a great deal of variety, differences.

Elma Meek and OLE MISS: She suggested the name OLE MISS be used for the first yearbook for the University in 1897. Within a couple of years, students and alumni were using the name of the yearbook as an affectionate name for the University.

Emergency Medical Treatment and Active Labor Act (EMTALA): this act is a federal law that requires anyone coming to an emergency department to be stabilized and treated, regardless of their insurance status or ability to pay.

Ethnicity: The Oxford English Dictionary defines ethnicity as the fact or state of belonging to a social group that has a common national or cultural tradition.

Exclusion: The Oxford English Dictionary defines exclusion as the process or state of excluding or being excluded, and exclude as to deny access to someone from a place, group, or a privilege.

Exercise: purposeful physical activity, designed to improve some aspect of physical fitness

Explanation of Benefit: paper or electronic form that notifies you of claims submitted to your insurance. It gives you details about what your insurance will pay for and what you are responsible for paying.

FAFSA: Free Application for Federal Student Aid. This is the single application for federal aid and must be filed yearly by visiting studentaid.gov or download the new mobile app.

Faculty: academic professionals of the University; persons who are full, associate, and assistant professors as well as instructors.

Fad Diets: a diet plan that makes promises of quick weight loss with minimal to no science background. These diets typically restrict one or more of the essential food groups, or recommend consumption of one type of food in excess at the expense of other foods. These diets typically do not result in long-term weight loss, can potentially be dangerous to your health, and are generally not endorsed by the medical profession.

Fall Convocation: a formal welcome to the University of Mississippi and presentation of all academic schools and colleges; at Convocation, students formally become student members of the University community.

Fats: a nutrient that supplies energy, promotes healthy skin and growth, and is a carrier of certain vitamins. Found in oils, butter, and lard.

Fiber: plant material that cannot be digested. It assists with digestion and bowel movements. There are two types: soluble and insoluble.

Flagship University: the finest, most important university that has the liberal arts education at its core; the University of Mississippi is the flagship university in Mississippi.

Flame war: A hostile dispute conducted on a public electronic forum such as a message board.

Fulton Chapel: auditorium located on the Circle. Named for Chancellor Robert Fulton, this historic building hosts performing arts events, University meetings, Orientation sessions, and large lecture classes.

GA: graduate assistant; a graduate student who receives a stipend for performing research, teaching, programming, or other assigned duties as part of his or her graduate education.

Galtney Center for Academic Computing: the 24/7 computer lab for students; this is especially helpful for students who have no laptops or whose laptops are broken.

General Education: sometimes referred to as "gen ed;" courses every student is required to take, regardless of major.

Gertrude C. Ford Center: the premier entertainment venue in the University and Oxford community area; used for theatre productions, lecture series, film screenings, Broadway shows, concerts, ballets, and more.

Gluten: gluten is a protein found in wheat, rye, and barley. It can also be in products such as vitamin and nutrient supplements, lip balms, and certain medicines.

Grace period: A short time period after graduation during which the borrower is not required to begin repaying his or her student loans. The grace period also may kick in if the borrower leaves school for a reason other than graduation or drops below half-time enrollment. For Federal Direct loans, you will have a grace period of six months before you must start making payments.

Greek: a term applied to members affiliated with social Greek-letter organizations.

HIV: Human Immunodeficiency Virus, virus that causes AIDS.

HPV: Human Papilloma Virus, also known as genital warts.

Health Insurance Portability and Accountability Act (HIPAA): created to stipulate how personal information is maintained and protected in health care and to address some gaps in insurance coverage.

Health Literacy: the degree to which individuals have the capacity to obtain, process, and understand basic health information and services needed to make appropriate health decisions.

Help Desk: located in Weir Hall; a phone and walk-in source of help for computer and IT problems; hours each day are 8:00 a.m. – 5:00 p.m., e-mail is helpdesk@olemiss.edu, and the phone number is 662-915-5222.

Heterosexual: an individual who is sexually oriented towards individuals of the opposite gender.

Hold: placed on a student's account or records and will not allow registration of courses, receipt of an academic transcript, graduation, etc. The student must contact the department from which the hold was placed to have it removed.

Homosexual: an individual who is sexually oriented towards individuals of the same gender.

Hotty Toddy: a cheer, greeting, and/or salutation embraced by all Ole Miss students, faculty, alumni, and friends; legend claims the phrase to be in mocking of the attitude of Ole Miss students in the 1920s as hoity toity which evolved into Heighty Tighty and later Hotty Toddy.

Hypertrophy: increased muscle size.

ID: student identification card, one of the most important possessions on campus; needed to access both Flex and Express accounts and meal plans; gain entrance to residence halls and recreation facilities; check-out library materials; buy tickets to athletic events and concerts; scan for class attendance, etc.

IHL Board: The Board of Trustees of the Institutions of Higher Education of the State of Mississippi is the constitutional governing body of the State Institutions of Higher Learning which includes the University of Mississippi.

Inclusion: The Oxford English Dictionary defines inclusion as the action or state of including or of being included within a group or structure.

Information Session: an event where students can gain in-depth knowledge about employers, companies, federal agencies, etc. Information sessions usually are held at the Career Center, although some are at other locations on campus.

Informational Interview: a short interview conducted with someone who works in a particular field to learn more about the realities of specific occupational choices.

Informed consent: your patient right to receive information and actively engage providers with questions about treatments so that you can make a well-informed decision about your health care.

In-network: refers to a provider having a contract with a health insurance provider and having negotiated rates for services.

Intake: the process of membership selection used by fraternities and sororities belonging to the National Pan-Hellenic Council (NPHC).

Internalized Racism: The misinformation and distortions that people may have about themselves and their cultures as a result of living in a racist society.*

Internship: a work immersion experience that allows students to gain first-hand experience of how a particular occupational choice will fit with their interests and personality. Internships may be paid or unpaid.

Intersession Course: compacted course that meets for only two weeks immediately before or after a semester but is the equivalent of a full semester course (May, August, and January).

Institutional Racism: The ways in which institutions: social, political, educational, cultural, financial, religious, medical, housing, jobs, criminal justice: create and/or perpetuate systems that advantage white people at the expense of people of color.*

iStudy: iStudy@OleMiss classes are flexible and self-paced. This distance learning program allows students to learn anytime, anywhere. Most courses are available online through Blackboard. There also are classes that are paper based. Many are available in both formats.

Jackson Avenue Center (JAC): multipurpose building located just northwest of the main campus on Jackson Avenue; Math Lab is located here.

James Alexander Ventress: Brought the bill before the Mississippi State legislature to establish a state university in 1840. Appointed first member of the original board of 13 trustees to oversee the newly chartered University in 1844. Because of this, Ventress is known as the "Father of the University" and Ventress Hall, which houses the College of Liberal Arts, was named in his honor.*

James Meredith and 1962: The young Air Force veteran from Koscuisko was the first African-American student to enter and integrate The University of Mississippi. Meredith enrolled October 1, 1962. Between September 30th and October 1st, a rebellious mob clashed with U. S. Marshalls and Federal troops in front of the Lyceum over the court-ordered admission of Meredith. Two people were killed, and the event marked a decisive turning point in the Civil Rights Movement and the history of public school desegregation in the South.

Jim Crow era and laws: State and local laws enacted in the United States between 1876 and 1965 that mandated segregation in all public facilities in the Southern states of the former Confederacy. Separate but equal laws during this time led to conditions for blacks that were inferior to those provided for whites, systematizing a number of economic, educational, and social disadvantages.*

Job Shadowing: the act of spending time (usually a day or so) with and observing an employee in his or her workplace to learn more about the tasks and responsibilities attached to a particular occupation or career.

John Howard Vaught: Head coach of the Ole Miss Rebel football team from 1947 to 1970. During his tenure, Vaught compiled an amazing record of 190 wins and only 61 losses. His teams won three national titles, six Southeastern Conference titles, and 18 bowl games. He coached 27 All-Americans and the 1959 Ole Miss team was voted the SEC Team of the Decade.

Liberal arts education: an approach to learning that empowers individuals and prepares them to deal with complexity, diversity, and change. It is an education needed to maintain a free society and enable the full development of individual talent.

Lyceum: Completed in 1848, the Lyceum was the first building constructed on campus. Over the years, it has served as both an academic and administrative center for the University. The Chancellor's Office, Provost's Office, and the Vice Chancellors' offices are located in the Lyceum.

Lynching: An execution conducted outside of legal authority by a mob, often by hanging, but also by burning at the stake, in order to punish an alleged transgressor and to intimidate, control, or manipulate a population of people.*

M Book: a compilation of many different policies that affect students both in and out of the classroom; it is every Ole Miss student's responsibility to be familiar with the contents of *The M Book.*

Martindale Student Services Center: student support offices are located in this building which is next to the J.D. Williams Library and across the street from the Turner Center; the Center for Student Success and First-Year Experience as well as the offices of the Bursar, Registrar, Student Disability Services, Career Center, Study Abroad, Financial Aid, International Programs, Health Professions Advising, Admissions, and Orientation can be found in Martindale.

Meredith Statue: This monument honoring James Meredith, the first African-American to enroll at Ole Miss, was unveiled in October 2006. The statue depicts Meredith passing through the doorway of campus as he was formally admitted to the University.

Metabolism: a measure of the number of calories a body expends per some unit of time.

Micro-aggresion: The everyday verbal, nonverbal, and environment slights, snubs, or insults, whether intentional or unintentional, which communicate hostile, derogatory, or negative messages to target persons based solely upon their marginalized group membership.*

Minerals: nutrients such as calcium, iron, and zinc; some regulate body processes while others become part of body tissues.

Multicultural Competency: A process of learning about and becoming allies with people from other cultures, thereby broadening our own understanding and ability to participate in a multicultural process. The key element to becoming more culturally competent is respect for the ways that others live in and organize the world and an openness to learn from them.*

myOleMiss: the online portal used to transact business with the University; it is accessed from the Ole Miss home page using your Web ID and password.

MyPlate: the current nutrition guide developed by the U. S. Department of Agriculture to guide healthful eating. MyPlate depicts a plate and glass divided into five food groups. It replaced the USDA's MyPyramid guide.

NPHC: National Pan-Hellenic Council; the governing body of the nine historically African-American fraternities and sororities.

Natatorium: an indoor swimming pool

Netiquette: A set of accepted practices that have evolved over the last twenty years defining good behavior on the Internet.

Networking: the exchange of information utilized to create meaningful relationships for business or everyday interactions.

Non-racist: Term used by those who consider themselves "color-blind," a claim that in effect denies any role in perpetuating systemic racism, or any responsibility to act to dismantle it. Institutional racism is perpetuated not only by those who actively discriminate, but also by those who fail to challenge it (silence = consent).*

Nutrients: substances in food that the body needs to function properly, to grow, to repair itself, and to supply energy.

Office Hours: specific times when faculty members are available for student questions, concerns, or just to talk about a course or other college issue. All faculty must provide office hours to their students. Office hours for a particular course will be included in the course syllabus.

Opiates: Drugs used to treat moderate to severe pain; may be prescribed after surgery.

OUT: (Oxford University Transit) public transportation available to all students, faculty, and staff at no cost; routes connect various locations in Oxford and on the campus; a schedule for the various routes can be found online.

Out-of-network: refers to a provider not having a contract with a health insurance provider and not being bound by negotiated rates for services.

Overload Principle: a principle of human performance that states that beneficial adaptations occur in response to demands applied to the body at levels beyond a certain threshold (overload), but within the limits of tolerance and safety

Pansexual: an individual who is sexually oriented towards individuals of any gender

Paris-Yates Chapel: completed in 2001, the ecumenical chapel seats approximately 200 individuals and is embellished with an elaborate handmade pipe organ and carillon. Paris-Yates Chapel is located on the west side of the Quadrangle.

Peer-to-Peer (P2P) File Sharing: A means for downloading files directly from other users on the Internet; often used to illegally download materials such as music and video without the owner's permission.

Pell Grant: a federal grant that provides funds up to a specific amount (determined annually) based on the student's financial need.

Phishing: An attempt to fraudulently acquire confidential information for use in identity theft, e.g., by sending an e-mail or setting up a website that resembles a well-known organization.

Physical Activity: any task involving physical movement

Physical Dependence: The need to continue substance use behaviors to avoid withdrawal.

Physical Fitness: a task-specific term used to describe an individual's ability to perform physical activity

Power: Access to individuals, social groups, and institutions that own and/or control the majority of a community's resources, as well as the ability to define norms and standards of behavior.* The Oxford English Dictionary defines power as the capacity or ability to direct or influence the behavior of others or the course of events; political or social authority or control; a person or organization that is strong or influential within a particular context.

Prejudice: An attitude or opinion: usually negative: about a socially defined group (racial, religious, nationality, etc.) or any person perceived to be a member of that group, formed with insufficient knowledge, reason, or deliberation.*

Pre-requisite: sometimes referred to as a "pre-req;" a course that must be satisfactorily completed prior to enrolling in another course.

Private loan: Education loan programs established by private lenders to supplement the student and parent education loan programs available from federal and state governments.

Privilege: The Oxford English Dictionary defines privilege as a special right, advantage, or immunity granted or available only to a particular person or group of people.

Protein: an essential nutrient that helps your body grow, repair itself, and fight disease; it can also provide energy if needed. We get proteins in our diet from meat, dairy products, beans, nuts, and grains.

Provost: Chief Academic Officer for the University.

Psychological Dependence: The need to continue substance use behaviors because of cravings for the pleasurable effects.

Quadrangle (Quad): green space with large fountain in the center bordered by J.D. Williams Library on the east, Bondurant Hall on the south, Paris-Yates Chapel on the west, and Paul B. Johnson Commons on the north.

Race: A social construct (with no biological validity) that divides people into distinct groups by categorizing them based on arbitrary elements of physical appearance, particularly skin color.*

Racial Stereotype: An image applied to an entire group of people (or a member of that group), assuming that those characteristics are rooted in significant and essential differences.*

Racism: Racism exists when one ethnic group or historical collectivity dominates, excludes, or seeks to eliminate another on the basis of differences that it believes are hereditary and unalterable. From George M. Frederickson's Racism: *A Short History*.*
An act by an individual or a group of individuals based on some bias or prejudice against another individual or group of individuals based on their race; a belief that based on racial categorizations, one group is superior to another group; attempts to deny a person or a group of persons' rights (including constitutionally granted rights) based on race.

RebAlert: The campus emergency notification system by which text messages are used to no- tify students and employees in campus emergency and alert situations (such as tornado watches).

Rebel Market: an all you care to eat dining facility open Monday through Friday for breakfast, lunch, and dinner. One swipe of the Student ID Card allows students to choose from different dining stations in a comfortable and social atmosphere. Rebel Market accepts Meal Plans, Flex Dollars, Cash, Credit Cards, Debit Cards, and Ole Miss Express.

Recovery: A voluntarily maintained lifestyle characterized by sobriety, personal health, and citizenship.

Recruitment: the mutual membership selection process in a Panhellenic or Interfraternity Council Greek organization.

Registrar's Office: located on the first floor of the Martindale Student Services Center, this office is responsible for registration of students for classes, recording of grades on official university records, maintaining and supplying transcripts of students' academic work, processing withdrawals, and Commencement.

Registered Dietitian (RD): an expert in human nutrition and the regulation of diet.

Reverse Racism: A term commonly used by white people to equate instances of hostile behavior toward them by people of color with the racism people of color face. This is a way of ignoring the issue of who has the power. *

Rubric: grading tool (sometimes called a scoring sheet or guide) that identifies specific criteria used in grading student work; used especially in writing courses.

Sarah Isom McGehee: Appointed the first female faculty member at The University of Mississippi in 1885. The Sarah Isom Center for Women and Gender Studies at the University was established in her honor in 1981

Saturated Fat: fats that are solid at room temperature and are typically found in animal products, such as meats, poultry skin, and foods made from whole milk. These fats increase the risk for heart disease.

Scantron: paper form used to record answers for quizzes, tests, and examinations; scantrons are available in the ASB Office or at local bookstores; scantrons come in a variety of versions and formats so the instructor should be consulted regarding the version needed for the course.

Section Number: identifies specific class (time, day, instructor) within a course.

Separate but equal: A legal doctrine in United States constitutional law that justified systems of segregation. Under this doctrine, services, facilities, public accommodations, and public schools were allowed to be separated by race, on the condition that the quality of each group's public facilities was the same.*

Simple Carbohydrates: carbohydrates that are digested quickly and include sugars found naturally in foods such as fruits, vegetables, milk, and milk products. They also include sugars added during food processing and refining.

Social construct: A mechanism, phenomenon, or category created and developed by society; a perception of an individual, group, or idea that is created or "constructed" through cultural or social practice.*

South Campus Recreation Center: the new 98,000 square foot facility has several innovative elements including a 6000 square foot functional training gym.

South Oxford Center: (SOC) Less than 2.5 miles from the center of the University of Mississippi's Oxford campus, the South Oxford Center is located at 2301 S. Lamar Blvd. The former site of Baptist Memorial Hospital – North Mississippi, the property was purchased by the University in 2017 and consists of a nearly 485,000-square-foot building, a parking garage and lot with ample parking for faculty, staff, students, and visitors. The South Oxford Center property allows UM to allocate adequate space to growing programs.

Stereotype: The Oxford English Dictionary describes stereotyping as something continued or constantly repeated without change.

Stimulants: Drugs used to treat narcolepsy, ADD/ADHD, and other conditions.

Student Disability Services Office: (SDS) located on the second floor of Martindale Student Services Center, SDS provides classroom accommodations to all students on campus who disclose a disability, request accommodations, and meet eligibility criteria.

Study Abroad Office: located on the third floor of Martindale Student Services Center, makes available opportunities to study abroad all over the world.

Subsidized loan: A loan for which the government pays the interest while the student is in school, during the six-month grace period, and during any deferment periods. Subsidized loans are awarded based on financial need.

Suicide: death caused by self-directed injurious behavior with an intent to die as a result of the behavior

Suicide attempt: a non-fatal, self-directed, potentially injurious behavior with an intent to die as a result of the behavior; might not result in injury

Suicidal ideation: thinking about, considering, or planning suicide.

Swayze Field: home field of Ole Miss baseball. The stadium at Swayze Field is known as Oxford/University Stadium (or OU Stadium).

Syllabus: an outline and summary of topics to be covered in a course; it will usually contain information about the instructor and his/her contact information, designated office hours, required textbooks, course requirements, due dates for assignments, test dates, and grading scale.

Tailgating: setting up tables, chairs, tents, and food to celebrate the gathering of Ole Miss fans and guests on campus before an athletic contest.

The Circle: the center of the University; the Lyceum stands at the apex of the Circle; original campus was laid out on the Circle to symbolize the Greek concepts of perfection and eternity which were the hopes held by founding trustees for the University.

The Daily Mississippian: (DM) founded in 1911, the campus newspaper is published four days per week; it is distributed free-of-charge throughout the campus and in Oxford.

The Forum: the hub of all campus involvement. This web-based platform streamlines communication and helps build a stronger campus community.

The Grove: 10 acres located in the center of campus; site of Commencement, peace and solace, and the greatest tailgating in America on gamedays in the fall.

The Inn at Ole Miss: the Ole Miss alumni's luxury hotel located on the east side of campus; available to alumni, students, their families, and other visitors to the University.

The Manning Center: (Indoor Practice Facility or IPF) athletic complex named for alumni Olivia and Archie Manning, the patriarchs of the first-family of football in America; contains in-door practice field, locker rooms, training facilities, weight rooms, team meeting rooms, and the Grill at 1810.

The Pavilion: state-of-the art, $96.5 million facility opened in January 2016. Site for basketball games, concerts, and academic convocation, The Pavilion also has the largest hung video display in college sports and includes Steak 'n' Shake, Raising Cane, and Rebel Locker Room.

The Square: Courthouse Square of the city of Oxford; home of smart retail stores, stylish boutiques, gourmet restaurants, and bars; some describe it as the Center of the Universe.

The Turner Center: located on All-American Drive across the street from Martindale Student Services Center; on-campus recreation center open to all students currently enrolled in classes.

TLO: (Transfer Leadership Organization) leadership organization for transfer students. tlo.olemiss.edu

Tolerance: The Oxford English Dictionary defines tolerance as the ability or willingness to tolerate something, in particular the existence of opinions or behavior that one does not necessarily agree with. Or, the need to continuously increase the amount of a substance used to gain a desired effect.

Trans Fat: trans fats are formed when liquid oils are made into solid fats like shortening and hard margarines. Trans fats can be found in processed foods such as crackers, cookies, snack foods, fried foods, and baked goods. It increases blood cholesterol levels and risk for heart disease.

Troll: Someone who initiates and encourages a flame war for the purpose of eliciting an emo- tional reaction.

UM Today: Important campus announcements sent as a daily e-mail message and also displayed in the campus portal, myOleMiss (my.olemiss.edu).

UMatter: Student Support and Advocacy - assists students facing challenges/crises includ- ing sexual harrassment; located in Suite H301 Student Union.

Universitas Scientiarum: Chancellor F. A. P. Barnard's far-reaching, comprehensive plan in 1858 to make The University of Mississippi "a true university that included all branches of science, medicine, agriculture, law, classical studies, civil and political history, and oriental learning."

University of Mississippi Museum: has its origins as the City of Oxford's Mary Buie Muse- um, built in 1939 as a WPA Federal Art Center, one of two in the state of Mississippi. Upon its transfer to the University in 1974, the construction of a large addition permitted de- partmental collections from across the campus to be consolidated in the new "University Museum" when it opened in February 1977. The Museum's collection holdings total over 20,000 artworks and cultural heritage artifacts, representing multiple continents and millennia. The Museum is steward of the largest collection of Greek and Roman Antiq- uities in the southern United States and also manages Rowan Oak, the National Historic Landmark home of novelist William Faulkner, and the Walton-Young House, home of novelist, playwright, and drama critic Stark Young.

Unsubsidized loan: A loan for which the government does not pay the interest. The bor- rower is responsible for the interest on an unsubsidized loan from the date the loan is disbursed, even while the student is still in school. Students may avoid paying the inter- est while they are in school by capitalizing the interest, which increases the loan amount. Unsubsidized loans are not based on financial need.

UPD: (University Police Department) University's police force with offices located in Kinard Hall.

USDA: the United States Department of Agriculture (USDA), also known as the Agriculture Department, is the U.S. federal executive department responsible for developing and executing federal government policy on farming, agriculture, forestry, and food.

Vaught-Hemingway Stadium: home of the Ole Miss football Rebels. Built in 1915, the stadium is named after Coach John Howard Vaught and Judge William Hemingway.

Vegan: a diet that excludes all meat and animal by-products, such as milk and eggs.

Vegetarian: a diet that excludes meat and sometimes other animal products.

Verification: A quality assurance process mandated by the Department of Education to confirm the accuracy of information submitted on the FAFSA. This review ensures fair and accurate distribution of federal funds during the financial aid awarding process. Examples of documentation collected by the school during the process include the verification worksheet (accessible through myOleMiss), student and parent IRS Tax Return Transcripts, and W2 forms.

Vice Chancellor: title for leader of a division of the University, i.e., Vice Chancellor for Academic Affairs, Vice Chancellor for Student Affairs; at many colleges and universities these positions are held by vice presidents.

Vitamins: nutrients that do not provide energy but help regulate body processes. These are essential for normal growth and are required in small quantities in the diet because they cannot be synthesized by the body.

Waitlist: when all seats in a class are full, some classes allow students to be put on a list to wait (hopefully) for others to drop the class, opening up seats for "waitlist" students.

WebID: this is a sign-on to access all UM web applications for taking care of University business, such as registering for classes, checking grades, and viewing other student oriented information; it is the first part of your UM e-mail address.

Wellness: quality or state of being in good health

White Privilege: Unearned advantages that benefit whites (whether they seek such benefits or not) by virtue of their skin color in a racist society.*

White Supremacy: Once used only by racist groups such as the Ku Klux Klan, the term also is used in anti-racism work to describe the historically based, institutionally perpetuated system of domination and exploitation of people of color by white people, and which maintains white peoples' position of relative wealth, power, and privilege.*

Whole Grain: whole grains contain the entire grain kernel – the bran, germ, and endosperm. Examples of whole grains include whole-wheat flour, oatmeal, and brown rice.

Withdrawal: Symptoms that are opposite to the effects the substance originally had on the body.

Work ethic: belief in the moral benefit and importance of work and its inherent ability to strengthen character.

These definitions were compiled over the last few years and are based on definitions originally created by the Challenging White Supremacy Workshops.